Essays in
Scottish Labour History

William Marwick

Essays in
Scottish Labour History

A Tribute to W. H. Marwick

Edited by

IAN MacDOUGALL

Secretary, Scottish Labour History Society

JOHN DONALD PUBLISHERS LTD

EDINBURGH

© John Donald Publishers Ltd.
All rights reserved
Published by John Donald Publishers Ltd.
138 St. Stephen Street, Edinburgh EH3 5AA

Printed in Great Britain by Bell & Bain Ltd., Glasgow

Preface

THANKS are due to Angus Calder for his support in initiating this volume, though he bears no responsibility for the actual contents.

The General Council and affiliated unions of the Scottish Trades Union Congress made a generous contribution toward the cost of publication, as did various private persons, many or most of whom know William Marwick and wished in that way to mark their appreciation of the man and his work. To all these sources of support, warm thanks are due.

No editor could wish for a more helpful and patient guide than John Tuckwell of John Donald Ltd. has shown himself to be.

Edinburgh, 1978.

Ian MacDougall.

Contents

WILLIAM HUTTON MARWICK

THIS collection of essays is offered as a tribute to the work of William Hutton Marwick in promoting and encouraging, during the past half century, the study of Scottish labour history. His book *A Short History of Labour in Scotland*, published a decade ago, marked a culmination of his prolonged and often pioneering research and teaching of that subject. Now, in his eighty-fourth year, it is fitting if long overdue that some formal recognition be accorded to William Marwick by some fellow students in the fields of economic and social history.

William Marwick is not only a scholar who continues in his middle eighties to take a close and active interest in an impressively wide range of scholarly subjects, but he is also a most unassuming, modest, honest, selfless man who constantly holds out a helping hand to new entrants in areas of study where he long ago pioneered. Those who know William Marwick value his friendship and his unfailing helpfulness and kindliness as well as his scholarship.

Though his characteristically modest manner might suggest the rather unworldly scholar, William Marwick early showed his equally characteristic moral courage by his refusal, as an objector on religious grounds to violence, to allow himself to be swept along on what he saw as a chauvinist tide into the 1914-18 War. Born on 16 October 1894 in the Calabar district of Nigeria, the eldest child of parents who had met and married there while both were missionaries of the United Presbyterian Church, William was a grand nephew of the well-known late nineteenth-century town clerk of Glasgow, Sir James Marwick. William's mother had gone from Scotland to Nigeria to work with Mary Slessor. His father was a minister in the United Presbyterian and later, after the union of 1900, in the United Free Church. Rev. Marwick, a christian socialist from his student days, became a prominent and highly respected figure in the labour movement in Edinburgh between the Wars as a result of his activity on behalf of the unemployed — 'the chaplain of the unemployed'. The young William Marwick, after spending most of his early years in Jamaica, where his father also worked for a time as a missionary, returned in 1905 to Edinburgh to complete his schooling at George Watson's College. There he learned French from a distinguished teacher and historian, Dr Henry Meikle, later Librarian of the National Library of Scotland: even now in his middle eighties William Marwick reads French literature almost every evening. At Watson's too his interest in politics was aroused and, before becoming a socialist, he was a Liberal Radical who took a prominent part in school debating societies. From Watson's he passed into Edinburgh University where he was first a student of classics and later of history. He graduated M.A. with first class honours in history in 1916, just as military conscription was introduced and the bloodbath on the Somme was beginning. His strong religious convictions had already led him in 1915 to refuse to attest under the Derby Scheme, and he had been accepted for war relief work in France by the Quaker Society of Friends. But a notoriously unsympathetic tribunal refused to exempt him from conscription despite his conscientious objection, and this quiet and gentle young man was, like so many others, arrested as a 'deserter' from the army, imprisoned in Stirling Castle, court martialled for refusing to don army uniform, sentenced to 112 days' hard labour in Wormwood Scrubs and subsequently, after he had agreed to accept work under the 'Home Office Scheme' for conscientious objectors, transferred to Wakefield prison. Eventually, in March 1918, he was permitted to join the Society of Friends war relief work in France, toiling finally as a builder's labourer in the Argonne until June 1919.

That William Marwick had shown the courage of his convictions and had undergone, like millions of others of his generation, some trying experiences between 1916 and 1919, did not in the least impress two eminent Edinburgh academics — professors both — who, at the end of the War, refused him testimonials and added gratuitously that they 'would not appoint him to any post'. A very different academic, however, J. F. Rees, then a lecturer at Edinburgh University in economic history (later, as Sir James Frederick Rees, Principal of the University College of Wales, Cardiff, and Vice-Chancellor of the University of Wales), helped William Marwick find employment at last in 1920 as a tutor-organiser in the Workers' Educational Association in the west of Scotland. That was an appointment which he held for the following twelve years. Those were busy years indeed, during which he lectured at classes and at meetings all over Scotland, although especially, of course, in the west. He was also politically active and stood as Labour candidate for Dumfriesshire in the 1929 general election. They were also happy years, since in 1923 he married Maeve Brereton, a descendant of 'the father of British socialism', Robert Owen. Maeve was a graduate in medicine from Edinburgh University, a pioneer in Scotland of the family planning movement, and like William, whom she first met at the University Fabian Society, a leading member of the Society of Friends. Five children were born to the Marwicks, of whom Arthur has followed the academic path trodden by his father and is now professor of history in the Open University. With characteristic modesty, William Marwick has remarked: 'I used to be known as the son of a famous father; now I am the father of a famous son.' The death of Maeve Marwick early in 1978 ended a long and happy marriage that, in addition to all else, provided their numerous friends and acquaintances with memorable hospitality, warm humanity, keen and sympathetic interest. Few who enjoyed the welcome accorded them by William and Maeve Marwick can have stepped out from No. 5 Northfield Crescent, Edinburgh (or their earlier homes in Glasgow), without feeling stimulated by their sympathy, their humanity, their modesty and good humour, their selflessness in the numerous causes in which they played an active, if often self-effacing, part.

William Marwick's contribution to historical scholarship increased with his appointment in 1932 as an extra-mural lecturer and Carnegie Fellow at Edinburgh University; he held the former appointment until he became a lecturer in economic history there in 1948. He retired in 1964, having taught for many years, in addition to his other classes, a final honours course in the history of working class movements — a pioneering course in the curricula of Scottish universities. These were the years in which he wrote his books, *Economic Developments in Victorian Scotland* (1936), *Scotland in Modern Times* (1964), and numerous pamphlets — including one for the Fabian Society in 1950 on Scottish Devolution — as well as articles on economic and labour history, adult education, and the Quakers. His book *A Short History of Labour in Scotland* was published in 1967, three years after he retired. He continues to make more or less daily the journey by bus from his home to the National Library of Scotland, the Central Public Library, and Edinburgh University Library (the last of which has particularly benefited by his generous donations of books), in order that he may keep abreast of the studies which have occupied him for almost the whole of this century.

The nine essays in this volume have been written by people of differing political and other beliefs. But what unites us all is the desire, through these essays, to pay our tribute to William Marwick, a historian of labour in Scotland, a kind and gentle man.

1978

Ian MacDougall

BIBLIOGRAPHY OF THE WORKS OF WILLIAM HUTTON MARWICK

Books

Economic Developments in Victorian Scotland London, 1936.
Scotland in Modern Times: Economic and Social Development since 1707
London, 1964.
A Short History of Labour in Scotland Edinburgh, 1967.

Pamphlets and booklets

The Economic Development of Scotland Workers' Educational Association,
Edinburgh, 1930.
The Present Position of Adult Education in Sweden London, 1938.
Scottish Local Government Fabian Society, London, 1939; rev. ed. 1951.
Labour in Scotland Scottish Secretariat, Glasgow, 1949.
Scottish Devolution Fabian Society, London, 1950.
The Social and Political Witness of Christianity: the Historical Approach
Society of Friends, London, 1944.
A Short History of Friends in Scotland Society of Friends, Leith, 1948.
The Story of Quakerism in Scotland, 1650-1850 By G. B. Burnet.
With an Epilogue in the Period 1850-1950 By W. H. Marwick.
London, 1952.
Ernest Bowman Ludlam (Quaker Biographies) Society of Friends, London,
1960.
The Life of Alexander Campbell Glasgow and District Co-operative Associa-
tion, Glasgow (1963).
Quaker Social Thought *(Woodbrooke Papers)* Society of Friends, London,
1969.
The Common Market and Scotland Scottish Secretariat, Carlops, 1971.
Conscientious Objection in Scotland in the First World War Scottish Secre-
tariat, Carlops, 1972.

Articles

'The Cotton Industry and the Industrial Revolution in Scotland', *Scottish
Historical Review*, xxi, No. 83, April 1924.
'Later Scots Worthies', *Scottish Educational Journal*, 13 (1930).
'Early Adult Education in the West of Scotland', *Journal of Adult Education*,
4, No. 2 (1930).
'Mechanics Institutes in Scotland', *Journal of Adult Education* (1930).
'Adult Education in Glasgow eighty years ago', *Proceedings of the Royal
Philosophical Society of Glasgow*, 59 (1931).

'Victorian Scots', *Scottish Educational Journal*, 14 (1931).

'Economics and the Reformation', *Scots Magazine*, August 1931.

'Bibliography of Scottish Economic History', *Economic History Review*, iii, No. 1, January 1931.

'Scottish Social Pioneers', *Scottish Educational Journal*, 15 (1932).

'Early Adult Education in Edinburgh', *Journal of Adult Education*, 5, No. 5 (1932).

'Dr John Taylor', *Glasgow Herald*, 23 September 1933.

'Adult Educationalists in Victorian Scotland', *Journal of Adult Education*, 6, No. 2 (1933).

'Scottish Chartist Leaders', *Glasgow Herald*, 10 February 1934.

'An Edinburgh Building Experiment', *Scottish Educational Journal*, 18 (1935).

'The Scottish Mineral Oil Industry', *Scotland*, i, No. 7, Autumn 1935.

'Scottish Overseas Investment in the Nineteenth Century', *Scottish Bankers Magazine*, 27 (1935).

'Early Trade Unionism in Scotland', *Economic History Review*, v, No. 2, April 1935.

'Paternalism in Victorian Scotland', *Juridical Review*, March 1935.

'The Hydropathic in Scotland', *Scottish Educational Journal*, 19 (1936).

'Housing in Scotland', *Scotland*, ii, No. 1, Spring 1936.

'Scottish Adult Education', *Scotland*, ii, No. 5, Spring 1937.

'Some Scottish Economic Writers', *Scottish Bankers Magazine*, 28 (1937).

'The Limited Company in Scottish Economic Development', *Economic History*, iii, No. 12 (1937).

'The University Extension Movement in Scotland', *University of Edinburgh Journal*, 8, Summer 1937.

'The Beginnings of the Scottish Working Class Movement in the Nineteenth Century', *International Review for Social History*, 3 (1938).

'The Incorporation of the Tailors of the Canongate', *Book of the Old Edinburgh Club*, xxii (1938).

'Scotland and Sweden', *Journal of Adult Education*, August 1939.

'Workers' Colleges in Scandinavia', *Journal of Adult Education*, June 1940.

'Functional Co-operation', *Friends Quarterly Examiner* (1944).

'Two Unorthodox Alumni of Aberdeen', *Aberdeen University Review*, xxx, No. 91, Summer 1944.

'Bibliography of Scottish Economic History, 1931-1951', *Economic History Review*, Second Series, iv, No. 3 (1952).

'Social Heretics in the Scottish Churches', *Records of the Scottish Church History Society*, xi, Pt. iii (1953).

'Friends in Nineteenth Century Scotland', *Friends Historical Society Journal*, Spring 1954.

'Friends and the State', *Friends Quarterly*, October 1957.

'Patrick Mathew', *Scottish Adult Education*, No. 23 (1958).

'Some Quaker firms of the Nineteenth Century', Pt. 1, *Journal of the Friends Historical Society*, 48, No. 6 (1958).

'Shops in Eighteenth and Nineteenth Century Edinburgh', *Book of the Old Edinburgh Club*, xxx (1959).

'The Scottish Reformation: a Quaker Commentary on Recent Literature', *Friends Quarterly*, October 1960.

'Some Quaker Firms of the Nineteenth Century', Pt. 2, *Journal of the Friends Historical Society*, 50, No. 1 (1962).

'Bibliography of Scottish Economic History, 1951-62', *Economic History Review*, Second Series, xvi, No. 1 (1963).

'Studies in Scottish Quakerism', *Records of the Scottish Church History Society*, xvi (1967).

'The Glasgow Study Circle', *Friends Historical Society Journal*, 51, No. 3 (1967).

'Carlyle and Quakerism', *Friends Quarterly*, 16, No. 1 (1968).

'Quakers in Victorian Scotland', *Friends Historical Society Journal*, 52, No. 2 (1969).

'Municipal Politics in Victorian Edinburgh', *Book of the Old Edinburgh Club*, xxxiii, Pt. 1 (1969).

'The Edinburgh Literary Institute', *Book of the Old Edinburgh Club*, xxxiii, Pt. 1 (1969).

'Quakers in Early Twentieth Century Scotland', *Friends Historical Society Journal*, 52, No. 3 (1970).

'Bibliography of Scottish Economic History, 1963-70', *Economic History Review*, Second Series, xxiv, No. 3 (1971).

'Arthur Ponsonby: a Centenary Tribute', *Friends Quarterly*, January 1971.

'Aristocrats Turned Proletarian: Ponsonby, Trevelyan and Pethick Lawrence', *Scottish Labour History Society Journal*, No. 5 (1972).

'Dugald Butler', *Records of the Scottish Church History Society* (1973).

'Workers' Education in Early Twentieth Century Scotland', *Scottish Labour History Society Journal*, No. 8 (1974).

'Rev. Dr William Morison', *University of Edinburgh Journal*, June 1977.

CONTRIBUTORS

Dr W. Hamish Fraser, a graduate of the Universities of Aberdeen and Sussex, is a senior lecturer in history at the University of Strathclyde. He is the author of *Trade Unions and Society. The Struggle for Acceptance 1850-1880* (1974), as well as of several articles on labour history. Since 1975 he has been chairman of the Scottish Labour History Society.

Dr Gordon M. Wilson, a graduate of the University of Glasgow, is principal lecturer in social studies at Hamilton College of Education. His previous publications include a book, *Teaching Local History in Lanarkshire* (1970), and various essays on local history. He is at present writing a biography of Alexander McDonald.

Ian Wood graduated in 1960 from the University of Edinburgh. He has taught in a comprehensive school, has been a lecturer in politics at the University of Strathclyde, and is at present a lecturer in history at Napier College of Commerce and Technology, Edinburgh, and a part-time tutor in the Open University. He is editor of the *Journal* of the Scottish Labour History Society.

Barbara W. Robertson, daughter of a Border shepherd, left school at fourteen and did wartime service as a staff sergeant in the A.T.S., from which, however, she was invalided out with tuberculosis. She graduated as a mature student in the 1960s from the University of Edinburgh with an honours degree in sociology, is now interested primarily in research, and hopes to complete a Ph.D. on Scottish farm workers.

Dr James H. Treble, a graduate of the University of Leeds, has been a lecturer in history at the University of Strathclyde since 1964. He is the author of a forthcoming book, *Urban Poverty in Britain 1830-1914*, and has published numerous articles and essays on social history. He is treasurer of the Scottish Labour History Society.

John Butt is professor of economic history and dean of the School of Arts and Social Studies at the University of Strathclyde. Formerly editor of *Industrial Archaeology Review*, he has published widely in the fields of industrial and business history, particularly on Scottish themes. He, like Dr Treble, contributed to the pioneer volume on *Working-class Housing*, edited by S. D. Chapman, in 1971, and has himself edited *Robert Owen: Prince of Cotton Spinners* (1971) and *Victorians and Social Protest* (1975). He is also author of

The Industrial Archaeology of Scotland (1967), and co-author with S. G. E. Lythe of *An Economic History of Scotland* (1975).

Ian MacDougall left school at fifteen, worked for some years as a newspaperman, graduated from the University of Edinburgh, and is at present tutor in history and trade union studies at Newbattle Abbey Adult College, Dalkeith. He edited (in 1969) *The Minutes of Edinburgh Trades Council 1859-73* and (in 1978) *A Catalogue of some Labour Records in Scotland.* He is secretary of the Scottish Labour History Society.

Dr William Thompson was born in 1939 and grew up in Shetland. As a student at the University of Aberdeen in the late 1950s and early 1960s he was active in the New Left Clubs and the Campaign for Nuclear Disarmament. He is at present senior lecturer in history at the Glasgow College of Technology. He is joint author of a book on the U.C.S. work-in and editor of the Communist Party quarterly, *Scottish Marxist.*

John T. Caldwell was born in Glasgow in 1911, moved with his family in 1915 to Belfast where he received a rudimentary education, and returned to Glasgow in 1925. He was a catering worker with Anchor Liners until 1938, when he became a full-time member of the United Socialist Movement. He worked in the Movement's associated Strickland Press until it closed in 1968. He first met Guy Aldred in 1932, was a member of Aldred's household for thirty years, and is his literary executor. He is author of a forthcoming biography of Guy Aldred, *The Red Evangel.*

Trades Councils in the Labour Movement in Nineteenth Century Scotland

W. Hamish Fraser

THE formation of trades councils in Scotland from the end of the 1850s was of vital importance for Scottish trade unionism. Trades councils played a much more crucial role in Scotland than they did south of the Tweed, largely because of the structure and the relative weakness of the Scottish unions.

The trial and harsh sentence on the officials of the Glasgow Cotton Spinners' Association in 1838 had the effect desired by Sheriff Alison and the Lord Advocate of breaking the confidence of the early Scottish unions and of deterring workers from associating with them. The depression of the early 1840s was a further hammer-blow to them and when conditions favoured revival in the 1850s most Scottish unions had to be rebuilt from scratch. The revived unions were small and localised. Attempts to link together local societies were made by tailors, bakers, slaters, printers, shoemakers, miners, ironmoulders and stonemasons, but the national organisations that were formed were federal in structure, with power and financial control remaining firmly in the hands of the local societies. Many of these national unions had a brief, insignificant existence, but when renewed attempts were made at consolidation in the 1880s it was once again the federal pattern that was adopted: the Operative Bakers' Scottish National Federal Union in 1886; the Scottish National Federation of House and Ship Painters in 1887; the Scottish National Operative Plasterers' Federal Union in 1888. Even the Associated Carpenters and Joiners' Society, which, as the nearest Scotland had to a 'new model' union, did at its foundation adopt central control of strike policy, abandoned centralisation after a few years and left major decisions to the branches. English unions with branches in Scotland from time to time came up against this insistence on local autonomy. The Greenock and Glasgow branches of the Amalgamated Society of Engineers were both suspended in 1857-8 for refusing to accept instructions from William Allan on equalisation of funds. In 1867 most of the Clyde boilermakers left the United Society 'because of the despotic character of the executive committee'.[1]

The stress on local autonomy arose fairly naturally from the structure of the Scottish economy. Glasgow had a dominating position, both in population and in concentration of industry. Clydeside workers were unwilling to accept decisions emanating from Aberdeen, Kirkcaldy or wherever, or to subordinate their own needs to those of other parts of the country. As soon as any efforts to form national unions were made, they came up against the imbalance between Glasgow and the rest of the country. A federal structure helped paper over the differences, but it meant that Scottish trade unionism remained relatively weak.

Central to the activities of English unions in the second half of the nineteenth century was the maintenance of the standard or uniform minimum rate and the regulation of entry through an apprenticeship system, or some modification of it. In Scotland, the stress on local autonomy seems to have discouraged the development of the minimum rate and hardly any Scottish union tried for it. In maintaining apprenticeship regulation, what limited success there had been in the 1850s and 1860s was lost during the following decades. The Scottish Iron Moulders' Union, one of the largest craft unions, possessed, by the end of the 1880s, hardly any trade regulation. The Associated Blacksmiths had no minimum rate, no regulation of piecework, of overtime or of the number of apprentices. Small sectional unions like the irongrinders, coppersmiths, brass-moulders, boltmakers, etc., were generally too busy blacklegging on the A.S.E. to achieve very much and, although all engineering unions were against piecework, it was firmly established on the Clyde by the 1870s. During the building boom of the 1870s, with work available for all, trade regulation by the building trade unions had broken down completely. Only compositors and tailors seem to have been able to restrict entry and even these steadily lost ground. After the *Scotsman* strike of 1872, more and more Edinburgh shops went non-union and the tailors' society only covered the small number in tailors' workshops and had nothing to do with the vast number of sweatshops in which the bulk of the trade was carried on. The one area in which there was some uniformity was in that of hours of work, but even this was not wholly successful. These weaknesses further militated against an effective national organisation.

This structure of Scottish trade unionism, which is so much more reminiscent of French unionism than of the increasingly centralised pattern in England (indeed, both the Scottish and French workers showed a similar resistance to paying dues of a level that would make their unions efficient and viable), gave trades councils (like *bourses du travail*) a peculiarly important role to play. Branches of a union could not look to a powerful national organisation for assistance at a time of dispute and had to look rather to the aid of other unions in their area. Major policy decisions could be made at local level without any reference to a central headquarters. Therefore, the position of an organisation that sought to link together societies in different trades was an important one.

Joint trades' committees to co-ordinate the activity of different societies have a long history in Scotland from general trades' committees in the early years of the nineteenth century through to the Clyde Workers' Committee of 1915 and beyond. Strike movements in Scotland tended to be local movements embracing a number of trades in an area, rather than national movements of one particular craft. The history of many Scottish societies is one of incompetence, maladministration and, occasionally, fraud. Qualities of leadership seem markedly lacking and not until the 1870s and 1880s do secretaries of some note appear, such as James Jack of the Iron Moulders, Matthew Allan of the Stonemasons and Henry Tait of the Railway Servants. From the end of the 1850s, it was the trades councils that attracted the most able unionists and it was trades councils that sought to give a voice to and make a movement from the weak, but fiercely independent, Scottish unions.

I

Glasgow can, with some justice, claim to have inaugurated the movement for permanent trades councils. The Glasgow Council of Trades' Delegates, formed in May 1858, 'to examine, devise and execute the best means of improving the condition of the working classes morally, socially and politically'[2] was not the first such. There was a Liverpool Trades' Guardians' Association, formed in 1848, which had probably fair claim to that distinction. It may not even have been the first in Scotland. A working men's committee, established in Edinburgh as a result of the half-holiday movement of 1853, seems to have continued in existence, dealing mainly with the organisation of the annual trades' holiday (usually a trip to Glasgow!). Certainly, by early 1859, a United Trades Delegates Association of Edinburgh and its Vicinity was well established.[3] However, neither the Liverpool nor the Edinburgh bodies made much general impact. Glasgow, in contrast, very quickly made its presence felt and other councils followed.

The Glasgow Trades Council consisted of two delegates from each affiliated society, irrespective of size, and met weekly. Affiliation fees depended on membership of the society: one with over 300 members paid 15s. per annum, one with under 300, 7/6d.[4] By the end of its first year there were 21 trades affiliated. In February 1859, the Scottish Miners' Association affiliated and Alexander McDonald attended meetings sporadically during the next few years. The man who quickly emerged as the dominating personality in the council was the vice-president, George Newton, representing a small local potters' society. Newton was young, intelligent and dedicated to showing that the working class was responsible and respectable. His death in 1867 deprived Scottish trade unionism of perhaps its most able figure.

At no time did the trades council include all the trade societies of Glasgow, but, in April 1861 there were delegates representing 30 societies, or about two-thirds of the organised trades of the city.[5] As with most trades councils, small craft societies — tailors, potters, shoemakers, bakers — provided the core of the membership and the bulk of the officers, with only an occasional iron-moulder or cotton spinner representing the more mechanised trades. Delegates attended from the local branches of the A.S.E. for a few months, but withdrew on the grounds that the time spent and the cost of attendance 'were not likely to be compensated by any practical benefit'.[6] Indeed the pattern of many societies was that they moved in and out of the council as unity seemed more or less important at the moment. This together with personal and political dissensions contributed to a sharp decline in the council's fortunes in the middle years of the 1860s. One withdrawal led to another and by June 1866 membership was reduced to a mere ten societies.

A similar pattern of rise and decline can be observed in the Edinburgh Trades Council during the decade, though the reasons for decline are not at all clear. Generally, there seems to have been little controversy, though as early as October 1862, the Edinburgh branch of the Associated Carpenters and Joiners of Scotland had been denied permission, by its executive committee, to join the trades council 'on the grounds that the objects of trades councils can never be realised until the associations composing them are each united in itself as a compact body over the whole country. . . . Besides, trades councils as at present constituted embody politics as part of their programme as well as other objects not strictly matters for trade societies'.[7] One main reason for the council's stagnation and decline was its failure to attract new societies. With meetings only monthly, it was difficult to maintain the momentum of agitation, and discussions dragged on for months until they had lost any relevance. Twice in 1865 there was no quorum and only five trades were represented at the annual delegate meeting in January 1866. A few stalwarts struggled to keep the council in being, but no efforts succeeded in attracting the larger and most important of the city's societies, and by the beginning of 1867 the demise of the Council was complete.

Other Scottish towns had sought to follow the example of Glasgow and Edinburgh. In November 1859, a trades' committee in Greenock informed the Glasgow Trades Council of its intention to form a council and four months later a Greenock United Trades Council was in existence.[8] In Dundee a trades council had a brief existence in 1864[9] but it was at the end of 1867 that a more permanent organisation was formed. A trades council was formed in Aberdeen in 1868, partly to give support to masons during a strike, but also to add its voice to the national demand for trade union legislation.

The Edinburgh Trades Council was successfully re-organised and revitalised during 1867 and by the end of 1868 twenty unions were affiliated, 'nearly the whole of the influential societies'. While the Glasgow Trades Council remained more or less moribund, it was Edinburgh that took the lead in Scottish trade union affairs, though fluctuations in attendance at meetings continued to be a problem. With the boom conditions of the early seventies, trades councils shared in the trade union 'explosion'. It was John Bennet, a founder member of the Glasgow Trades Council, who, in 1871, called a meeting to resuscitate the council in time to condemn the new Trade Union Act and the Criminal Law Amendment Act.[10] The council flourished. 'Few important branches were not represented in 1872', and by 1875, 41 societies and branches sent delegates. Matthew Allan, the secretary of the Scottish United Operative Masons' Association, was the moving force behind a revived Greenock United Trades Council in 1872, which grew out of meetings held in protest at the Criminal Law

Amendment Act,[11] and in Fife, Kirkcaldy Trades Council was formed at the end of 1873, modelling itself on Dundee.[12] Of the three councils which sent delegates to the T.U.C. in January 1875, Dundee claimed to speak for 4,000 unionists, Edinburgh for 10,000 and Glasgow for 140,000.

The boom conditions came sharply to an end in 1878 when Glasgow was hit by 'the greatest disaster that had ever befallen the commercial community of Great Britain', when the City of Glasgow Bank failed with debts of £6 million. It had a paralysing effect on Scottish enterprise, with the building trades, that had enjoyed an unprecedented boom, being the most badly hit. The average standard wage of a Glasgow stonemason in 1877 was 40/4d, and in the following year it had fallen to 27/7d, the lowest it had been since 1871. The strength of the Glasgow Trades Council suffered accordingly. In 1880 affiliation had fallen to 38 societies and, though there was a slight recovery in 1882 and 1883, the trend continued downwards to a trough in 1886, with only 32 affiliations. Bad as this was, however, it was not disastrous and the 32 societies of 1886 is the same number as in 1873. In other words, the really spectacular increase in membership in the mid-seventies caused the position in the early 1880s to appear very much more serious than it was. Branches of some large and important societies like the A.S.E. and the Associated Carpenters were conspicuously absent from the council. Nonetheless, more than most trades councils, the Glasgow one represented a cross section of the local trades and an unusually high proportion of the societies affiliated sent their local secretary as delegate.[13] In 1887 there were three general secretaries of national unions on the Council: John Inglis of the Associated Blacksmiths, Henry Tait of the Amalgamated Society of Railway Servants of Scotland, and Alexander Wilkie of the Associated Shipwrights.

The building trades continued to provide a high proportion of the office-bearers. Daniel Ferguson, a mason, was president in 1877, Campbell, a plumber, in 1878, Thomas Macduff, secretary of the Bricklayers, in 1879, and, from 1881 to 1887, R. C. Grant, a joiner. Duncan Kennedy, a housepainter, was the council's secretary from 1877 to 1880. The most prominent member in these years, however, was a member of the Scottish Typographical Association, John Battersby. He was president of the council in 1875 and as such chaired the Glasgow meeting of the T.U.C. in October of that year and was a member of the Parliamentary Committee of the T.U.C. until 1877. In 1880, the secretaryship was taken over by A. J. Hunter, a baker, and he held the position continuously until 1902. He was chief spokesman for the council over these years, though he increasingly fell out of touch with the younger, more militant members.

The depression seems to have hit the Edinburgh trades a little later than those in Glasgow, though the failure of the City of Glasgow Bank was felt in Edinburgh also. The worst years were the first half of the eighties, when 'all trades, with scarcely an exception' were more depressed than at any period in the previous twenty years. Indeed, the council in its evidence to the Royal Commission on the Depression of Trade and Industry in 1886 went so far as to claim that, although in many trades there had been an apparent increase in wages, 'real wages were lower than for many years',[14] a view hardly supported by the facts. In 1875 there were 26 societies, representing about ten thousand unionists, affiliated. In 1880 affiliations had shrunk to 21 societies and continued to decline until 1884, when there were only 16. However, that was the turning point and growth proceeded fairly rapidly from then on. The tailors were one of the largest societies in Edinburgh and provided some of the most active members of the council. Donald McAllen was president in 1875 and 1876, and Neil McLean, local secretary of the Tailors' Society, was secretary to the council from 1880 to 1887.

The decade after 1885 saw an unprecedented growth in trade unionism throughout the United Kingdom. This was especially so among the unskilled workers, but many skilled trades were organised effectively for the first time, and there was a large increase in the membership of many old-established unions. The spread of unionism was accomplished by new demands and a more militant attitude among unionists, changes which were reflected in trades councils. Affiliations rose: in Glasgow from 54 in 1889 to 113 in 1895; in Edinburgh from 34 to 51; in Aberdeen from 30 to 40. In a few years there were fundamental changes in the personnel, the power structure, the role and the policies of trades councils. In addition, there was an outcrop of new councils. Dundee's early council had had but a short life and a new one was formed in 1885. Greenock revived in 1889 and councils were formed at Motherwell, Port Glasgow and Arbroath in the same year. The following year, Falkirk Trades Council was formed thanks to the efforts of R. Chisholm Robertson, secretary of the Stirlingshire Miners and a member of the Glasgow Trades Council.[15] A Kirkcaldy Council was re-formed, while others were established at Govan in 1890 and at Paisley in 1891. A year later one was inaugurated in Inverness and there were others at Hawick, Dunfermline and Montrose sometime during the decade. Not all of these survived, but the Labour Correspondent of the Board of Trade reported 15 Scottish trades councils in 1897.

II

The main activities of all trades councils can be summarised as 'organising', 'agitating' and 'political campaigning'. The Scottish councils were involved in all three.

The part played by Scottish trades councils in organising new societies was both distinctive and pioneering. It took some time before the councils accepted that they had an organising role, since they saw themselves as representative of the already organised trades. However, the revived Edinburgh Trades Council of 1867 wrote into its new rules that one of the means of securing the moral and social advancement of labour was to be 'by assisting to organise trade societies for friendly and other purposes'.[16] An Organising and Agitating Committee was formed and, early in 1868, it helped in the formation of a Labourers'

Association. The Association joined the Council in 1868, after being invited to do so.[17] There were similar efforts at about the same time to organise the horse shoers.[18]

Glasgow Trades Council had no such committee but societies of labourers were affiliated to the council at its foundation. Indoor and Outdoor Labourers' Societies attended the inaugural meeting and a society of harbour labourers affiliated later in 1858,[19] though all of these seem to have dropped out at quite an early stage. There is no further mention of the unskilled in the council until 1874, when the Glasgow Causewaylayers' Association affiliated[20] and, in the next year, a Marine Stokers' Society joined.[21]

Few of the unions of unskilled workers survived the onset of the depression at the end of the 1870s, but immediately there was an improvement in the economic situation, unions of the unskilled reappeared. In Glasgow, for example, a society of outside labourers was again represented at the trades council in 1883.[22] In 1886, Alex. Wilkie of the Shipwrights, with the backing of the council, organised an Associated Mariners' Society to provide witnesses to a Select Committee on the extension of employers' liability to seamen.[23] Neil McLean, the secretary of the Edinburgh Trades Council, gave assistance to the tramwaymen, who were forming a union.[24] On the other hand, a few years later, the Edinburgh Council declined to assist the shop girls to reduce their hours: 'As the persons concerned have no union we can take no action.'[25] The pattern seems to have been that at the first sign of spontaneous action by a group of workers the trades council was likely to involve itself.

As early as 1883, the Aberdeen Trades Council granted £5 to the shore labourers who were on strike. When the strike ended successfully the labourers formed a union and sent three delegates to the trades council.[26] In the following year it was the seamen who organised themselves into a branch of the South Shields' Union and James Annand, a mason, the secretary of the council, spoke at their inaugural meeting 'with the utmost approval of the Trades Council'.[27] A Workmen's Protective and Benefit Society sent two women delegates a few months later, and, at the same meeting, a deputation from the gas-stokers asked the council to assist them to form a protective society.[28] A deputation from the council was appointed to meet with the stokers and, at the December meeting of the council, three delegates were present from the Gas Stokers' Society. In September 1885, Brown, one of the Stokers' delegates, was elected to the Executive Committee. At the beginning of January 1886 Davidson, a shore labourer, replaced him on the committee.

Farm servants in the surrounding countryside also received the benefit of the council's aid, when they made moves towards forming a union. The initiative came from the farm servants themselves, but the trades council immediately assisted them.[29] As a result of a conference organised by the Aberdeen Trades Council, a Scottish Farm Servants' Union was formed. Dr K. D. Buckley describes the role of one of the most active of the council's members, J. C. Thompson, an ironmoulder, president of the council from 1883 to 1885. He was one of the main supporters of the farm servants, and became first general secretary of the Scottish Farm Servants' Union. 'By 1888, he was also secretary of the Shore Labourers' Society, and had added to this the position of secretary of the newly-formed branch of the Amalgamated Union of Seamen and Firemen, whilst still representing the ironmoulders at the Trades Council.'[30]

The annual report of the Glasgow Trades Council for 1889-90, reviewing the great expansion of trade unionism that had taken place during the year, commented,

> It is in this connection a matter of sincere thankfulness that so much has been attempted, and that what has been termed the New Trade Unionism has during the year affected so much, although we doubt the wisdom of attempting to establish any hard and fast line of difference between old and new. So far as we can judge the new are the same as the old, and their modes of procedure are not different in striving for the general good of the class to which they belong. If this is so it will surely be unwise in any way to hinder the good work now being done by all bodies of Unionists by making invidious comparisons. It may be said once and for all, that so far as the Glasgow Trades Council is concerned, during the 32 years of its existence it has known no difference between what is called skilled and unskilled labour, so far as giving help is concerned.[31]

This was fair comment on the trades council's attitude. A. J. Hunter, who wrote the report, had acted as treasurer of the Associated Mariners' Society in 1886. In the autumn of 1888, the council took the part of the harbour labourers against the stevedores. A labourers' society, numbering five hundred members, had been formed some twelve months previously, and the stevedores had tried to break it by importing blacklegs from Belfast. The council unanimously condemned 'the malicious action of said stevedores in endeavouring to import into the present struggle a spirit of sectarianism'.[32] They agreed to help the labourers procure a licence from the Clyde Trust to do both loading and unloading, but they were only successful in getting a limited licence, to unload.[33] The Labourers' Society did not survive, but in February 1889, Havelock Wilson and two Glasgow Irishmen, Edward McHugh and Richard McGhee, formed in Glasgow the National Union of Dock Labourers, assisted by another member of the council, Duncan McPherson, a tinplate worker.[34] In May, the union sent two delegates to the council.

At the end of 1888, the Glasgow Council co-operated with Darby, who had come from North Shields to re-organise the seamen and firemen on the Clyde,[35] and by January the new society was sending delegates to council meetings. By February, the seamen were on strike, and on the proposal of Chisholm Robertson, the secretary of the Forth and Clyde Miners, an appeal to the societies was issued by the trades council on their behalf. Robertson was also authorised to use the council's name when he went to Belfast to assist Darby in organising the seamen there.[36] Robertson was probably the most active organiser of new unions. He presided at meetings of the workmen employed by the American-owned tramway company, and helped form a tramwaymen's union. But other council members were active also. William Eddy, for example, presided over a council committee that was responsible for setting up a union of women workers in the city.[37]

Regular reports were made to the council on the state of organisation. At the end of 1889, Darby reported on the 1,500 members of the Gas Stokers'

Union, and George Carson, a tinplate worker and secretary of the recently formed Scottish Labour Party, on the Postmen and Paviors.[38] A small committee of the council organised a union of quarriers and the Maltmen's Society was formed with the assistance of Henry Tait, secretary of the Railway Servants, and A. J. Hunter. This work of organising continued through the nineties. At times, there were problems. The Operative Bricklayers' Society and the Slaters strongly opposed a motion from a labourers' delegate that

... the time has arrived when the different skilled trades represented should in all cases where labourers are required to help or attend to them, take legal steps to have those labourers organised, and thereby give practical effect to the resolution in reference thereto passed by the T.U.C. sitting in Glasgow.[39]

A similar situation arose in the following year when the Plasterers' Society withdrew from the council after they had been criticised for failing to support their labourers in a dispute.

The pattern of development in Edinburgh was not so very different. An investigation by the trades council, at the end of 1888, 'showed the necessity of some steps being taken without delay to improve the position of labour in the city.'[40] Once again, attention was turned to the tramwaymen, as a body of men most obviously in need of a protective organisation, since they were still being subjected to exceptionally long hours. The leading officials of the council acted as office-bearers in a tramwaymen's society in 1889. The council's organisation committee was also involved in the formation of societies of dock labourers, of gas workers and of masons' labourers in the early summer of 1889,[41] and the committee continued in existence during the nineties. It is found, for example, launching a labourers' union in 1893 and again in 1897.[42]

There is no evidence in the activities of the Scottish trades councils of any deep-seated hostility between skilled and unskilled workers. Indeed, the Scottish councils went out of their way to assist new unions. The weakness of the Scottish unions may have contributed to the lack of hostility, since the lines between skilled and unskilled in Scotland were less sharply drawn. Trades council activity among the unskilled in Scotland preceded 1889 and the influx of 'new unionists' into trades councils and antedated any really extensive socialist influence on trades councils. The really remarkable developments were in Aberdeen, where each year from 1883 saw members of the trades council involved in organising. No trades council in Britain compares with it. Presumably a great deal depended upon the personality of a few local leaders and upon the fact that Aberdeen escaped the worst effects of the depression of 1884-7.

III

Trades councils provided a forum for the general demands of labour. Conditions of work could be discussed and improvements demanded in general terms, as they could not be at union branch meetings. They were a place where grievances could be aired and a means whereby demands could be brought before the general public. This was particularly important in Scotland, where the councils often took the lead in agitations. Among the most important of these was the demand for shorter hours.

While there was unanimity on the need for shorter hours of labour, there were differences of opinion on how this was to be achieved. Already in 1858, when the matter was first raised at the Glasgow Trades Council, the main lines of the division of opinion could be discerned. The question was raised by Smith, a labourers' delegate:

> He had long felt that a great cause of evil among the industrious classes was the overtime worked, and the too long hours that many had to labour. The remedy was to shorten their hours, by which a more just and equitable share of employment might be obtained by all. He had no definite plan by which to shorten the hours of labour, but he thought as a beginning of agitation on the subject, a memorial to the legislature should be numerously signed and presented.[43]

McKay, a mason, took the opposite line, and asserted that 'the shortening of the hours of labour was a measure which the working classes must carry themselves'. This division was to bedevil discussion on shorter hours for the next forty years. In 1858, apart from a general declaration in favour of an eight-hour day, nothing was done.

As befitted a council that had grown out of a short-time movement, Edinburgh took the lead in advocating a general nine-hour day. The movement originated among the masons — no doubt inspired by events in London in 1861 — but the council followed up their initiative by calling a public meeting, addressed by George Potter.[44] Only the Carpenters' Society seems to have joined the movement and, confronted by a lock-out organised by the Master Builders' Association, the movement collapsed.

In 1869, the reconstituted council again embarked on a short-time movement, 'with a view to instituting a national agitation for the adoption of fifty hours as a week's work'.[45] In fact, when the movement was launched, it was for a fifty-one hour week (probably to get greater support) as 'the only practical method of giving employment to our surplus labour and thereby enabling the workmen to influence the labour market in their favour, so as to secure a more reasonable share of the wealth which labour produces, and thus prevents the working man sinking into processes of social and national deterioration which will eventually subvert the best interests of the community'.[46]

The campaign aroused considerable interest. George Potter, who had a regular column in the Edinburgh radical weekly, *The Reformer*, was very much in favour and urged the calling of a national conference on the question. Eccarius wrote from the General Council of the International welcoming the move:

> Either the work people must insist upon a reduction of the working hours, or they must surrender all benefits, derivable from our improved hours of production, to the non-producing rich and perish from want in the midst of rapidly increasing wealth.[47]

Within three years, a fifty-one hour week had been obtained by blacksmiths, engineers, moulders, brassfounders and tinplate workers, and a fifty-four hour week by printers, bookbinders and typefounders.[48] As depression deepened at the end of the 1870s, the council organised a 51 Hours Defence League, but found among the societies little will to fight.[49]

When the demand for shortening of hours was revived in the eighties, it was for an eight-hour working day. Again, in Scotland, the Edinburgh Trades Council was at the forefront, when James Wood, a masons' delegate, in 1884 proposed that 'owing to the depressed state of trade and the large numbers of men who were idle . . . the time has arrived when the working day should be reduced to 8 hours.'[50] It was carried unanimously and some discussion took place among the trades. In 1887, the council's delegate to the T.U.C. was instructed to support a motion in favour of an eight-hour bill. However, from 1888, a reaction set in. The Lib-Lab elements in the council dug in their heels and until 1891 a majority of the council was against a legislative eight hours. What altered things was the influx of new societies into the council during 1890 and 1891. Even more important, however, was the Scottish Railway Strike of 1891, 'due to the withering indifference of the respective general managers and their directorates to the appeals of the men for a readjustment of their conditions of service, very specially working hours from 144 per fortnight to a sixty-hour week'.[51] In August 1891, the council's delegate was again instructed to vote for legislation. By the spring of 1893 they were marching with James Connolly and the Socialist Federation in the May Day procession, announcing that 'relief from our industrial drudgery can be best secured by legislative enactment' and calling for 'the democratic administration of the industries by which they live'.[52]

Nowhere was the eight-hour day so vital an issue as in Aberdeen. The trades council there was the first to declare itself in favour of legislation, early in 1888.[53] They were the only trades council to agree to this in the replies to the T.U.C.'s plebiscite on the issue. Aberdeen's attitude is explained by its enthusiasm for that maverick officer and gentleman, Henry Hyde Champion. To Champion a legislative eight-hour day was the key issue, upon which his whole political philosophy was based. He envisaged himself playing the role of Parnell in a party based on support of an eight-hour bill. He found staunch support in Aberdeen.

It was the trades council that organised the first May Day in Aberdeen in 1890, ensuring its success by confining their resolution to a general eight-hour demand. But the council itself was firmly committed to legislative action. Although it was still possible for them to pull out of the May Day celebration when the Socialists insisted on their being held on a Sunday, there was no doubt about their position. This was Champion's panacea and as they stuck to Champion, so they stuck to an eight-hour bill. To them it was the obvious basis for a labour party in Parliament and, in 1894, they urged that 'all labour candidates returned to Parliament pledged to support an eight hours day form themselves into a separate and distinct party who will sit in opposition to the Government of the day.'[54]

The Glasgow Trades Council moved cautiously on the question of legislative action. In discussions on the issue in 1887 and 1888 the council was fairly evenly divided on the issue. In 1889, by 15 votes to 13, the delegate to the T.U.C. was instructed to support an eight-hour bill. A year later, however, there was 'practical unanimity' and from 1892 the council was taking part in the annual May Day rally, alongside the Scottish Labour Party, the Social Democratic Federation, the Socialist League and the Labour Army.[55] The course of events was very similar in Dundee, where the delegates to the 1889 Congress were instructed to vote for eight hours by legislation.

The marked lack of success that had met efforts to get a general eight-hour bill through the House of Commons caused the Govan Trades and Labour Council to suggest a conference of Scottish Labour bodies 'for the purpose of endeavouring to obtain an eight hours working day, or a maximum of 48 hours per week, in the shipbuilding and engineering industries'.[56] The conference was held in October 1894 and delegates attended from fourteen trades councils. Any sectional effort was condemned, and it was unanimously carried that legal enactment of an eight-hour day be made a test question at the next general election.[57]

It is clear from the activities of trades councils over the issue of the eight-hour day that there was, as Clegg, Fox and Thompson point out, 'no clear-cut division between the new socialists and an "old gang" hopelessly bound to the doctrines of non-interference'.[58] Most councils swung round to supporting a bill before there was a significant influx of either socialists or new unionists. Aberdeen, Dundee and Glasgow all came out in support of an eight-hour bill before the T.U.C. of 1889. In the case of Glasgow, the majority was small and involved only two people changing their minds. In Aberdeen, on the other hand, a large majority of the council declared in favour of a bill in 1888. The contrast to this is Edinburgh, where a majority held out against legislative action until the end of 1891.

Aberdeen's early support of legislation can be seen as part of its generally sympathetic attitude towards the unskilled. But the Edinburgh council certainly could not be regarded as unsympathetic. Much seems to have depended on the views and effectiveness of a few key individuals who guided the meetings. John Mallinson, an Edinburgh shoemaker, very effectively held up the Edinburgh conversion. One thing does emerge clearly. The debate for or against a legislative shortening of the working day was being carried on among the members of the 'old unions'. The conversion of trades councils to legislative action took place, not as a result of new unionists gaining a majority, but through members of the old unions changing their opinions on the issue. This was part of a much wider change in attitude that was also reflected in political activity.

IV

All trades councils engaged in multifarious pressure-group activities, particularly on local issues. A careful eye was kept on the salaries and perquisites of local officials. The Glasgow Trades Council protested in 1881 against superannuation of Parochial Board officials from the rates. In 1885 they objected to the proposed increase in the salary of the Water Commissioner. Edinburgh protested at increases for the city superintendent in 1884 and for the city chamberlain in the following year.[59]

The local courts were also closely supervised. In 1874, the Glasgow Trades Council protested at the allegedly excessive penalties being imposed by one of the bailies,[60] and, a few years later, the Edinburgh Trades Council was complaining that sheriff court decisions in cases of dispute between employers and employed revealed 'very doubtful justice'.[61]

In spite of a certain basic unwillingness to see any increase in the city expenditure, trades councils generally were in favour of city improvements. Among the earliest resolutions of the Glasgow Trades Council was one commending the town council's efforts 'to beautify and improve the city' by the acquisition of public parks and a picture gallery.[62] With support of public improvements went the campaign for free public libraries. The Glasgow Trades Council raised the matter in 1860[63] and Edinburgh took up the movement in 1864.[64] The campaigns of the sixties met with scant success. The defeat of the proposal in Edinburgh was attributed, by the trades council's library committee, to the activities of the 'independent liberal shopkeepers', though the full council caused this to be deleted from their report.[65] The issue of libraries revived again in the eighties. The Glasgow Trades Council approached the Corporation on the issue in 1883, and as a result a committee of citizens was formed. Again, however, free libraries were rejected in a poll, due to the 'indifference of the workers' and the 'antagonism of petty shop-keepers'.[66] The council continued to agitate for the adoption of the Free Libraries Act into the nineties.[67] The Edinburgh Trades Council was similarly active on the issue in the 1880s, urging the acceptance of Andrew Carnegie's offer of £50,000 to establish a library.[68] Because of Carnegie, the movement in Scotland was pursued more actively and met with wider success than was the case in England.

Another matter upon which trades councils exerted pressure upon the local authorities and on which Scottish councils were particularly active was the municipalisation of public utilities. The Aberdeen Trades Council seems to have led the way in this field when, in July 1870, the council unanimously declared itself in favour of the purchase of the gas works by the town council on the ground that 'the community should have the control of supplying gas to the city and suburbs in their own hands'.[69] It was from the eighties, however, that there were intensified demands for further municipalisation. By a majority of 23 to 4, the Edinburgh Trades Council called for the municipalisation of the gas works in 1885. Two years later the call was repeated, this time unanimously. The town council was already making moves in that direction and when, later in the year, the gas works were bought over, the trades council protested at the excessive compensation paid and found that the city had got a 'bad bargain'.[70] The Glasgow Trades Council expressed similar sentiments when Glasgow Corporation bought over three gas works.[71]

Glasgow's main concern was over its tramways. The American-owned tramway company had long been a source of dissatisfaction. The company refused to extend the service — rental to the corporation being by mile of track — or to improve the hours and conditions of their men. In the spring of 1889 members of the council had organised the tramwaymen into a union and when the company started dismissing unionists, the council decided to 'take such steps as are calculated to prevent the renewal of the Tramway Company's lease'.[72] There were demonstrations and questions asked at municipal election meetings. The agitation had its effect, as a contemporary noted:

> For some time this proposal [to municipalise the tramways] was treated as 'rank socialism'. But it was not long in commending itself to the citizens. As often happens, the citizen tail wagged the corporation dog, and a speedy *volte face* was made by Councillors who had been most backward in the matter.[73]

The corporation took over the tramways when the lease expired in 1894.

On many such local issues the trades councils were acting in conjunction with other groups, and it is difficult to estimate the specific significance of trades council pressure. On one issue, however, trades councils can claim most honour. They successfully persuaded local authorities to adopt fair contracts resolutions. Both the Edinburgh and the Glasgow Trades Councils had published exposés of 'sweating' in the tailoring trade in the 1860s. But it was as a result of the House of Lords' Committee on the subject in 1888 that a co-ordinated agitation developed.

The Glasgow Trades Council memorialised the corporation on the conditions under which police uniforms were produced, and called on it to ensure that all contractors paid the standard rate of wages.[74] At about the same time the Edinburgh Trades Council asked the city fathers 'to insert a clause in [clothing] contracts to prevent sub-contracting and to provide that all work shall be done in the contractor's workshop'.[75] By 1892 Edinburgh had persuaded the corporation to adopt a fair wages resolution and Glasgow followed soon afterwards. But the struggle did not end there. A group in Glasgow Town Council were trying to get the resolution rescinded in 1895[76] and in Edinburgh there were complaints that the resolution was being largely disregarded.[77]

During the 1860s trades councils tended to concentrate on trade union matters. If they did look outside it was usually to political matters. However, from the 1870s onwards, a new interest in a wide range of local matters is observable. It is a sign of a growing confidence on the part of trades councils and of a readiness to speak for the whole of the working class in their town. It is also evidence of the willingness of local officials to accept the leaders of trades councils as spokesmen of the workers. Finally, it showed a growing awareness on the part of trade unionists that unions had to be more than merely bodies for protecting wages and conditions of work, but had to be responsible for, and take action on behalf of, the wider working class.

V

In the nineteenth century, trades councils were the only trade union forum for political debate and rallying point for political pressure. The campaign of the 1860s against the Master and Servant Act, initiated, led and co-ordinated by the Glasgow Trades Council, is too well-known to need examining in detail here.[78] It provided an important example of the possibilities of united action and was followed on many later issues.

The trades councils in Glasgow and in Edinburgh had parliamentary bills committees in the early 1870s, to supervise legislation affecting labour and to draw attention to any important matters.[79] At the instigation of the Glasgow Trades Council in 1878 a campaign, based on the trades councils, for an extension of the hours of polling, was launched, and Glasgow again led the successful campaign for public inquiries into fatal accidents in Scotland.[80] Another favourite theme of Scottish trades councils was temperance and they moved from support of permissive bills,[81] to loval veto,[82] ending, in the nineties, by favouring the municipalisation of the drink trade.[83]

The question of direct involvement in party politics caused major crises in most trades councils. For some members it was impossible to deal with the problems of labour without becoming involved in political activity. For others, any political activity was likely to divide and weaken the trades councils. Yet, in all councils, there was a hard core of activists who were keen to take up political activities. There is some evidence that to George Newton and John Bennet and other founder-members of the Glasgow Trades Council the main purpose of the organisation was to develop into a forum for political debate. Time and again, in the early 1860s, the leaders of the council sought to light some spark of enthusiasm for parliamentary reform in the ranks of their constituents, only to meet with a smothering apathy.

In 1861, Newton, overcoming considerable opposition, managed to persuade the council to issue an *Address to the Workingmen of the United Kingdom*, calling on them 'to put forth your energies once more for the attainment of that share of political power which is our due' and to use trade societies and trades councils as 'the best machinery for carrying out a successful movement of this kind'.[84] It was a crucial step on the road to 1867, welcomed by John Bright and stimulating a political debate in London and elsewhere. Yet, for Glasgow, the effects were near disastrous. The council was left with a debt of £10 and a greatly reduced membership, as bricklayers', ironmoulders', and ropespinners' societies withdrew in protest. Continuing political activities, including the Master and Servant Act campaign, caused such difficulties that in a final effort to save the council from extinction the word 'political' was dropped from the constitution. Just as the parliamentary reform campaign was reaching its peak, the council had to decline to take part in it as it had 'given up its political character'.[85] On the other hand, individual council members were actively involved.[86]

Edinburgh's pattern was almost the exact opposite. At first the council generally avoided political discussion and declined to consider the issue of parliamentary reform.[87] However, with the revitalised reform movement in 1866, the Edinburgh council took a more positive attitude. It called an open meeting out of which grew a Working Men's Political Union, and it was the council that organised a trades' demonstration in November 1866, out of which emerged a branch of the Scottish Reform League.

With reform achieved, the council issued questions to the candidates, but took no part in the general election of 1868. In local politics, on the other hand, the council became increasingly active. It publicised division lists of relevant debates in the town council, such as that which had defeated the move to have an inspector appointed under the Workshops' Act,[88] or the one which refused a rise of a shilling per week in the wages of the scavengers.[89] The activities culminated in the council's decision 'to use its best endeavours to secure the direct representation of labour in the Edinburgh Town Council'.[90] The initiative which led to this decision had come from William Paterson, secretary of the Joiners' Association, and it was he who was asked to stand. A decision to contest the Canongate Ward was altered when the Independent Liberals (the group associated with the city's radical member Duncan McLaren) offered to support a working man as a candidate in Broughton Ward, in opposition to the retiring councillor, Bailie Millar, who had deserted the camp of the Independent Liberals. Less than a fortnight before the election, however, Millar returned to the fold and was accepted as the Independent Liberals' candidate. The trades council tried to transfer their effort to Canongate Ward, but they had little time available to make an impact.[91]

The episode left a residue of bitterness and resulted in the declaration that 'this Council in future connect itself with none of the present political parties but confine itself to the representation of labour'.[92] Nevertheless, the following year the council was again communicating with the Independent Liberals. A general meeting of trades' delegates declared their belief in the need for the return of *bona fide* working men to the town council and a Trades Council Municipal Election Committee was formed. Eventually, two candidates, Paterson and J. H. Waterston, went to the poll with the support of the council, unopposed by the Independent Liberals. Both were convincingly defeated.[93] One result, however, was that the Municipal Election Committee formed itself into a permanent body, 'the Scottish Reform Union', as 'an advocate of the political rights of labour', though its fortunes are obscure.[94]

The Edinburgh Trades Council's political activity at this time was by no means unanimously approved of and the printers detected some dangerous tendencies, as was made apparent in the *Scottish Typographical Circular* of 1871:

A local election instantly transforms the Council into a democratic election committee; the marriage of a member of the reigning family reveals the real tendencies of the men; the visit of a free-thinking Republican lecturer is hailed with delight, and his sage utterances passed from lip to lip as morsels of unsurpassing sweetness; Communist insurgents are sympathised with in their most objectionable transactions and the doctrine seriously enunciated, that 'until there is a universal Republic the workers can never enjoy the blessings of peace'.[95]

Not many of the trades councillors would have recognised themselves in this description and, indeed, the high political excitement of 1869 and 1870 was not maintained. There was division in the council between those who sought an independent line and those closely tied to the Advanced Liberal supporters of Duncan McLaren. Although there were frequent criticisms of the views of McLaren on issues like the Criminal Law Amendment Act, generally it was the latter who won within the council.

It was the fury aroused by the Criminal Law Amendment Act of 1871 that revived political discussion in the Glasgow Trades Council: a new generation of activists talked of 'arranging for the election of a working man as one of the three members of the House of Commons for Glasgow'. [96] Predictably, discussion became bogged down in a debate on 'what would be the religious opinion of the candidate', with warnings from some delegates that they would not give 'aid to return a secularist working man candidate'. [97] A 'plebiscite' to sound out working-class opinion was planned, but Gladstone's snap election of 1874 put paid to all schemes.

During the election of 1868, the newly formed Aberdeen Trades Council made no move against the sitting candidate. The council did take an active interest in local affairs and was an active proponent of a scheme for the expansion of the city south of the River Dee. The issue of whether or not to buy land for this purpose remained the subject of acrimonious debate at the municipal elections, and, because the parties were so evenly balanced, the council found it 'impracticable to put forward any *bona fide* working men, this year, as candidates'. [98] The pattern was repeated in the following years.

Any gratitude for the labour legislation from the Conservative government of 1874 to 1880 was short-lived, and unionists aligned firmly with the Liberal opposition and stirred to the ringing moral utterances of Mr Gladstone. However, during Gladstone's second ministry, some doubts began to appear. Scottish radicals and trade unionists were particularly disturbed by the crofters' agitation and the failure of the government to implement the recommendations of the Napier Commission. There was a growing questioning of the economic system. Indeed, the Edinburgh Trades Council warned the Royal Commission on the Depression of Trade and Industry that there was a real danger of 'social revolution' and 'a great uprising of the people in the demand for justice', 'unless steps are at once taken to bring about a general diffusion of the soil among the people, and to reduce the number of non-producers'. [99] Socialist propaganda was important also in opening unionists' eyes to the inadequacies of Liberalism, though the Glasgow Trades Council was at pains in 1885 to distinguish itself from the socialist Scottish Land Restoration League. None of the five League candidates in the election received support from the trades council and lack of money was consistently used by the council as an excuse for not taking a more active part in politics. However, in 1888, by 23 votes to 9, the council agreed to support Keir Hardie's candidature at the Mid-Lanark by-election. Yet, a few months later, they declined to send a delegate to the founding conference of the Scottish Labour Party. On more

than one occasion in 1889, Hardie addressed the council and sought its affiliation, but the Lib-Lab element, led by Henry Tait of the Railwaymen's Union,
successfully blocked this move.[100] Rather desultory efforts to elect labour
candidates to the town council and the school board came to nothing.

The Aberdeen Trades Council took part from time to time in local elections,
to the extent of approving of certain candidates, but in 1884 two of the council's
members were elected as Labour candidates, largely as a protest against
increased salaries for public officials. A few months later, at the School Board
election, the council's six nominees were elected.[101] It was therefore in a
position of considerable strength to demand the nomination of a working-class
candidate at the approaching general election. When the Radical Association
pointed out to the council that the time had come to choose candidates for the
election, the council regarded it as an invitation to nominate a labour candidate. An approach was made to Henry Broadhurst, the secretary of the
T.U.C., but he had already accepted a Birmingham nomination. The
Liberal Association now made it clear that they would not share the responsibility of nominating a candidate with either the trades council or the Radical
Association. The council's response was 'we must look to ourselves to get men
to represent ourselves'. Together with the Radical Association the council
nominated Dr W. A. Hunter, a leading advocate of free education, which had
long been one of the council's enthusiasms, as their candidate and prepared to
run him against Liberal opposition. However, the Liberal Association caved in
and Hunter was duly elected Member for North Aberdeen.[102]

When the redistribution of seats in Edinburgh took place, the trades council
made efforts to organise the return of a working man. They still hoped to work
through the Liberal party, but the local association declined to accept any of
the council's nominees.[103] Political activities were not resumed until early in
1888, when three candidates, backed by a predominantly trades council
committee, were elected to the school board.[104] Flushed with this success, they
began to look towards the municipal elections in November, but were unable to
find any working man willing to stand. Neil McLean, the council's secretary,
was sent as delegate to the inaugural conference of the Scottish Labour Party in
August 1888[105] and although there was general support in the council for the
programme of the new party, with the exception of state interference with the
hours of labour, the council did not in fact affiliate, claiming that there already
was a labour electoral association. However, the council's delegate to the 1889
T.U.C. was instructed to support 'any proposal tending towards the formation
of a distinct Labour Party in Parliament'. In November, the Trades Council
nominated two candidates, both backed by the Liberals and one, A. C. Telfer,
was returned for St Cuthbert's Ward.[106]

Everywhere 1885 was the key year. With the redistribution of seats, trade
unionists were, with increasing insistence, demanding the return of working
men to local bodies and to Parliament. The demands coincided with the growth
of socialist organisations and the spread of socialist ideas. They coincided also
with crisis within the Liberal Party. In Scotland, the party was torn apart by the

bitter debate on disestablishment of the church, which led many radical members of parliament along increasingly sterile by-ways, and by the split on the issue of Irish Home Rule. At a time when working-class aspirations were growing, the Liberal Party, and particularly the local Liberal associations, were unwilling and frequently unable to respond to them. As a result, snubbed by those whom they had regarded as their natural allies, trade unionists found that they were being pushed towards independent labour politics. It was not easy, and time and again efforts at independence came up against a lack of financial backing or a lack of enthusiasm, but the trend was unmistakable.

A new initiative came from the Aberdeen Trades Council in 1891 when, at its suggestion, a conference was called in Edinburgh to consider the question of labour representation. The *eminence grise* of Aberdeen labour was H. H. Champion. His family background was in Aberdeenshire and he had visited the city, under the auspices of the Scottish Land and Labour League and the Scottish Socialist Federation, in 1887 and 1888. On these occasions he had made contact with some of the more radical members of the Aberdeen Junior Liberal Association, impressing, in particular, the secretary, George Gerrie, a young bank clerk. Champion returned in 1890 to address the May Day rally, stressing in his speech the importance of the eight-hour day and of independent labour representation. A labour committee around Gerrie was established as an independent body, but the main agitation for an eight-hour day remained in the hands of the trades council. The members of the council unanimously agreed to 'pledge themselves to make the interests of labour the first and determining question in all their political action, imperial and local'.[107]

At the beginning of 1891, a committee of three from the council was appointed to co-operate with the same number from the Labour Committee 'to draw up a programme of labour questions of pressing importance'.[108] This joint committee recommended that the council call a national conference of delegates from trades and labour councils. Hardie wrote showing an interest, stating that he himself had intended calling a conference but was willing to fall in with Aberdeen's arrangements, and the council agreed that 'anyone could take part in the conference who was favourable to the labour interest but who was precluded from becoming a trade unionist'.[109]

The conference was held in Edinburgh on 8 August 1891. Aberdeen had intended it to be only a preliminary to a larger conference, but, sixty-seven delegates, representing 84,000 members, attended. Andrew Purdie, the president of the Edinburgh Trades Council, was chairman and Hardie was among those present. It had already been decided by Aberdeen that five issues were to be given prominence at the conference: (a) What means might be taken to secure the return of a body of labour members for Scotland; (b) payment of members of parliament; (c) payment of election expenses out of the rates; (d) a legislative eight-hour day; and (e) abolition of the conspiracy laws. Rightly, many delegates saw Gladstone as a major obstacle to weaning the working class away from liberalism and there were denunciations of the 'Grand Old Humbug'. The motion eventually adopted recommended that unions should support those candidates nominated by 'recognised local labour organisation' who were 'in no wise connected with either of the great political parties'. An executive, consisting of one representative from each trades council and one from the Scottish Labour party, was appointed to prepare a report on political organisation.[110]

A second conference was held in Glasgow on 5 March 1892, when the structure of a new political party was proposed, firmly based on trades councils:

> As the present movement for the better representation of labour on all public bodies and in Parliament has been initiated by the Trades Councils, and as we expect to obtain the chief aid to it from these organisations, we recommend that the trades councils in their respective centres should be responsible, recognised managers of the branches of the proposed Labour Representation Party, that the Trades Councils be looked upon as the head of the branches in which each exists, that no branch should be recognised in any centre unless it has the approval of the Trades Council in that centre.[111]

Thus was established the Scottish United Trades Councils Independent Labour Party, with an executive consisting of delegates from each of the affiliated councils — Aberdeen, Edinburgh, Falkirk, Glasgow, Arbroath, Dunfermline, Govan, Kilmarnock and Paisley, with George Carson representing the Scottish Labour Party. The secretary of the party was R. Chisholm Robertson, whom Page Arnot had called the 'stormy petrel' of the Scottish miners and to whom R. B. Cunninghame Graham referred as 'Robespierre'.[112] Chisholm Robertson had clashed with Hardie at the T.U.C. in 1889, and clearly there was a great deal of personal rivalry between the two for the leadership of the Scottish miners. However, it would be wrong to see the S.T.C.L.P. as being founded with the intention of rivalling the S.L.P.; rather it was an attempt to give the independent labour movement a firm trade union basis, something which Hardie had always regarded as vitally important to the success of a labour party.

The programme of the party consisted of demands for a legal eight-hour day, adult suffrage, one man, one vote, reform of the registration laws, payment of M.P.s, payment of official election expenses from the rates, nationalisation of land, mines and railways, amendment of the factory laws, employers' liability amendment act, local option, triennial parliaments, and a second ballot.[113] The party was poised somewhere between liberalism and full independence, as became clear from Chisholm Robertson's answer to questions in August 1892:

Q.   Does the assertion of independence by the S.T.C.L.P. imply antagonism to all political parties?

A.   No, not necessarily antagonism to both, but independence of either.

Q.   Should the S.T.C.L.P. be willing to co-operate with the Liberal Party, as a matter of policy, in securing their aims?

A.   The party are willing to co-operate with any party which goes furthest in advancing the programme which the needs of the workers most urgently demand.

Q.   Would the S.T.C.L.P. at any time recommend working men to support Parliamentary Labour candidates when it was quite apparent that by so doing they would split the Liberal vote and be likely to secure the return of unionists?

A.   The circumstances of the case shall determine the action of the party.[114]

The limitations to independence came out at the general election of 1892 when the party issued its list of approved candidates. These included labour candidates like John Wilson, the Broxburn miners' leader, at Edinburgh Central, Robert Brodie at Glasgow College, Cunninghame Graham at Camlachie, H. H. Champion at South Aberdeen, and Chisholm Robertson in Stirlingshire. But, they also included liberals, in some cases of doubtful radicalism, like Peter Esslemont in East Aberdeenshire, Sir William Wedderburn in North Ayrshire, Seymour Keay at Nairn and William Birkmyre at Ayr Burghs.[115]

The results for the labour men were fairly disappointing. In Glasgow, Cunninghame Graham was the most successful with 906 votes, while Brodie, standing against the well-entrenched radical member Charles Cameron, who was in fact helped by some of the trades councillors, received a mere 225.[116] Chisholm Robertson in Stirlingshire came a poor third with 663 votes. John Wilson, who stood in Edinburgh, with the backing of a branch of the S.T.C.L.P., polled 783 votes. In Aberdeen the Labour Committee had dissolved itself into a branch of the S.T.C.L.P. and backed Champion, who was the most successful of the independent labour candidates in Scotland with 991 votes.[117]

During the election campaign there had been many accusations about 'Tory gold' used against the Labour Party candidates, and these continued after the election. At the Edinburgh Trades Council, John Mallinson, an arch-opponent of independent labour action, claimed to have evidence that the S.T.C.L.P. had been offered £1,000 by the Tory Party on condition that it would contest certain Liberal seats. Another delegate raised the figure to £3,000.[118] Chisholm Robertson wrote indignantly denying such accusations, but because of the link with Champion, who was becoming an increasingly suspect figure in many labour circles, largely because of his association with the enigmatic 'Tory Socialist' Maltman Barry, there were doubts about the party's future. However, it continued to grow for some time, and at the annual conference in March 1893 it was claimed that the party had thirty branches. But, already the signs of decline were clear to see from the poor attendance at the conference. In January 1893 the I.L.P. had been established at Bradford, and for many activists this at last seemed to offer a coherent organisation for independent labour. The executive of the S.T.C.L.P. recommended dissolution of the party into the I.L.P. In October 1893 Champion sought to revive the S.T.C.L.P. as a rival to Hardie and the I.L.P., which he regarded as still too closely associated with Liberalism. The effort failed and Champion, discredited, departed for the Antipodes.[119]

After 1893 the initiatives for independent political activity passed to the Scottish Labour Party and the I.L.P., with trades councils playing a secondary role. There was still considerable resistance to socialism and to the I.L.P. within all trades councils and, indeed, the mid-1890s saw a revival of the Liberal elements in both Aberdeen and Edinburgh, and to a lesser extent in Glasgow. Although a majority in all trades councils were committed to independent labour politics by the mid-1890s, they were far from convincing a majority of the working class. The early promise of Scottish independent labour activity was not fulfilled. Although there were still some victories in local council elections in most cities, there was a long way to travel before anything like labour majorities appeared in sight. The initiatives in national politics, the S.L.P., the S.T.C.L.P. and, in January 1900, the Scottish Workers' Representation Committee, bore little fruit. Two Labour M.P.s by 1914 was surprisingly little to show for thirty years of effort.

VI

A recurring hope in Scottish trades councils was that they would in time form the basis for some kind of national federation of unions. The Glasgow Trades Council had got the length of issuing a discussion pamphlet in 1861, but since the Edinburgh Trades Council thought the trades 'were not ripe for such a scheme', it was abandoned.[120] The re-formed council took it up again in 1871 and in June 1872 a United Trades Confederation of Scotland was launched. The primary aim was 'to levy a small sum of each trade, according to its numerical strength, for the purpose of supplementing the aliment of those who already have a protective fund, and generally assisting trades in the throes of a lock-out, or strike that could not be averted without loss or degradation, instead of at present depending partly if not wholly on eleemosynary aid'.[121] The Confederation survived until the end of 1873, but collapsed largely because it failed to get the support of the larger societies.[122]

From time to time there were further discussions of federation. The Edinburgh Trades Council looked at the possibilities of a local federation, but found a lack of interest. Schemes for British federations foundered on the hostility of the big societies, who had no desire to subsidise what they regarded as the often irresponsible militancy of small unions. A West of Scotland trade union conference in 1887 again discussed federation but felt there were still too many difficulties in the way.[123] Aberdeen Trades Council raised the issue in 1889, but again found no enthusiasm, and an East of Scotland Federation planned by the Edinburgh Trades Council foundered on the rocks of apathy within months.[124]

The situation altered in 1895, when a sub-committee of the Parliamentary Committee of the T.U.C. announced the alteration of standing orders, with the effect that trades councils would now be excluded from meetings of Congress. It was the culmination of long drawn out efforts to eliminate the double representation which trades councils often produced and to give greater influence to the large societies. Already trades council representation had been sharply reduced by the raising of affiliation fees. The decision to exclude trades councils naturally caused a flurry among them and the London Trades Council sought to organise a rival 'Labour Parliament', but without success.

In Scotland, however, the proposals for a conference of trades councils were greeted with much more enthusiasm. In November 1895, a meeting summoned by the Aberdeen Trades Council in Dundee, and consisting of representatives of trades councils of Aberdeen, Dundee, Edinburgh, Glasgow, Govan and Paisley, agreed to support the London Trades Council in establishing a conference of trades councils. The exclusion was condemned as being at the expense of the small societies and as transferring all power to the paid secretaries, and ending local involvement.[125]

The prevailing opinion among the majority of the English councils was that efforts to alter the standing order to re-admit trades councils ought to be persisted with. The Scottish trades councils rapidly discarded any hope of revision, however, and, at a conference called by the Falkirk Trades Council in April 1896 once again to take up the question of a confederation of Scottish unions, a resolution was passed recommending the formation of a 'trades union conference for Scotland, which would include the trades unions and trades councils of Scotland, and which would arrange for united action on Scottish labour questions'.[126] A further meeting in Edinburgh confirmed the decision and the first meeting of the Scottish Trades Union Congress was called for March 1897.

The formation of the S.T.U.C. in 1897 was not solely in response to the exclusion of trades councils from the T.U.C. This was the immediate cause, but it succeeded in Scotland, while it failed to get off the ground in England, because it satisfied the frequently expressed belief in the need for united effort in Scotland, and was one answer to the frequent Scottish protests that not enough attention was paid to Scottish matters. The Glasgow Trades Council's annual report explained:

Considering the existing differences between Scottish and English labour conditions, and in view of the fact that in nearly every bill brought before Parliament, special provisions have to be made for Scotland, it is obviously desirable that Scottish labour men should have a full opportunity for ventilation of their views on such matters, and that there should be some organisation of Scottish labour opinion on questions of local and national importance, and some common understanding in respect of them. In the limited time at the disposal of the British Congress, obviously, in the nature of things, this cannot be had.[127]

Duncan McPherson, the president of the first congress, continued in the same vein in his address to the delegates:

. . . the Congress was not, as some imagined, got up in opposition to the British Trades Union Congress, but because they believed that if they wanted anything well-done they had to do it themselves, and in doing their own work they were in some degree lightening the work of the British Congress. Then there were many questions which affected Scotland particularly to which their English fellow unionists could not be expected to devote the amount of time and attention they deserved.

He stressed the need for trades councils to be represented to put the question of the smaller trades, and spoke against a method of voting which 'placed the decision of almost all questions in the hands of a few of the large trades'.[128]

Trades councils, the central organisation in Scottish trade unionism, were, therefore, fully represented at the new organisation which was to co-ordinate nationally the activities of Scottish unions. The first parliamentary committee of the S.T.U.C. included five delegates from trades councils, and they have continued to play a major role in the organisation.

VII

That sharp observer of the labour scene, Mrs Beatrice Webb, visited Glasgow for the meeting of the T.U.C. in August 1892. She has left in her diary a few acid comments on her observations:

> I leave Glasgow with no regrets. The working-men leaders here are an uninteresting lot; without enthusiasm or much intelligence. The Scottish nature does not lend itself to combination; the strong men seek to rise and push for themselves and not to serve others. And apparently the Co-operators have absorbed the finer intelligence and warmer hearts among the Scotch working men of the official cast.[129]

While much of that indictment was grossly unfair, there was undoubtedly a certain perceptiveness in her comments. What Mrs Webb was really critical of was the failure of the Scottish unions to produce national figures of the calibre of Knight or Maudsley, the kind of trade union administrator whom she so much admired. To expect such a figure in Scotland was totally to misunderstand the nature of Scottish trade unionism. Its core lay, not in national headquarters, but at local level and there, in the trades councils, Mrs Webb would have found the enthusiasm, the intelligence and the service to others.

Suggestions for further reading

Ian MacDougall, *Minutes of Edinburgh Trades Council 1859-73* (Scottish History Society, Edinburgh, 1968)

Kenneth D. Buckley, *Trade Unionism in Aberdeen 1878 to 1900* (Edinburgh, 1955)

W. H. Marwick, *A Short History of Labour in Scotland* (Edinburgh, 1967)

Glasgow Trades Council, *Centenary Brochure 1858-1958: A Hundred Years of Progress* (Glasgow, n.d.)

Hamish McKinven, *Edinburgh and District Trades Council Centenary, 1859-1959* (Edinburgh, 1959)

Notes

1. A.S.E., *Annual Report, 1859*; *Glasgow Sentinel*, 31 Aug. 1867.
2. MS Minute Books of the Glasgow Trades Council, 23 July 1858. (Henceforth referred to as Glasgow Mins). The surviving minute books, including the first one, are in the Mitchell Library, Glasgow.
3. MS Minute Books of the Edinburgh Trades Council are held by the Council, but *The Minutes of Edinburgh Trades Council 1859-1873*, edited by Ian MacDougall, have been printed by the Scottish History Society (1968). All references in the footnotes are to the MS Minutes and are cited as Edinburgh Mins.
4. *Glasgow Sentinel*, 3 July 1858.
5. Ibid., 6 Apr. 1861; *Bee-hive*, 3 Sep. 1864.
6. *Glasgow Sentinel*, 26 Jan. 1861.
7. Quoted in S. Higgenbottam, *Our Society's History* (Manchester, 1939), 59.
8. *Glasgow Sentinel*, 19 Nov. 1859, 10 Mar. 1860.
9. *Bee-hive*, 3 Dec. 1864.
10. *Reformer*, 11 Mar. 1871; *North British Daily Mail*, 6 Apr. 1871.
11. *North British Daily Mail*, 18 Apr. 1872; *Reformer*, 8 June, 14 Dec. 1872.
12. *Reformer*, 25 Oct. 1873, 3 Jan., 2 May 1874.
13. Glasgow Trades Council, *Annual Report 1881-82*.
14. *Royal Commission on Depression of Trade and Industry*. P.P. 1886 xxii, 97.
15. *North British Daily Mail*, 28 Aug. 1890.
16. *Reformer*, 26 Dec. 1868.
17. Edinburgh Mins, 28 Apr., 12 May, 23 Nov. 1868.
18. Ibid., 22 Sep. 1868.
19. *Glasgow Sentinel*, 22 May, 21 Aug., 16 Oct. 1858.
20. Ibid., 5 Sep. 1874.
21. *North British Daily Mail*, 15 Apr. 1875.
22. Glasgow Trades Council, *Annual Report 1882-83*.
23. Ibid., *1885-86*; *North British Daily Mail*, 15 July, 28, 30 Oct. 1886.
24. Edinburgh Mins, 24 Apr. 1883.
25. Ibid., 31 May 1887.
26. MS Minute Books of the Aberdeen Trades Council, 4 July, 15 Aug. 1883. (Henceforth cited as Aberdeen Mins). These are held in the library of King's College, University of Aberdeen.
27. *Aberdeen Daily Free Press*, 9 June 1884; Aberdeen Mins, 17 June 1884.
28. Aberdeen Mins, 30 Oct. 1884.
29. K. D. Buckley, *Trade Unionism in Aberdeen 1878-1900* (Edinburgh, 1955), 30-31.
30. Ibid., 33.

31. Glasgow Trades Council, *Annual Report 1889-90*.
32. Glasgow Mins, 19 Sep. 1888.
33. Ibid., 12 Nov. 1888.
34. Ibid., 3 Apr., 15 May 1889.
35. Ibid., 7 Nov. 1888; *North British Daily Mail*, 22 Nov. 1888.
36. Glasgow Mins, 7 Feb. 1889.
37. *North British Daily Mail*, 22 Nov. 1888.
38. Ibid., 19 Nov., 5 Dec. 1889.
39. Ibid., 3 Aug. 1893.
40. Edinburgh Mins, 4 Dec. 1888.
41. Ibid., 28 May, 11 June, 3 Sep. 1889.
42. Ibid., 17 Oct. 1893, 25 Jan. 1897.
43. *Glasgow Sentinel*, 4 Sep. 1858.
44. Edinburgh Mins, 20 Feb. 1861; *Scotsman*, 21 Feb. 1861.
45. Edinburgh Mins, 19 Jan. 1869.
46. *Bee-hive*, 20 Mar. 1869.
47. *Reformer*, 27 Mar. 1869.
48. Edinburgh Trades Council, *Annual Report 1871-72*.
49. Edinburgh Mins, 12, 17 Sep., 15, 29 Oct., 26 Nov. 1878.
50. Ibid., 11 Jan. 1885.
51. Edinburgh Trades Council, *Annual Report 1890-91*.
52. Edinburgh Mins, 7 May 1894.
53. Aberdeen Mins, 18 Jan. 1888.
54. Aberdeen Trades Council, *Annual Report 1894*.
55. *North British Daily Mail*, 2 May 1892.
56. *Glasgow Echo*, 6 Sep. 1894.
57. Ibid., 22 Oct. 1894.
58. H. A. Clegg, A. Fox, P. Thompson, *British Trade Unions since 1889* (Oxford, 1964), 54.
59. *North British Daily Mail*, 24 Mar. 1881, 15 Jan. 1885; Edinburgh Mins, 12 Feb. 1884.
60. *North British Daily Mail*, 8 Oct. 1874.
61. Edinburgh Mins, 5 Aug. 1879.
62. Glasgow Mins, 20 Nov. 1858.
63. *Glasgow Sentinel*, 3, 17 Mar. 1860.
64. Edinburgh Mins, 23 Feb., 8 Mar. 1864.
65. Ibid., 7 July 1868.
66. Glasgow Trades Council, *Annual Report 1884-85*.
67. *Glasgow Echo*, 13 Sep. 1894; J. D. Marwick, *Glasgow: The Water Supply of the City from the Earliest period of Record* (Glasgow, 1901), 223.
68. Edinburgh Mins, 7, 11 Sep. 1886.
69. *Aberdeen Daily Free Press*, 8 July 1870.
70. Edinburgh Mins, 14 July 1885, 18 Oct. 1887, 17 Apr. 1888.
71. Glasgow Mins, 5 June 1888.
72. Ibid., 5 June 1889.

73.   G. Fisher, 'Glasgow — A Model Municipality', *Fortnightly Review* cvii (1895), 611.

74.   *Glasgow Citizen*, 5 July 1888.

75.   Edinburgh Mins, 19 June 1888.

76.   *Glasgow Echo*, 7 Feb. 1895.

77.   Edinburgh Trades Council, *Annual Report 1897-98*.

78.   The best account of it is the essay by D. Simon in *Democracy and the Labour Movement*, ed. J. Saville (London, 1954).

79.   *North British Daily Mail*, 25 Apr. 1872; Edinburgh Mins, 9 Nov. 1875.

80.   Glasgow Mins, 16 Feb. 1887; *North British Daily Mail*, 17 Feb. 1887, 4 Apr., 27 July 1893; Edinburgh Mins, 11 Apr. 1893; Aberdeen Mins, 25 Apr. 1893; *Glasgow Echo*, 13 June 1895; *North British Daily Mail*, 17 Oct. 1895; Edinburgh Mins, 17 Sep. 1895, 18 Feb. 1896.

81.   *North British Daily Mail*, 4 Apr. 1872, 22 Apr. 1875; Edinburgh Mins, 3 Sep. 1878.

82.   *North British Daily Mail*, 26 Apr. 1886; Aberdeen Mins, 6 June 1883.

83.   *North British Daily Mail*, 13 Apr. 1893; Aberdeen Mins, 5 July 1893; Glasgow Trades Council, *Annual Report 1896*.

84.   *Glasgow Sentinel*, 26 Oct. 1861.

85.   Ibid., 18 Aug. 1866.

86.   See W. H. Fraser, 'Trade Unions, Reform and the General Election of 1868 in Scotland', *Scottish Historical Review*, 1 (1971).

87.   Edinburgh Mins, 13 Mar. 1860.

88.   Ibid., 16 Feb. 1869.

89.   Ibid., 10 Aug. 1869.

90.   Ibid., 5 Oct. 1869.

91.   Ibid., 5 to 26 Oct. 1869.

92.   Ibid., 26 Oct. 1869.

93.   *Reformer*, 22 Oct., 5 Nov. 1870.

94.   Edinburgh Mins, 27 Dec. 1870.

95.   *Scottish Typographical Circular*, iii, 1 July 1871.

96.   *Reformer*, 18 Oct. 1873.

97.   *Glasgow Sentinel*, 6 Dec. 1873.

98.   *Aberdeen Herald*, 6 Mar. 1869; *Reformer*, 6 Mar. 1869.

99.   *Royal Commission on the Depression of Trade and Industry, Second Report*, Appendix D., part 2, 97. P.P. 1886 xxii.

100.   Glasgow Mins, 6 June, 12 June 1889.

101.   Buckley, op. cit., 122-4.

102.   *Aberdeen Daily Free Press*, 4 June 1885; Buckley, op. cit., 125-6.

103.   *Edinburgh Courant*, 13 Apr. 1884.

104.   Edinburgh Mins, 21 Feb., 17 Apr. 1887; *Scottish Leader*, 7 Apr. 1888.

105.   Edinburgh Mins, 21 Aug. 1888. The very full instructions given to him are printed in the *Edinburgh Trades Council Centenary 1859-1959* (Edinburgh, 1959), 48-50.

106.   *Scottish Leader*, 6 Nov. 1889.

107.   Aberdeen Mins, 8 May, 2 July 1890.

108.   Ibid., 28 Jan. 1891.

109.   Ibid., 3 May 1891.

110.   *Aberdeen Daily Free Press*, 10 Aug. 1891; *Scotsman*, 10 Aug. 1891; *Trade Unionist*, 15 Aug. 1891.

111.   *North British Daily Mail*, 7 Mar. 1892.

112.   Cunninghame Graham to John Burns, 29 Oct. 1891. British Museum, Add. MSS 46,284 f. 175.

113.   *Aberdeen Daily Free Press*, 7 Mar. 1892.

114.   *North British Daily Mail*, 1 Aug. 1892.

115.   *Workman's Times*, 16 July 1892.

116.   Ibid., 21 Aug. 1892.

117.   Ibid.

118.   Edinburgh Mins, 11 Oct., 18 Oct. 1892; *Workman's Times*, 22 Oct. 1888.

119.   *Aberdeen Daily Free Press*, 9 Oct. 1893; *Labour Leader*, Oct. 1893; Buckley, op. cit., 158-9.

120.   *Glasgow Sentinel*, 4 Sep. 1858, 27 Aug. 1859, 25 Feb. 1860; Edinburgh Mins, 31 Jan. 1860, 28 Feb. 1860, 24 Apr. 1860; *Glasgow Sentinel*, 5 Oct. 1861.

121.   *To the Trade Unionists of Scotland*, pamphlet in the Edinburgh Bookbinders' Correspondence, National Library of Scotland.

122.   *Reformer*, 28 June 1873.

123.   Glasgow Trades Council, *Annual Report 1886-87*.

124.   Aberdeen Mins, 13 Nov. 1889; *Scottish Leader*, 2 June 1891; *Scotsman*, 28 Sep., 26 Oct. 1891.

125.   *Scotsman*, 11 Nov. 1895; *Aberdeen Daily Free Pesss*, 11 Nov. 1895.

126.   *Aberdeen Daily Free Press*, 27 Apr. 1896.

127.   Glasgow Trades Council, *Annual Report 1895-96*.

128.   *North British Daily Mail*, 26 Mar. 1897.

129.   B. Webb, *Our Partnership*, ed. B. Drake and M. I. Cole (London, 1948), 33.

The Strike Policy of the Miners of the West of Scotland, 1842-74

Gordon M. Wilson

THE spectacular growth of ironstone and coal mining along the Clyde Valley in the mid-nineteenth century was accompanied predictably by frequent industrial disputes and almost constant tension between mineowners and mineworkers. As a result trade unionism became relatively strong among the mining population of the region, and W. H. Marwick has argued that it was Scottish miners who made the most important advances in union organisation in Scotland during the period of 'mid century revival'.[1] These unions were influential in comparison to other groups of industrial workers, but most attempts at unionisation among the miners of Lanarkshire and Ayrshire were short-lived and limited to certain mining districts. Trade unionism was merely one of several manifestations of discontent in the industry, one of several strategies used by miners to defend themselves in the hurly-burly of industrialism. Other defensive strategies included friendly societies, emigration, agitation for legislative reforms in working conditions, and restricted output — the 'darg' policy. All of these strategies were implemented by mining unions but they were not the policies of these unions exclusively. Friendly societies existed outside as well as within trade unions, and the same could be said of emigration, parliamentary legislation and the restricted 'darg'. But of all the tactics used by miners, whether organised by unions or not, lifting their 'graith' or tools and coming out on strike was seen to be the ultimate, most damaging and most controversial. The contemporary middle-class observers of mining in the West of Scotland like Seymour Tremenheere, the government commissioner for mining districts, Sir Archibald Alison, sheriff of Lanarkshire, David Bremner, author and journalist, A. G. Miller, author and ironworks manager, and numerous newspapers, all agreed about the frequency of strikes in the industry and about what they thought to be their detrimental effects.

This essay is a study of the miners' strikes of which there are records or reports between 1842 and 1874 in West Central Scotland, that is, in the coalfields of the Clyde Valley in Lanarkshire, and in those of Ayrshire, Renfrewshire, West Stirlingshire and Dunbartonshire. The study moves from a tabulated classification of these strikes according to their size and their dates to an analysis and comparison of their causes. The fact that strikes were more frequent in some mining districts than in others will be discussed, and reasons for this will be examined. The attitudes and ideology of union leaders and of rank and file members will be examined and compared and their influence on the organisation of strikes with particular reference to those in 1842, 1856 and 1860 will be analysed. A consideration of the counter-measures used by employers will be followed by a summary of the successes and failures of the miners' use of strike action.

The period 1842-74 began and ended with a widespread strike of miners in the Clyde Valley. In 1842 there was the most substantial turnout that had ever taken place in the region, occurring at a time when the coal and iron industries were expanding rapidly. The strike gave rise to more widespread co-operation and organisation among the miners than had ever existed there before. By its spontaneity as well as its bitterness and even violence it seemed to mark a new level of class consciousness among the mining population. The strike of 1874 was the West of Scotland miners' reaction to the onset of the 'Great Depression'. The period of expansion and prosperity in the coal and iron industries seemed to be on the wane as prices and wages dropped. This strike and its failure marked the end of an era in the mining history of the Clyde Valley, an era in which persistent attempts were made by miners' leaders like Alexander MacDonald to organise the miners into a union or unions which aspired to a similar type of organisation and similar policies to those of the craft unions like the A.S.E. After the 1874 strike trade unionism among Clyde Valley miners was in the doldrums for over five years. Hence the significance of the period 1842-74.

In the whole region the number of miners increased during the period as shown in Table One.

Table One: Number of Miners in West Central Scotland 1841-71

Year	Coal	Ironstone	Unspecified	Total
1841	11,901	2,024	643	14,568
1851	25,213	5,908		31,121
1861	26,634	9,322	2,300	38,256
1871	35,761	7,814	3,070	46,645

The very rapid growth in the 1840s compared with that of the two following decades indicates not only the state of the industry but also the implicit problems of miners' leaders in trying to organise unions or strikes. When new labour could be recruited as readily as it was in the forties, the ability of workers to defend themselves against employers was clearly limited.

The rate of growth of coalmining in the region from the middle fifties is shown in rather more detail in the numbers of collieries shown in Figure One. From this it can be seen that the expansion was by no means constant, with peaks in 1857, 1866 and 1874 and troughs in 1859 and 1870-1. Collieries were closing frequently during the period to be replaced by new ones, so that the workforce had to be mobile. The migratory nature of the mining population made it still more difficult for union leaders to organise.

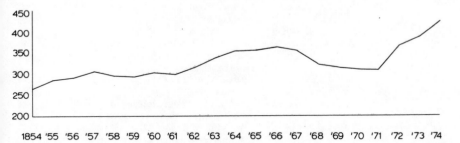

FIG.1. NUMBERS OF COLLIERIES IN THE WEST OF SCOTLAND 1854-1874

Before proceeding to examine the strikes, a cautionary comment must be made about the sources. While important information about individual major strikes is to be found in Home Office Papers, Lord Advocates' Papers, individual company records and Parliamentary Papers, nevertheless for a year-by-year account of the incidence and location of strikes the press has to be the main source. This presents some problems. Local newspapers in the West of Scotland were only beginning to appear in the middle of this period, from the 1850s onwards, with papers like the *Airdrie and Coatbridge Advertiser* in 1855, the *Hamilton Advertiser* in 1856 and the *Kilmarnock Standard* in 1863. While some national papers such as the *Northern Star*, the *Miners' Advocate* and the *Colliery Guardian* reported major strikes, as did Glasgow newspapers like the *Glasgow Argus* and the *Glasgow Herald*, it was only with the coming of smaller local newspapers and with the coming of the *Glasgow Sentinel*, which was sympathetic to trade unions, that there was frequent reporting of small-scale local strikes. Nor was every strike reported fully and accurately. What can be said is that every major strike from 1842 to 1874 was reported in most newspapers which, together with other sources, give us a fairly full account. Smaller strikes were only reported regularly from about 1856 onwards. Not every newspaper mentioned every strike, but from the whole range there emerge references to a sufficient number of small strikes — over 130 — from the period 1856-74 to provide a picture of their frequency, location, causes, organisation and outcomes.

To measure and compare the extent of strikes it is most convenient to divide them into four categories, those extending over several districts, strikes in one district, strikes in two, three or four mines, and strikes in only one mine. In the first category there were eleven in the period from 1842 until 1874. Some details of each strike are compared in Table Two.

D

Table Two: Miners' Strikes Which Involved Several Districts of West of Scotland 1842-74

Year	Months	Length	Districts Involved	Estimated No. of Strikers
1842	Aug.-Nov.	c. 10 weeks	Airdrie, Coatbridge, Holytown, Glasgow, Dalry, Kilmarnock, Ayr, Barrhead	c. 12,000
1843	Jan.-Feb.	c. 3 weeks	Airdrie, Coatbridge, Holytown	
1844	June-Aug.	c. 12 weeks	Airdrie, Coatbridge, Holytown, Glasgow	875
1847	July-Sep.	c. 12 weeks	Airdrie, Coatbridge, Dalry	
1850	Mar.-July	c. 15 weeks	Airdrie, Coatbridge, Holytown, Glasgow, Dalry, Kilmarnock, Stirlingshire	c. 10,000-12,000
1855	Sep.	2 weeks	Airdrie, Coatbridge, Holytown, Wishaw	
1856	Mar.-June	c. 14 weeks	Airdrie, Coatbridge, Baillieston, Holytown, Wishaw, Glasgow, Maryhill, Cumnock, Dalry, Kilmarnock, Pollokshaws, Johnstone	c. 15,000
1860	Jan.-Mar.	c. 10 weeks	Bishopbriggs, Govan, Coatbridge, Holytown, Johnstone	c. 900
1866	Aug.-Sep.	4-5 weeks	Hamilton, Larkhall, Wishaw	
1867	June-Aug.	c. 11 weeks (2 weeks for locked out mines)	Hamilton, Larkhall, Motherwell (locked out), Wishaw (strike)	c. 1,800
1874	March	c. 12 weeks	Maryhill, Glasgow, Airdrie, Coatbridge, Holytown, Hamilton, Wishaw, Motherwell, Larkhall, Kilmarnock, Dalry	

Although the figures for estimated numbers of strikers are very vague, often the conjecture of contemporary observers, they help to point up the most extensive of these strikes. They were those in 1842, 1850, 1856 and 1874, as the lists of districts involved show. These strikes are also shown to have been among those of longest duration in this category.

About strikes in the second category, those involving the mines of only one district, our information is much more fragmentary. None were recorded before 1854, and from 1854 to 1874 there are references to six, the details of which are given in Table Three.

Table Three: Miners' Strikes Which Involved One District in West Central Scotland 1854-74

Year	Month	Length	District
1854			Airdrie
1861	November		Kilmarnock
1863	Mar.-Apr.		Hamilton-Larkhall
1867	May	2 weeks	Larkhall
1870	July-Sep.	7 weeks	Airdrie
1872	July		Hamilton

For the same period, 1854-74, Table Two shows that there were also six strikes covering several districts so that the single-district strike seems to have been as regular an occurrence as the more widespread stoppage. All of these in Table Two and Table Three were major industrial disputes and that there should have been so many during this period is a reflection of the disturbed condition of industrial relations in West of Scotland mines.

But between these major upheavals there were frequent smaller-scale strikes. Of those in the third category strikes involving two, three or four mines, from 1855 until 1874, there are references to twenty-four, as outlined in Table Four.

Table Four: Miners' Strikes Which Involved Two, Three or Four Mines in West Central Scotland 1854-74

Year	Number of Strikes	Districts
1858	1	Airdrie
1859	1	Larkhall
1862	4	Glasgow, Holytown, Kilmarnock
1863	2	Johnstone, Glasgow
1864	1	Glasgow
1865	1	Kilmarnock
1866	5	Cambuslang, Kilmarnock, Hamilton, Wishaw and Airdrie
1867	4	Motherwell, Hamilton, Kilmarnock, Wishaw
1868	2	Wishaw, Kilmarnock
1870	1	Kilmarnock
1872	1	Motherwell
1873	1	Larkhall

Strikes of this smaller scale are seen to have been quite regular in those decades and particularly frequent in the years 1862 and 1867. But these should be seen as occasional combinations of the men of a few neighbouring mines and therefore as an extension of the much more frequent single-mine strikes, the fourth category which is enumerated year by year in Table Five.

Table Five: Miners' Strikes in Single Mines in West Central Scotland 1854-74

Year	Number of Strikes	Districts
1855	3	Kilmarnock (2), Muirkirk
1856	2	Dalry, Glasgow
1857	3	Dalry, Carluke, Hamilton
1858	2	Nitshill, Wishaw
1859	5	Glasgow, Wishaw (3), Larkhall
1861	7	Larkhall, Hamilton, Cambuslang (2), Pollokshaws, Wishaw, Baillieston
1862	15	Larkhall, Dalry, Maryhill (3), Glasgow (2), Baillieston (3), Cambuslang, Hamilton, Wishaw, Coatbridge (2)

Year	Number of Strikes	Districts
1863	8	Paisley, Wishaw, Kilmarnock, Hamilton, Maryhill (2), Ayr, Johnstone
1864	6	Kilmarnock, Hamilton (2), Glasgow (2), Holytown
1865	3	Dalry, Glasgow, Kilmarnock
1866	10	Glasgow (3), Holytown, Hamilton, Ayr, Coatbridge, Wishaw, Stonehouse, Kilmarnock
1867	7	Wishaw (2), Glasgow, Hamilton (2), Larkhall, Motherwell
1868	7	Kilmarnock, Holytown, Wishaw, Glasgow, Maryhill (2), Hamilton
1869	7	Motherwell (2), Hamilton (2), Coatbridge, Wishaw, Cambuslang
1870	3	Motherwell (2), Coatbridge
1871	2	Douglas, Glasgow
1872	4	Johnstone, Kilmarnock, Motherwell, Maryhill
1873	3	Wishaw, Glasgow, Airdrie

The total for Table Five is ninety-seven strikes taking place in twenty years, an average of almost five per year. The years of most frequent strikes are seen to have been 1862 and 1866, similar to the evidence of Table Four. But the numbers of strikes in 1861, 1863, 1864, 1867, 1868 and 1869 were also above the average and only in 1854 and 1860 were no such stoppages recorded.

Because of the inadequacy of information about the period before 1854 it is possible to attempt a summarising statistical profile of all types of strike from only 1854 to 1874. This is done in Table Six, where the totals for each category show that over the twenty years there was an average of one (1.2) major strike as in categories One and Two every two years and six lesser strikes as in categories Three and Four every year. The years which can be seen to have been most troubled were 1855-6, 1862-3, 1866-7 and 1874. These represent peaks in a fluctuating graph of strike incidence. The troughs, the years of fewer than average strikes, were 1854, 1857-8, 1865, 1870-1 and 1873. The reasons for these peaks and troughs are to be found partly in the causes of the disputes.

Table Six: Summary of All Types of Miners' Strikes in West of Scotland 1854-74

Year	Category 1	Category 2	Category 3	Category 4
1854		1		
1855	1			3
1856	1			2
1857				3
1858			1	2
1859			1	5
1860	1			
1861		1		7

Year	Category 1	Category 2	Category 3	Category 4
1862			4	15
1863		1	2	8
1864			1	6
1865			1	3
1866	1		5	10
1867	1	1	4	7
1868			2	7
1869				7
1870		1	1	3
1871				2
1872		1	1	4
1873			1	3
1874	1			
Totals	6	6	24	97

Most of the disputes were about wages, sometimes over employers' refusal to agree to demands for wage increases and sometimes over miners' refusal to accept wage cuts. These were the causes of all but one of the major strikes in the whole period 1842-74. The one exception was in Airdrie District in 1854, when the cause was apparently religious. The district miners were reported to have gone on strike 'until all the Roman Catholics should be expelled'.[2] This appears to have been the only example of a strike among miners caused by religion, and David Bremner, writing some fifteen years after the event, is the only source of information about it. There may therefore be a reasonable doubt about the accuracy of the information. The general (and more credible) causes of strikes are listed in Table Seven.

Table Seven: Causes of Major Strikes of Miners in West Central Scotland 1842-74

Wage Rise Demand Refused by Employers	Wage Cut by Employers Opposed by Miners
1842	1847
1843	1856
1844	1863
1850	1866
1855	1867
1860	1874
1861	
1867	
1870	
1872	

Although wage rise demands caused ten major strikes, compared to six caused by wage cuts, it is important to note that of the latter six those in 1856 and 1874 were the most extensive strikes of the whole period. In some of these disputes the miners professed to be striking over other grievances as well as wages. In 1844, for example, the Lanarkshire miners also demanded a fairer system of weighing their output and the abolition of truck stores or company stores.[3]

The Airdrie miners on strike in 1870 wanted shorter hours as well as a wage increase.[4] But in each of these cases the wage demands were the principal causes, and when they were conceded the strikes ended and the other objectives were forgotten.

The majority of smaller strikes also stemmed from wage rise demands or from wage cuts. There were, however, nineteen out of the total of 121 which had other causes. These nineteen strikes are included in the column headed 'Other Causes' in Table Eight, which shows the pattern of causes of lesser strikes.

Table Eight: Causes of Lesser Strikes of Miners in West Central Scotland 1854-74

Year	Numbers of Strikes Caused by			
	Wage Rise Demands Refused	Wage Cuts Opposed	Other Causes	Unknown
1854				
1855	2	1		
1856		1	1	
1857		1	2	
1858	1	1	1	
1859	4		1	1
1860				
1861	3	3	1	
1862	17		2	
1863	3	5	1	1
1864	6		1	
1865		2		2
1866	8	4	2	1
1867	6	5		
1868	6	2		1
1869	3		3	1
1870	4			
1871	1			1
1872	4		2	
1873			2	1
1874				
Totals	68	25	19	9

As percentages of the total, these causes were in the following order of importance:

Strikes in support of wage rise demands	56.5 per cent
Strikes opposing wage cuts	20.5 per cent
Strikes arising from other causes	15.5 per cent
Strikes when causes are unknown	7.5 per cent

Over seventy-seven per cent of lesser strikes and virtually all major strikes were about wages, but there was clearly an important difference in circumstances between those in support of wage rise demands and those in opposition to wage cuts. Table Eight shows that these circumstances were constantly changing as causes of strikes altered from year to year from 1858 until 1868. Wages were fluctuating even within individual years, as in 1861, 1863, 1866, 1867 and 1868. This points to the fundamental central reason for the frequency of these strikes and for the bitterness which characterised industrial relations in West of Scotland mining in this mid-Victorian period. Miners' wages were fluctuating almost constantly and, in spite of all their other grievances such as weighing, truck shops and bad ventilation, this was what most often brought miners to take their most serious industrial action.

Contemporary evidence about miners' wages, imprecise though it is, confirms this impression. It is impossible to have a completely accurate account of the changes in these wages because not all employers paid at the same rate and not all miners produced the same output and earned the same wage. Some employers deducted more than others from the men's wages for such services as pick sharpening, house rents and colliery doctors. In spite of these variations there were regular references to a notional common or average daily wage for miners at that period. The references appeared in newspapers and in numerous books and pamphlets. Although these notional figures cannot be regarded as universally accurate, they can be used as a rough guide for measuring pay fluctuations. The graph in Figure Two brings together several contemporary estimates of miners' daily wage rates which show a measure of general agreement. The figures quoted in newspapers were collected from six different sources and they show that, in addition to fluctuations in annual average wages, there were often changes several times per year from 1855 onwards.

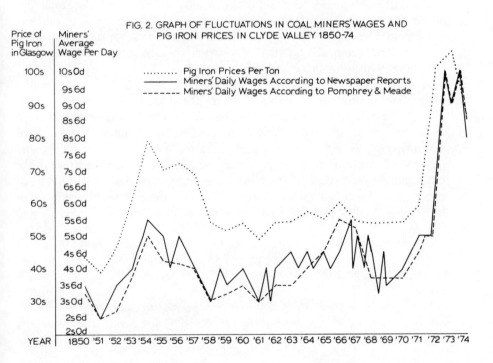

FIG. 2. GRAPH OF FLUCTUATIONS IN COAL MINERS' WAGES AND PIG IRON PRICES IN CLYDE VALLEY 1850-74

The major peaks and troughs shown in Figure Two conform almost exactly to those of pig iron prices at the same period, with peak years in 1854, 1866 and 1873 and trough years in 1858, 1861, 1868 and 1874. Various studies have shown the correlation between miners' wages, pig iron prices and the cycles of the British economy, and Professor Campbell has also shown that the fluctuations in pig iron prices were particularly frequent, being intensified probably by speculation in the Glasgow Pig Iron Market.[5]

From Tables Seven and Eight it can be seen that strikes in support of wage rise demands were most widespread in 1855, 1861-2, 1866-8 and 1872. Of these years, 1855, 1861-2 and 1866-8 were periods of particularly frequent fluctuations in wages, as the newspaper evidence in the graph in Figure Two shows. In 1872, on the other hand, there was a quite regular and rapid rise in wages.

The periods of most strike activity against wage cuts, according to Tables Six and Seven, were 1856, 1863, 1866-7 and 1874. Figure Two shows that in 1856 and in 1874 wages were dropping quite rapidly, from 5/- per day to 4/- in 1856 and from 9/- per day to 8/- in 1874. In 1863, however, wages dropped only during the first half of the year, during which time all these strikes took place. They were to rise again later in the year. The strike-torn years of 1866-7 saw no fewer than three substantial wage cuts, each being followed after an interval of several months by comparable increases.

The years of comparative peace, from Tables Seven and Eight, were 1857-60, 1864-5 and 1869-71. During the first and second of these periods, wages can be seen, from Figure Two, to have risen and fallen but never more than once a year and usually only by 6d. per day. In 1857-60 it is clear from the graph that the mean wage was lower than in 1864-5 and indeed it was as low as at any time between 1855 and 1874. Yet in spite of this it was a period comparatively free of wage strikes. From 1869 until 1871 wages climbed almost continuously, apparently with little strike action.

On the strength of the evidence provided in Tables Seven and Eight and Figure Two, several observations can be made in conclusion about these wage strikes. The majority of the disputes were about miners' wage rise demands. These happened most often and most extensively at times of rapid wage fluctuation or, as in 1872, when wages and pig iron prices were rising. The periods of fluctuation also produced widespread strikes against wage reductions, as did periods of steep decline in wages. These turnouts took place irrespective of whether miners' wages were generally high or low, and one of the most strike-free periods occurred when wages were comparatively low in 1857-60.

Second only to wages, the issue which most often caused miners in the Clyde Valley to lift their graith and go on strike was the system of weighing output. Between 1852 and 1874 at least ten strikes were recorded in the region which were caused by disputes over weighing. Four of these were in Dalry, two in Ayr and one each in Wishaw, Hamilton, Coatbridge and Larkhall.[6] Because miners were paid according to the weight of coal they produced, the issue was obviously an important one and since the 1840s it had produced regular complaints, the most common being that miners were paid nothing for hutches or carts of coal which were found at the pithead to be below a standard weight. Nor did they receive payment for extra coal in a hutch which was over the required weight. The decision as to whether or not hutches were up to weight was often an arbitrary one resting with pitheadmen, who before 1860 were usually employees of the mineowners.[7]

Although the Mines Act of 1860 granted miners the right to appoint their own checkweighmen in each pit to supervise and ensure fair weighing, disputes continued to occur up to 1874. They led to strikes in collieries at Wishaw in 1861,[8] at Ayr in 1863[9] and 1866,[10] at Coatbridge in 1869[11] and at Larkhall in 1872-3.[12] When employers resisted the appointment of miners' checkweighmen, or 'justicemen', this caused further strikes at Dalry in 1862,[13] Ayr in 1866[14] and Hamilton in 1869.[15] The miners also complained about weighing machines which were sometimes thought to be faulty,[16] but according to Lord Elcho, the Tory M.P., the mineowners in Scotland were opposed to the imposition of a uniformly accurate weighing system because of the expense of the machines and the weighers' wages.[17]

The collectivist spirit of the miners which made such frequent and widespread strikes possible was itself sometimes the cause of disputes. This spirit manifested itself in strikes in defence of trade unions, their rules and leaders, or in defence of colleagues who were being victimised. For example the men of Braidwood Colliery, Carluke, struck in 1852, as did the men of Sunnyside Colliery, Wishaw, in 1858, in both cases because they refused to sign colliery rules which restricted their freedom to organise unions.[18] When three colliers at Muirhouse Colliery, Wishaw, were sacked in November 1859 after asking for a rise of sixpence per day, the whole colliery came out in support of them.[19] The same happened at Woodhall Colliery, Coatbridge, in October 1862 when miners who had attended union meetings had been sacked,[20] and at Darnconnar Colliery, Kilmarnock, in January 1864 when twelve of the miners' leaders were dismissed after asking for a wage increase.[21] There were even strikes in defence of a 'closed shop' and against the employment of non-unionists at a colliery in Airdrie and at one in Maryhill, both in November 1873.[22]

Disputes at individual collieries about working conditions occasionally led to withdrawal of labour. Miners struck at Newton Colliery, Cambuslang, in 1853 against the use of new riddles,[23] at Bonnyton Colliery, Kilmarnock, in 1866 over the cutting of pit props,[24] at North Motherwell Colliery over pay differentials between men at different workings of the mine,[25] and at Portland Colliery, Kilmarnock, over the need to give warning before leaving employment or withdrawing labour.[26]

Before leaving the subject of the causes of strikes, mention must be made of a very sensitive issue in industrial relations of the time which surprisingly did not produce strike action. The issue was truck. Local miners' leaders often denounced it, and in spite of anti-truck legislation the Truck Commission in 1871 provided voluminous evidence of its extent and injustices in the West of

Scotland.[27] And yet although it was mentioned as one of several grievances leading to strike action on a few occasions, there is no evidence of the truck system having been the sole cause of withdrawal of labour on any occasion during this period in the West of Scotland. This was perhaps because truck was a traditional feature of many mines. It was always there and its effect was constant and therefore easier to learn to accept, unlike wage fluctuations which persistently altered miners' standard of living. Nor did truck have the direct effect of reducing miners' 'take-home pay' as the weighing system did. Furthermore the employers who operated truck systems in their mines most widely were ironmasters. Over thirteen thousand miners employed by ironmasters were subjected to the truck system compared to only 3,280 employed by coalmasters.[28]

The unique strength of the ironmasters in the West of Scotland mining industry also explains the apparent lack of strike action by miners against their truck policy. These employers were the dominant mineowners in several districts such as Dalmellington, Dalry and Cumnock in Ayrshire and in the Glasgow, Coatbridge and Holytown districts of Lanarkshire. Employing as they did large numbers of miners in most of their pits, they were able to control work prospects for whole mining communities, as Merry and Cunninghame did in Dalry and Johnstone and as the Monkland Iron and Steel Company did at Chapelhall. Power like this was bound to deter miners from striking against the truck system, a system which many men had come to accept as part of their working conditions.

The question now arises — were some districts of the West of Scotland more 'strike-prone' than others and if so, why? Table Nine shows the incidence of strikes in the main districts during this period. It must still be remembered that the information for the period 1842-54 is fragmentary and refers only to major strikes. For the remainder of the period, i.e. 1855-74, the figures are more complete. The table shows that there were marked differences between districts in the frequency of strikes. Two districts — Ayr/Dalmellington and Cumnock/Muirkirk — had only three strikes each in the whole period. Two other districts — Kilmarnock and Glasgow/Rutherglen — show a fairly consistent record of participation in major strikes, five in Glasgow and seven in Glasgow/Rutherglen along with quite regular minor turnouts from 1855, fourteen in Kilmarnock and twenty-seven in Glasgow/Rutherglen. The two districts of Wishaw/Motherwell and Hamilton/Larkhall saw rather later development of large-scale mining operations, and it was not until the 1850s that mining populations were established there. But one feature of these new mining communities seems to have been their readiness to strike. There were three major strikes in each district from 1855 until 1874, thirty lesser ones in Wishaw/Motherwell and twenty-two in Hamilton/Larkhall.

A quite different pattern from any of these can be seen in the three districts of Dalry, Airdrie/Coatbridge and Holytown. There the miners were extensively involved in several major strikes, particularly in the first half of the period. In Dalry there were four major strikes between 1842 and 1856, in

Table Nine: Incidence of Miners' Strikes Shown District by District in the West of Scotland 1842-74. (Category A — major strikes of more than four mines: Category B — minor strikes of 1-4 mines)

	Ayr & Dalmellington		Dalry		Kilmarnock & Cumnock/ Muirkirk		Renfrewshire		Glasgow & Rutherglen		
	A	B	A	B	A	B	A	B	A	B	
1842	1		1		1		1		1		1842
1843											1843
1844									1		1844
1845											1845
1846											1846
1847			1		1						1847
1848											1848
1849											1849
1850			1		1				1	1	1850
1851											1851
1852				1							1852
1853										1	1853
1854											1854
1855						3					1855
1856			1	1	1		1		1	1	1856
1857				1							1857
1858								1			1858
1859										1	1859
1860							1		1		1860
1861				1			1			3	1861
1862				1	2				1	4	1862
1863		1			1		3			3	1863
1864					1					2	1864
1865				1	1					1	1865
1866		1			2					4	1866
1867					1					1	1867
1868					2					3	1868
1869										1	1869
1870					1						1870
1871										1	1871
1872					1			1		1	1872
1873										1	1873
1874			1		1				1		1874

	Airdrie & Coatbridge		Holytown		Wishaw & Motherwell		Hamilton, Larkhall, etc.		
	A	B	A	B	A	B	A	B	
1842	1		1						1842
1843	1		1						1843
1844	1		1						1844
1845									1845
1846									1846
1847	1								1847
1848									1848
1849									1849
1850	1		1						1850

	Airdrie & Coatbridge		Holytown		Wishaw & Motherwell		Hamilton, Larkhall, etc.		
	A	B	A	B	A	B	A	B	
1851									1851
1852								1	1852
1853									1853
1854	1								1854
1855	1		1		1				1855
1856	1		1		1				1856
1857						1		1	1857
1858		1				1			1858
1859						3		2	1859
1860		1	1						1860
1861						1		2	1861
1862		2	2			1		2	1862
1863			1			1		3	1863
1864			1					2	1864
1865									1865
1866		2	1			3	1	2	1866
1867						7	1	3	1867
1868			1			3			1868
1869		1				3		2	1869
1870	1	1				2			1870
1871								1	1871
1872						3		2	1872
1873		1				1			1873
1874	1		1		1		1		1874

Airdrie/Coatbridge eight, and in Holytown six. But thereafter, until 1874 there was one in Dalry and two each in the other two districts. The number of smaller disputes from 1856 in these districts was also lower than in most other districts, four in Dalry, nine in Airdrie/Coatbridge and six in Holytown. From having been centres of quite intensive strike activity, as in 1842, these districts by the second half of the period had become comparatively strike-free.

How are these differences between districts and changes within some districts to be explained? It seems clear, in the first place, that the differences in strike incidence sprang not from differences in working conditions but rather from differences in ability to organise collective action. There is no evidence that miners in districts like Ayr and Cumnock were free of the wage fluctuations which were the cause of most strikes. Nor did wages become more stable in Dalry, Airdrie and Holytown after 1856 when strikes there became less frequent. The grievances which caused strikes existed throughout the West Central Scotland mining districts during most of the period 1842-74. But for a grievance to become a strike a measure of collectivism among the miners and some form of organisation were necessary. For this reason it is not surprising that strike action was most frequently used in districts where trade union organisation was strongest. So in Ayr and Cumnock — districts where unionism had seldom if ever caught on — strikes were particularly infrequent. In Glasgow and Kilmarnock, shown by regular reports in the *Glasgow Sentinel* and *Kilmarnock Standard* to have been centres of union activity, miners lifted their graith quite regularly. The growth and strength of miners' unions in Wishaw, Hamilton and Larkhall in the 1860s and 1870s was parallel to the frequency of strikes in these districts. In Airdrie, Coatbridge and Holytown there existed relatively strong union organisation from the time of the 1842 strike.[29] By the early sixties, however, these organisations had all but died there,[30] and a list of district organisations produced by Alexander MacDonald in December 1862 makes no mention of any union in existence in Airdrie, Coatbridge or Dalry.[31] Although the list includes a reference to a union of Holytown miners with 500 members, in the following month MacDonald agreed with a statement by John Muir, a Glasgow Union leader, that Holytown was the worst organised mining district in the West of Scotland.[32]

One study of trade unionism among Lanarkshire miners suggests that colliery ownership influenced miners' ability to organise themselves.[33] Large iron companies, it is suggested, imposed rigid industrial discipline and suppressed trade unionism. This can probably be seen to have been the case in Ayr, where the Dalmellington Iron Company was predominant, in Cumnock, Muirkirk and Dalry, dominated by the Eglinton Iron Company (owned by Baird of Gartsherrie), and by the end of the period in Coatbridge, where Bairds and the Summerlee Iron Company were the biggest employers. The theory does not appear to hold good, however, for Airdrie, adjacent to Coatbridge but with quite a different pattern of colliery ownership in which coalmasters owned more collieries than did ironmasters.

Another and more important explanation suggested for district variations is the difference in population structure. Irish immigrant labour may have been more difficult to organise in unions, and districts such as Coatbridge with a high density of Irish population may for that reason have lacked a strong union among the miners.[34] The historian who has written at greatest length about Irish immigration into Scotland agrees that Irish miners did not play as big a part in trade unionism as did their Scottish counterparts.[35]

The mobility or stability of a mining community also affected the way in which unions and strikes could be organised. Furthermore those communities which were close to larger, more diversified industrial towns, such as Glasgow or Kilmarnock, could usually rely upon moral support and occasionally material support from local trade unions in other industries. Finally, some districts had better leaders than others. Holytown miners, for example, were led by William Cloughan in the forties, and by Alexander MacDonald in the early fifties. When MacDonald turned his attention to Scottish and British affairs in the sixties, the district failed to produce an effective replacement as leader — and thereafter the local union organisation declined. Small local organisations such as trade unions, or political parties at the present day, still depend upon a few dedicated organisers. In the mid-nineteenth century local trade union leaders required not only dedication but also courage in the face of widespread condemnation and the threat of victimisation by employers. Several mineowners pursued a policy of dismissing miners who emerged as leaders of strikes or unions,[36] so it is hardly surprising that strong effective leaders did not emerge in every mining district.

The use which any group of workers make of industrial action depends on their attitudes to the economic order in which they find themselves — their ideology. Any discussion of the ideology of these Scottish miners must proceed from the fundamentally important fact that their strikes were so frequent by the standards of mid-Victorian Britain. With an average of six involving one or more mines every year and one involving several districts every two years, it cannot be argued that the miners saw strike action as an exceptional policy to be resorted to only very occasionally. They were quite a regular feature of the way of life of mining communities, more regular in some communities than in others, as Table Nine has shown. Two separate but related observations about miners' ideology follow from this. The frequency of strikes indicates first the non-acceptance by miners of conventional economic orthodoxy of mid-Victorian capitalism and second a relatively strong class consciousness among these mining populations. Several historians have made the point that strike action was contrary to the Victorian economic theories of the wages fund, the sanctity of supply and demand, and unfettered competition.[37] To strike as often as Clyde Valley miners did was to reject capitalist ideology of the time through collective action in self-defence. It is the collective nature of this rejection, involving the risk of victimisation and the likelihood of financial hardship, sometimes alleviated by subscriptions from miners elsewhere, which is the mark of strong class consciousness.

This consciousness created an ideology which, although it is not clearly articulated in any set of doctrines, was not any less potent as an influence on miners' industrial action. It was when attempts were made by miners' leaders to spell it out that confusion arose — and has continued to arise — about its consistency. This is because these leaders frequently expressed themselves in public as being opposed to strike action. William Cloughan, in a pamphlet published in 1846, looked forward to the miners' abandonment of strike action:

> Give us more education on the part of the working classes and strikes will soon become a matter of history. Why? Because intelligent men will not risk their all in a foolish contest with their employers unless they are sure of success.[38]

An Ayrshire miners' leader, Peter Wyper of Galston, was of the same opinion and, like Cloughan his opposition was based not on a reverence for orthodox economics but on the belief that all too often strikes failed. Wyper went on to argue for a more radical alternative: co-operative ownership of mines by the miners.[39] It is not difficult to find examples of other leaders in the region who publicly opposed strike action. At a meeting of Lanarkshire miners in Hamilton in July 1866, both Robert Steel, district union agent in Wishaw, and Henry Malcolm of Shotts advised their members to be cautious about striking at that time.[40] Thomas Smith, an Ayrshire miner who succeeded Steel as agent in Wishaw, advised Wishaw miners in January 1868 against strike action in pursuit of a wage rise, and again in December 1869 he declared a general preference for constant agitation about wages rather than strike action.[41] Even after he had left Wishaw in 1870, he wrote from his home in Kilmarnock urging the Wishaw men to avoid strike action.[42]

This cautious attitude was a recurring feature of the unions. The rules of the Coal and Iron Miners Association of Scotland, formed at Holytown in 1855, declared that, in the event of a dispute between employers and workmen 'for an advance of wages or from any other necessary cause', the matter was to be handled by the district committee who would refer it to arbitration. If the employers refused, the union would support the men on strike. If the men refused arbitration, they would 'place themselves beyond the pale of the association'.[43] Similarly the Coal and Ironstone Miners Association of Scotland, whose rules were announced in Glasgow in 1862, insisted that the strike weapon be used with great caution and that no mine was to strike without consulting the district committee.[44] By 1874 the attempt to organise a Scottish union of miners had been virtually abandoned, but several well organised district unions existed in the West of Scotland, of which seven had formulated sets of rules. These unions were in Wishaw (1873), Motherwell (1873), Carluke (1873), Larkhall (1874), Hamilton (1874), Stonehouse (1875) and Maryhill (1875). All of them held the same attitudes to strikes. Arbitration was always to be tried in a dispute. No pit was to strike without the permission of the executive and, when that permission was given, strikers would receive financial support from the union.[45]

A great deal of attention was given to the opinions of Alexander MacDonald and he frequently expressed opposition, in public, to strikes. In 1856 he wrote that his aim was 'to have strikes blotted for ever from the book of the employers' and miners' experiences'.[46] Earlier that year he had proposed a sliding scale of miners' wages related to coal prices, with the specific intention of preventing strikes.[47] In 1863 he strongly discouraged Maryhill miners from striking against a wage cut, arguing that economic circumstances were not favourable.[48] He advised against strike action in Lanarkshire in 1868, when a wage demand had been rejected by employers. Instead he urged further discussion between both sides.[49] Again in 1870 MacDonald tried to dissuade Wishaw miners from striking in support of a wage demand and once more he pressed the men to try further discussion and agitation rather than striking.[50] Finally in 1874, as pressure for a massive strike of West of Scotland miners built up, MacDonald again opposed it, urging the miners to 'let the word "strike" become obsolete'.[51] His advice in 1874 went unheeded and his opposition to the widespread strike of that year caused him to lose much of his prestige and popularity.[52]

Public statements of the kind quoted above have been taken by some historians to indicate an acceptance by MacDonald of the economic theories of capitalism and of the need for class harmony. But MacDonald's standpoint was more complex than that. When he spoke at a meeting of miners in Wishaw public park in August 1864, he said again how he deplored strikes. But he went on to raise the question of who was to blame for their taking place, suggesting that they were an unavoidable consequence of the poor industrial relations in the mining industry.[53] A thorough study of MacDonald's many public statements reveals a substantial number of declarations of support and encouragement for strikes and of statements which were contrary to contemporary economic doctrines. At a meeting in Glasgow in May 1862, for example, MacDonald denied the argument of political economists that the prosperity of the nation depended on the prosperity of the employers. He argued, almost in Keynesian terms, that higher wages for workers meant more money in circulation and therefore greater general prosperity. On this basis he went on to encourage miners at Clyde Iron Works, currently on strike, to stand firm by their demands for a wage increase.[54] He used the same economic argument at a meeting in Wishaw in June 1862 to encourage support for miners on strike in several collieries in the district.[55] In October of the following year he urged support for miners on strike in four collieries in North Glasgow,[56] and in January 1864 he urged miners at Westmuir Colliery near Rutherglen to strike if their employer refused to give a wage rise.[57] Later in 1864 he recalled in a speech that he had advised miners in 1857 to accept wage reductions. But now in 1864 he strongly recommended united agitation and strike action in support of demands for increased wages.[58] He committed himself to organise union support for miners on strike in Motherwell in July of 1866 and in Wishaw in 1867.[59] Peter Wyper of Galston even accused MacDonald of making excessive use of strikes, bringing miners out against their own better judgment.[60]

Among his many public statements MacDonald occasionally ventured a comment on economics and society, and these were by no means orthodox, conventional mid-Victorian opinions which he expressed. In May 1868, for example, at a meeting in Maryhill, he declared that the depressed condition of miners was not caused by the state of trade but by unbridled competition in industry to produce goods at any cost to the workmen. He went on to urge united action by miners to agitate for 'a fair day's pay for a fair day's work',[61] and in 1870 he urged the miners of Hamilton 'to form a society to protect themselves against the inroads of capital upon labour'.[62]

If MacDonald's attitudes were complex, this does not mean that they were inconsistent. He opposed strike action on certain occasions when it seemed to him that it would fail. He was in general rather cautious about using it because of the damage which it could do to the finances and morale of a trade union if it failed. In this his views were in line with those of earlier miners' leaders in the region and with the whole tenor of union organisation in the industry. When he gave evidence to the Royal Commission on Trade Unions in 1868, he summarised with honesty and consistency his attitude to strikes:

I am satisfied upon the whole and am able to show on the whole, that strikes, although in those periods to which I have referred they have proved disastrous, yet as a whole they have been a gain to the men in wages. I will put it thus: I am satisfied upon the whole that combinations have given more to the workmen by an advance of wages than the loss has been on the other side in the way of privations or in the way of destitution caused by them.[63]

It is therefore too simple to argue, as at least one historian has done, that 'the whole emphasis of his (MacDonald's) message was on achieving class harmony; to go on strike was the original sin. For strikes were wasteful, costly, involved suffering and social strife, endangered the well being of the union and more likely to alienate influential friends who could assist in getting legislation through Parliament'.[64] Even this last point about the danger of alienating influential friends is not valid. MacDonald's defence of strikes in his statement to the Royal Commission on Trade Unions did his cause no harm, and indeed his complete evidence impressed Lord Elcho and other members of the Commission. In a letter about the Commission to MacDonald in the following year Elcho wrote, 'I was very much pleased with your speech — it was the best of the lot and did credit to my countrymen and I am not the only member of the Commission who thinks so'.[65]

In being neither wholly opposed to strikes nor absolutely in favour of them, MacDonald may have shown a certain duality of mind in which he was torn between two apparently contradictory points of view. His humble origins, his experiences as a miner and his constant contact with the mining population probably gave him an almost instinctive sympathy for the collective defiance involved in strike action. On the other hand, his university education, his comfortable financial circumstances and his elevation to a position of national prominence in regular contact with parliamentarians like Lord Elcho must have had the opposite influence on him. He was often concerned about 'respectability', both for himself and for his miners' unions and he saw this as an effective means of bringing about legislative reforms.

This double attitude is a not uncommon characteristic of men and women who move away from their working class background. It has also been argued recently that duality of outlook was a feature of several eminent Scotsmen like Lord Cockburn, R. L. Stevenson, Edwin Muir and Hugh MacDiarmid.[66] Although the idea of 'the Caledonian Antisyzygy' referred particularly to some aspects of the Scottish split mind on literature, it could be seen to be a feature of the personality of a political figure like Cockburn and perhaps of MacDonald.

In spite of the fact that nearly all of their leaders expressed reservations about the policy, the West of Scotland miners made frequent use of strike action. Does this lend weight to the argument, put forward by more than one historian, that non-unionists were frequently more militant than unionists?[67] There were certainly occasions when miners lifted their graith against the advice of union leaders, and some of MacDonald's attempts to prevent strikes were referred to above. The 1874 strike was the most extensive example of this kind of divergence of views. But it has been mentioned that there were also occasions when miners were encouraged to withdraw their labour when economic circumstances seemed favourable. Militancy in any event cannot always be equated with willingness to take strike action. Although union leaders may have discouraged this on some occasions, they constantly urged other forms of industrial action, particularly the 'darg' policy of restricting output. This was potentially just as subversive in its economic and social implications as strike action. It interfered with the flow of production and by affecting supply could affect prices. It also involved collective agreement and sacrifice over long periods of time. By their organisation of strikes union leaders can be seen to have been both more moderate in their determination to discourage law breaking and more radical in their efforts to make strikes more successful. This needs more detailed examination at this stage.

Between 1842 and 1874 the two most important developments in strike organisation in the industry were a decline in violence and an increase in collective financial support for strikers. These changes were the result of the growing influence of union leaders like the men quoted above. Their policy was that if there were to be strikes, then they should be conducted in such a way as to have some likelihood of success. It was therefore important first that their timing should be right. It was also important that they should be in accordance with the law and supported by money from non-striking miners.

Sir Archibald Alison, sheriff of Lanarkshire, remarked in 1860 upon the decline of violence in disputes in the industry in West Central Scotland. He contrasted the violence of the strike of 1842 with the peacefulness and orderliness of disputes in the 1850s. 'I conclude therefore', he said, 'that there is a great and growing improvement in this respect'.[68] From 1842 until the time of Alison's speech in 1860 there were three occasions when large-scale strikes of miners in West Central Scotland caused him and the Home Office in London such alarm that they called out the local militia and summoned military reinforcements from Edinburgh and elsewhere.[69] After 1860 none of the mining disputes in the region was felt to be jeopardising law and order sufficiently to justify the use of military force. A comparison of these three strikes illustrates the increasingly law-abiding form of organisation which the miners were adopting.

The 1842 strike began on the morning of Monday the first of August, when the coal and ironstone miners of 147 pits in the Airdrie and Coatbridge districts struck work.[70] Soon more men came out in Holytown, Bellshill, Chapelhall, Baillieston, Kirkintilloch, Cambuslang and in parts of Ayrshire.[71] One estimate of the number of strikers was between 10,000 and 12,000.[72] Almost twenty years later in his memoirs Sheriff Alison put the figure at 20,000.[73] This seems unlikely, however, as there were only 14,568 miners in the West of Scotland recorded in the census of 1841.[74] The Lanarkshire men stayed out for two and a half months and in October they returned to work, first in Airdrie, Coatbridge and Holytown.[75] By early December the Ayrshire men too were back in the pits.[76]

In addition to the concern about the strike shown by Alison and by the Home Office there was great apprehension among the gentlemen of the press. The comment of the *Glasgow Saturday Post* was, 'This turn-out would seem to be the most alarming that has ever taken place in the mining districts of the West of Scotland'.[77] As well as being worried about the extent of the strike, the authorities were very alarmed by the fact that groups of these miners were reported to be roaming the area, armed with sticks and stealing food, mainly potatoes from fields, but also livestock, bread and milk.[78]

The reaction of Sheriff Alison and the Home Office was swift and firm. On the third day of the strike Alison moved to Airdrie with a troop of dragoons and two companies of infantry.[79] Three days later two more troops of dragoons and two troops of cavalry came by rail from Edinburgh to Castlecary station. A short nine-mile march brought them to Airdrie.[80] A force of fifty police substitutes came by rail to Airdrie from Glasgow.[81] When Alison reported to the Home Office that despite their show of force the 'nightly depredations . . . by bands of marauders' were continuing, the Lanarkshire Yeomanry were called out and the Home Secretary, Sir James Graham, ordered an additional regiment of cavalry from Ireland to the trouble spots.[82]

As a result of nightly patrols of Yeomanry in the mining districts with frequent searches of miners' houses, the foraging raids by strikers on potato fields and elsewhere gradually tailed off by the end of August.[83] But this was not the end of violence during the dispute. As well as occasional demonstrations of hostility towards the police in Airdrie and Coatbridge, there was intimidation, or attempted intimidation, of working miners by strikers in Campsie, Hurlford and at Clyde Iron Works.[84] There was even a riot in Airdrie on 21 September when a mob of about 400 people attacked the police headquarters and released five prisoners.[85]

The dispute of 1856, from the last week of March until the first week of June, was even more extensive than that of 1842. About 15,000 miners from the Lanarkshire districts of Airdrie, Coatbridge, Holytown, Baillieston, Glasgow, Maryhill and Wishaw were out[86] along with 2,000 in Renfrewshire,[87] 1,500 in Stirlingshire[88] and an indeterminate number in Ayrshire.[89] Although there were numerous reports of intimidation of non-strikers and several riots against the police, there appears to have been little or no theft and from the middle of April Sheriff Alison and the military authorities reported that the strikers were acting quite peaceably.[90]

The strikers in 1856 were much more effectively organised by their leaders than they had been in 1842 and this helps to explain their more orderly conduct. Most of the organisation in 1842 was done by district strike committees,[91] with occasional meetings of delegates from other districts.[92] There were regular mass meetings of strikers to boost morale and to vote on broad tactical decisions.[93] But this form of organisation proved to be too loose to be effective. The leadership was uncertain, divided and somewhat anonymous. As a result of this, the stealing of food continued in spite of opposition and disclaimers by the leaders.[94] Here lay the most serious failure of the 1842 leadership, the failure to provide financial or material support for the strikers.

By 1856 these weaknesses of organisation and leadership were being rectified by the new union of Scottish miners based on the West of Scotland and with a set of rules which made detailed provision for raising finance and for strong district organisations.[95] This was to prove more effective in the Clyde Valley than the growing but unstructured solidarity which had existed in 1842.[96] Throughout the 1856 dispute there were regular delegate meetings in Glasgow at which all districts on strike were represented. It was at these meetings that most of the important tactical decisions were taken, such as the appointment of negotiators to meet employers and the final concession of victory to the employers.[97] The delegates at these meetings were nevertheless acting on the instructions of their local districts, so that the organisation of the whole strike involved a much greater degree of co-operation and exchange of opinions between districts than had existed in 1842.

The unity and discipline of the men in 1856 were the results not only of the form of union structure which had emerged but also of the personal influence of leading union officials like Alexander MacDonald. He travelled from district to district addressing large meetings of strikers, sustaining morale and giving advice. A constant theme in this advice was the need for peaceful, lawful behaviour showing a 'respect of property and persons'.[98] This 'respectable' policy of the miners won the admiration and sympathy of the principal spokesmen of the labour aristocracy of the West of Scotland, including the United Trades Committee of Glasgow,[99] and the editor of the *Glasgow Sentinel*.[100]

The strike leaders took the view that if the turn-out was to be successful it should be as widespread as possible, with financial support provided for the strikers. Among the collieries which were reluctant to take part in the strike were Gartsherrie and Dundyvan in Coatbridge, and Chapelhall near Airdrie. The men from these mines were persuaded to come out at a large meeting at Baillieston on 14 April.[101] Many of the Gartsherrie and Dundyvan men returned to work after a week, however, with police protection provided by Sir Archibald Alison.[102] This led some strikers to resort to threats, intimidation and even violence in their efforts to bring them back out.[103] Although these methods were not what MacDonald advised, they were smoothly organised, as Alison reported to the Lord Advocate:

The general practice of the men on strike has been to hold midnight meetings . . . at them the men are told off in bands to intimidate workmen at the various points, and perhaps in an hour afterwards they swoop down upon a place, attack the workmen, and are off in a few minutes.[104]

But it is probable that there were only a few cases of physical violence, or threats of violence, and simple persuasion was used more often than intimidation. The Procurator Fiscal of Airdrie said, 'If the men are only asked civilly whether they are going to attend the meeting today, I don't consider this intimidation'.[105] Such intimidation as there was can hardly have been serious or widespread, since the Sheriff substitute of Airdrie reported in the middle of the strike that his area was satisfactorily quiet and that there was no need to call out cavalry.[106] This was confirmed by James Baird of Gartsherrie, the largest employer of miners in Lanarkshire, when he wrote at the end of April that the strikers were quite well behaved and that the peace-keeping forces were adequate.[107] Although the leaders were successful in sustaining solidarity among the strikers throughout most of the West of Scotland, they were less successful in raising money to support the men who were out. It was agreed that miners who had won a wage rise as a result of the strike should return to work and give one shilling in every five to help the strikers. Little came of this, however, because it was not effectively organised and probably because of a reluctance among the working miners to co-operate.[108] MacDonald also issued appeals to other trade unions and to the general public for financial support. His trade union appeal made overt use of the language of class conflict:

> We therefore appeal to you in this struggle of labour against capital, to ask for your sympathy and aid and we trust that should a struggle come to your lot it will be ours to stand by you in your day of trial.[109]

Promise of help came from some trades and from some of the public meetings which MacDonald addressed during May. But it all proved to be rather haphazard, inadequate and probably too late to be useful. Very few strikers were to receive financial support, so when the dispute was virtually over MacDonald recommended that the union should levy three shillings from every member when he returned to work and thereafter ask sixpence a week 'to accumulate a fund for the support of their just rights in the future'.[110] Although subsequent meetings altered the sums which MacDonald had suggested, the principle of the creation of a strike fund was accepted.

By their conduct of the strike of 1856, the newly formed union can be accredited with substantial changes in the organisation of this form of industrial action, changes which were to affect most subsequent strikes in the region until 1874.

In 1860, the last occasion when troops were used against striking miners during the period 1842-74, over 900 men employed by William Dixon came out from the middle of January until the end of March. During February several ironmasters in the Clyde Valley locked out their miners and stopped production in support of Dixon. Although the Glasgow miners' leader James Blee remarked in February, 'if the struggle continued much longer it would be a difficult matter to maintain the peace when thousands of men, women and children were starving',[111] and although Lord Belhaven and the Solicitor General persuaded the Home Office to move troops into possible trouble spots in early February,[112] the miners proved to be orderly and peaceful, with little or no law-breaking, violence, theft or intimidation.

Further refinements and improvements in strike organisation were made during the 1860 dispute. The district meetings and regional delegate meetings which had operated in 1856 continued to do so in 1860 with the same democratic processes and the influence of MacDonald, James Blee and men of that ilk being felt as much as ever. This time a strike committee was set up by the union which issued appeals and sent deputations to various individuals and organisations in an effort to win support.[113] An unusual feature of this strike was that it was initiated by non-unionists, employees of William Dixon being expressly forbidden to join a trade union. Instead they were enrolled in a 'Friendly and Free Labour Society' run by the company for which money was deducted from their wages.[114] But the strike came about in spite of this society and it was quickly supported by the union, which became responsible for most of its organisation, with only two of Dixon's employees on the strike committee.

Once again MacDonald and the other leaders travelled around the mining districts addressing meetings, drumming up support for the strikers and pouring scorn and contempt on collieries whose miners were not contributing to the strike fund.[115]

Dixon's miners were sustained during the dispute in two ways, by money raised from other mining districts and by finding temporary employment in other pits. These were both policies which MacDonald supported vigorously in this and subsequent strikes, and he supervised the collection and distribution of money on behalf of the strike committee. A levy of one shilling per man per week from all working miners was agreed to provide the strike fund. The men from Dixon's mines at Springfield and Huntershill, Bishopbriggs, were to be sustained by subscriptions from miners in Maryhill district, while the strikers from Dixon's large mines at Govan and Carfin were supported by the rest of the Scottish miners.[116] Every week MacDonald published in the *Glasgow Sentinel* a statement of money received from each district or colliery. This was a complicated exercise involving regular communication between scattered mining districts and requiring honesty, efficiency and a sense of collective responsibility among the miners and their officials. In spite of this it was felt in the business community that the help being given to the strikers by their working brethren was being so effectively organised that it was prolonging the dispute.[117] Yet at the end of the strike there were complaints by miners that the fund was inefficiently organised and the sums paid to strikers were inadequate.[118] Not all of them had needed help, as they had found work in other mines. By the middle of February, for example, only thirty-six of the 135 Bishopbriggs strikers were out of work.[119] This was partly why the other iron-masters enforced a lock-out in February as one of the simplest means of ensuring that striking miners were not being re-employed in their mines. But the coalmasters did not join the lock-out and it was not difficult for more of Dixon's men to find work in their collieries.

The comparison of these three major strikes appears to confirm Sir Archibald Alison's opinion that the miners were adopting a more peaceful policy. Further confirmation is found in the conduct of smaller strikes. During the 1840s and early fifties reports of violence in strikes were quite frequent — at Beith, for example, in 1847, at Coatbridge in 1850 and at Airdrie in 1855.[120] But throughout all the more detailed press reporting of miners' strikes between 1856 and 1874 only three cases of intimidation were mentioned, all in 1868. The first was at Addie's colliery, Maryhill, in April, the second at Dixon's Govan colliery in August, and the third at Galston when colliers' wives tried to force those who were returning to work to come back out on strike.[121] With the exception of these three minor incidents, the peaceful law-abiding policy of MacDonald and the union prevailed after 1856 until the end of this period. This was part of the process by which their strikes were more efficiently organised with stronger leadership and more vigorous attempts to provide money or alternative work for strikers. The size of a strike fund and the opportunities of re-employment were in inverse proportion to the number of men on strike so that the more strikers there were, the smaller the strike fund and the fewer jobs available in the region.

But the Clyde Valley miners continued to provide money for strikers throughout the 1860s, and from 1858 until 1874 there were thirty-nine occasions on which this policy was adopted. Thirty of these were limited to one or two collieries and therefore relatively simple to finance. The other nine were more extensive, covering several collieries in a district, and at least three of these ended with complaints and recriminations that the sums paid were too small to be of help. These were at Larkhall in 1863,[122] at the Eglinton Iron Works collieries in Kilmarnock in 1865,[123] and at Rosehall and Gartsherrie collieries in Coatbridge in 1866.[124]

Usually the money for strikers came from working miners in the local district and its collection and distribution were organised at district level. Twenty-seven of the thirty-nine strikes received this more limited district support, and Kilmarnock district miners even established their own district strike fund for these occasions.[125] But the more widespread or larger strikes required help from other districts and hence more complex co-operation and organisation. This was the case in the remaining twelve of these disputes. Often the support provided was substantial and came from widely scattered sources. In 1861, for example, when the men of Titwood Colliery in Pollokshaws lifted their graith, they received money from all other mining districts in the West of Scotland, with threepence being levied from each working miner per week.[126] But the collection could lead to disagreement and bickering between districts. When 320 striking miners of two collieries in Holytown required support, a levy of sixpence per week was raised from working miners in neighbouring districts. Glasgow district failed to respond, giving rise to some criticism at delegate meetings. The total sum raised on this occasion was £74.10/-, being 2,980 sixpenny contributions.[127] Of the 20,500 miners in Lanarkshire,[128] only a small proportion had contributed to support the Holytown strikers.

During these years the miners often tried a policy of selective strikes within a district. One colliery would be chosen to strike in support of a wage claim, the strikers being paid 'strike aliment' by the other miners of the district. If and when the wage rise was granted, then the same claim could be put to the rest of the employers. Of the thirty-nine supported strikes between 1858 and 1874, at least six were organised in this way.[129]

But what of the employers' reactions to these frequent and often carefully organised withdrawals of labour? While almost all middle class opinion saw strikes as dangerous, subversive and economically ruinous, it was left to mine-owners to devise tactics to oppose them. During the period 1842-74 they made use of a variety of strategies: eviction of strikers and their families from company houses, locking out the workforce of several collieries in support of employers whose mines were striking, bringing in blackleg labour, dismissing or taking other action against strike leaders and forbidding employees to join a trade union.

Of these strategies, the one which was adpoted most often throughout the period was eviction. From 1842 until 1874 mineowners used it on at least eighteen occasions. The advantages from the employers' point of view of this course of action were that it was legal and was often enforced by local sheriff courts and that it could bring strong pressure to bear on strikers through the hardship it could cause. Miners' families on some occasions had to camp in neighbouring fields, as they did at Lugar in August 1847 and at Airdrie in August 1870.[130] The greater hardship in winter months could quickly bring strikers to heel. It also gave rise to angry resentment and could prolong and exacerbate a strike, as Captain John Davidson, the commander of the 1st Royal Lanark Militia, feared during the 1856 strike. He reported, 'I do not apprehend any disturbance unless the masters carry out their intention of ejecting their workmen from their dwelling houses'.[131] Alison reported to the Lord Advocate that several orders for ejectment of Lanarkshire miners had been issued: 'I have strongly recommended to the Masters not to enforce these Decrees as likely to lead to painful scenes and violent collisions'.[132] Some unrepentant employers proceeded, however, and one of them, Lord Belhaven, reported that he believed they had the desired effect of forcing the miners back to work.[133]

During the 1860s employers were frequently obliged to adopt the lock-out as another method of collective self-defence. This was intended to prevent strikers from finding work in other mines and also, by causing widespread hardship, to bring collective pressure to bear on strikers to return to work. The lock-out of 1860, when ironmasters in Coatbridge, Holytown and Johnstone closed their collieries in support of William Dixon against his strikers, was one of the first examples of this kind of collaboration in the West of Scotland.[134] Its effectiveness probably induced employers to repeat the policy on five further occasions during the following six years. To be successful, a lock-out had to cover most of a mining district, or more than one district, and in these five subsequent disputes when mineowners resorted to the tactic, they made sure that it was on a wide scale. In 1861, for example, all the miners in Kilmarnock district were locked out after a strike. The miners were defeated and it was this experience which led them to establish a district strike fund.[135] In the following year a strike by 107 miners at Sunnyside Colliery, Wishaw, led to 400 other men being locked out at six other collieries in the district.[136] The mineowners of Rutherglen district used the policy a month after the Wishaw lock-out of 1862 in response to the attempt by the miners at a selective strike at Stonelaw colliery to force a wage increase. On this occasion many of the miners moved to Wishaw at MacDonald's suggestion to find work, and by August the Rutherglen employers were ready to concede a rise of one shilling per day to their employees.[137]

A more extensive lock-out was enforced in March and April of 1863 by mineowners in Wishaw, Larkhall and Hamilton. It grew from a strike at

Scott and Gilmour's colliery, Wishaw, against a wage cut to four shillings per day. Because of the extent of the lock-out, other jobs were difficult to find for the miners. The eviction policy of some employers, together with the inability of the union to provide enough money to relieve hardship, all helped to bring about victory for the employers by April, when the men accepted the wage and returned to work.[138]

When the Wishaw miners attempted a selective strike at Scott and Gilmour's in June of 1867 to bring about a wage rise, the employers of Wishaw, Larkhall and Hamilton with those of Motherwell again combined to lock out their workers for two weeks and again they were successful. No wage increase was given.[139]

These lock-outs of the 1860s were the result of a growing co-operative spirit among the employers of the region. During the strike of 1856 the sheriff of Ayrshire remarked that 'the miners seem more skilled in combination than their Masters'.[140] This was hardly surprising, given the variety of companies of different sizes, run by individual entrepreneurs in competition with one another. There was a particular divergence of interests between ironmasters and coal or sale masters. They produced for different markets and the price and wages policies of the one group could have adverse effects on the other. And yet by the sixties, although the first major lock-out in 1860 was carried out entirely by ironmasters, the subsequent uses of the policy in Kilmarnock, Rutherglen, Wishaw, Motherwell, Larkhall and Hamilton all involved co-operation by all mineowners, whatever their scale or whatever their market.

There were examples of mutual support among employers of an informal nature, like the letter sent by Bairds' manager at Gartsherrie, J. Alexander, to all contractors of Bairds' pits in April 1863:

> We are desirous that none of the men at present on strike against the coalmasters should be employed at our works. . . . Employ nobody if you have the slightest reason to think he is from a colliery on strike. Any at present employed please dismiss.[141]

But this supportive relationship was also becoming more institutionalised, and a Coalmasters and Ironmasters Defence Association was formed.[142] The employers met more frequently in district groups and it was at a meeting of the Wishaw district coalmasters in March 1865 that the lock-out of the district collieries was agreed upon.[143] But this unity of spirit was short-lived and by 1866 the *Colliery Guardian* was urging the need for mineowners to unite again for self-protection. 'Unless this is done', said the writer, 'and is done speedily, labour will have the supremacy of capital and total disorganisation and decay will be the result'.[144]

The masters could take individual action against strikes, and a method widely used during the 1840s was simply to recruit new labour. At that period it was quite a feasible policy because the constant flow of Irish immigrants into the West of Scotland provided a ready labour force and also because the miners' attempts at trade unionism were so sporadic that there was often no opposition to blackleg or 'nob' labour as it was called in the region.[145] By the 1860s, however, employers made only infrequent use of nob labour, with only six reports of their employment between 1856 and 1874. These men were recruited sometimes from the local population, as at Portland Colliery, Kilmarnock, in 1863, and at Caprington in the same district in 1865 when unemployed weavers were used to break strikes.[146] Nob labour was brought from Cornwall to Wishaw during the lock-out of 1867 and William Dixon brought men from Staffordshire to Govan during a strike in 1868.[147] But the policy had serious disadvantages for the owners. The new recruits, if they were local weavers or from some other occupation, could not be expected to learn the work quickly enough to produce sufficient coal to break the strike. The other drawback was the fierce resistance of the miners to nobs and the hostility which the policy could engender. On five of the six reported occasions when nobs were recruited between 1856 and 1874, they had to be dismissed again as a result of vigorous opposition by the regular miners.

A few employers tried forbidding trade unionism and sacking all strike leaders or potential leaders. Dixon used this policy at Govan in 1860 and the company sacked more strike leaders in 1862,[148] but the policy does not seem to have been effective because the Govan miners withdrew their labour again in 1863, 1865, 1866, 1868, 1871 and 1874. Not many other owners used this form of victimisation because it could have the opposite of the desired effect by causing further strike action. It has been mentioned above that the sacking of miners' leaders produced this result at Davidson's Colliery, Wishaw, in November 1859, at Woodhall Colliery, Coatbridge, in October 1862 and at Darnconner Colliery, Kilmarnock, in January 1864. Bairds of Gartsherrie, on the other hand, appear to have been comparatively successful in discouraging strikes among their workforce. This was achieved by a combination of legal action against strikers, refusal to employ strikers from other collieries, the creation of a disciplined, controlled workforce by use of contractors and by enforcing a firm, paternalist regime through company housing and schools (but not by means of truck stores).[149]

Apart from these counter-measures which the owners could adopt, they could simply 'sit out' a strike, hoping that they could survive for longer than the strikers. This depended on the coal stocks which they had available or upon other sources of coal, which most ironmasters had from their other collieries. MacDonald realised that the success or failure of a strike could depend upon the coal stocks and upon the current market price for coal and iron. If stocks were low, then a strike could cause embarrassment and expense for mineowners. In January 1850, for example, because of a strike at Cambuslang colliery, the owner, the Duke of Hamilton, was obliged to buy coal to meet some of his own requirements.[150] Even the mighty Bairds of Gartsherrie were unable to supply coal to a client company because of a colliers' strike in June 1866.[151]

How successful, then, was the strike weapon in achieving the miners' objectives? Unfortunately, when newspapers reported these disputes they did not always record how they were settled. Of the seventeen major strikes tabulated above in Tables Two and Three, the results of thirteen are known and of the 121 smaller strikes in Tables Four and Five the outcomes of fifty-seven were reported.

The major strikes in the period 1842-74 ended in failure slightly more often than in success. The successful turnouts were in 1842, 1844, 1855, 1866 and 1870 and the failures in 1847, 1856, 1860, 1863, 1867 (two strikes) and 1874. The widespread strike of 1850 ended with success in Lanarkshire but failure in Ayrshire. During the period from 1856 until 1874 there were many more failures for the miners, the only two successes in 1866 and 1870 being in strikes of a relatively smaller scale. Their disastrous defeat in 1856, and lock-outs of 1860, 1863 and 1867 and the other disastrous defeat in 1874 showed that their employers were in a stronger situation in disputes of this scale.

The fifty-seven smaller strikes in the period 1855-74 had quite a different pattern of results, with thirty-seven ending in victory for the miners and twenty in defeat. The smaller strike was easier to organise and to support from outside sources. It could be used selectively and rapidly when the time seemed appropriate and therefore had more chance of success.

But success or failure could be influenced by the nature of the miners' demands in any strike. They succeeded more often when they were pressing wage rises and they failed more often when they were opposing wage cuts, as the following tables show.

Table Ten: The Successes and Failures of Major Strikes 1842-74

	Successes	Failures
Strikes Pressing Wage Rises	4½	2½
Strikes Opposing Wage Cuts	1	5
Totals	5½	7½

(The ½ strike referred to in two columns was in 1850 which succeeded in Lanarkshire and failed in Ayrshire.)

Table Eleven: The Successes and Failures of Lesser Strikes 1855-74

	Successes	Failures
Strikes Pressing Wage Rises	27	10
Strikes Opposing Wage Cuts	5	10
Other demands	5	—
Totals	37	20

In general the miners of the region had little success in opposing wage cuts, but their strikes did have the effect of forcing wages up quite frequently during the period. A relationship had emerged between owners and men whereby wage rises were often refused until after a strike had taken place. This relationship was demonstrated particularly blatantly from 1870 until 1872 when, despite the fact that coal and iron prices were rising, a district strike of Airdrie miners and six individual colliery strikes in other districts were necessary before wage rises were given. This was symptomatic of the tension and mistrust which existed in the industry.

In conclusion, the picture which emerges is of a system of industrial relations of which the strike was a regular feature. The miners lifted their graith most often over wage disputes and particularly in support of demands for wage increases. But in the more isolated mining districts of the Clyde Valley, particularly those where employment was dominated by ironmasters, strikes were less frequent. The large districts with more diversified industry like Glasgow, Kilmarnock and later Wishaw and Hamilton had a constantly high strike level, whereas Airdrie, Coatbridge and Holytown, which were active districts in the strikes of the 1840s and fifties, became much less so in the sixties and seventies. This variation is explained by different levels of union organisation between districts, by different standards of leadership emerging in each and perhaps by differences in numbers of immigrant workers.

The use which these miners made of the strike weapon represented a consistent and regular rejection of Victorian economic theory and a collectivist philosophy of self-defence. Although most miners' leaders urged caution and restraint upon their followers, it was not because they opposed strikes for ideological reasons but rather because they feared the consequences of failure. Alexander MacDonald was a frequent advocate and organiser of strikes and an exponent of social and economic opinions which contemporary Victorians thought of as subversive and anti-capitalist. Despite his occasional disagreement with working miners about strike policy, he was usually in harmony with the men. This harmony enabled him and other miners' leaders from 1856 until 1874 to influence the organisation of strikes and the conduct of strikes so that they were better co-ordinated, less violent and in many cases more adequately financed than before.

In spite of eviction from company houses and lock-outs by their masters, the miners persistently withdrew their labour and even the use of 'nob' workers and victimisation could not succeed as retaliatory tactics. Although the majority of the large-scale strikes were failures, this was not the case with smaller one or two-colliery turn-outs, over sixty per cent of which ended with victory for the miners, usually producing a wage rise. This record of success helped to persuade miners to make regular use of the policy which also had the effect of strengthening their solidarity. When strike meetings in the 1850s and sixties began to include banners and bands, cultural trappings of class consciousness, they symbolised communities which were finding a unity and identity, although they had been thrown together so hurriedly and carelessly during the previous two decades.[152]

Suggestions for further reading

R. Page Arnot, *A History of the Scottish Miners* (London, 1955)
Raymond C. Challinor and Brian Ripley, *The Miners' Association: A Trade Union in the Age of the Chartists* (London, 1969)
W. Hamish Fraser, *Trade Unions and Society* (London, 1974)
Thomas Johnston, *The History of the Working Classes in Scotland* (Glasgow, 1920)
W. H. Marwick, *A Short History of Labour in Scotland* (Edinburgh, 1967)
A. J. Youngson Brown, 'Trade Union Policy in the Scots Coalfields, 1855-85', *Economic History Review*, vi (1953), 35-50

Notes

1. W. H. Marwick, *A Short History of Labour in Scotland* (Edinburgh, 1967), 24.
2. D. Bremner, *Industries of Scotland* (Edinburgh, 1869), 20.
3. *Glasgow Argus*, 17 June 1844; *Miners' Advocate*, 24 Aug. 1844.
4. *Hamilton Advertiser*, 6 Aug. 1870.
5. R. H. Campbell, 'Growth and Fluctuations of the Scottish Pig Iron Trade 1828-1873' (Unpublished thesis, Aberdeen University, 1956), 26, 112; A. Slaven, 'Earnings and Productivity', *Studies in Scottish Business History*, ed. P. Payne (London, 1967), 235.
6. *Glasgow Sentinel*, 18 Dec. 1852, 13 Sep. 1856, 28 Feb. 1859; *Colliery Guardian*, 2 Feb. 1861, 28 June 1862, 5 Dec. 1863; *Hamilton Advertiser*, 12 May 1866, 6 Feb. 1869, 17 Apr. 1869; *Glasgow Herald*, 18 Feb. 1873.
7. William Cloughan, *A Series of Letters on the Restriction of Labour and Its Effects in the Mines of Lanarkshire* (Coatbridge, 1846), 1-3, pamphlets in National Library of Scotland.
8. *Colliery Guardian*, 2 Feb. 1861.
9. *Miners' and Workmen's Advocate*, 24 Oct. 1863.
10. *Hamilton Advertiser*, 12 May 1866.
11. Ibid., 17 Apr. 1869.
12. *Glasgow Herald*, 18 Feb. 1873.
13. *Colliery Guardian*, 12 July 1862.
14. *Hamilton Advertiser*, 12 May 1866.
15. Ibid., 6 Feb. 1869.
16. *Report of Select Committee on Mines, Minutes of Evidence 1866* (P.P. 431), q. 7172.
17. Letter Lord Elcho to Alexander MacDonald, 11 July 1870, in Wemyss MSS (microfilm), Scottish Record Office, RH 4/40.
18. *Glasgow Sentinel*, 5 Sep. 1857; *Hamilton Advertiser*. 11 Dec. 1858.
19. *Hamilton Advertiser*, 19 Nov. 1859.

20. *Colliery Guardian*, 18 Oct. 1862.
21. Ibid., 9 Jan. 1864.
22. *Glasgow Herald*, 18 Nov. 1873.
23. *Glasgow Sentinel*, 27 Aug. 1853.
24. *Hamilton Advertiser*, 1 Sep. 1866.
25. Ibid., 24 July 1869.
26. Ibid., 31 Aug. 1872.
27. *Report of Commissioners Appointed to Inquire into the Truck System*, 1871 (P.P., C. 327).
28. Manuscript tables in MacDonald's handwriting in University of Glasgow Library. Simplified form of this information in *Report of Select Committee on Mines*, 1866 (P.P., 431).
29. *Glasgow Argus*, 15 Aug. 1842.
30. *Hamilton Advertiser*, 16 Aug. 1862.
31. Ibid., 20 Dec. 1862.
32. Ibid., 17 Jan. 1863.
33. Alan Campbell, 'Honourable Men and Degraded Slaves: Comparative Study of Trade Unionism in Two Lanarkshire Mining Communities 1841-1871', *Bulletin of Society for Study of Labour History*, No. 28, Spring 1974, 10.
34. A. Campbell, op. cit., 9-10.
35. J. E. Handley, *The Irish in Modern Scotland* (Cork, 1947), 320.
36. Letter from J. Alexander, Works Manager, Gartsherrie Iron Works, to Colliery Contractors, 18 Apr. 1863, in Letter Books of Messrs. Bairds of Gartsherrie, 1853, vol. 14, 561, in Coatbridge Public Library. I am grateful to Dr Robert Corrins for this and subsequent Gartsherrie references; *Hamilton Advertiser*, 19 Nov. 1859, 11 May 1861, 6 Feb. 1869; *Colliery Guardian*, 18 Oct. 1862.
37. R. V. Clements, 'British Trade Unions and Popular Political Economy 1850-1857', *Economic History Review*, 2nd ser., xiv, 1961-2, 94, 101-2; Harold Perkin, *The Origins of Modern English Society 1780-1880* (London, 1969), 405-7; Royden Harrison, *Before the Socialists* (London, 1965), 12-13.
38. Cloughan, *A Series of Letters*, 7.
39. *Kilmarnock Standard*, 13 May, 3 June 1865.
40. *Hamilton Advertiser*, 21 July 1866.
41. Ibid., 18 Jan. 1868, 4 Dec. 1869.
42. Ibid., 28 May 1870.
43. *Glasgow Sentinel*, 13 Oct. 1855, article iv.
44. *Hamilton Advertiser*, 4 Oct. 1862, article 11.
45. Rules of Amalgamated Coal Miners Mutual Protection Society of Wishaw and District, 1873, F.S. 7-35, rules 8-10; Rules of Amalgamated Coal Miners Mutual Protection Society of Motherwell 1873-4, F.S. 7-43, rules 8-10; Rules of Larkhall Miners Mutual Protection, Accident and Funeral Association 1874, F.S. 7-1, rules 29-30; Rules of Stonehouse Miners Mutual Protection, Accident and Funeral Association 1874, F.S. 7-34, rules 29-30; Rules of Carluke Miners Association 1873, F.S. 7-39, rules 8-10; Rules of

Maryhill Miners Labour Protection and Benefit Association 1875, F.S. 7-23, rules 14-16, all in Records of Assistant Registrar of Friendly Societies for Scotland, in Scottish Record Office (Register House).

46. *Glasgow Sentinel*, 25 Oct. 1856.
47. Ibid., 29 Mar. 1856.
48. *Colliery Guardian*, 18 July 1863.
49. *Hamilton Advertiser*, 10 Oct. 1868.
50. Ibid., 4 June 1870.
51. *Airdrie and Coatbridge Advertiser*, 14 Feb. 1874.
52. R. Page Arnot, *A History of the Scottish Miners* (London, 1955), 57.
53. *Hamilton Advertiser*, 20 Aug. 1864.
54. Ibid., 31 May 1862.
55. Ibid., 14 June 1862.
56. Ibid., 17 Oct. 1863.
57. Ibid., 23 Jan. 1864.
58. Ibid., 10 Sep. 1864.
59. Ibid., 7 July 1866, 22 June 1867.
60. *Kilmarnock Standard*, 3 June 1865.
61. *Hamilton Advertiser*, 23 May 1868.
62. Ibid., 9 July 1870.
63. *Royal Commission on Trade Unions* 1868, (P.P. 3980) q. 16,346.
64. Raymond Challinor, *Alexander MacDonald and the Miners* (London 1967), 22.
65. Letter from Lord Elcho to Alexander MacDonald, Mar. 1869, in Wemyss MSS (microfilm), Scottish Record Office, RH 4/40.
66. Karl Miller, *Cockburn's Millennium* (London, 1975), 215-17.
67. Raphael Samuel, reviewing Raymond Challinor, *The Lancashire and Cheshire Miners* in *New Society*, 7 Dec. 1972, 587.
68. National Association for Promotion of Social Science, *Trades' Society and Strikes* (London, 1860), 602.
69. Letter from Home Office to Sir Archibald Alison, 12 Aug. 1842, in Home Office (Scotland) Entry Books Domestic, H.O. 103, vol. 9, in Scottish Record Office, RH 2/4, vol. 235, 241 and 243.
70. *Glasgow Argus*, 4 and 8 Aug. 1842.
71. Ibid.; Duke of Hamilton's Lanarkshire Coal Accounts, 1842, Cambuslang Colliery, in Hamilton District Library, 220970/10LC, Aug. 1842; *Ayr Advertiser*, 18 Aug. 1842.
72. *Glasgow Argus*, 8 Aug. 1842.
73. Sir Archibald Alison, *Some Account of My Life and Writings* (Edinburgh, 1883), 487.
74. Above, Table One.
75. *Glasgow Chronicle*, 10 Oct. 1842.
76. *Glasgow Herald*, 12 Dec. 1842.
77. *Glasgow Saturday Post and Renfrewshire Reformer*, 13 Aug. 1842.
78. *Glasgow Argus*, 4, 8, 11, 15 Aug. 1842; *Glasgow Chronicle*, and

Glasgow Herald, 5 Aug. 1842; *Glasgow Saturday Post*, 6 Aug. 1842.

79.   Alison, *Some Account of My Life*, 487.

80.   *Glasgow Argus*, 8 Aug. 1842, and Alison, op cit., 487.

81.   *Glasgow Argus*, 8 Aug. 1842.

82.   Letters from Alison to Home Office, 9 Aug. 1842, and letter from Sir James Graham to Duke of Hamilton, 11 Aug. 1842, in H.O. (Scotland) Entry Books, RH 2/4, vol. 235, 442, 444, 445-6.

83.   Letter from H. Manners Sutton at Home Office to Alison, 19 Aug. 1842, in H.O. (Scotland) Entry Books, R.H. 2/4, vol. 235, 462; *Glasgow Argus*, 22 and 25 Aug. 1842.

84.   *Glasgow Argus*, 8 and 18 Aug. and 10 Oct. 1842; *Glasgow Saturday Post*, 17 Sep. 1842.

85.   Alison, *Some Account of My Life*, 499; *Glasgow Chronicle*, 22 Sep. 1842.

86.   Letter from Sir Archibald Alison to Lord Advocate, 5 May 1856, in Lord Advocate's Papers, Box 117, Letters Relating to Miners Strike in Linlithgowshire, Stirlingshire and Lanarkshire 1856, in Scottish Record Office, West Register House, Edinburgh (hereafter cited as L.A. Strike Letters, 1856).

87.   Letter from N. McFarlane, Edinburgh, to Lord Advocate, 9 May 1856, in L.A. Strike Letters, 1856.

88.   Letter from Charles Baillie, sheriff of Stirlingshire, to Lord Advocate, May 1856, in L.A. Strike Letters, 1856.

89.   Letter from John Christison, sheriff of Ayrshire, to Lord Advocate, 2 May 1856, in L.A. Strike Letters, 1856.

90.   Letter from Captain Davidson, Coatbridge, to Home Office, 20 Apr. 1856; Alison to Lord Advocate, 5 May 1856, in L.A. Strike Letters, 1856.

91.   *Glasgow Argus*, 11 Aug. 1842.

92.   *Northern Star*, 16 July 1842; Raymond Challinor and Brian Ripley, *The Miners' Association — A Trade Union in the Age of the Chartists* (London, 1968), 72.

93.   *Glasgow Argus*, 4 and 8 Aug. 1842; *Glasgow Saturday Post*, 6 Aug. 1842.

94.   *Glasgow Argus*, 11 Aug. 1842.

95.   *Glasgow Sentinel*, 13 Oct. 1855.

96.   Challinor and Ripley, op. cit., 72.

97.   *Glasgow Sentinel*, 3 May and 7 June 1856.

98.   Ibid., 12 and 26 Apr., 3 May 1856.

99.   Ibid., 14 June 1856.

100.   Ibid., 7 June 1856; W. Hamish Fraser, 'A Newspaper for its Generation: the *Glasgow Sentinel*', *Journal of the Scottish Labour History Society*, No. 4, July 1971.

101.   *Glasgow Sentinel*, 19 Apr. 1856.

102.   Ibid., 26 Apr. 1856.

103.   Letters from Hugh Tennent to Alison, 28 Apr.; J. N. Dyce, sheriff

substitute at Lanark, to Alison, 28 Apr.; Alison to Lord Advocate, 5 and 7 May 1856, in L.A. Strike Letters, 1856.

104.   Letter from Alison to Lord Advocate, 17 May 1856, in L.A. Strike Letters, 1856.

105.   *Report of Commissioner for Mining Districts*, 1856 (P.P. 2125) 47.

106.   Letter from Hugh Tennent to Alison, 23 Apr., in L.A. Strike Letters, 1856.

107.   Letter from James Baird to Lord Advocate, 30 Apr., in L.A. Strike Letters, 1856.

108.   *Glasgow Sentinel*, 19 Apr., 7 June 1856.

109.   Ibid., 4 May 1856.

110.   Ibid., 7 June 1856.

111.   Ibid., 25 Feb. 1860.

112.   Letters from H. Waddington, Home Office, to Lt. Gen. Sir Charles Yorke and to Lord Belhaven, 30 Jan. and 7 Feb. 1860, in H.O. (Scotland) Entry Books, R.H. 2/4, vol. 243, 294.

113.   *Glasgow Sentinel*, 25 Feb.; *Airdrie and Coatbridge Advertiser*, 18 Feb., 17 Mar. 1860.

114.   *Govan Colliery Pay Book* 1859-61, in Glasgow University Department of Economic History.

115.   *Glasgow Sentinel*, 28 Jan., 25 Feb., 10, 17 Mar. 1860.

116.   Ibid., 11 Feb., 3 Mar. 1860.

117.   *Airdrie and Coatbridge Advertiser*, 10 Mar. 1860, report of monthly business circular of Messrs. Woodrow and Sons dated 2 Mar. 1860.

118.   *Glasgow Sentinel*, 31 Mar. 1860.

119.   Ibid., 11 Feb. 1860.

120.   *Glasgow Argus*, 20 Sep. 1847; Letter from D. Wallace, Gartsherrie, to J. Johnstone, factor of Colts of Gartsherrie, 3 May 1850, in Gartsherrie Letter Book, vol. 3, 323; *Glasgow Sentinel*, 22 Sep. 1855.

121.   *Hamilton Advertiser*, 11 Apr., 8 Aug. 1868; *Kilmarnock Standard*, 22 Aug. 1868.

122.   *Hamilton Advertiser*, 28 Mar. 1863; *Colliery Guardian*, 28 Mar. 1863; *The Miner*, 21 Mar. 1863.

123.   *Kilmarnock Standard*, 20 May 1865.

124.   *Airdrie Advertiser*, 26 May 1866; *Colliery Guardian*, 28 July 1866.

125.   *Kilmarnock Standard*, 17 Sep. 1870.

126.   *Hamilton Advertiser*, 6 July 1861.

127.   *Colliery Guardian*, 14 Mar. 1863.

128.   *Census of Scotland*, 1861, vol. ii, 256.

129.   *Hamilton Advertiser*, 10 Sep. 1859.

130.   *Glasgow Argus*, 16 Aug. 1847; *Hamilton Advertiser*, 26 Aug. 1870.

131.   Report of John Davidson, Coatbridge, to Lord Advocate, 20 Apr. 1856, in L.A. Strike Letters, 1856.

132.   Letter from Alison to Lord Advocate, 25 Apr. 1856, in L.A. Strike Letters, 1856.

133. Letter from Lord Belhaven, Wishaw, to Lord Advocate, 6 June 1856, in L.A. Strike Letters, 1856.

134. *Hamilton Advertiser*, 4, 11 Feb. 1860.

135. *Colliery Guardian*, 23 Nov. 1861.

136. *Hamilton Advertiser*, 28 June, 5 July 1862.

137. Ibid., 26 July, 30 Aug. 1862; *Colliery Guardian*, 26 July, 30 Aug. 1862.

138. *Hamilton Advertiser*, 7 Mar., 11 Apr. 1863; *The Miner*, 21 Mar. 1863.

139. *Hamilton Advertiser*, 20 July, 10 Aug. 1867.

140. Letter from J. Christison, Ayr, to Solicitor General, 13 May 1856, in L.A. Strike Letters, 1856.

141. Letter from J. Alexander, Gartsherrie, to all contractors, 18 Apr. 1863, in Gartsherrie Letter Books, vol. 14, 423.

142. *Colliery Guardian*, 19 Jan. 1861.

143. *Hamilton Advertiser*, 14 Mar. 1863.

144. *Colliery Guardian*, 4 Aug. 1866.

145. *Report of Commissioner on Mining Districts*, 1844 (P.P. 592), 32-3; James E. Handley, *The Irish in Scotland* (Cork, 1943), 111-112.

146. *Colliery Guardian*, 25 Apr., 11 July 1863; *Hamilton Advertiser*, 11 Nov. 1865.

147. *Hamilton Advertiser*, 10 Aug. 1867, 8 Aug. 1868.

148. *Colliery Guardian*, 13 Sep. 1862.

149. Letters from David Wallace, Gartsherrie, to Robert Watt, writer, Airdrie, 24 and 25 Apr. 1855; J. Alexander, Gartsherrie, to all Bairds' contractors, 28 Aug. 1863; John Campbell, cashier, Gartsherrie, to all contractors, 14 Feb. 1854; J. Alexander to R. Angus, Lugar, 25 June 1870 (all in Gartsherrie Letter Books, vols. 6, 8, 14, 21).

150. Duke of Hamilton's Mineral Accounts, 1849-50, 53-67, in Hamilton Library Local Collection.

151. Letter from R. Munro, Gartsherrie, to Garnkirk Fireclay Company, 15 June 1866, in Gartsherrie Letter Book, vol. 18, 568.

152. Gordon M. Wilson, 'The Miners of the West of Scotland and their Trade Unions, 1842-74' (Unpublished Ph.D. thesis, University of Glasgow, 1977), 232-66, contains most of this essay and sets it in a wider context.

Irish Immigrants and Scottish Radicalism, 1880-1906

Ian Wood

WHEN political nationalism is gaining support as rapidly as it is at the time of writing, the task of defining a clear Scottish identity, assuming that this can be done, takes on a new urgency. Modern Scotland, above all its central industrial belt which is of such importance demographically and politically, has been the melting-pot of diverse cultures — highland, Calvinist and Catholic Irish. The impact of this last tradition has been a matter of recurrent concern in Scottish nationalist writing. In 1968 H. J. Paton's *The Claim of Scotland*[1] was well-received by much of the Scottish press and its arguments for self-government were widely quoted editorially and by leading figures in the Scottish National Party.

Its author's view of Irish immigration into Scotland was never much in doubt however: 'few reasonable Scotsmen will regard it as an unmixed blessing than an unusually homogeneous country should be split up into two nations'.[2] Later we are told that 'the untrammelled benefits provided by the welfare state have played no small part in bringing into this country too many of the less valuable elements in the Irish invasion'.[3] Paton's contention was that Irish immigration has been a lesser evil than native Scottish emigration, but still for all that an evil, for the damage done to an (unclearly defined) Scottish identity which predated it.

Paton's book cannot, of course, be taken as any guide to what immigration policy, if any, an independent Scotland might pursue but his stereotypes of Irish poverty and Irish criminality point to a layer of Scottish xenophobia which has for long co-existed with the real or imagined facts of the Irish presence in Scotland. Polemicists much more virulent than Paton have, in the recent past, reacted to this Irish 'threat'. One of them was Andrew Dewar Gibb, who held the Regius chair of law at Glasgow University between the wars. He wrote extensively on the theme of Scotland's decline, and his attacks on the Irish reached a climax in his *Scotland in Eclipse*, published in 1930.

A savage chapter in this book concerns itself exclusively with the 'running sore' of Irish immigration and Gibb resorts to every kind of accusation against the Irish in one of the most paranoid racialist outbursts ever produced by a Scottish nationalist writer. 'As a rule quite unprosperous [to Gibb an apparent proof in itself of vice] they have in some places displayed special abilities.

Thus in Glasgow, they are fast developing a monopoly of the priesthood, the pawnshops, and the public houses. They form an appreciable proportion of the population of Scotland, breeding as they do not merely unchecked but actually encouraged by their own medicine-men. . . . They are responsible for most of the crime committed in Scotland, which otherwise would be the most law-abiding country in the world. Wheresoever knives and razors are used, wheresoever sneak thefts and mean pilfering are easy and safe, wheresoever dirty acts of sexual baseness are committed there you will find the Irishman in Scotland with all but a monopoly of the business'.[4]

Gibb's concern with, in his own words, the 'proper disposal and treatment of the deplorable Irish colony in Scotland' was paradoxical at a time when the National Party which he supported so actively all his adult life was itself accused of being manipulated by Irish Catholics.[5] Writing of the period after the nationalist triumph in securing Compton Mackenzie's election in 1931 as rector of Glasgow University, Dr John MacCormick referred to how 'the lie that our Party was under Catholic control took firm root and spread all over the country like some foul weed'.[6] MacCormick's reaction to the Irish question in Scotland was, however, a balanced one compared with Gibb's. He saw the failure to assimilate the Irish as a product of the Scottish people's lack of any clearly perceived identity of their own and grasped the cultural shock and brutal exploitation which had so often been the immigrants' lot in industrial Scotland. 'When Scotland has developed a sufficiently healthy national life of her own she will find no difficulty in absorbing strangers in her midst and turning them into good Scottish citizens'.[7]

Scottish literature would be a useful seam to mine for evidence on the Irish presence and responses to it, whether popular or individual ones, by particular authors. John Buchan, for example, was never a nationalist, though his feeling for things Scottish comes through strongly in some of his best work. His antagonism to Irish nationalism, even the moderate Home Rule it was demanding before 1914, is well documented by his most recent biographer, Janet Adam Smith. A vivid passage in *Mr Standfast*, one of the Richard Hannay adventures set during the first world war, captures the deep-seated working class suspicion on the Clyde of Irish war-workers and their families. 'Glasgow's stinkin' nowadays, with two things, money and Irish', Hannay is told by the disillusioned border radical, Andrew Amos, who goes on to make clear to Hannay exactly whom he means: 'I'm not speaking about Ulster, which is a dour, ill-natured den, but our own folk all the same. But men that will not do a hand's turn to help the war and take the chance of our necessities to set up a bawbee rebellion are hateful to God and man'.[8]

The Irish dimension to modern Scottish experience is a topic rich in possibilities but this essay will confine itself to the political involvement of the immigrant Irish, and to the question of whether their identity as an immigrant community was a serious obstacle to their assimilation to the struggles of an emergent labour movement in Scotland.

To begin by stressing the importance to labour of the Catholic vote in west and central Scotland is to state a truism for anyone actively interested in labour politics. It is now some years moreover since Budge and Urwin, in *Scottish Political Behaviour*, set out to quantify the matter. One result of this research was to show that, in one area surveyed, the Catholic labour vote was conspicuously *more* solid than that of the working class taken as a whole.[9] Offsetting the long-term asset to labour that this reservoir of Catholic support has been are the tensions it has created, for example on the school issue, but Labour could not have been a real power in Scotland without it. The extent of this support must be seen as the product of the social assimilation of Irish-Catholic immigrants, a process the political logic of which was first pointed to by the young John Wheatley in his celebrated controversy with the church in 1907 about whether Catholics could be Socialists. Middlemas in 1965 gave some rather superficial coverage to this episode in *The Clydesiders*,[10] and this article will seek to fill in some at least of the historical background to it.

The overall pattern of Irish immigration into nineteenth-century Scotland has been described and to some extent documented elsewhere, and census figures help to quantify the picture. A problem arising from their use is, of course, that they deal in figures for those of Irish birth (although, of course, making no distinctions between Catholics and Ulster Protestants). They do not include persons of Irish parentage. This is important: modern work on Irish-American nationalism[11] serves to underline the fact that people with no direct personal memories of the homeland may develop even deeper politically expressed loyalty to it, whether as a result of parental example or the influence of an immigrant sub-culture.

An additional problem is that overall figures on Irish immigration and on persons resident in Scotland but of Irish parentage are not in themselves reliable as denominational statistics in that they do not distinguish between Catholics and Ulster Protestants. For more specific evidence about the growth of a Catholic population in Victorian Scotland Catholic sources themselves have had to be explored, like the parish returns already drawn on in a recent exercise in quantifying the Irish vote in Glasgow.[12]

The year 1878 saw the restoration of a Catholic hierarchy to Scotland, Glasgow becoming one of two archdioceses in Scotland. Catholic life in Glasgow particularly took on an increasingly organised form, structured, of course, around the parish. Standard (but non-Catholic) sources on the period stress and indeed pay tribute to the role of the church in providing religious and secular education, social activity and relief for the aged and the very poor. Catholic life in Glasgow and in Scotland revealed itself in other ways, in the rapid spread of the Ancient Order of Hibernians (despite the local hostility of the hierarchy) and other friendly societies like the Irish Foresters. There was also the revival of Gaelic sports which met a response in the Scottish immigrant community, though some no doubt would view the rapid growth of the Glasgow Celtic as equal proof of a desire to assimilate with the social life of industrial Scotland.

William Walker in a recent article has carried out a valuable examination of Irish immigrant culture in Victorian Scotland. His thesis is that the church-centred organisations which controlled immigrant social life and education to such an extent militated against any realisation of Engels' prediction that the Irish would give a new dynamism and militancy to the indigenous working class. Political nationalism when it did begin to develop was, Walker argues, endorsed by the Catholic clergy as an antidote to the influence of a secular working-class radicalism apathetic or hostile to the claims of any church.[13] Whether Irish nationalism in Scotland was always inimical to any immigrant rapport on class issues with Scottish trade unionists and radical movements is, however, a matter in need of further exploration.

Irish communities in Scotland had been mobilised politically as early as the 1820s behind the Catholic Emancipation campaign, and Daniel O'Connell's birthday continued for long to be a major celebration, especially in Glasgow. After O'Connell had moved on to a campaign for repeal of the Act of Union, Irish repeal associations for a time grew rapidly and in the 1830s and 1840s were represented on platforms and demonstrations alongside the Chartists, but Irishmen in Scotland do not seem to have risen to positions of prominence within the Chartist movement. After the Second Reform Act, from which the Irish community was also in some degree a beneficiary, well-publicised meetings, notably in Glasgow, were held to deliberate on how Irish votes should be deployed.

Prior to this, however, ward-level attempts to mobilise Catholic votes and to put up Catholic candidates were not unknown. These usually tried to stand on purely local issues without party labels, conforming to the then agreed view that Scottish local government was and should remain non-political. Race and religion, particularly in Glasgow contests, could never be kept at bay for long. This can be seen in the role of James Lynch, a well-known Glasgow undertaker who sought to campaign for a council seat in 1872, on issues like local jobbery, threats to the amenity of Glasgow Green and the need for more economical administration of the city's Improvement Trust. Some of his meetings were violently disrupted, as were those of other candidates supported by a fairly short-lived Catholic Association whose activities get periodic mention in the Glasgow press up to 1873. Some ward-level Irish and Catholic organisations did nonetheless linger on to be incorporated in the Irish National League, and the 1872 Education Act prompted a certain amount of organisation of the Catholic vote at local School Board Elections.

Sectarian prejudice of the virulence just mentioned was perhaps in part a product of the fact that attempts to organise politically Irish Catholics in Scottish cities were paralleled or provoked by the role of militant Protestantism, especially in the form of the Orange Order. A Parliamentary Select Committee of 1835 pointed to its strength in Glasgow even then; witnesses before this Committee set up by the Whig reform ministry claimed the existence of twelve active lodges in Glasgow.[14] There were also many belligerently Protestant and patriotic clubs to whom the standing of O'Connell among the Glasgow Irish was an ever-present provocation. The Glasgow Conservative

Operatives Association, formed with Peel's blessing, was almost wholly Orange in its orientation and also in sympathy with the Evangelical party in the Church of Scotland.[15] A standard view has been that working-class Orangeism was in abeyance in Scotland (and indeed in Protestant Ulster too) until Gladstone's espousal of Home Rule gave the order a glorious resurrection.

More work must be done on this, but some evidence would suggest that militant Orangeism was in no great need of any new stimulus from Home Rule in the 1880s. References in Government papers make clear that its activities in working-class areas in the west of Scotland were a matter of concern right through the 1850s and 1860s.[16] In Glasgow itself sectarian violence never assumed the form of recurrent and large-scale rioting as in Belfast, but special Catholic Irish celebrations could act as the flashpoint for serious trouble. O'Connell in his lifetime had been at the centre of much tension created by his speaking tours. After his death, the invocation of his memory continued to provoke Orangemen in Ireland and Scotland. Above all, the centenary of his birth in 1875 was fraught with danger, something which the Catholic church in the west of Scotland sensed right away, for the attempt was made to keep the commemoration under wholly clerical control. In this the church failed, and separate clerical and political demonstrations were held on the same Sunday within a short distance of each other to honour the memory of the 'liberator'.[17] It was the return of demonstrators to the working-class suburban burgh of Partick which precipitated bloodshed, for as a Glasgow newspaper commented, the Orange Order 'enjoy the full sympathies of the lower class of the Scotch population of the burgh'. At the height of what turned out to be an extended weekend of rioting in which pikes, daggers, and axes were used, spokesmen of Partick's Orangemen asked the provost and baillies of the burgh that lodge brethren be sworn in as special constables. This was a request too provocative for the authorities to grant, even had they wished to, for the Glasgow press was full of reports of organised Orange bands hunting Catholics off the streets. Yet it was a request significant of the relationship which the Order imagined it could and should have with the authorities. The most important contribution to limiting the scale of this outburst probably came from the nearby Catholic parish of Maryhill, whose priest intercepted some thousand of his flock who were marching — many of them well-armed — into Partick to avenge the imagined death (for remarkably, no loss of life resulted) of a Catholic at the hands of the Partick Orangemen. The eloquence of his appeal, reinforced with assurances of the curse of God on those who defied him, had its effect and the Maryhill crowd dispersed.

Effective organisation of the Irish in Glasgow and in Scotland in the nationalist cause came with the arrival in the city of John Ferguson, a Protestant of farming stock born near Belfast. He settled in 1860 in Glasgow, where he was apprenticed to the book and stationery trade. It time he became a partner in a successful publishing firm and latterly lived in apparently comfortable circumstances in Lenzie outside Glasgow, naming his house there

'Benburb' after Owen Roe O'Neill's great victory in 1646. Ferguson emerged in the Reform League's agitation of 1866 but was not so immersed in domestic radical politics as to forget the national cause. He was instrumental in publishing *The Green Flag of Erin*, an anthology of patriotic verse and song, which received the accolade of confiscation by the Dublin Castle authorities when copies of it crossed the Irish Sea for distribution.

Ferguson's real impact on Irish politics in Scotland, however, came with the preparations for Isaac Butt's visit to Glasgow in 1871. Ferguson had a major role in forming a committee to welcome Butt to the city, out of which a more permanent organisation took shape in the form of a nationalist society affiliated to the Home Government Association which Butt had already founded in Dublin. The Glasgow Home Government branch was in fact the first to be formed outside Ireland and quickly became a power in its own right in Irish nationalist politics, remaining bigger than many of the branches subsequently formed in Glasgow and elsewhere. It tended also to a distinctive line on some issues and was regarded with suspicion by Catholics inspired by Cardinal Manning's conversion to the temperance cause on account of the alleged publican influence in its membership.

The years following upon the emergence of Ferguson and the Glasgow Home Government association were ones in which the Irish M.P.s at Westminster operated without any very permanent organisational base either in Ireland or in Scottish or English constituencies. They were indeed, in Dr Conor Cruise O'Brien's words, very much a 'Catholic's particularist fringe' of the Liberal party. Militant agrarian agitation in Ireland, followed by Parnell's election to the chairmanship of the Irish Parliamentary group, changed this and in 1882 the Irish National League was founded to mobilise Irish opinion and Irish votes behind the Home Rule cause.

The most important and illuminating comments on the organisation of the Irish National League are still those by Dr Conor Cruise O'Brien. He stresses that 'the foundation of the National League had, in effect, turned the active Home Rule movement from a loose conglomeration of independent and sometimes discrepant elements into a well-knit political party of a modern type', but that it was always, in Healy's phrase, an 'auxiliary' of the Parliamentary party and one whose role both in candidate selection and policy formulation was a declining one in the period of Parnell's leadership.[18] Dr O'Brien's concern is, of course, primarily with the League as an arm of the Parliamentary party in constituencies which could be won for Home Rule, i.e. in Ireland. Only one Home Ruler was ever elected for a British constituency, but League activists like John Denvir were well aware of the large Irish electorate which nonetheless existed in Britain, albeit not strongly enough concentrated in most constituencies actually to be able to elect candidates.[19]

The new League first attempted to organise at ward level, where elected ward committees had an important though not always decisive role in nominating council candidates and in requiring sitting councillors to render an account of their stewardship. The *Glasgow Observer* in its debut as an assiduous and well-informed journal of Irish opinion in Scotland gave its blessing to these efforts to mobilise the Irish vote, as to renewed efforts to capture Catholic School Board places. By 1885, however, the most pressing task was preparations for general elections in which the Irish vote would have to be deployed to the best advantage.

This was no mean task, and press reports nearly always erred on the side of optimism, or at any rate exaggeration, in their claims for what League activists were achieving. The problem lay both in the nature of the franchise and of the Irish community itself — a ratepayers' and residential franchise, one moreover demanding personal rate payment, contained built-in obstacles to the registration of the Irish poor. Over and above this, to be in receipt of poor relief in the twelve months before registration was in itself a disqualification. The system in other words made unrealistic demands on a largely poor and necessarily mobile working-class community, of whom at least one in two managed to get a vote.[20]

The illiteracy of Irish voters could present serious problems too, though figures for this are not immediately to hand. In the 1892 general election, the defeat in north-west Lanarkshire of a Liberal Home Ruler by a narrow margin of votes was attributed by the Irish nationalist press in Glasgow to over a hundred ballot papers being spoiled by Irish voters. These, it was claimed, feared to make known their illiteracy to polling agents who would then have to record their preference for them. Since many poll clerks and agents were released from their work for the day by the constituency's predominantly Unionist employers, Irish voters were believed to fear subsequent victimisation if they gave away their allegiance in this way.

The National League could claim from 1885 to be the fastest growing political organisation in Scotland. At the peak of its strength it had well over a hundred branches, the vast majority of these in the west of Scotland, although Irish communities in Edinburgh, Dundee and Dumfries also formed branches. West Lothian and Lanarkshire, with a large Irish labour force in mining, had numerous branches. Glasgow branches numbered just over a dozen of this total, but, judged from press coverage, tended to have larger membership and to provide a base for the movement's best-known activists in Scotland like Ferguson. The controlling body of the League's branches in Scotland, as in England and Ireland, was the Irish Parliamentary party, acting through the executive committee which it elected. This London-based executive could make considerable demands on local branches, for example for regular reports and quarterly returns to central funds of any financial surplus achieved by local branch efforts. Full-time organisers were appointed by the London executive and often arrogated to themselves extensive powers in matters like the suspension or suppression of branches whose affairs were deemed to be in disarray. Yet the branches were not consulted in the appointment of these officers. Some Glasgow branches waged a campaign in 1885 and 1886 against one organiser, Owen Kiernan, whom they claimed had been foisted on them in this way, and whose financial integrity had previously been in question. The

November 1885 convention of Irish National League branches from the Glasgow area heard many motions critical of the central organisation of the League and of the way it denied branch autonomy.[21]

Criticism of top-heavy centralism in organisation became inextricably caught up in disagreement over substantive issues of League policy. Early in 1886, the executive ruled in London that the Glasgow branches' St Patrick's Day rally must not be chaired by John Ferguson, despite his seniority in the movement, and indeed in Scottish radical politics (two years later he was to be one of the co-founders of the Scottish Labour Party). The point of contention was precisely Ferguson's radicalism which had led him publicly to entertain his doubts about executive directives to Scottish branches that, in the November 1885 general election, they should, in conformity with Parnell's policy, deploy their votes behind Tory candidates. As a bargaining strategy at that time this may have had some merit, but it meant in effect opposing Liberal and radical candidates with views on Irish and more general social questions acceptable to many branches of the League.

In the election campaign, Ferguson had in fact appeared on some radical platforms, notably that of James Shaw Maxwell, an executive member of the Scottish Land Restoration League who had contested a Glasgow constituency. Maxwell was particularly popular with many of the Glasgow Irish for his conscientious support for the agrarian struggle in the western counties of their homeland, which he saw as a fight against the common enemy of Irish tenants and Scottish crofters. Maxwell received a telegram of support from Michael Davitt, the sentiments of which Ferguson endorsed. Ferguson's support for Maxwell was not held against him by a majority of branches in the Glasgow area who agreed to his chairmanship of the 1886 rally as a routine matter only to be confronted with hostile executive intervention. Some branches' first reaction was to call for protest action but, as the *Glasgow Observer* pointed out on 13 March 1886, the League executive was acting within its constitutional rights.[22] Delegates from League branches planning to attend the rally forced the issue to a vote, and obedience to executive action was agreed to by a 30-16 vote, not without strong attacks being made on the slight administered to Ferguson. Feeling on this episode lingered on and there was a demonstration from the floor in Ferguson's support when the rally was held.[23]

The episode most likely to have tested relations between League branches in Scotland and the London executive and perhaps to have forced a re-structuring of those relations, was the Parnell divorce case. Parnell's prestige in Scotland on the eve of the divorce was high, not just among the League's active membership but with much of the Liberal party well to the left of the leadership on issues like land reform, church disestablishment, and Home Rule itself. Not for nothing did Parnell pay Scotland the compliment of taking his famous action against the *Times* in 1888 to Parliament House in Edinburgh. Edinburgh repaid the compliment by granting him the freedom of the city once the charges originally brought against him were comprehensively refuted. Yet once the storm broke over the O'Shea divorce the vast majority of League branches in

Scotland repudiated their leader and accepted the view of the majority of the Irish Parliamentary party. In this new situation, advocates of more autonomy for the League and its branches in Scotland were quick to make the connection between the consequences of Parnell's autocracy and the highly centralised nature of the League itself.

Some Glasgow branches were outspoken in the campaign for a radical re-shaping of the League, and the *Glasgow Observer* gave them strong support, a move away from its previously cautious position on this matter. Matters came to a head at the 1891 Newcastle convention to which over four hundred branches from Scotland and England sent delegates. The Glasgow delegation, in which members of the Home Government branch were prominent, tabled resolutions calling for a democratic executive, half of whose members were to be elected from local branches and half by the Parliamentary party. These resolutions, however, were all defeated and an opportunity lost to give a measure of what was becoming known as home rule to League members themselves.[24]

This is not the place to evaluate the overall extent to which Irish Home Rule was set back by the divorce split. In Scotland the national movement's organisation and its relationship with the anti-Parnell majority of the Parliamentary party survived and the National League was retained in Scotland until William O'Brien's creation of the United Irish League in 1898 provided a basis for reuniting the whole national movement. The new designation was thereafter adopted in Scotland and it was in the United Irish League that, for example, Wheatley served his political apprenticeship in Shettleston at the beginning of the new century.

Sectarianism and clerical control were charges often made against the National League, and not always by Unionist opponents of Home Rule for Ireland. Given the prestige of priests in Catholic working-class communities, it followed that they did often play a central role in the launching of League branches, and providing church halls as meeting places once a branch had been formed (few could match the generous facilities with which the Glasgow Home Government branch could afford to provide itself). In the then small mining village of Baillieston, where a new branch was set up in 1886, the local priest took the chair at the inaugural meeting in the parish hall, and the sectarian import of his remarks was unmistakable. He spoke on the theme of faith and fatherland and declared that 'he could not separate the Irish cause from Catholicity, and he always considered, speaking in a general sense, that when he met an Irishman he met a Catholic'.[25]

The policy of a party with a Protestant like Parnell as its revered leader could never have been sectarian as to matters of membership, but some evidence would suggest that the executive may not have been as ready to apply pressure at a local level on this issue as on others. The way in which the Dalmellington branch in Ayrshire voted to admit non-Catholics to its St Patrick's night concert and dance (provided each was accompanied by a Catholic friend) suggested that Protestants were not normally being received into membership. Other branches might refuse certain privileges of membership to non-Catholics, like the Robert Emmet branch in Irvine which carried a motion confirming membership of its band to Catholics only.

Hardship facing members through sickness and unemployment often engaged the concern of branches, even although membership often over-lapped with that of the Catholic friendly societies. It was not uncommon for branches to suspend other business in order to set up concerts or other fund-raising activities for the benefit of a member in distress or to provide immedi-ately needed financial help to widows and children of branch members. Such initiatives did, however, represent a departure from the principal *raison d'etre* of League branches, which was political.

When economic recession in the mid-1880s set in, concern with the relief of the Catholic poor became the overriding concern of some branches, and after 1887 something closer to a working relationship in the relief of distress developed between the Parkhead branch and the newly formed football and athletic association associated with the district ever since. Charities not under Catholic control were often held in suspicion by Scottish Catholics and this was voiced by some of the League's Glasgow branches, for example in their attacks on the city's Quarrier Homes for the allegedly large-scale 'conversion' of Catholic orphans or abandoned children.

Local school boards created under the 1872 Act also aroused the suspicion of some branches. The problem was essentially that Catholic schools were not directly a charge on local school rates and could only claim aid on a 'direct grant' basis from the Scottish Education Department once they were actually built and equipped. In practice, a proportion of Board school places were always filled by Catholic pupils, and in some schools in Glasgow's working-class areas there could be a Catholic preponderance. This latter was a situation fraught with tension, though much depended on the teachers concerned. In 1885, controversy with a clearly sectarian edge to it flared in Glasgow when the League's Northern branch attacked a local school for requiring a daily singing of *God Save the Queen* from its mainly Catholic pupils. The fact remains none-theless that a proportion at least of Catholic and Protestant children were at this time being educated under the same roof and in the same class-rooms.

Clerical influence in a mainly Catholic movement was a reality which had to be taken into account by anyone seeking an active career in it. This was especially so for a Protestant like Ferguson who had good contacts with radical elements in the Liberal party liable to be distrustful of clericalism in any shape or form. Standard work on the Home Rule movement, however, makes clear that clerical influence was not tantamount to clerical control. Had it been, it is questionable whether Parnell could have achieved the ascendancy that he did. At the height of his power over the Parliamentary Party and the League, there were local Catholics ready to ignore even their priest in deference to the leader.

After the general election of 1885 the Wishaw branch voted by a substantial majority to expel a member who had openly disobeyed Parnell's directive to give votes and all other aid to the Tories. Admittedly, this had created widespread tension, as evidenced by the controversy referred to earlier over Ferguson's actions in the same election campaign. This particular branch remained adamant in its view that a directive from the leader ought to have been carried out, even when Father McCoy, the local priest, intervened. He used his pulpit to censure branch members concerned, and also refused the branch any further use of his school-rooms for their meetings. The response in this instance was a spirited one, the branch carrying a defiant motion upholding the expulsion and declaring roundly that 'they would be pleased to sit under Father McCoy in religion, but in politics we will be guided by the leaders of the Irish people'.[26]

The power which Parnell for a time achieved over the national movement, and some of the policies behind which he threw his influence and support like the 'plan of campaign', are enough in themselves to cast doubt on charges of clerical control. By the same token, his fall from power cannot be explained in terms of the kind of drastic clerical intervention which was central to the beliefs of the relatives of the young Stephen Daedalus in their famous Christmas quarrel. The vast majority of League branches in Scotland repudiated Parnell after the divorce case without any appearance of sudden deference to the views of the Church. After all there was a clear political case against Parnell's attempts to retain the leadership and also control over party funds and newspapers, once the Parliamentary party had voted by a majority for his resignation.

In a few branches of the League outside Glasgow there were local splits precipitated by the national one over the O'Shea episode, but the *Glasgow Observer* claimed to represent a majority view of the League's membership in Scotland in its own denunciation of Parnell. It carried out a poll among its readership to substantiate its claim that Parnell's authority over the movement in Scotland was at an end, and this poll produced the desired verdict in agreement with the editorial view.[27] It is worth emphasising again, however, that in Scotland at any rate the campaign against Parnell was motivated very much by a belief, already voiced by local activists, especially in the Glasgow area, that under new leadership the Home Rule movement could become a much less over-centralised and authoritarian organisation.

Evidence seems to be lacking to support the view that the League in Scotland was in any oppressive sense a vehicle for clericalism in politics. In the remainder of this essay some evidence will be offered to suggest that, far from pursuing simply sectarian ends, it assumed an increasingly important role in the labour and radical politics of west and central Scotland in the late nineteenth and early twentieth centuries.

When local branches were not dealing with immediate problems of elections and Home Rule, their role could become one of simply reinforcing the immigrant community's sense of Irish identity. Irish history loomed large at all branches in the shape of lectures and dramatic readings, while evenings of national song and music were common. Socially branches were a focus of much activity, like dances and Gaelic sports, but also summer outings for members and their families, children's picnics, etc. One branch is on record as having enrolled in full membership a member's three and a half year old child. This was reported without comment in the Glasgow Irish press.[28]

The League's rapid growth in central Scotland coincided with a surge of militancy among highland crofters which for a time seemed a major challenge to the power of landlordism. As early as 1881 Irish rallies in Glasgow were raising funds for Skye crofters fighting eviction, and Irish support continued once the Highland Land League came into being with aims broadly similar to the Irish Land League. Irish Home Rule in turn never lost the support of activists in the crofters' struggle.[29] Possibly misleading attempts have been made to relate the crofters' movement to the mainstream of labour history. It should perhaps be assessed primarily in terms of whether it met adequately the aspirations of the crofters themselves.

The one man who argued most clearly that the agrarian struggle was one in which there were common Scottish and Irish interests at stake was Henry George. Central to his analysis of the land question in *Progress and Poverty* was his advocacy of the taxation of all land values as a necessary strategy to unite tenants and labourers in the expropriation of the owners whether of agricultural or of urban land. His rapport with Scottish radical audiences was apparent from the time he first came to Scotland in 1881 and on his subsequent speaking tour to Britain of 1884-5, the bulk of his meetings were again held in Scotland. Irish League activists were prominent among an audience of over two thousand who heard George in Glasgow in 1884 at a rally which led to the formation of the Scottish Land Restoration League. Its creation was, for agrarian radicalism in Scotland, a lurch to the left of the existing land leagues and the crofters' candidates who contested a significant number of seats in the 1885 and 1886 general elections.

The Land Restoration League's base remained in industrial central Scotland, where it broke less electoral ground than the 'crofters' party in highland seats in 1885. The appeal of George's doctrines was a potent one to Irish activists like Ferguson, who until the end of his life used his base in Scottish radicalism to press for taxation of land values, though he did not join the Land Restoration League. Irish National League branches gave a ready hearing to speakers who espoused George's views, comprising as they did so many immigrants either born on the land or whose parents had been, and who either in person or through relatives identified with the fight against Irish landlordism. Such identification could be strong precisely at the point where the conversion of the immigrant Irish into a mainly urban labour force was irrevocable.

Potent though the call of agrarian radicalism still was to many of its branches, the Irish National League was a body seeking to give expression to the views of a heavily working-class immigrant community. Many branches had practical need of information on legislation affecting members. In 1886, branches in the Cambuslang area recruited lawyers from Glasgow to lecture on up-to-date aspects of the law on underground safety in coal mines and on the 1880 Employers Liability Act. The League's main Edinburgh branch met permanently in trade union premises and was outspoken (as were others) in suport for the militant strike of Scottish railwaymen in the winter of 1890-1 when in central Scotland eviction of strikers from railway company houses was carried out with the backing of cavalry and the Riot Act.

Chisholm Robertson, a leader of the Scottish miners and himself a Catholic, was the guest of branches anxious to devote evenings to social and class questions. The *Glasgow Observer* did not miss the significance of such matters infiltrating local agendas: 'With the Home Rule question satisfactorily solved and out of the way the Irishmen of these islands would be released from the claims their country has upon them and take that leading role in the social movement which characterises their countrymen in other parts of the globe'. The comment was perhaps a cautious one — the possible political impact of this sort of change was not directly touched on.[30]

Overtly class-conscious feelings could break the surface of branch activity in unexpected ways. A move was initiated in Tradeston early in 1886 to set up a commercial branch of the League for local Irishmen established in business and retail trade with the high affiliation fee of five shillings. The response from neighbouring branches was sarcastic. Attacks at the John Dillon branch were aimed at the 'presumptions of one particular class', who were in any case latecomers to the national cause, and jokes were made at the expense of the new 'kid-glove branch' which seems in fact to have had only a short life after its unpropitious inception.[31] Yet the fact remains that some of the Irish community's most important political leaders were self-employed or owners of businesses like Ferguson, whose publishing interests expanded throughout his active political life.

Given the central importance of this period to radical and labour politics in Scotland, the problem which must now be examined is how far the working-class nature of League membership complicated its overall political strategy. The tensions created by Parnell's decision that Irish votes in Britain be thrown behind Conservative candidates in 1885 have already been referred to: but this represented a departure for a brief period only from the Liberal alliance which took on a new strength once Gladstone espoused the cause of Home Rule. The temptation in this relationship became for the Liberals to take Irish support at the polls very much for granted. Scottish Liberal Association records are disappointingly sparse in reference to co-operation with the Irish. Where they occur they tend to deal in a matter of fact way with co-operation with National League branches, for example in the matter of preventing votes being lost by making sure that Irishmen in important constituencies did not get into arrears with their payment of poor rates, something which could easily happen in times of slack trade.[32]

Liberal leaders in private could be outrightly disdainful of their Irish allies: a disdain caught for a moment when Ronald Munro-Ferguson, a leading Scottish Liberal, writing to Rosebery after the great Home Rule split, commented (on Parnell and his colleagues), 'there is a marvellous change in the Irishmen — they have almost learnt to cheer properly and are quite well-mannered. I think we should incorporate them along with the party as much as possible . . . the same whips might do for both'. . . .[33]

This kind of complacency was to be somewhat shaken when John Ferguson, himself an active Liberal and delegate from his own constituency to the Scottish Liberal Association, came out in support of Keir Hardie's independent candidature at the famous mid-Lanark by-election of 1888. The circumstances of this local challenge to Liberal hegemony have been well documented elsewhere.[34] Ferguson's role could not have been a more open one, for he was present with Cunninghame Graham at Hardie's formal nomination and subsequently at some of his campaign meetings. League members from Glasgow followed his example and the Home Government branch found itself considerably embarrassed by a telegram of gratitude from Hardie, although its own policy was continued support for the Liberal alliance despite the action of some members in the by-election.

A majority of the Home Government branch in fact voted to endorse the official Liberal candidature, as did several other branches (nine at least can be counted from press reports). Ferguson's action was a departure from an agreed policy laid down by the League's full-time agents in Scotland and by the *Glasgow Observer* of 14 and 21 April,[35] but his prestige in the movement seems to have given him immunity from anything more than formal censure.

Identical issues to those posed in the mid-Lanark by-election faced Irish organisations when Parliament was dissolved in 1892. There was Labour intervention in a number of Scottish constituencies, though Keir Hardie himself was invited to stand in West Ham by local trade unions and radical clubs. This complicated Ferguson's position, since he had been a co-founder of the Scottish Labour Party in 1888 and was one of its senior elected office-bearers, but in an election where Gladstone was clearly committed to a new attempt at Irish Home Rule, he gave priority to supporting Home Rule Liberals even when Labour candidates stood against them. This was a strategy in conformity with the view of the National League as a whole, which was echoed in an editorial in the *Glasgow Observer* setting out the view that 'once Home Rule were out of the way, the Labour cause would be our own. The Catholics of Great Britain, are, in the mass, mostly workers, so that our interest in the redress of Labour grievances is substantial and real'.[36]

Labour intervention in 1892 was in fact attacked with quite noticeable venom by many League branches, particularly in Glasgow, where in three seats won by the Unionists there had been Labour candidates. R. B. Cunninghame Graham was the recipient of some of the bitterest denunciations, partly because it was believed that some League activists had in fact worked for him. Camlachie, where he stood, was lost to the Liberals by only a narrow margin, as was Tradeston, the other seat where a Labour candidate had entered the race. The *Glasgow Observer* subsequently calculated that Labour had won the 'beggarly' total of 3,747 votes out of over 51,000 cast in the six Scottish constituencies where it had fielded candidates. The damaging effect of this apparently low poll was argued to be out of proportion to its total.[37]

Gladstone was sufficiently exercised by the apparent Labour challenge in Scotland to make public his thoughts on the matter to Liberal candidates. He chose the Stirlingshire constituency as his pretext for this, and wrote a letter to W. Jacks, an embattled Liberal candidate, which was then circulated to the press. This merits attention because Gladstone came as close as he ever did to putting the case for the Liberal and Irish alliance in class terms. He began with the standard accusation that Labour's impact on the campaign was merely to run 'bogus candidates for every purpose except the purpose of putting Tories into Liberal seats'.

More significant is the unfolding of Gladstone's argument when he declared that 'to punish the Liberal party at this moment is to punish when they, far beyond any of these I.L.P. candidates, are in charge of the interests of Labour, for their first object now is the Irish question. The Irish question is a labour question for the Irishmen are, as I have shown, a nation of labourers, and this is the most urgent part of the Irish question, for the Irish are the most needy and the most suffering: they are oppressed by unequal laws, devised to place them under their landlords; they are insulted by the open breach of pledges; they are utterly deprived even of the institutions of local self-government. Let it then be understood that every Liberal voter who co-operates in bringing about the return of a Tory candidate votes against the Irish nation and especially against the Irish labourer — he votes against Labour, and against Labour in Ireland, where it has the greatest needs and the highest of all its claims'.[38]

Gladstone's language on this occasion was not too far removed from that of Michael Davitt, whose very different background of land agitation and long imprisonment for Fenianism made it easy for him to argue the nationalist case in socially radical terms. This he did soon after the 1892 elections at a conference of Glasgow National League delegates which endorsed a series of resolutions against landlordism and evictions. Davitt's contribution was to issue a warning that 'they would not confine their attack to Irish landlordism. The time was ripe for a movement on this side of the Channel to give to the farmers of England, Wales and Scotland the protection of judicial leases and the benefits of land courts and the revision and reduction of rents'.[39] Yet for all the closeness of his own relationship with the British labour movement, Davitt never moved far from the conviction that the balance of political power in Britain made continued alliance with the Gladstonian Liberal party the key to Home Rule.

The League continued to be anxious to justify itself to the labour movement in Britain, whatever tensions elections might arouse. When in the winter of 1892 the 'plan of campaign' was launched to apply new pressure on Irish landlords by the collective refusal of rent above levels set by tenants themselves, nearly all Scottish League branches endorsed the national organisation's support for the new tactics. At a large and enthusiastic meeting of the League's Glasgow members, with Ferguson in the chair, speakers from the floor put the case for the plan in terms which made it clear that they saw it as analogous to industrial action by workers.[40]

G

The failure of the Liberal cabinet to go to the country after the Lords' rejection of Gladstone's second Home Rule Bill in 1894 has been described as the first major Liberal retreat on the whole issue.[41] It was certainly in this light that the Irish party in Parliament saw the decision to avoid a confrontation with the Lords and after 1894 the 'Union of Hearts' of which Parnell had spoken was generally agreed to be a thing of the past. Despite this cooling of relations and indeed the emergence of sharp differences of opinion with the Liberal party over questions like the endowment of a Catholic University in Dublin and rate support for church schools (an especially contentious issue in Scotland where Catholic payers of schol rates received no school board maintenance of their own schools), some kind of working arrangement for elections survived disillusionment with the Liberals.

This was apparent in the 1895 general election, despite Gladstone's resignation as Prime Minister a year earlier and his replacement by Rosebery. Irish National League policy still rested on faith in the Liberal alliance. Scottish Catholic voters received a predictable reminder of their duties from the *Glasgow Observer*, but significantly its first election issue was more taken up with the church school question than Home Rule as such. 'Wrecking' intervention by the I.L.P. was again the target for attack by League branches in Scotland, particularly in Glasgow, where I.L.P. candidates stood in five of the city's seven constituencies. None of these was able to better Robert Smillie's performance in Camlachie, where he won just under 700 votes. Moribund Liberal organisations in some seats, notably Kilmarnock burghs, were also alleged to be placing an unfair burden on the National League's resources in supplying canvassers and workers. The inference to be drawn was that Irish help at elections was accepted much more readily than it was acknowledged by the Liberal organisation in Scotland.

In the immediate aftermath of the Liberal defeat in the 1900 general election, Campbell-Bannerman expressed in writing a personal reaction: 'we shall never have so many adverse conditions again; and in the circumstances have not done badly. Scotland has been horrid; for one thing the Catholics voted against us for the first time — this is the main cause of the reduced majority in my own case'.[42] This assertion by the opposition leader of course discounted the unusual circumstances of the 1885 general election. Moreover, the author of what still stands as a major biography of Campbell-Bannerman puts this sort of explanation in a proper perspective by pointing out that war-fever had been as effectively whipped up in Scottish constituencies as anywhere else and that the Irish vote did not in itself decide the outcome.[43] Nonetheless, there were interesting instances of independent Irish action in one or two Scottish contests which might be seen as symptomatic of how far the 'Union of Hearts' had lost much of its warmth.

Campbell-Bannerman, in conjunction with Herbert Gladstone, his chief whip, had formulated a policy of what has been called 'disengagement' from any firm commitment to Home Rule legislation by a Liberal Government being given immediate priority: Home Rule was not dropped as an ultimate objective, but the formula had been designed to unite the party by giving the maximum of latitude on the whole tormented issue to party candidates in any forthcoming general election. In the Blackfriars and Hutchesontown division of Glasgow which, like all other seats in the city was won by the Unionists, the local Irish organisation went so far as to throw its support behind the Unionist candidate. This was an extreme case of Irish disaffection from the Liberal cause. Provand, the Liberal defending the seat, was comprehensively denounced by the William Smith O'Brien branch of the United Irish League as a traitor to Home Rule and as a pledged opponent of any endowment with public funds of a Catholic university in Dublin. As far as the local branch was concerned, the kiss of death for Provand probably came in the form of endorsement of his candidature from the *Glasgow Herald*[44] (in its 5 October 1900 issue). Ironically, the victorious Unionist on whose behalf the O'Brien branch placarded the constituency with emerald green posters was Andrew Bonar Law, later to loom large in the demonology of Irish nationalism.

Irish associations in Edinburgh showed themselves less than fervent about committing their efforts to Liberal candidates. Their delegates agreed to draw up a list of questions for submission to the Liberal candidates on Home Rule and educational policy. One speaker argued presciently that Irish preferences were going to be immaterial in this contest, given the certainty of the Unionist government being returned. In the end, it was agreed that branches should give support to Liberal candidates ready to declare themselves on Home Rule as a matter of high priority for a future Liberal ministry.[45]

The neighbouring constituency of Leith Burghs was held by Ronald Munro-Ferguson for the Liberals after a campaign in which Irish support had been completely withdrawn. Ferguson at his campaign meetings came under continual pressure from Irish questioners and went to some pains to set out his own position. He denied that he had reneged on Home Rule but 'had not insisted on it as remaining a leading plank in the Liberal platform just now because it was outside practical politics to have an Irish Parliament in Dublin'. Endowment of a Catholic university got his reluctant support but he refused to shift his ground on rate support for denominational schooling, which he feared would drive 'a nail into the coffin of the Scottish national system'.[46]

Campbell-Bannerman may well have been right in seeing 1900 as less of a disaster than it might have been, but his analysis of the reason for Liberal setbacks in Scotland, though shared by other Scottish Liberals like Munro-Ferguson, is less sure. There are few constituencies across central Scotland in which the United Irish League overtly turned against Liberal candidates, and in only the one mentioned already did a branch urge actual support for a Unionist. There is no way of knowing how far disillusionment with the Liberals kept Irishmen away from the polls altogether. Liberal claims that the poll would be a low one because the elections were being held on an almost expired register were not borne out. In the Glasgow constituencies it was higher than in 1895, but this did not save the Liberals from defeat in all the seats contested.[47]

Perhaps the most striking feature of the 1900 election was the altered attitude of the *Glasgow Observer*, once so unswerving in its support for the Liberal alliance. It now urged a policy of only the most qualified support for the Liberals, warning Irish voters off certain candidates altogether. In the case of West Renfrew, where a Rosberyite Liberal lukewarm on Home Rule was standing, the paper urged that 'in his case, as in Blackfriars & Hutchesontown, we hope the Irish voters will not make a half job of it but that they will vote solidly for the Tory and show recalcitrant Liberals that the Irish voters are not a mere tail of the Liberal party but an intelligent, organised, alert political force keen to perceive treachery and swift to punish it'.[48] It can be added that clerical intervention in 1900 was very apparent, for example in the form of a circular letter sent by Archbishop Eyre of Glasgow to every priest in his archdiocese. This was to be read to all parish congregations, reminding them of church advocacy of rate support for Catholic schools in Scotland and of a Catholic university in Ireland. Parishioners were reminded of their duty as voters to ascertain in detail where election candidates stood on these issues.

What was not a major factor in siphoning off Irish votes in Scottish seats was Labour intervention, however closely many local Irish associations identified themselves with the Scottish working class. The dissolution of Parliament in the autumn of 1900 gave the new Labour Representation Committee in England scant time to organise itself for an election, and the same was true of the Scottish Workers Representation Committee.

This kind of dilemma, however, did present itself to a sizeable community of Irish and Catholic electors in 1904, when the Labour Representation Committee fielded a candidate in a seat traditionally Liberal until a Unionist had taken it in a by-election in 1901. The campaign coincided with a major speech by Redmond to a Glasgow Irish rally, in which his theme was that Labour was the friend of Home Rule. He expressed the hope that any forthcoming General Election would see major Labour gains. Any hopes that this might have raised among Irish miners in North-East Lanarkshire of the local Labour candidate receiving a blessing from the U.I.L.'s executive were soon to be dashed. The executive's directive made an unequivocal recommendation of support for Provost Findlay, the Liberal candidate.[49]

The outcome of this contest was significant and was treated as such in some extended press comment and analysis. The Liberals won back the seat with a minority of the total vote cast, while the Labour candidate ran a close third to the Unionist, polling just under 4,000 votes despite the U.I.L.'s clear directive to its members in the North-East Lanarkshire coalfield. The obvious allegations followed that the U.I.L. had lost control of its members. Its branch in Hamilton, which had done much to co-ordinate the Irish campaign in the constituency, denied this, but the size of the Labour vote needed more explanation than they were able to provide.

The Liberal concordat on Home Rule which had been hammered out for the 1900 general election was a short-lived one; it soon gave way after 1900 to a prolonged and acrimonious debate on Home Rule which threatened at times to disrupt the party far more seriously than the Boer War ever had. The outcome of this was that Campbell-Bannerman and his supporters fought off attempts by the party's Liberal Imperialist wing to jettison Home Rule altogether from the party's declared aims. The policy of non-committal gradualism embodied in the formula of 'step by step' Home Rule was probably the best Redmond and the Irish National movement could hope for at the time of the 1905 general election. To give support to it was at least an effective way of securing Campbell-Bannerman's position against those who agreed with Rosebery that the party slate be wiped clean of Home Rule.[50]

Another major development of the years between the two general elections was the 1903 agreement on electoral co-operation achieved between the Liberals and the Labour Representation Committee. In readiness for the general election which was imminent once Campbell-Bannerman was invited to form a Government at the end of 1905, the United Irish League issued a directive urging Irish support for Labour Representation Committee candidates, provided they held sound views on Home Rule and were not standing against Liberals with equally well-established Home Rule credentials.[51]

Ferguson, in one of the last actions in a career spanning an extended period in the history of radical and Irish nationalist politics, had no hesitation this time in commending the League's directive to all branches in Scotland: 'the day has come to prove your loyalty to the motherland and the power of your position here in the strongholds of your nation's destroyer. . . . We cast to the winds all our public and private privileges and rights as Scottish citizens and press on, as our fathers did before us, and as our Celtic race demands, for helpless Ireland's nationhood'.[52]

League involvement in the general election proved not to be without friction. The Blackfriars-Hutchesontown constituency in Glasgow was again conspicuous, this time for a major split within the Smith O'Brien branch of the U.I.L. A majority of the branch voted its support for George Barnes, an active trade unionist who was the Labour candidate. This accorded with the League's national directive, but dissidents in the branch urged a repetition of the 1900 strategy of supporting Bonar Law's Unionist candidature. Their major reason for this was the extent to which the T.U.C. and the I.L.P. had moved, since 1900, towards a wholly secular educational policy, and intervention by Ferguson in the dispute had the main effect of displeasing the branch majority who took it as a reflection on their own ability to deliver the Irish working-class vote in the seat for Barnes.[53]

Ferguson came under much stronger attack for his role in North-West Lanarkshire, a constituency which registered the phenomenon of a Unionist gain in 1906. Dr C. M. Douglas, a Roseberyite Liberal with predictably lukewarm views on Home Rule, was opposed by a Unionist and a Catholic Labour candidate who, as in North-East Lanarkshire two years before, split the anti-Unionist vote. Ferguson certainly took an active part in the contest, as he managed to do in numerous others in this campaign, but with the full support of local U.I.L. branches who claimed this was merely in accord with the policy formulated by Redmond of punishing wherever possible Liberal renegades. Again the poll was a significant indicator of what could happen when local Irish organisations threw their resources behind Labour candidates.[54]

Ferguson's death as a result of a Glasgow tramway accident soon after the Liberal landslide of 1906 came at a moment when Liberal and Irish relations in Scotland, and England too, had for the moment been restored. The Liberals in Scotland owed no small debt to Ferguson for his strenuous work in encouraging the implementation in Scottish constituencies of the U.I.L.'s directives. He had become by the time of his death a figure whose importance extended beyond Scotland. In February of 1906 he had been a leading speaker on the taxation of land values at a London conference of municipal and rating authorities from all over the United Kingdom and was given much credit for Parliament's decision to go ahead with legislation on this matter in the 1906 session.[55] Glasgow Corporation, on which he was still a councillor at the time of his death, had proved an effective forum for him to press his views on the land question and to expose local land speculation.

Over and above the requirements of Parliamentary contests, the Irish vote had to be deployed at municipal elections as well, and in Liverpool this was done with notable success. There the Irish vote was sufficiently concentrated to elect a Nationalist M.P., so it followed that in the wards which comprised his constituency, League colours could be confidently hoisted at local council contests. In Scotland the problem initially facing individual Irish candidates was in securing adoption in the local ward committees, bodies open to all ward electors which met periodically to air local views and to hear councillors rendering an account of their stewardship. In the majority of local wards in Glasgow and other Scottish towns Liberal associations were in control, as, though not in name, they always were of Glasgow council itself. The reigning consensus of view had been, since the sharply polarised Whig-Tory contests for control of local government after the 1832 Burgh Reform Act, that local authorities could best be run without the intrusion of politics.

In fact, Liberal-Irish relations deteriorated sharply in Glasgow over the question of Irish candidates being given a free run in local contests. In 1891 some timely organisation of Irish electors secured an I.N.L. candidate's adoption by the Fourth Ward electors' meeting. The local Liberal association's response was to put up its own candidate who defeated him. Irish League reaction was resentful and was voiced quickly: 'We are quite good enough to be used as instruments by these gentlemen but when we seek the rights of allies the answer is to be that given to Mr Francis Henry [the defeated Irish candidate] in the Fourth Ward'.[56]

The dilemma of Irish political activists in local politics was made a much sharper one by the beginnings of trade union intervention. An important role here was taken early on by trades councils. In 1891 Glasgow and Aberdeen Trades Councils issued a joint programme for the extension of municipal ownership and the protection of municipal workers. That same year four of the candidates for election to council seats in Glasgow who had secured trades council endorsement got active Irish backing at ward level. Two years later in 1893, the Trades Council endorsed Ferguson's candidature for Calton Ward in the city's heavily populated industrial East End. Ferguson fought his campaign on local issues, especially on the rights of municipal employees (and the sweating involved in contract work to make uniforms for the police and tramway workers). His election for Calton was certainly helped by his having built up a position in Scottish politics which straddled the Irish, Liberal and Labour movements, while he could not be attacked on simple sectarian grounds as a Catholic infiltrator of the council.

The other two Irish candidates whom the Glasgow Trades Council endorsed in the 1893 local elections were both Catholics and both were defeated. One of them, MacKenzie, standing in a heavily Irish ward, claimed his opponent had capitalised on his connections with local Orange Lodges, and neither of them was entirely able to keep the campaign free from sectarian controversy. The other Irish candidate, Caldwell, found himself encumbered with a ward committee chairman who was prepared to declare to a meeting that any Protestant elector voting for him would be 'a traitor to the cause of freedom'.[57]

Two years later the Glasgow Irish achieved a measure of recognition from the Labour movement in the city. In 1895 the United Irish League in Glasgow was invited to affiliate to a Workers Municipal Election Committee. This comprised representatives of the main working-class organisations in the city and, over the whole period up to the outbreak of war in 1914, played an important role in achieving Labour and working-class representation in the government of the city.[58]

A Glasgow council election in 1897 produced quite a notable victory for Irish and Labour co-operation in Springburn, an area with several strong Orange Lodges at the time. John O'Hare, later to represent County Monaghan in Parliament after 1906, fought a determined campaign on local issues in conjunction with James Johnstone of the I.L.P., there being two vacant seats. This alliance survived the attentions of the local Church of Scotland minister, who described it from his pulpit as the unholy collusion of 'Papist with atheist'.[59]

Fear of an Orange backlash was certainly a factor in complicating reciprocal action by I.L.P. and trades councils in repaying Irish electoral help by endorsing U.I.L. candidates who were also Catholics. In 1900 the I.L.P. endorsed the Glasgow council candidature of Hugh Murphy, a veteran U.I.L. activist in the city. This was in Mile End, a heavily working-class ward, where I.L.P. and trades councils candidates had polled well on previous occasions. On this occasion, after a stormy campaign in which local Orangemen in some numbers took to the streets, the Labour vote slumped disastrously and Murphy was beaten. The Irish press was in doubt as to the reason: 'a Catholic come into the field on any ticket and at once, like mercury plunged into boiling water, up leaps the poll of his opponent'.[60] This episode, however, cannot in itself be taken as a basis for arguing that the Protestant working class were more sectarian than the Catholic, unless evidence becomes available to prove that the political pressure from Orange Lodges was more effective than was that of priests on local Irish associations.

Nineteenth and early twentieth century Glasgow did not see the rise of a militant working-class Protestant organisation which sought a base for itself in local politics. This development did not take place until the inter-war period, but the fear of an Orange working-class vote was an important contributory cause of the Irish Nationalists' links with the organised working class not yielding more in local representation commensurate with the size of Irish communities in Glasgow or indeed in industrial Scotland. Ferguson's election in Glasgow was an exception that proved the rule, made possible by his own Protestantism and by his prestige achieved in battles other than purely Irish ones.

During his time as a Glasgow councillor Ferguson co-operated effectively with Labour and radical Liberal colleagues on a wide range of issues. Perhaps his most important work here was to keep Glasgow Corporation as a forum for debate and agitation on the taxation of land values. Henry George on his tours of Scotland had tapped much support among the Labour movement and the Irish in Scotland for his single tax formula to expropriate the landowners. He saw the political climate in Glasgow as being particularly ripe for the propagation of his views and recognised the importance of the city council as a means for this. Ferguson was not a councillor at this time, but once elected proved George to have been right and was instrumental in keeping Glasgow in the forefront of the struggle for land taxation. Not for nothing were the abortive (because emasculated in the Lords) bills on Scottish land values presented in Parliament between 1906-8 known as the 'Glasgow bills'.

The developments covered in this essay coincide with a time of ferment within the Catholic Church on social issues, culminating in Leo XIII's encyclical *Rerum Novarum* of May 1891. This, of course, was much concerned with poverty and social injustice and the worker's right to industrial action, but it was also a lengthy condemnation of socialism as a heresy leading to the state robbing lawful possessors of property and creating schisms within the community. For this reason the encyclical formed a central theme in Wheatley's debates with the Jesuit Order in 1907. Yet this debate was being anticipated in the dilemma of working-class activists in the Irish Nationalist movement over Labour and independent working-class intervention in local and Parliamentary elections some years before.

In 1891, before *Rerum Novarum*'s publication, the *Glasgow Observer* delivered itself of an attack on German Socialism and its alleged danger to the faith of Catholics: 'It means a nation of paramours, bastards and profligates. It is Manichaeism, Montanism, Waldensianism, Mormonism and Divorce Court Protestantism rolled into one'. The same editorial went on, however, to accept that a distinction could be drawn between the beliefs of the existing Labour movement in Britain and that of Socialist parties on the continent.[61] The *Observer* was often in fact ready to accept that in matters like representation in the local government of Glasgow common class interest gave most

Catholics good reason to support in elections candidates who had Labour and trade union endorsement. It was when Labour began to move over to what in church eyes seemed a position of ideological secularism on education that doubt set in, even although Labour was ready to keep faith with the Irish on Home Rule.

Whether at this stage of its development it was accurate to think of the Labour movement in Scotland or Britain as a whole as being a socialist movement was less important than that the historic anti-clericalism of the European left had a conditioning effect on much articulate Catholic opinion in Scotland. In 1891 a speaker put the matter clearly to the Catholic Literary Association of Glasgow: 'As Catholics I maintain we can have nothing to do with the aims and aspirations of the Socialists. To assist them to gain a voice in the government of the city and country is to enable them to deal more effec-tively, a destructive blow at some of our more cherished institutions . . . to associate with them is to endanger our faith'.[62]

The audience given this warning was not one composed of working-class Catholics and trade unionists, and it has been the chief concern of this essay to suggest that not all the Catholic Irish in Scotland were ready to be warned off in these terms from the politics of class co-operation across sectarian lines. Activists like Ferguson and later Wheatley clearly foresaw a time when the Irish working-class vote could become a permanent reservoir of support for the left in Scotland. This could not happen, however, until a measure of Irish self-government had been won, and this was to be the work of men who revived the Fenian tradition and turned their back on the patient groundwork of local and parliamentary elections and weekly League meetings which ate up so much of the time of those who have been this essay's chief concern. Yet those who worked to create and keep in being a legal and constitutional Irish political organisation in Scotland deserve to be remembered. Their dilemma was to secure justice for what they still felt to be their homeland, while at the same time joining in other battles which their rapid absorption into a Scottish working class required them to fight.

Suggestions for further reading

J. E. Handley, *The Irish in Scotland* (Cork, 1943)

J. E. Handley, *The Irish in Modern Scotland* (Cork, 1947)

J. Denvir, *The Irish in Britain from the earliest times to the fall and death of Parnell* (London, 1892)

C. C. O'Brien, *Parnell and his Party* (Oxford, 1957)

E. P. Lawrence, *Henry George in the British Isles* (Michigan, 1957)

F. S. L. Lyons, *Ireland Since the Famine* (London, 1971)

H. Pelling, *The Social Geography of British Elections 1885-1910* (London, 1967)

H. Senior, *Orangeism in Ireland and Britain* (London, 1966)
T. W. Moody, 'Michael Davitt and the British Labour Movement', *Transactions of the Royal Historical Society*, 3 (1953), 57-77

Notes

1. H. J. Paton, *The Claim of Scotland* (London, 1968).
2. Ibid., 177-80.
3. Ibid., 181-2.
4. A. Dewar Gibb, *Scotland in Eclipse* (London, 1930), 54-5.
5. Ibid.
6. J. M. MacCormick, *The Flag in the Wind* (London, 1955), 51.
7. Ibid., 58.
8. J. Buchan, *Mr Standfast* (London, 1919), 86.
9. I. Budge and D. Urwin, *Scottish Political Behaviour* (London, 1966), 60-3.
10. R. K. Middlemas, *The Clydesiders* (London, 1965), 36-40.
11. T. N. Brown, *Irish-American Nationalism* (Philadelphia and New York, 1966), 21-3.
12. J. McCaffrey, 'The Irish Vote in Glasgow in the Later Nineteenth Century', *Innes Review*, xxi (1970), 30-6.
13. W. Walker, 'Irish Immigrants in Scotland', *Historical Journal*, xv (1972), 649-67.
14. Report of the Select Committee appointed to inquire into the origins, nature, extent and tendency of Orange institutions in Great Britain and the colonies, H.C. 1835 (605), xvii, app. 20, p. 45.
15. D. Urwin, 'The Development of Conservative Party Organisation in Scotland until 1912', *Scottish Historical Review*, xliv (1965).
16. Scottish Record Office, *Lord Advocates' Correspondence 1857-73*, Book 117.
17. *North British Daily Mail*, 9 Aug. 1875.
18. C. C. O'Brien, *Parnell and His Party* (Oxford, 1957), 126-33.
19. J. Denvir, *The Irish in Britain* (London, 1892), 449.
20. McCaffrey, op. cit., 36.
21. *Glasgow Observer*, 25 July and 7 Nov. 1885.
22. Ibid., 13 Mar. 1886.
23. Ibid., 27 Mar. 1886.
24. Ibid., 18 Apr. 1891.
25. Ibid., 27 Feb. 1886.
26. Ibid., 26 Dec. 1885.
27. Ibid., 24 Jan. 1891.
28. Ibid., 13 Oct. 1890.

29.   J. Hunter, 'The Politics of Highland Land Reform', *Scottish Historical Review*, 53 (1974), 45-68.

30.   *Glasgow Observer*, 5 Sep. 1891.

31.   Ibid., 10 Apr. 1886.

32.   Edinburgh University Library, Scottish Liberal Association Minutes, 5 June 1895, 170-1.

33.   National Library of Scotland, Rosebery MSS, Munro-Ferguson to Rosebery, 26 Aug. 1886.

34.   J. G. Kellas, 'The Mid-Lanark By-election', *Parliamentary Affairs*, 18 (1964-5), 318-29.

35.   *Glasgow Observer*, 14 and 21 Apr., also 5 May 1888.

36.   Ibid., 8 June 1892.

37.   Ibid., 18 June, also 9 and 23 July 1892.

38.   Ibid., 16 July 1892.

39.   Ibid., 8 Oct. 1892.

40.   Ibid., 19 Nov. 1892.

41.   H. W. C. McCready, 'Home Rule and the Liberal Party', *Irish Historical Studies*, xiii (1962-3), 316-48.

42.   J. Wilson, *C.B. — A Life of Sir Henry Campbell-Bannerman* (London, 1973), 335.

43.   J. A. Spender, *A Life of the Rt. Hon. Sir Henry Campbell-Bannerman* (London, 1923), i, 244.

44.   *Glasgow Herald*, 10 Oct. 1900.

45.   *Scotsman*, 24 Sep. and 1 Oct. 1900.

46.   *Glasgow Herald*, 10 Oct. 1900.

47.   H. Pelling, *The Social Geography of British Elections 1885-1910* (London, 1967), 401.

48.   *Glasgow Observer*, 6 Oct. 1900.

49.   *Glasgow Herald*, 15 and 19 Aug. 1904.

50.   McCready, op cit., 347-8.

51.   *Glasgow Observer*, 6 Jan. 1906.

52.   Ibid., 13 Jan, 1906.

53.   Ibid.

54.   Ibid., 27 Jan. 1906.

55.   Ibid., 10 Feb. 1906.

56.   Ibid., 7 Nov. 1891.

57.   *Glasgow Herald*, 7 Nov. 1893.

58.   W. H. Marwick, *Labour in Scotland* (Edinburgh, 1967), 84.

59.   *Glasgow Observer*, 5 Nov. 1897.

60.   Ibid., 10 Nov. 1900.

61.   Ibid., 17 Jan. 1891.

62.   Ibid.

The Scottish Farm Servant and his Union: from Encapsulation to Integration

Barbara W. Robertson

THE Scottish Farm Servants' Union was founded in 1912, in Aberdeenshire. Twenty years later, in 1932, it was affiliated to the Transport and General Workers' Union, and in 1942 a complete amalgamation was carried through and the Union became the Scottish Farm Servants' Section of the Transport and General Workers' Union but with its own headquarters, and staff, and autonomy in the conduct of its agricultural activities.[1] Since 1969 it has become the Scottish Agricultural and Forestry Section of the Transport and General Workers' Union, with headquarters now in the Borders.

This opening statement is, in précis form, a reflection of Scottish agricultural trade union history over the past 150 years. The movement of twentieth century Union headquarters from the north-east to the south-east of the country implies the growth and inclusion of members in the geographical area within these two points. It also infers that what started out as a local desire for agricultural unionisation ultimately became a national agricultural reality. The Union, having thus become established in the agricultural community, then became part of an even wider organisation, a major national union, while at the same time retaining its own sectional individuality.

I

The outstanding feature of agricultural unionisation is the late date of formation at national level,[2] and the obvious corollary to this is the question why it was so much later in developing than were the urban-oriented combinations. To attempt an explanation of this involves not only some understanding of the agricultural scene but an awareness of what was taking place in the non-agricultural sectors of British society. As no event takes place in a vacuum, an overview of the decades prior to the twentieth century is therefore called for, and this in turn has to be treated at two different levels: local and agricultural, and national.

More than a hundred years before the Scottish Farm Servants' Union was founded, some Scottish farm workers were already making tentative attempts at combination. One occurred in the Carse of Gowrie in 1805[3] and, although this first effort appears to have been suppressed before it got off the ground, other attempts in 1834 at Inchture and Forteviot caused wider ripples, several local newspapers reporting them in some detail.[4] A decade later in 1845, East Lothian was the scene of some further, short-lived stirrings, and again in 1860 when a Farm Servants' Union was formed at Dunbar.[5] Not until the mid-1860s, however, was a more permanent combination started, this time in Midlothian, where a Farm Servants' Protection Society emerged in 1865. Branches were formed in various counties stretching from Berwickshire to Perthshire, and though many of them probably had a life-span of only a few months, the Midlothian branch lasted for at least seven years.[6] That these organisations, whether short-lived or not, were regarded at national level as being of some importance is deducible from the fact that one at least was called upon to give evidence before the Royal Commission on the Employment of Children, Young Persons and Women in Agriculture in 1867. This was the Border Farm Servants' Protection Association, formed in 1866, with head-quarters in Jedburgh, whose chief object, according to the secretary in his evidence to the Royal Commission, was the abolition of the bondage system.[7]

What might be termed the penultimate outburst of nineteenth century activity was that of the 1870s which, to some extent, coincided with the English activity in Warwickshire, led by Joseph Arch, though the Scottish was of much briefer duration. This time it was in the north-east of Scotland where, following a meeting of farm servants at Longside in 1872, a proposed Aberdeenshire Farm Servants' and Agricultural Labourers' Society was mooted. Though several branches were formed and some trade union activity did take place, the movement lasted for a short time only. A further attempt at combination, with the initiative this time coming from well-wishers in Aberdeen, was made in 1880, and though this appears to have been better organised and of longer duration, it too was relatively short-lived.[8]

A major breakthrough, however, took place at last in 1886, probably on the initiative of the farm servants themselves but also with the interest and support of the Aberdeen Trades Council behind the scenes. The aim here was not parochial, but rather was the establishment of a union of farm servants covering the whole of Scotland. Furthermore, the organisers on this occasion were in touch with the leader of the English Agricultural Labourers' Union, Joseph Arch, and had as potential guidance a copy of the rules of that Union. And thus was born the Scottish Farm Servants' Union, registered as such in 1887, with the motto 'United we stand, divided we fall'.[9] Despite its national aims, however, the Union did not appear to spread beyond the county, and the most prominent branch was in the city of Aberdeen itself, where its member-ship was made up of carters and general labourers, many of whom were ex-farm workers who had left or been forced off the land and were thus utilising in the urban setting the only transferable skill they had, namely, that of horsemen.[10]

The 1887 union was primarily a provident society and contributed little towards improving the position of farm servants. In an attempt to meet this

need, it amalgamated with the Perth-based Ploughmen's Federal Union in
1895 to become the Scottish Ploughmen and General Labourers' Union.
It appears to have failed in this aim, however, for although it was in existence
for another five years and the carters' and general labourers' branch in the city
of Aberdeen was fairly strong, there is no evidence to show that the union was
similarly active in rural life after 1895: by 1901 it had officially ceased to exist.[11]

The foregoing is by no means an exhaustive survey of agricultural trade
union actitivy in Scotland in the nineteenth century — the complete history
of which is yet to be written[12] — but it does show that pro-combination stirrings
were taking place all over the country, or at least in those areas where hired
labour was the norm. Other forms of co-operation such as friendly societies
should also be mentioned. These were in existence from before the nineteenth
century and mention of them is made time and time again in the *New Statistical
Account* of 1845. In Berwickshire alone, for instance, with a population which
was largely agricultural, more than a score of friendly societies are listed in the
thirty-two parish accounts. A few, like the 'Dunse' one, are described as 'not
founded on the most approved principles of calculation', while others are
spoken of as being 'of great advantage to the members' or, as in the case of
Channelkirk, 'seeming to promote a desire for independence'.[13]

As de Tocqueville pointed out in the 1830s, voluntary associations generally,
whether they be large or small, are an important vehicle in a democratic society
for the expression and satisfaction of sectional needs. In *Democracy in America*
he laid great stress on the importance of this English principle of association
which the Americans of his day had extended to all spheres of society, and
pointed out that if men were to remain civilised or to become so, then the art of
associating together must grow and improve in the same ratio in which the
equality of conditions was increased.[14] Many such associations, with varying
objectives, existed also in Scotland for long or short periods of time throughout
the nineteenth century. Included under this miscellaneous grouping, for
instance, were the voluntary associations of small numbers of Border hill
shepherds for the purpose of educating their children, as described in the
evidence to the Royal Commission of 1867.[15] Other voluntary associations,
however, may not have had such 'desirable' objectives, and that appears to
have been the case with the Kelso Society of Whipmen and Ploughmen. This
Society consisted of farmers' servants, ploughmen, husbandmen, or whipmen,
'call them what you please', and was in existence from at least 1789 to 1839.
John Mason, writing about Kelso traditions of the past, mentions secret articles
and various bloodthirsty 'shameful' rituals carried out by the organisation,
adding that 'the advantages of the society are a mystery to everyone but the
brotherhood'.[16] Horsemen's Societies, on the other hand, probably acted as a
form of apprenticeship, though E. P. Thompson has pointed out a possible
connection between these societies in England and illegal trade union
activity.[17] Taken all together, these various associations, whatever their
objectives, must have played a not unimportant part in furthering the
education of the often inarticulate worker in the art of making his claims heard,

and suggesting to him that not by individual effort but by concerted action could betterment of his condition be obtained.

The aims of the nineteenth century short-lived unions were in many instances little different from those of friendly societies. Conversely, a friendly society might have trade union aims, as for instance the Berwickshire Farm Servants' Friendly Society in 1872, with its resolution to demand the same minimum terms of wages and conditions.[18] Houston, writing about the attempt to form a union in Perthshire in 1834, quotes a newspaper account which shows that the purpose of forming the association was to procure a reduction in working hours, 'which are admitted by every reasonable person to be unnecessarily long'.[19] In the north-east the Kintore meeting of 1886 also aimed at a reduction in working hours, so that the men could attend evening classes and so effect their 'laudable object of self culture'.[20] Activity in the Borders in the 1860s on the other hand was geared towards abolition of the bondager system though, in the evidence given to the Royal Commission of 1867, the secretary of the Border Farm Servants' Protection Association stated that the Association was also interested in 'petitioning Parliament for household suffrage or at all events an extension of the borough franchise'.[21] The north-east pioneers of 1872 had aims likewise associated with local conditions such as improvement of the bothy and chaumer system, but also had more general ones including a shorter working week and the subsidising of emigration.[22] This latter is of some interest, being similar to a major aim of a newly formed English union in Herefordshire whose watchword was 'Emigration, migration but no strikes'.[23] Again, the aims of the 1887 Scottish Farm Servants', Carters' and General Labourers' Union were similar to the earlier 1872 organisation, being part economic, part friendly society but, as already mentioned, with a national goal in view:

Rule 1: Objects of the Union
The establishment of Branches throughout Scotland. To consolidate and strengthen the influence and power of Farm Servants, Carters, and Labourers generally. To reform and improve our relation with employers, and to obtain for Farm Servants Monthly Payments with Indefinite Engagement; Weekly Half Holiday, except six weeks in Harvest. The abolition of the Bothy System; the Improvement of our Kitchen Dietary scale, and of our House and Sleeping Accommodation. To protect the Interests of the Members of the Union by securing redress against oppression. To establish a Sick and Funeral Benefit Society, and Superannuation Fund for Trade Members.[24]

This Union in practice, however, was primarily a provident society, and even after amalgamating with the Scottish Ploughmen's Federal Union in 1895, itself mainly a benefit society though seeking a weekly half holiday and abolition of long-term engagements, any militant action taken was in Aberdeen and on behalf of the City members only.[25]

Though few if any of the aims of these early combinations were achieved and the organisations failed to establish themselves as permanent bodies, the nineteenth century movement as a whole had done much towards publicising the working conditions in agriculture as well as providing a collective voice from time to time for the farm servant, and so prepared the ground for the emergence of a truly national union in the twentieth century.

This started at Turriff in Aberdeenshire in April 1912, that peak year of labour unrest throughout the country. The tailors in Turriff, as part of general labour unrest, had made a move for an increase in wages, and had got their increase. The farm workers in the district, having learned of this, approached the tailors for help towards getting an increase also for farm workers. Following some publicity of this proposed action, the chairman of the Aberdeen Trades Council, Joseph Duncan, offered help in organising meetings and starting branches, and within a few weeks several branches had been formed with almost 1,000 members.[26] The Scottish Farm Servants' Union had arrived on the agricultural scene at last.

Brief mention of attempts at agricultural unionisation in England must also be made. Here a very similar pattern appears of localised outbursts of activity, from the Dorchester Martyrs' efforts of 1834 to the upsurge of movement in the early 1870s in Warwickshire and elsewhere, culminating in the formation of the National Agricultural Labourers' Union in 1872. This latter, unlike the Aberdeen combination of the same year, expanded rapidly and also lasted for several years, but ultimately quietly died away over the years of agricultural depression in the eighties and nineties.[27] Its members, however, did play some part in the attainment of the franchise for rural labourers in 1884, and the movement as a whole, like the Scottish, was to lead ultimately to the foundation of a permanent, national union. This was in 1906, with George Edwards, himself a farm labourer's son but with trade union experience, as organiser.[28]

'A trade union,' wrote the Webbs at the end of the nineteenth century, 'is a continuous association of wage earners for the purpose of maintaining or improving the conditions of their employment.'[29] Trade unionism, therefore, as exemplified by a continuous association, did not appear on the agricultural scene until 1906 in England and 1912 in Scotland. Unlike many Continental agricultural unions, the two in Britain have both emerged from the land workers themselves.[30] The late date of the emergence of agricultural trade unions — late that is in comparison with urban trade unions — can be explained at least in part by the peculiar situation of agriculture as an industry.[31] Writing about the British scene in the first half of the nineteenth century, Orwin and Whetham also stress industrial factors, such as separation of farm workers from town life and their dispersal in small scattered groups under the eyes of their employers.[32] These two factors still existed in the second half of the century, though the geographical separation from urban life became less with the coming of the railways, this providing not only a new source of work for some country people but at the same time opening up the possibility of travel. By the end of the century a network of routes, both local and long distance, was in use not merely for transporting people but also agricultural produce including stock,[33] and this new form of locomotion not only shortened the geographical distance between town and country but in no small measure was also to help bridge the cultural gap. But this latter was still far from bridged at the end of the century, and several reasons for the Scottish farm workers' encapsulation in the farming community until then, and indeed until well into the twentieth century, can be mentioned.

Firstly, there was the work situation itself: long hours and often heavy manual work left little time or energy for other activities. Mechanisation had still a very long way to go before it was to take the labour out of the farm labourer's lot. Leisure in the modern sense was unknown: the majority of workers had animals of some kind to look after, whether horses, cattle or sheep, and these tied the men not only to a seven-day week but to a day stretching from early morning to late evening. 'The reformers seem to forget that a ploughman's tools, if I may call them so, comprise living animals, which cannot be thrown aside like a mason's mallet whenever the day's work is done.'[34]

Secondly, within the work situation, at least on the larger farms employing a fair amount of labour, there was a form of differentiation by worker typology as well as stratification within the ploughman typology itself. The ploughmen were a group, the women workers (or bondagers) were another, the cattleman and/or byrewoman was slightly apart, and the shepherds were quite distinctly apart from the main workforce.[35] The workers, said Joseph Duncan, the Union's secretary, 'not infrequently are very sensitive about their rights and distinctions. A Lothian ploughman would feel insulted if asked to pull turnips; any ploughman would refuse to allow another ploughman to work his pair of horse; most ploughmen would refuse to do any byre work; cattlemen would refuse to allow ploughmen to handle their cattle . . .' In addition to inter-typology separation there was a clear hierarchical structure within the plough-men group. 'On the larger farms, when a number of ploughmen turn out to plough together or to do any other work as a team, they are very punctilious to keep their due order, from the first ploughman who leads to the halflin or callant who has been promoted to his first pair, who brings up the rear. Each man has his place and keeps it.'[36] The shepherd members of the farms, whether in the Borders or in Caithness, tended to be put on the higher rungs of the status ladder.[37] The picture emerging from the literature is one in which, in many instances, the individual farm unit could be viewed as a social system on its own. Any attempts at combination, therefore, given these demarcation lines in the work situation, plus the status ranking by worker of fellow worker, would tend to be that of worker typology across farms, as for example ploughmen associations, rather than of all workers on the same farm.

A third factor, relating particularly to the Lothians and Borders, and also to Caithness though to a lesser extent, was that the workforce included a high proportion of women, or bondagers.[38] This bondager system was said to be dying out in the third quarter of the nineteenth century, but the family hiring system prevalent in the south-east and lasting in modified form up to World War II, still included numerous women workers, still often called bondagers, though usually these were female members of the family rather than strangers hired by the hind or ploughman as previously.[39] Female labour is reputedly

H

less union-conscious than male, and this too may have been a factor militating against the development and growth of a farm servants' union. On the other hand, when asked if he had had difficulty in getting the women to join the Union, Joseph Duncan replied that although the married women tended not to join the Union as they 'thought they were entitled to that as part of the marriage contract', there was a fairly considerable membership amongst the outdoor women in the Lothians and Borders together with quite a number of women in dairying in the south-west, but these latter were women who hired direct and not simply as part of their husband's contract.[40]

Fourthly, there was the Scottish hiring system. Broadly speaking, the system was such that when Speaking Time came round, usually in January or February, farmer and worker arranged with each other the terms of contract for the following year. If no agreement was made, then both worker and farmer would sally forth to the appropriate Hirings some weeks later to find someone with whom a suitable arrangement could be reached. These Hirings are an interesting subject on their own, and take on a dual role of social gatherings plus collectivity of individual bargain-making. Several were usually held in each county, and the wages arrived at at the earlier Hirings, usually reported in the local press, frequently acted as a standard against which any subsequent hiring arrangements would be set. The actual conditions under which hirings were held, that is, in the open street or market place, were often regarded as degrading, with the workers 'standing around like cattle' waiting to be hired, or 'bought'.[41] On the other hand, this passive interpretation of the worker's role at the Hiring Fairs is balanced by other reports wherein he is shown at times to be equally active with the farmer in this contract-making process, not only checking up on the farmer's reputation — as the farmer did on the worker's — but at the same time turning down an offer if this appeared unsuitable.[42] The subject of hiring markets was one which exercised the minds of many throughout the nineteenth century: the Highland and Agricultural Society, for instance, reported on these in 1849, 1860 and again in 1874. It would appear, however, that the system was being looked at more from the point of view of the attendant insobriety which these occasions sometimes engendered rather than the more fundamental one of the relationship of master and servant in general. Obviously, however, this long established custom of individual bargain-making could not be altered overnight, and its existence was clearly a factor militating against the formation of a trade union (or trade unions). Joseph Arch, president of the English Union, for instance, when giving evidence to the Royal Commission in 1881, specifically mentioned the hiring system in Northumberland (where it was similar to that of the Scottish Border counties and Lothians) as one of the principal reasons for his Union's lack of appeal there.[43]

A fifth factor was undoubtedly the tied cottage, almost universal on Scottish farms. Writing in 1939 about trade unionism in agriculture, J. Pointing, editor of *The Land Worker*, gives the figure of about 97 per cent of Scottish farm cottages as being tied, compared with about 60 per cent of English, and states quite categorically that 'the tied cottage has been a grave obstacle to Trade Unionism'.[44] Self and Storing, summing up the English farm worker's position in the 1960s, have this to say about his tied cottage: 'Apart from the genuine hardships which the tied cottage system does sometimes produce, it is identified with the continuation of a dependent social status for the agricultural worker. By means of the tied cottage, in the Union's opinion, the farmer's influence extends beyond employment to the private and family life of his workers. The tied cottage system both strengthens and symbolises the unusually close relations between farm workers and their employers. . . . Whether or not this relationship is a good one, it is certainly not helpful to unionisation.'[45] In general, these remarks are applicable to Scotland also, though it should be emphasised that the topic of tied agricultural cottages is a much less emotive one north of the Border.[46]

Finally, a major factor militating against the formation of a union was the excessive geographical mobility of the Scottish farm servant.[47] It is constantly referred to right up to the Second World War, and varying views are held regarding this semi-nomadism. For instance, in favour, is the suggestion that the worker, by changing farms from time to time, saw different farming practices and thus learned more. Further, though the movement was rarely very far — often a circulation within a 10-15 mile radius — it could be argued that the worker therefore developed a sense of belonging to a wider community than otherwise he would have done had he stayed too long on the same farm. Conversely, there was an equally strong viewpoint held that this pattern of more or less annual flitting on the part of the farm worker had unfortunate effects on the children's formal schooling and possible educational advancement. But whatever the viewpoint held, this continual movement from farm to farm was a factor of Scottish farm life rarely found on the English scene. It was indeed more than a fact of life, it was almost a way of life: 'The long hiring system induced an unsettled state of mind as "flitting time" approached. The result was a psychological compulsion to move and take a chance of betterment in wages or conditions'.[48] It must be pointed out, however, that even after the union was formed in 1912, and flourishing, this mobility pattern of the Scottish farm servant was still the norm, and though again it was undoubtedly a factor making branch organisation and maintenance an extremely difficult task for any organiser, it must not have been the only nor necessarily the prime factor in delaying the workers from combining at a national level 'for the purpose of improving the conditions of their working lives'. Other forces must have been at work in delaying the emergence of a national union, forces that have to be looked for at the national rather than local or agricultural level.

II

Professor A. V. Dicey, that expert on constitutional law, divided nineteenth century legislation into three broad periods, these three periods corresponding to three main currents of legislative opinion. In his *Lectures on the Relation between Law and Opinion*, published in 1905, he equated the first three decades of the century with Tory repression and paternalism, which in turn was followed by a period of Benthamism or Individualism from 1825 to 1870. The third period, 1865 to 1900, he describes as a period of collectivism, when legislation became increasingly socialistic, and one aspect of national life after another became the subject of state interference.[49]

Some of the major legislation affecting not only trade unions but also agriculture, and in particular the worker, shows a fairly similar time division. The obvious example for the early decades of the century are the Combination Acts and their repeal in 1824, while for the *laissez faire* period the repeal of the Corn Laws is an outstanding example of this philosophy. It was in the later decades, however, that the biggest changes took place. For trade unionism there were two important Acts of far-reaching consequence: the Trade Union Act of 1871 which gave unions legal recognition and the right to register as friendly societies, thus protecting their funds; and the Conspiracy and Protection of Property Act, 1875, which allowed peaceful picketing during a strike, previously regarded as a criminal offence. For, as Benn and Peters point out, freedom to associate is not enough, and if associations are to fulfil the functions suggested, then they must be recognised by the law.[50] Wade and Phillips, in turn, sum up the nineteenth century as the period when, broadly speaking, the status of trade unions and similar industrial associations evolved.[51]

If trade unions, then, were legally established by the end of the century and given a status of some importance, what of the worker's position? The extension of the franchise to the urban worker in 1867 and to the rural in 1884 — and the time lag has to be noted, reflecting as it does the lesser importance of the rural worker in the eyes of the legislators of the earlier date — together with the Ballot Act of 1872, gave the majority of workers the legal right of participating in this aspect of the democratic process. A further major improvement in the status of the worker, and one which strongly affected the Scottish farm servant whose engagement was usually on a contractual basis of six months or a year, was the replacement of the Master and Servant Act by the Employers and Workmen Act of 1875. Up to then the law was such that if a servant, such as the Scottish farm servant, broke his contract, it was a criminal offence for which he could be sent to prison, whereas if the farmer broke his side of the contract and dismissed the servant it was only a civil offence.[52] The change of terminology in the Act inferred a change of attitude or public opinion towards the lower ranking members of society, a tacit acknowledgment that they were no longer pieces of property and objects of servitude being paid mainly in kind, but were the co-parties in a more rational, cash-nexus based relationship of employer and employee. Passing an Act, however, was one thing: implementing it was another. Nor was there necessarily widespread knowledge or understanding of the conditions with which it dealt. The Royal Commission of 1867, with its various Reports in the early 1870s, therefore played an important educative role and, together with the subsequent comment on these Reports in newspapers and journals, brought to a wide public some awareness at last of the conditions of the agricultural community.[53] Although material conditions of the agricultural worker were still little improved by the end of the century he had nevertheless, like trade unionism itself, been given a measure of legal status and was thus enabled to take a small step forward towards integration into the national scene.

Mention should also be made here of certain changes in the tenant farmer's position, for his legal relationship with his landlord was in some respects as vulnerable as was that of the servant to farmer, and he too in the last quarter of the nineteenth century gained in security via the legislative process. In addition to the 1872 Ballot Act, which affected tenant farmers as much as workers, three Acts relating to agriculture, of varying importance, could be mentioned: the Hypothec Abolition Act of 1894 by which the landlord's precedence over all others having claims on a bankrupt tenant's estate was abolished; the Ground Game Act of 1880, which gave occupiers of farms the right to kill game and so enabled them to protect their crops; and the Agricultural Holdings (Scotland) Act of 1883, which made compensation for tenants' improvements compulsory. This ultimately led to the 1908 Agricultural Holdings Act, a further refinement — 'The Tenant Farmers' Magna Carta' — and this took away the last vestiges of landlord control of tenant farmer operations.[54] Farmers, like their workers, had moved, legally, out of a feudal relationship into a more independent status.

A piece of legislation also of this third period of Dicey's but relating to farm stock is of interest, introducing as it did an entirely new principle into agriculture. Cattle Plague, or rinderpest, had broken out in 1865, and in the following year a Cattle Diseases Prevention Act was passed relating to the slaughter of diseased animals. This laid down that compensation be paid to farmers when such slaughter took place in the public interest in order to control a major epidemic. The principle here being applied to the agricultural industry was in keeping with that already to the fore in various public health measures of the period and earlier. Agriculture therefore was beginning to be regarded at national level as an industry liable to state intervention like any urban-based industry.

The overall picture of the last decades of the nineteenth century is not only one of increasing state intervention in all aspects of agriculture but of a changing balance of relationships between landlord, tenant and worker, the beginning of a gradual levelling process whereby the worker emerges from his state of near-servitude towards that of a fellow citizen not only of the farmer and landlord, but also of the urban worker and urban employer. In short, it was the start of a breach in the farm servant's encapsulation in the agricultural community, and the beginning of a tacit acknowledgement of his status as a member of a wider grouping, not merely of fellow workers but of fellow citizens, and of his gradual integration into that wider national society.

III

The formation of the Scottish Farm Servants' Union in 1912 was a major step forward in this movement towards acknowledged citizenship, tangible evidence to the ranks in the agricultural labour force as well as to the non-agricultural community that the clod hopper image, if such still existed, was no longer acceptable. 'Probably the most striking and interesting of recent developments in Trade Unionism', wrote James Maxton in 1914, 'is the establishment of the Scottish Farm Servants' Union, a vigorous and purely national organisation. . . . It organises a body of men who previous to the advent of this Union were unorganised, and brings them into closer touch with other sections of the working classes, which cannot but be for the good of the rural population'.[56]

It required the emergency situations of two wars, however, to further the farm servant's standing and to bring forth an open acknowledgment of his importance to the nation. His different position in the two wars, in relation to conscription, sums this up. In the 1914-18 war his was not at first regarded as an essential occupation, with the result that farm workers in their hundreds answered the call of 'Your Country Needs You' by joining the armed forces. By 1917 almost a third of the farm workers of Scotland were in the army, and these were, of course, predominantly the younger members of the industry.[57] Compare this with World War II, when the importance of the industry and its labour force was early acknowledged. On the outbreak of war the age of reservation had been reduced to twenty-one for the most important classes of agricultural workers; in 1940 the Undertakings (Restriction on Engagements) Order limited the freedom of agricultural workers to move out of the industry, and the following year the Essential Work (Agriculture) (Scotland) Order made it impossible for Scottish male farm workers to terminate their engagement without the consent of the National Service Officer. In the 1939-45 war both the agricultural industry and its workers were regarded from the outset as of vital importance to the war effort.[58]

This brief comparison of wartime regulations may represent the attitude of the state towards the farm servant at these two periods: what of the attitude of the servant himself towards his own position? In the Introduction to *Rural Scotland during the War*, W. R. Scott sums up the effect of the 1914-18 war thus: 'The war had left a deep impress on the Scottish farm worker. He was made conscious of his place in the social organism. He felt, more deeply than some other classes of workers, the patriotic appeals made to him. This awakened his sense of citizenship. His social importance was increased, and he ceased to be wholly inarticulate. The formation of the Scottish Farm Servants' Union is the external sign of this awakening, which, however, is a much bigger thing than a class-consciousness in the narrow sense'.[59]

Such indeed may have been the effect of the 1914-18 war on the farm servant and his union but, as the twenties advanced, agriculture was once more in the doldrums and remained thus until well into the thirties, by which time another factor, one previously unknown to the Scottish farming scene, that of unemployment among farm workers, was also to the fore. In previous decades surplus farm labour had tended to utilise emigration schemes as escape routes, but with the shutting down of these and at the same time a general economic depression throughout the country, a willingness to work no longer equated with the possibility of work. And the farm servant had no unemployment insurance: legislation of 1920 had extended this social right to every other worker except the worker in agriculture — he was not included until 1937, and then at rates of contribution and benefit which were lower than in other industries.[60] 'It is a most difficult thing to get people to consider farm workers as citizens. The emphasis is always on the farm, and not on the workers . . . if he comes into social legislation he comes in later and on different terms. I submit that it is much safer for the agricultural worker to stand along with his fellow workers in other industries and not to be segregated from them or to be cut off from the general social provision that we are making.'[61] Not until the Agricultural Wages (Regulations) Scotland Act, 1937, was there some standardisation of wages and hours of work; until then his terms of service had been little changed from nineteenth century conditions, with yearly engagements and wages a matter of individual bargaining. This Act, which laid down a minimum wage structure, had become necessary when unemployment appeared among farm workers for the first time in the thirties. Because of this surplus labour the individual's bargaining power over wages was lowered, and this led to the Union asking for wages legislation for Scotland:[62] England had had a minimum wage structure since 1924.[63]

In addition to wage structure, his housing, despite numerous Acts of the interwar years, had likewise little improved, as was shown by the *Report on Rural Housing* of 1937, which included the statement that in general no section of the population was compelled to live in such consistently bad housing conditions as farm servants.[64] This finding merely repeated what Joseph Duncan had been saying for years, namely, that the attitude towards agriculture was the reverse of the attitude towards other industries and that this resulted in definitely lower standards being accepted for those engaged in it. Agricultural workers, he maintained, were regarded as second-class citizens and were denied the same social and political rights as other workers.[65]

It has often been said that wars effect the greatest changes and speeding-up of improvements in the two spheres of medicine and agriculture, both closely associated with life-saving activities. And World War II is an outstanding example of this, the improvements in agriculture including not only material improvements to the worker's work situation but also an enhancement of his status generally. It has already been mentioned that by the outbreak of war, plans had been made to ensure that his work would be treated as of equal importance to that of the armed forces, and this in itself was an indication of the stature the farm worker had suddenly gained. His tools, which had been gradually changing in the inter-war years from horse and horse-associated implements to those of tractor and equivalent extensions, were now of top priority, and under Lend-Lease arrangements introduced in 1941 there was an additional flow of machinery from America to supplement the home products. 'In 1939 there were 6,250 tractors at work on Scottish farms. In 1944 the number was 20,158.'[66] The internal combustion engine had taken over the farming scene, and the farm worker. He had now, in terms of his working week, definite off-duty periods, with conditions more akin to those of the urban worker: for the majority of workers their tools of trade no longer required a seven-day servitude. Also, of course, much of the labour aspect of the work was removed, leaving him with some energy with which to make use of the new-found leisure. In 1945 the long engagement system was at last abolished, and another step towards assimilation into the mainstream of working class conditions of work was taken. This had been one of the objectives of the 1887 Scottish Farm Servants' Union: the time lag is 'a measure of the obstacles which had to be overcome'.[67]

Dicey, as mentioned earlier, had noted the increased state intervention in various aspects of national life during the last decades of the nineteenth century, and this activity increased and developed further in the twentieth century, especially during the Second World War. Self and Storing, in their overview of postwar agricultural policies and politics in Britain, 1945-61, use a slightly different term from Professor Dicey's 'intervention', and this in itself is of some interest. The distinctive feature of this period, they state, has been agricultural 'partnership' — 'a close and pervasive pattern of co-operation between the Government and the principal agricultural organisations'.[68] In short, a subtle change in the relationship between state and industry is inferred, a relationship of two equals rather than of super and sub-ordinates: a similar change to that of a previous decade when the relationship of master and servant with its connotations of subservience had altered to the contractual one of employer and employee. At pragmatic level, and in relation to agricultural workers' conditions, Joseph Duncan listed the three most important changes following the 1939-45 war as being improvement in wages, increase in mechanisation, and the suspension of the term changes. This last, the outcome of the Essential Work Order, had produced a more settled rural population than had ever been known, and everybody had benefited by the fact that the terms passed without the former general upheaval. It had been 'a game of musical chairs which, for three-fourths of those playing it, served no more useful purpose than to change the chairs they sat in'. The years of war had secured a more settled farm population and if this continued in peacetime it would provide the basis for a more satisfying social life: 'Where people remain settled and let their roots down', Dr Duncan maintained, 'they become members of a society which can provide a better life for its members'.[69]

IV

'By class I understand an historical phenomenon, unifying a number of disparate and seemingly unconnected events, both in the raw material of experience and in consciousness. I emphasise that it is an *historical* phenomenon. I do not see class as a "struggle" nor even a "category", but as something which in fact happens (and can be shown to have happened) in human relationships.' Thus E. P. Thompson defines his theme in *The Making of the English Working Class*, and later in the book he places the historical phenomenon of working class formation as having taken place in the decades at the end of the eighteenth and the beginning of the nineteenth centuries between 1790 and 1830. This formation is revealed in the growth of class-consciousness; that is to say in the consciousness of an identity of interests as between all these diverse groups of working people and as against the interests of other classes. It is also shown in the growth of corresponding forms of political and industrial organisation. 'The making of the working class is a fact of political and cultural, as much as of economic, history. . . . The working class made itself as much as it was made.'[70]

Thompson may well be right in his thesis that the formation of the English working class was an historical phenomenon of the period 1790 to 1830, but some qualification is needed regarding the agricultural sector of the population. In relation to the English agricultural worker, Orwin and Whetham point out that farm workers were hardly touched by the campaign for the Repeal of the Corn Laws, Chartism, or the movements for factory inspection, shorter working hours, and trade union recognition which loomed so large in the 1840s. By the nature of the industry they were isolated from the mainstream of working class life concentrated in the town. Furthermore, the labour force in agriculture had always contained a number of farmers' relatives, whose incomes and aspirations depended on the general level of farm profits rather than on wages.[71] The development of a working class consciousness and identity of interests was therefore most unlikely, particularly among these latter members of the labour force.

Much of this general agricultural statement applies equally to conditions north of the Border, but in addition there are Scottish agricultural as well as Scottish cultural factors to be taken into account. There was, for instance, the large proportion of long-term engagements in Scotland, six-monthly or yearly, as opposed to the system of much day labour which was more prevalent in England, particularly in the southern areas. By 'belonging' to the farm, even if on the basis of 'servant' to the 'master', for at least a twelve month during which the complete cycle of land-crop or stock-crop occurred, a receptive and responsible worker might develop a pride of semi-ownership of land or stock. Phrases such as 'my horses', 'my sheep' were frequently used by workers. There was also, of course, a proportion of workers who stayed on the same farm with the same employer for many years. Exactly what proportion of the total labour force this was is difficult to assess but, despite what has already been said about the excessive mobility of the majority of the hired workers, this section of more 'permanent' as opposed to 'nomadic' workers is of some importance. The fact was formally recognised by the Highland and

Agricultural Society when in 1914 it instituted, in addition to its already long-standing awards to farm workers for ploughing skills, etc., a new award, that of a long-service medal. These awards still continue and are in two categories: (a) to workers with 45 years' service on the same farm and (b) to those with 30 and more years' service on the same farm. In the sixty-odd years since the inception of this long-service medal award, thousands of workers have been eligible,[72] a fact which can be interpreted, at least in part, as an indication of good relationships existing between farmer and worker on many Scottish farms. Amicable relationships infer a certain identity of interests, and even if this relates to the good of the land and the stock rather than the social conditions of the worker, it is still nevertheless a bond between farmer and worker. A third point is that in the Scottish Border counties, for instance, many of the shepherds, especially the out-bye hill herds, actually owned sheep, their wage often including 'a pack' of so many sheep plus some cash payment. They were in a sense small-scale capitalists, and quite a few of these hill shepherds ultimately became farmers. In terms both of personality and of work conditions generally, the hill herds were most unlikely indeed to have either any 'working class consciousness' or be at all interested in unionisation.

But perhaps more fundamental cultural factors rather than purely agriculture-associated ones should be looked at. Brief mention has already been made of the independent character of the farm servant as evidenced, for instance, in the individual bargaining system of the hiring fairs. This has deeper roots than those of nineteenth century farm organisation, and reference to this Scottish characteristic of independence — not always in complimentary terms — can be found in numerous writings. Perhaps the sixteenth century is a little too early for the purpose of this essay, but the Bishop of Chichester's opinion then of 'the devellysche dyspocion of a Scottysh man' is worthy of a passing mention at least.[73] More specifically on the rural scene, however, Orwin and Whetham, when comparing the difference between agricultural conditions in England and Scotland in the first half of the nineteenth century, bring out a very fundamental point, namely, that in Scotland domination of the great house over a docile village was rarely to be found.[74] This same point is mentioned by Dunbabin regarding conditions in North Northumberland in the 1890s,[75] where the agricultural labour conditions and organisation were very similar to those of the Scottish Border counties, with family hiring system, bondagers, and much geographical mobility, some of this latter taking place into Scotland. This lack of docility, or of deferential behaviour on the part of the Scottish worker towards his farmer was also noted, in 1871, by A. G. Bradley, one of the many pupils who went to Fenton Barns in East Lothian to learn the system of husbandry there from George Hope. In his book, *When Squires and Farmers Thrived*, Bradley has left a vivid account of the farm and the district in the heyday of nineteenth century agriculture, prior to the Depression years. Hailing as he did from south of the Border, his comparison of the Scottish and English worker is of some interest. The Scottish man, he noted, lacked the manners of the south country sort that he was used to;

there was no touching of caps and no 'sir-ring', even of the master, but they were skilful and willing, strong and loyal, and 'they were then about the best farm hands in the world'.[76] And in more recent years Carter, in his studies of north-east Scotland farm servants, also discusses this factor of lack of deference.[77]

In short, it could be said that this relationship of Scottish farmer and farm servant — and at one time the laird too would be included — whether described as lacking in deference, or minus class antagonism, or of showing an independence of character was, in Galbraithian terms, part of the 'conventional wisdom' in Scottish rural life.[78] The last word, however, on the differences between Scottish and English farm workers in their attitude to their 'betters' is left to Tom Johnston. In his *History of the Working Classes in Scotland*, he notes that although the disturbances during the crofting clearances were dramatic enough, 'we have nothing analogous to the long drawn out class war pictured for England in Hammonds' *The Village Labourer'.*[79] So, as a corollary to this picture of an independent and apparently non-subservient attitude of the Scottish farm servant, we must now ask the question why it should be so.

J. A. Symon, in his excellent account of Scottish farming past and present,[80] provides the clue when he describes the interaction of laird and tenant in the mid-eighteenth century, how each spoke the same broad Lowland Scots and had doubtless sat on the same bench at school, attended the same kirk, and probably knew a good deal about the other's affairs. Some two or so generations later than this, however, following on the Scottish agricultural revolution and resultant material improvements, the landlord's children were being sent to private schools away from home, many of the small tenants of a previous generation had become landless farm workers, and a social gap had begun to develop between landlord and tenant, tenant and worker. But two generations is not long in rural memories, especially at a time when the oral tradition was still to the fore, with family trees and family traditions frequently topics of discussions,[81] and when the disrespectful Scotticism of 'I kent his grandfaither'[82] would no doubt be used as a levelling element on occasion. To take more pragmatic factors, however, and look again at the school system, it is clear that although the laird's son might now have his education further afield, the majority of farmers' sons still sat with the workers' children on the same parish school bench at least for their early school years. In sum, it is the education system in Scotland prior to 1872 which could be the democratising or anti-class formation factor in Scottish rural life.

No doubt the education facilities of parishes varied tremendously both in quantity and quality, but the evidence obtainable from the *New Statistical Account*, for example, suggests that a great amount of educational activity was going on throughout the country, and that many work people had the opportunity of living up to the Knoxian dictum of self-improvement. The areas of the country reputedly with the poorest educational facilities were the Glasgow slums and the Western Isles. Other parts of the country, including the areas of hired farm labour, were well catered for, and literacy was especially high in the south-east.[83]

The long-term potential of this educational facility, this early social service to the Scottish people, cannot be measured in accurate quantitative terms, but there is no doubt that it had an effect on the individual's self-respect and developed the belief that he was as good a man as the next. As already mentioned, one of the early union attempts had been aimed at evening class attendance and improvement of self-culture. The 1867 Royal Commission evidence includes many instances of a similar attitude towards education on the part of the Scottish agricultural worker, and this is a point highlighted in the Fourth Report, where a comparison is drawn between the indifference and at times open opposition to education in English rural districts and the wide-spread desire for education in Scotland combined with co-operation from members of all classes towards securing it.[84] In more precise vein, James Scotland sums up the 1870 situation and differences between the two countries in these words: 'The 1870 Act was an attempt to battle through to general literacy in England, to establish a national system of schools; Scotland by that time was ninety per cent literate, and she already had a national system'.[85]

As already stated, Thompson has placed the formation of the English working class in the period 1790 to 1830. He adds, however, that generalisation of his thesis to Scotland does not necessarily follow. Class is a cultural as much as an economic formation, and though the Scottish story is quite as dramatic and as tormented as the English, it is nevertheless significantly different. He then comes to the crux of the matter, namely, that 'Calvinism was not the same thing as Methodism'.[86]

If class-consciousness in the Thompson sense was not a major factor on the Scottish agricultural scene or one likely to be a motivator of trade union formation, and individualism rather than collectivism was the prevailing ethos in the country in the nineteenth century, what other 'historical phenomenon' may then be explanation or part explanation? For this we must turn to T. H. Marshall, that elder statesman of British sociology, and to his concept of citizenship.[87]

Citizenship is likewise to Marshall as class-consciousness is to Thompson, an historical phenomenon, but one whose development spans three centuries as opposed to four decades. Marshall defines citizenship as a status bestowed on those who are full members of a community. There are three strands to this status: civil, political, and social, and when placed in historical perspective these three strands were 'wound in a single thread' in an estate society where there was 'no principle of equality of citizens to set against the principle of inequality of classes'. The first of the three strands to emerge from the 'single thread' is the civil, and this action takes place against the backcloth of the eighteenth century, the outward manifestation being the growth of freedom of speech, the right to justice, and the right of liberty of the person. 'But the right to freedom of speech has little real substance if, through lack of education, you have nothing to say that is worth saying and no means of making yourself heard if you say it.' Not until the nineteenth century, therefore, is the civil right a reality for many, by which time the second strand in the Marshall trinity, the political, is beginning to emerge. Political rights, a feature of the nineteenth century, are those of participation in the exercise of political power, for example Parliamentary and local government. The twentieth century is the period Marshall associates with the emergence of social rights. This component of citizenship is defined as the right to a modicum of economic welfare and security, of living the life of a civilised being according to standards prevailing in society, and sharing to the full in the social heritage. The social heritage includes education and social services, and the former is the most important right of all. Citizenship, then, is a concept of equality, as opposed to social class wherein is inferred a system of inequality; and the inequality of the social class system may be acceptable provided the equality of citizenship is recognised.[88]

How near to this ideal of full citizenship status had agriculture workers in general, and the Scottish farm servant in particular, travelled by 1912 and the formation of the latter's Union? In general, it was not until after the 1914-18 war that farm workers in many European countries gained the legal right to form unions, for instance, even though these rights were accorded to industrial workers. In Scotland the farm servant had achieved civil rights, though not fully until the nineteenth century and especially the abolition of the Master and Servant Act in 1875. He had also achieved political rights through extension of the franchise in 1884 combined with the Secret Ballot Act of 1872, though the universal implementation of these, as for example participation in local government, was not attained. His actual work conditions and the economic corollary, plus his geographical mobility, were some of the counter-factors to this participation. 'The character mask of the citizen', according to Dahrendorf, 'is its bearer's title to participation: citizenship rights are so many chances of participation'.[89] The Scottish farm servant was still minus full chances of participation: he was still too much encapsulated in the agricultural community.

And what of the third strand of the Marshall concept, that of social rights, of the right to a modicum of economic welfare and security, of education and a share in the social services? The right of education he had had, in modified form, much earlier than many; indeed this was more than a right, it was also a duty and, it would seem, a duty which was willingly performed as well as the circumstances allowed. The Scottish farm servant of the nineteenth century may have been lagging behind other workers in the development of a working class consciousness as defined by Thompson, but he was a step ahead in citizenship terms. Marshall recognised one very definite citizenship right, the right of children to be educated, and this same recognition of the importance of education had been a factor in much of Scottish life for generations. But other elements of social rights had not been won by 1912, and it was to take many years of Union activity plus the effects of two major wars to achieve improvement in meeting basic human needs, such as a realistic wage structure and civilised housing accommodation, and thus to effect the necessary changes in the farm servant's life to bring it more into line with the 'standards prevailing in the society'. For until the industry itself gained its rightful status in the eyes of those outside it, the workers within agriculture were likewise afforded similar lowly status and treated accordingly in the distribution of social rights in general: consequently they did not 'share to the full in the social heritage'. It was not until the Second World War that the industry and its workers achieved full recognition. 'The history of farming is one of long periods of stagnation interspersed with periods of marked progress. Future historians may well record the 1939-45 period and the postwar era as one of the greatest progress. . . . Agriculture, long the Cinderella of British industries, had assumed an importance which no Government could ignore'.[90]

V

Marshall's citizenship concept, as we have shown, comprises three strands of different rights, each gradually emerging into the national scene and national consciousness over a long period of time; for Marshall thought of citizenship as a way of life, growing within a man, rather than as something presented from without. In relating this concept to the Scottish agricultural scene, a tripartite system of worker, union, and industry, has been looked at. All three components have been involved in an historical movement towards a situation akin to the achievement of citizenship. The workers, in the movement from within the agricultural community which spanned several generations, had as motivator the Calvin-inspired ideal of self-improvement, exemplified for instance not only in their independence of outlook but also in their thirst for education. The movement from without, resulting from the growing national consciousness of citizenship rights, led to legislation and state-initiated material improvements from time to time, such as public health measures or the legal right to collective action. The Scottish Farm Servants' Union, as a result of these two movements, became a reality in the twentieth century, and from then on two components of the agricultural trinity, worker and union, travelled towards the same goal, though hampered by the low status of the industry itself and the resultant reflection of this low status on both worker and union. Since the last war, however, the industry is no longer a Cinderella; its labour force is not now composed of farm servants but of agricultural workers whose working conditions and wages are agreed at national level between state, industry and union. The Scottish agricultural worker is no longer a semi-nomad and member only of the agricultural community, but takes his place in the wider, national society, able to participate in such as a full and acknowledged member.

If, therefore, the farm worker has now broken free of his encapsulation in the agricultural community, what then of his union?

When the Scottish Farm Servants' Union was formed in 1912 with the help of Joseph Duncan, his knowledge of farm life plus his experience of and involvement in trade unionism in Aberdeen made him well qualified not only to understand the Scottish farm servant personality, but to nurse the newly born union — of which he was to become secretary in 1914 — through the period of infancy, the 1914-18 war and the hard times of the twenties.[91] In 1932 the Union, as already mentioned, affiliated to the Transport and General Workers' Union, which itself had been formed in 1922 on the basis of the dockers' and carters' unions.[92] Why was the Transport and General Workers' Union chosen rather than the National Union of Agricultural Workers? Dr Duncan's answer to this was that amalgamation with the latter had never been considered, as their method of working was entirely different from that of the Scottish union. The matter was discussed with the secretary of the Scottish Trades Union Congress, and the Transport and General Workers' Union had been suggested. Unlike the ordinary national union this latter, composed of all different types, would allow the farm servants a measure of freedom, including freedom to act on their own industrial questions.[93]

Symbolically, then, when the time came for the Scottish Farm Servants' Union to become part of a wider organisation, it was not that of the National Union of Agricultural and Allied Workers, representing a similar class of workers in England, which it opted to join, but a union with more varied components which not only had some historical links, albeit tenuous, with Scottish agriculture via the earlier carters, but was also prepared to allow its varied components, including the present Scottish Agricultural and Forestry Section, retention of a certain individuality.

The twentieth century has seen the Scottish farm servant emerge from his encapsulation in the farming community. He has shed this title of 'servant', with its connotations at least of subservience, and become the agricultural worker of an important national industry. He is more than that: he is now also an acknowledged member of the wider national society in general. His Union has likewise developed from a purely farming combination to become part of the largest national union, which is also the largest general union. Citizenship is a much bigger thing than class-consciousness, W. R. Scott had said in the inter-war years, and the integration of both worker and union from agricultural into national status can be regarded, it is suggested, as another step towards the full attainment of this goal.

Notes

1. Transport and General Workers' Union, Scottish Farm Servants' Section, *Then and Now 1912-1946* (Airdrie, n.d.), 1, 8.
2. The equivalent union in England was founded in 1906 as the New Union, later becoming the National Agricultural Labourers' and Rural Workers' Union and affiliated to the Trades Union Congress. (Christabel S. Orwin and Edith H. Whetham, *History of British Agriculture, 1845-1914*

(London, 1964), 336-7.) It is now the National Union of Agricultural and Allied Workers.

3.   George Houston, 'Labour relations in Scottish agriculture before 1870', *Agricultural History Review*, vi (1958), 34-5.

4.   Houston, op. cit., 35-8. *The Dundee Advertiser*, for instance, was sympathetically interested in trade unionism at this time, whereas the *Perthshire Courier* was antagonistic. Houston also mentions that at the Inchture meeting on 5 June 1834 two of the speakers were men prominent in the trade union movement in Dundee. See also Note 6 below where similar urban-rural connections are noted.

5.   Thomas Johnston, *The History of the Working Classes in Scotland* (Glasgow, 1929), 355.

6.   Johnston, op. cit., 355-6. Johnston mentions that this 1865 Society, at its formation, was addressed by an official of a Mason's Union from Edinburgh. See Note 4 above for similar urban-rural connection.

7.   *Royal Commission on the Employment of Children, Young Persons and Women in Agriculture (1867)*, Parliamentary Papers 1870, xiii, Appendix Part II to Fourth Report, 145, 193.

8.   Gwenllian Evans, 'Farm Servants' Unions in Aberdeenshire from 1870-1900', *Scottish Historical Review*, xxxi (1952), 29-33. On p. 30 she notes that the Feb. 1872 meeting at Longside coincided with Joseph Arch's first meeting in Warwickshire on 7 Feb. 1872, but that this seems to be no more than a coincidence.

9.   Evans, op. cit., 33-5.

10.   Evans, op. cit., 36. Angela Tuckett, *The Scottish Carter: The History of the Scottish Horse and Motormen's Association, 1898-1964* (London, 1967), 22-3, 32.

11.   Evans, op. cit., 35-40. See also Tuckett, op. cit., 31, 32, 39, 58, for the other side of the coin, that is, activities of the Aberdeen carter members of this Scottish Ploughmen and General Labourers' Union.

12.   J. P. D. Dunbabin, *Rural Discontent in Nineteenth Century Britain* (London, 1974), Ch. vi deals with the Scottish scene.

13.   *New Statistical Account of Scotland* (Edinburgh, 1845), ii, Berwick, 47, 92, 260.

14.   Alexis de Tocqueville, *Democracy in America* (London, 1840), Part the Second, iii, Second Book, Ch. v, 'Of the use which the Americans make of public associations in civil life', especially 221, 228.

15.   *Royal Commission*, op. cit., Appendix Part I to Fourth Report, 71. See also 136 for details of similar associations in Caithness.

16.   John Mason, *Kelso Records, being Traditions and Recollections of Kelso* (Edinburgh, 1839), 64.

17.   E. P. Thompson, *The Making of the English Working Class* (London, 1968), 517-521, 531, 540, 556-561.

18.   J. P. D. Dunbabin, 'The incidence and organisation of agricultural trades unionism in the 1870s', *Agricultural History Review*, xvi (1968), 121.

19. Houston, op. cit., 36.

20. Evans, op. cit., 33.

21. *Royal Commission*, op. cit., Appendix Part II to Fourth Report, 194.

22. Evans, op. cit., 29.

23. W. Hasbach, *A History of the English Agricultural Labourer* (1894, reissued London, 1966), 277.

24. Scottish Farm Servants, Carters and General Labourers' Union, *Objects, Constitution, Rules and Scales of Contributions and Benefit* (Aberdeen 1887, Amended 1890), 5. (Copy of pamphlet is in the National Museum of Antiquities of Scotland, Edinburgh.)

25. W. H. Marwick, *A Short History of Labour in Scotland* (Edinburgh, 1967), 66.

26. Joseph F. Duncan. Tape recording of recollections of Dr Joseph F. Duncan made by J. H. Smith, 1964. Tape 1, side 1. (In possession of the Scottish Labour History Society.) See also J. H. Smith, *Joe Duncan: The Scottish Farm Servants and British Agriculture* (Edinburgh, 1973), 31-4.

27. Hasbach, op. cit., 276-303. See also: Joseph Arch, *Joseph Arch, the Story of his Life* (London, 1966); and Pamela L. R. Horn, *Joseph Arch 1826-1919, the farm workers leader* (Kineton, Warwickshire, 1971).

28. Reg Groves, *Sharpen the Sickle: The History of the Farm Workers' Union* (London, 1949), 95-127. See also George Edwards, *From Crow-Scaring to Westminster* (London, 1922).

29. Sidney and Beatrice Webb, *The History of Trade Unionism* (London, 1894), 1. In later editions they substituted 'working lives' for 'employment'.

30. J. F. Duncan, 'Organising farm workers', *Journal of Agricultural Economics*, iv (1936), 252.

31. Louise E. Howard, *Labour in Agriculture, an International Survey* (Oxford, 1935), 182-3.

32. Orwin and Whetham, op. cit., 94.

33. Orwin and Whetham, op. cit., 23-8. See also A. R. B. Haldane, *The Drove Roads of Scotland* (Edinburgh, 1952), Ch. 12, especially 219-221. Instead of the old trysts, markets developed at the railway heads, near rearing districts, and as the drovers decreased so did the auctioneers increase.

34. J. G. Dow, 'The Scottish Ploughmen's Union and its reforms', *Scottish Review*, xviii (1891), 203.

35. B. W. Robertson, 'The Border farm worker 1871-1971: Industrial attitudes and behaviour', *Journal of Agricultural Labour Science*, ii (1973), 73-4.

36. Joseph F. Duncan, 'The Scottish agricultural labourer'. In D. T. Jones, J. F. Duncan, H. M. Conacher, W. R. Scott, *Rural Scotland During the War* (Oxford, 1926), 194-5.

37. *Royal Commission*, op. cit., Appendix Part I to Fourth Report, 65. See also George Tancred, *Rulewater and its People: an Account of the Rule and its Inhabitants* (Edinburgh, 1907), 283-5; and Donald Omand, *The Caithness Book* (Inverness, 1972), 148.

38. *New Statistical Account of Scotland*, op. cit., 78, 96, 157. See also W. S. Gilly, *The Peasantry of the Border* (1842, reissued Edinburgh, 1973), 6, 19, 20, App. 2. Though primarily about Norham area in Northumberland, the remarks are also in part pertinent to the bondager counties north of the Border such as Berwickshire, Roxburghshire and East Lothian. *Royal Commission*, op. cit., Appendix Part I to Fourth Report, 53-60.

39. *Royal Commission*, op. cit., Appendix Part I to Fourth Report, 23. See also R. Shirra Gibb, *A Farmer's Fifty Years in Lauderdale* (Edinburgh, 1927), 31.

40. Joseph F. Duncan, op. cit. (1964), Tape recording, Tape 2, side 2.

41. Personal communication from 90-year-old Berwickshire farm worker, female (1972).

42. J. W. Robertson Scott, *The Dying Peasant and the Future of his Sons* (London, 1926), 218. See also William Alexander, *Johnny Gibb of Gushetneuk* (Edinburgh, 1881), 45-7, 93-5, for description of North-East hiring markets in the 1840s, and R. Shirra Gibb, op. cit., 12-15, for details of a Border hiring market, 1870s.

43. Parliamentary Papers 1882, xiv, Questions 60, 227-60, 232.

44. J. Pointing, 'Trade unionism in agriculture', in G. D. H. Cole, *British Trade Unionism Today: A Survey* (London, 1939), 441.

45. P. Self and H. J. Storing, *The State and the Farmer* (London, 1962), 173.

46. Ruth Gasson, *Provision of Tied Cottages* (Cambridge, 1975), 86, 90, 108, App. A.6.3.

47. B. W. Robertson, op. cit., 77-81.

48. R. Molland and C. Evans, 'Scottish farm wages from 1870 to 1900', *Journal of the Royal Statistical Society*, cxiii (1950), 221. But see B. W. Robertson, op. cit., 80-1, for other more pragmatic family- or farm-related reasons for moving. Note, however, the exception, item 11.

49. A. V. Dicey, *Lectures on the Relation between Law and Public Opinion in England during the Nineteenth Century* (London, 1905), Lecture iv, 62-9.

50. S. I. Benn and R. S. Peters, *Social Principles and the Democratic State* (London, 1959), 281.

51. E. C. S. Wade and G. G. Phillips, *Constitutional Law* (London, 1931), 489.

52. Henry Pelling, *A History of British Trade Unionism* (London, 1963), 75-6. See also Houston, op. cit., 31-4, for some Scottish examples of the Master and Servant law in action.

53. Hasbach, op. cit., 275.

54. Orwin and Whetham, op. cit., 164-7, 170-7, 298, 300. See also John Clay, *John Clay, a Scottish Farmer* (Chicago, 1906), 70-82, 91-116; and J. A. Scott Watson and M. E. Hobbs, *Great Farmers* (London, 1937), 106, 111.

55. *Oxford English Dictionary:* 'Clod hopper: one who walks over ploughed land; a ploughman or agricultural labourer; a country lout; hence a clumsy, awkward boor, a clown'.

56. James Maxton, 'The working-class movement', *Scottish Review*, xxxvii (1914), 563-4. Maxton was a Labour candidate at the time of writing.

57. W. R. Scott, Introduction to Jones, Duncan, Conacher, Scott, *Rural Scotland during the War*, op. cit., 16.

58. Keith A. H. Murray, 'Agriculture', in *History of the Second World War*, ed. Sir Keith Hancock (London, 1955), 82, 84, 125, 304.

59. Scott, op. cit., 12.

60. Murray, op. cit., 27, f.n.

61. J. F. Duncan, Discussion on paper by Louise E. Howard, 'Contemporary efforts on behalf of agricultural workers', *Journal of Agricultural Economics*, v (1937), 84.

62. Louise E. Howard, 'Contemporary efforts on behalf of agricultural workers', *Journal of Agricultural Economics*, v (1937), 74. See also J. F. Duncan, Discussion on paper by Howard, 83-4.

63. Murray, op. cit., 27.

64. Scottish Housing Advisory Committee, *Report on Rural Housing, 1937*, quoted in Transport and General Workers' Union, op. cit., 7.

65. Joseph Duncan, 'The political economy of agriculture', *Journal of Agricultural Economics*, ii (1932), 89.

66. Joseph F. Duncan, 'The farm worker', *Scottish Journal of Agriculture*, xxv (1946), 200. See also Murray, op. cit., 161, 173, 275, App. Table viii; and Ministry of Agriculture, Fisheries and Food and Department of Agriculture for Scotland, *A Century of Agricultural Statistics 1866-1966* (H.M.S.O., 1968), 72-4, for further details.

67. Evans, op. cit., 35.

68. Self and Storing, op. cit., 9. The book is dedicated 'To Partnership properly understood'.

69. Duncan, op. cit. (1946), 202-3.

70. Thompson, op. cit., 9, 194.

71. Orwin and Whetham, op. cit., 94.

72. *Berwickshire News*, 5 Feb. 1974, reporting on recent local awards, has a statement by the chairman of the directors of the Highland and Agricultural Society to the effect that some 5,500 long service awards had by then been given out.

73. Robertson Scott, op. cit., 245.

74. Orwin and Whetham, op. cit., 56.

75. Dunbabin, op. cit. (1968), 141.

76. A. G. Bradley, *When Squires and Farmers Thrived* (London, 1927), 79. See also Allan Fraser, *Hansel Craig* (Edinburgh, 1937), especially 111-113, speeches at Border kirn. The book is mainly autobiographical and gives an authentic picture of relationships between Scottish Border farmer and workers.

77. Ian Carter, 'Agricultural workers in the class structure', *Sociological Review*, xxii (1974), 271-9. See also Ian Carter, 'Class and Culture among Farm Servants in the North-East, 1840-1914', in A. Allan MacLaren, *Social Class in Scotland* (Edinburgh, 1976), 105-127.

78. J. K. Galbraith, *The Affluent Society* (Harmondsworth, 1962), 18.

79. Johnston, op. cit., 350.

80. J. A. Symon, *Scottish Farming Past and Present* (Edinburgh, 1959), 106.

81. Eric Cregeen, 'Oral sources for the social history of the Scottish Highlands and Islands', *Oral History*, ii (1974), 25-6.

82. Kurt Wittig, *The Scottish Tradition in Literature* (Edinburgh, 1958), 64.

83. James Scotland, *History of Scottish Education*, i (London, 1969), 358. See also Robert Harvey Smith, *An Aberdeenshire Village Propaganda Forty Years Ago* (Edinburgh, 1889), describing the Mutual Instruction Movement which swept across north-east counties in the mid-nineteenth century.

84. *Royal Commission*, op. cit., Appendix Part I to Fourth Report, 17, 67-73.

85. Scotland, op. cit., ii, 261.

86. Thompson, op. cit., 13.

87. David Lockwood, 'For T. H. Marshall', *Sociology*, viii (1974), 363-7.

88. T. H. Marshall, *Citizenship and Social Class* (Cambridge, 1950). See also T. H. Marshall, *Sociology at the Crossroads and Other Essays* (London, 1963).

89. Ralph Dahrendorf, *Society and Democracy in Germany* (London, English translation, 1968), 67. The other side of the medal of citizenship, obligations and duties is, of course, of equal if not more importance. It is, however, outwith the boundary of this present paper.

90. Symon, op. cit., 269.

91. Smith, op. cit., especially Chs. 1 and 11. See also G. F. Hendry, 'Labour in Scottish Agriculture', *Journal of Agricultural Economics*, xi (1956), 431.

92. Pelling, op. cit., 168.

93. Duncan, op. cit. (1964), Tape recording, Tape 2, side 1. Membership of the Union in fact never accounted for more than between a quarter and a third of all hired farm workers in Scotland. It never reached 40,000 and was, for the greater part of the period between 1912 and 1945, well under 10,000. See Smith, op. cit., 38.

The Market for Unskilled Male Labour in Glasgow, 1891-1914

James H. Treble

ONE of the most vigorously debated issues in late Victorian and early Edwardian society was the question of unemployment. Indeed the plethora of extant material not merely bears eloquent testimony to the catholic nature of a protracted debate; it also serves as a reminder that contemporary opinion was by no means as unaware of the existence of a pressing social evil as the relative lack of government legislation might otherwise tend to suggest. For instance, it might be argued that the institutional framework approved by Parliament for alleviating the needs of the unemployed between the first issuing of Chamberlain's Local Government Board Circular in 1886 and the Unemployed Workmen Act of 1905 conveys the impression that the legislature was exclusively concerned with the provision of 'make work' schemes for the deserving artisan class during short-lived, but acute, periods of cyclical unemployment. Such a thesis, however, could only be sustained if one ignored the fact that successive administrations increasingly realised — even if appropriate remedial action was not forthcoming — that the parameters of the problem were not simply coterminous with the boundaries of the market for skilled labour. Nor were the broadening intellectual horizons of contemporary society surprising, since over time evidence accumulated from disparate sources to highlight the presence of chronic underemployment within the unskilled labour market. Although it can be accepted that the dimensions and pervasive nature of casual and seasonal work had been explored much earlier in the nineteenth century — in such studies as the Hand-loom Weavers' Inquiries of 1834-5 and 1839-41; in Henry Mayhew's monumental survey of London outworkers in 1849; and in the proceedings of the National Association for the Promotion of the Social Sciences — it was only effectively from the late 1880s onwards that the volume of literature on the 'reserve of labour' question ensured that the topic would secure close scrutiny from all those who were interested in the condition of the working-classes.

In this context the social historian can point to three distinct contributions to the debate. In the first place, long before Beveridge's 1909 analysis of the returns of Distress Committees set up under the Unemployed Workmen Act, it was realised that the vast majority of 'make work' projects promoted by municipalities — as in Glasgow, where deficits on such undertakings were usually underwritten by the Common Good Fund — catered for the unskilled worker suffering not from economic hardships imposed by 'dull trade' but from the adverse consequences of under-employment. Secondly, data gathered from a variety of government blue books enable a clearer picture of the nature of the unskilled labour market to be constructed. For example, the *House of Lords Select Committee on the Sweated Trades* (1888-90) and the subsequent investigation into *Home Work* in 1907-8 underlined the point that irregular employment and low wages which characterised the sweating system were casually related to a market in which the supply of labour permanently outstripped demand. But the problem was, of course, of much broader scope than this narrowly circumscribed and, indeed, contracting area. As the *Royal Commission on Labour* (1891-4), the *Select Committees on Distress from Want of Employment* (1895-6) and the voluminous *Royal Commission on the Poor Laws* of 1905-9 demonstrated, the same pattern occurred with monotonous frequency among dockers, carmen, vanmen, barbers, general labourers and building trade workers. Where unskilled labour was to be found, it was inextricably linked with the social and economic sufferings of 'a residuum' of under-employed workmen. Finally, the testimony of parliamentary-sponsored inquiries was reinforced by the painstaking research of private individuals. Beatrice Webb's early work was largely devoted to an analysis of dock labour; Charles Booth had examined in massive detail the multifarious outlets for unskilled labour in the metropolis; while General William Booth's *In Darkest England and the Way Out* (1890), despite its preoccupation with farm colonies and emigration schemes as a means of easing intolerable pressures upon the labour market, tacitly acknowledged that 'surplus hands' within the unskilled sector deprived whole sections of the working-classes of the modest standard of subsistence embodied in the 'cab horse' charter.[1]

In the early years of this century such London-oriented investigations grew in number and to some extent in sophistication. Pre-eminent among them was Beveridge's classic delineation of under-employment, which rested on evidence culled largely from London sources, and Dearle's 1908 study, which pointed to the presence of a reserve of labour as one of the salient characteristics of the metropolitan building trades.[2] It is a mistake, however, to concentrate too heavily on the London dimension. Inquiries mounted in other areas are equally important for any understanding of what was a national phenomenon. For instance, the 1893 *Report* of the Charity Organisation Society in Dundee went to considerable pains to discriminate between different kinds of unemployment and to assess the extent to which they affected different social groupings in society.[3] In York, Rowntree demonstrated that his Class A represented an unskilled fringe which could not, even at the peak of the trade cycle, be guaranteed full work, while Eleanor Rathbone's 1909 survey discussed in depth the social deprivation and economic dislocation associated with intermittent patterns of employment among Liverpool's dockers.[4]

Nevertheless, despite the copious nature of the material — and the above list could be considerably extended — there has been until recent years a marked reluctance among social historians to examine the contours of the market for unskilled labour at the micro-economic level of the individual town or city. In part such neglect can be attributed to deficiencies of much of the late nineteenth century evidence; for a considerable volume of the literature was devoted less to the market *per se* and much more to an evaluation of the hallmarks, and treatment, of 'the unemployable', an amorphous grouping whose catalogue of 'failures' strongly suggested that the reserve of labour could best be understood in moral rather than economic terms. Similarly, much of the statistical data relating to unskilled workmen stems from sources — *inter alia*, Distress Committee reports and analyses of the socio-economic background of applicants to municipal and private relief schemes — which are also by very definition concerned with the unemployed rather than with the broader issues of the structure of the local labour market. But even when these drawbacks have been taken fully into account, sufficient material still exists, as the writings of Hobsbawm, Hall, Stedman Jones and Harris amply demonstrate, to enable some of the more fundamental problems in this field to be adequately answered.[5] Hitherto, however, virtually all of the pioneering research has largely been confined to London, which possessed a radically different socio-economic structure to the major industrial communities of the North of England and the West of Scotland. It is the aim of this essay to begin the process of filling one of the many large gaps in our knowledge by examining the market for unskilled male labour in Glasgow during the period 1891-1914.

I

During these years Glasgow's prosperity depended to a considerable extent upon the fluctuating fortunes of the engineering, iron and steel, and shipbuilding trades — and this despite the fact that until the absorption of the burghs of Partick and Govan in 1912 the city possessed no major shipyards within its municipal boundaries. For if these industries covered a vast range of skills — among them heavy engineering, iron moulding and dressing, brass finishing, boilermaking, the production of textile machinery, locomotive and vehicle construction, and machine tools — the local economy in these fields was nonetheless, with one or two prominent exceptions, an essentially integrated structure in which a decline in orders in one sector would have adverse multiplier effects over the whole spectrum. This close and continuing interrelationship can in fact be amply demonstrated by an analysis of those extant 'all union' unemployment returns which relate to engineering and shipbuilding craftsmen in the greater Glasgow area. With few exceptions these data reveal a remarkable degree of symmetry both in terms of their chronology and the amplitude of their fluctuations, highlighting the years of good trade —

particularly 1895-1902 and 1911-13 — as well as the acute and prolonged crises of 1903-5 and 1907-10.[6] Yet if Glasgow's international reputation largely depended upon the degree of expertise embodied in these three staple industries, it is important to emphasise that the city's occupational pattern was bound to reflect not merely the pull of a demand generated in national and international markets; it would also by very definition mirror the more parochial but necessarily inter-dependent needs of the city and its hinterland. Thus the building industry (although encountering substantial problems in the post-1903 era), coalmining, and a heterogeneous collection of transport undertakings — from shipping lines and railway companies to tramways and the motley collection of concerns providing work for carters, vanmen and cabmen — continued to be major employers of male labour in what were largely traditional fields. The same function was fulfilled for women by domestic service and a variegated textile industry, in spite of the fact that by the 1890s Glasgow had already lost its struggle with Lancashire in cotton spinning and the production of cotton fabrics. In areas of more recent growth, the number of openings for commercial clerks and schoolteachers continued to expand between 1891 and 1911 in the increasingly important tertiary sector, while a bewildering multiplicity of trades — jam and sweet-making, baking, gasworks, steam laundries, tailoring, tobacco-making, dressmaking, hairdressing, the provision of food and drink — attempted to meet the requirements of a more sophisticated local market for goods and services.[7]

But if Glasgow's economy possessed skill and tertiary sectors of impressive size, contemporary opinion encountered few problems in identifying the principal outlets for unskilled labour in the city. In general terms they were thought to consist of either those occupations where the principal test of competence was physical strength or of trades in which the sub-division of individual processes, powerfully abetted by machinery, had created a 'dishonourable' element within an established craft. All types, for example, of heavy manual work — in gasworks, foundries, engineering workshops, shipyards, sawmills, brickyards, docks, as well as such jobs as coalheavers, coal porters, paviours', builders', railway and railway contractors' labourers — were placed under this broad classification. Reinforcing these elements were warehousemen, newsboys, cabmen, carters, vanboys, assorted grades of messengers, hawkers, scavengers, billposters, barmen, milkmen, and inn servants as well as a proportion of tailors and shoemakers.

While, however, it is easy enough to identify most of the unskilled trades, the problem of quantifying them presents formidable methodological difficulties. For example, major groups within the unskilled market were often classified in a manner which obscured rather than clarified the underlying trend in employment. In some cases — as with engineering labourers and the numerically small contingents of newsboys and billposters — an occupation was initially listed in the 1911 Census, which effectively precluded all possibility of measuring over time any shifts in its significance as a work outlet for the unskilled. In other cases lack of precision in the published Census data means that it is impossible to illuminate certain aspects of the problem under review. For instance, the vague category 'Other or undefined Workers in Engine and Machine Making', introduced in 1901, gives no indication as to whether or not it covered any segment of the unskilled workforce. In yet other trades, where there were substantial socio-economic differences between a skilled artisan element and a largely unskilled sector, little insight into the respective strengths of these disparate groups can be gained from the published returns, since they merely record the numbers of those engaged in the same occupation without any regard to the proficiency and status of its different members. This was true of tailoring, which consisted of craftsmen employed in 'first class' shops in the bespoke section of the trade and those individuals — mainly but by no means exclusively female — who toiled in the 'slop' workshops of the 'ready-made' sector; of dock work, where there was a considerable gulf between stevedores and foremen of squads on the one hand and the general mass of unskilled dock and quay labourers on the other; and of all those working in the gas industry who were classified upon an undifferentiated industrial basis. Again, if the 1911 Census explicitly recognised shipyard labourers as an important element of the workforce for the first time, it is still not possible to evaluate their numerical strength from the printed source since they are incorporated, under one broad heading, along with ship-painters, a skilled and unionised part of the labour force. Two final illustrations of the ambiguity which so frequently surrounds these data must suffice. Firstly, a substantial refinement in clarification between 1891 and 1901 in those trades concerned with the manufacture of steel and pig-iron not merely destroys any hope of analysing short-term trends in the employment patterns of this sector of the labour market other than in crude aggregate terms; but the continuing adherence to a system of industrial categorisation also frustrates all attempts at measuring that component among those in iron-founding and steel-smelting who fulfilled essentially unskilled functions. The same problem confronts us when we examine that umbrella term 'general labourers'. Outwardly the evidence seems uncompromisingly clear. Whereas 6.09 per cent of Glasgow's occupied male population was placed in the grouping in 1891, that figure was to fall slightly to 5.37 per cent in 1901 and more spectacularly to 2.88 per cent by 1911. In reality, however, it is far from apparent whether the sharp decline encapsulated within this last decade cannot in part be accounted for by the classification of engineering labourers — 1.10 per cent of employed males — as a separate category for the first time in 1911.[8]

But in addition to obstacles of this nature there are two further complicating factors of which we should take account. In the first place, there was a vigorous debate in certain narrowly demarcated areas about whether or not an occupation could be designated, in the classic sense, unskilled. In relation to shipbuilding, for instance, George Carson clearly distinguished between the labourer proper and the plater's helper; 'it is not every man that is physically fit to make a plater's helper; he must be a particularly strong man to do that'.[9] But the difference between the two reflected not merely the possession or absence of a good physique; it also denoted the fact that in the eyes of many, the plater's helper was a semi-skilled worker. This was essentially the verdict of A. McGregor Smith, secretary of the Clyde Shipbuilders' Association, when he defined helpers in the 'black squads' as 'not wholly unskilled men, though not to be ranked with tradesmen',[10] and of W. J. Lewington who in his submission to the Royal Commission on Labour was at pains to differentiate between 'skilled' and 'unskilled' labourers employed in naval dockyards. In Lewington's words, 'a skilled labourer is doing work requiring technical knowledge and such men as those, who are doing work which if it was not done by a labourer would be done by a mechanic, are skilled labourers . . . we call a man able to assist a mechanic a skilled labourer'.[11] The same claim was to be forcibly advanced in the early 1890s by the Amalgamated Shipyard Helpers' Association on the Clyde. For while it acknowledged that 'the work is termed unskilled', it argued that its members were 'frequently more skilled than men who have served an apprenticeship to setting or plating'.[12] There are equally strong grounds for placing gas-stokers in the semi-skilled category, while in the iron-moulding trades there was an indeterminate contingent of workers — sometimes styled 'labourers' — who 'are somewhat above the ordinary foundry labourer, and are close on the heels of the ordinary moulder'.[13] Over time these men had 'gradually gained sufficient experience, being intelligent enough and apt to take the matter up', to enable them to produce iron-piping, although 'their knowledge of moulding stops there, as they are not qualified to make other castings'.[14] Finally, and quite apart from this blurring of the difference between the unskilled and semi-skilled, the social historian cannot chart with any degree of accuracy either those short-term reallocations of labour which took place among several of the major unskilled occupations or quantify skilled and semi-skilled workers — customer tailors, for example — who helped to swell the unskilled labour market when their own crafts were experiencing periods of slackness. Beside these difficulties it is safe to conclude that the problem of assessing the impact of the principal extension of the city's boundaries in these two decades — the absorption of the burgh of Kinning Park in 1905 — upon its overall structure of employment pales into insignificance.

Nonetheless, having made these qualifications, it must, of course, be conceded that they are by no means of universal application. In particular it is possible to obtain a static view of the proportion of the male population in certain trades which were unmistakably the preserve of the unskilled. Thus the percentage of occupied males who were employed as carters, lorrymen, carriers and vanmen rose on trend from 3.58 per cent in 1891 to 4.35 per cent in 1911. Again, those labourers in the building industry who serviced masons, bricklayers, builders and plasterers fluctuated between two relatively narrow points representing 0.66 per cent of the working male population in 1891 and achieving their high-point of 1.20 per cent ten years later. Other unskilled outlets which can be analysed in the same fashion include 'messengers, porters and watchmen', with their substantial numbers of adolescents (2.87 per cent of the total male workforce in 1891, 2.90 per cent in 1911); coalheavers, coal porters and labourers (0.22 per cent in 1891, 0.30 per cent in 1911); coster-mongers, hawkers and street sellers (0.24 per cent in 1891, 0.35 per cent in 1911); and navvies, platelayers and railway contract labourers (0.37 per cent in 1891, 0.10 per cent in 1911). Shorter-term comparisons can be made between 1901 and 1911 in such occupations as railway labourers who were not linked with outside contractors (0.27 per cent in 1901, 0.91 per cent in 1911), scavengers (0.11 per cent in 1901, 0.24 per cent in 1911) and barmen (0.80 per cent in 1901, 0.46 per cent in 1911).[15] In the last analysis, however, not-withstanding the utility and accuracy of these findings, the gaps which remain are formidable. At best the Appendix to this essay can only serve as a general indication of some of the principal areas where the unskilled were located. Beyond that and the obvious point that, for reasons which have already been enumerated, the aggregate percentage for each Census almost certainly inflates the significance of the unskilled within Glasgow, it is not at present possible to proceed.

But if it is impossible to delimit with absolute precision the outer boundaries of the unskilled labour market, the problem of identifying the sources from which it drew its recruits is more easily resolved. In this sphere there are three principal areas upon which the historian should focus his attention. Firstly there was the role played by those incomers into the city who could perform only jobs which demanded little more than a modicum of physical strength and/or reasonable health. Thus in the late 1880s and early 1890s Jewish sweaters in the wholesale tailoring trade were actively employing their co-religionists — usually female labour — in considerable numbers to the detriment of indigenous workers of both sexes in what was already an overstocked market.[16] But of greater significance than the Jewish immigrant who was principally to be located in this one sector of the sweated industries was the impact of Irish, Highland and Lowland immigration upon the labour market.

Although, expressed in percentage terms, the Irish-born inhabitants of Glasgow reached their peak in the quarter of a century which followed the 'Great Hunger', the total of Irish adult males of twenty years of age and above who had made their home in the city was still of impressive proportions in the period under review. At the 1891 Census this figure stood at 30,687; ten years later it had risen by roughly ten per cent to 33,997. By 1911, however, and in spite of boundary extensions, it had fallen dramatically to 26,562. Never-theless, the existence of these sharp inter-censal fluctuations should not disguise the fact that the vast majority of the Irish male community tended to conform to a pattern of employment which diverged only marginally from that which had characterised the immediate post-Famine years. In the early 1890s, for instance, it was openly acknowledged that those Irishmen who formed the bulk of the local membership of the newly constituted National Union of Dock Labourers, were largely restricted to the least skilled categories of dock work.[17] But it was not merely at the quayside that the immigrant made his presence felt; he also constituted an important component of that army of general labourers which serviced a wide variety of industries, as the testimony of the *Report* on the Glasgow Unemployed Relief Fund of 1878-9 and A. V. Woodworth's 1895-6 inquiry into the condition of that section of the workless which lay 'between the organised trades and the semi-criminal or vagabond population' made abundantly plain.[18] Finally, if surnames can be employed as a criterion of nationality, Irish-born workers were actively involved in the lower grades of tailoring and among the casual elements within the boot and shoe trade.[19] Viewed against this backcloth, it is scarcely surprising that as late as 1909 one commentator was moved to assert that the Irish constituted 'the great body of unskilled casual labour in Glasgow'.[20] As with most generalisations, due account must be taken of the element of hyperbole in this evaluation — for the casual element of the workforce possessed a considerably more complex racial structure than was here being implied — but once that qualification has been made, there can be little doubt that the statement itself can be accepted as a shrewd qualitative insight into the importance of the role of the Irishman in the market for unskilled labour within the city.

Highland and rural Lowland immigration, on the other hand, diverged in one crucial respect from the Irish experience. For among those who made the transition from rural to urban society were groups of craftsmen who came to fill vacancies in skilled and well-remunerated occupations. As R. H. Tawney remarked in his submission to the Royal Commission on the Scottish Poor Laws, an important factor in this migration pattern was 'the inability of Glasgow employers to get as many tradesmen as they want in Glasgow. Thus, in the bread-making trade nearly all the "all-round" men are recruited from the country. The same is said to be the case in tailoring. In particular, the building trades in Glasgow . . . draw masons, bricklayers, carpenters, plumbers, and painters from all over the Kingdon. . . . The reason given for the immigration of country tradesmen, and the preference they obtain with employers is, first, the fact that a better all-round training is given in country shops, and second, that town-bred boys do not make satisfactory learners'.[21] Supplementing this list, it should also be noted that a considerable proportion of Glasgow's policemen and blacksmiths employed by local engineering and shipbuilding firms were from a rural background, while Dr Alexander Scott implied that the bulk of the country-bred boys he was required to inspect in the Finnieston district of the city, in his capacity as a Certifying Factory Surgeon, went into skilled occupations.[22] Nonetheless this element, although difficult to quantify, must have represented a very minor part of the total Highland and rural Lowland influx. As A. J. Hunter, secretary of the Glasgow Trades Council, pointed out in 1895, while he had 'known a considerable number of joiners come from the Highlands', the vast majority of the newcomers to city life were young and unskilled.[23] And if such assorted sources as *Organised Help* — the official journal of the Glasgow Charity Organisation Society — and the 1904 *Inter-Departmental Committee on Physical Deterioration* can be relied upon, this conclusion was equally valid for the opening years of this century.[24] What this meant in concrete terms was that many of these first-generation city-dwellers gravitated towards dock work, and a wide variety of labouring jobs including employment within the municipal gas-works, as well as those parts of the transport industry — above all carting — for which an agricultural background would have provided a particularly apt training.[25] In other words, once they had transferred to an urban environment, they tended to be placed near the foot of the socio-economic ladder in much the same way as had occurred to rural-born workers in the cotton town of Preston in the middle decades of the nineteenth century.

The second source from which employers of unskilled workmen derived part of their labour requirements stemmed from what may be styled the operation of a process equivalent to 'the impoverishment of gentility' among those who had toiled for much or part of their lives as members of the artisan class. This kind of downward social mobility was the product of several factors. In the first place the increasing spread of mechanisation could be attended with deleterious consequences for those who earned their livelihood in both old and relatively new crafts. The rise, for example, of large integrated firms such as Bilsland's in the bread-making industry was accompanied by the fairly rapid adoption of dough-making and other machinery which resulted in the shedding of labour and the creation of a permanent class of under-employed 'jobbers'.[26] In Glasgow's pottery factories, on the other hand, mechanisation in certain cases meant that the production of plates and other items which had hitherto been handmade by adult male workmen came to be largely the preserve of a female workforce.[27] By the early 1900s a similar pattern — the replacement of male labour by machinery and/or women — could also be discerned in some of the major clay-pipe establishments in the city.[28] The strength, therefore, of local union opposition to the spread of female workers in these industries cannot be simply attributed to an irrational display of male chauvinism; rather it represented an attempt to safeguard jobs and a traditional way of life from forces over which it had relatively little direct control. As Margaret Irwin, secretary of the Scottish Council of Women's Trades, remarked in 1903, 'one of the great features of our present industrial position [is] to transfer skilled hand work from men to machines worked by women'.[29] In other industries, however, it was technological innovation *per se* — rather than female competition — which posed a fundamental challenge to groups of artisans. In Glasgow's building trades, for instance, it was claimed that the introduction of stone-cutting and polishing machinery had by the early 1890s produced a considerable decline in the demand for masons.[30] In shipbuilding the triumph of iron and steel threatened to affect adversely joiners, since shipwrights 'in consequence . . . lost the hull of the ship, and then they naturally fell upon the work of the joiners', while ship-painters complained that their average working season had been shortened as a result of the employment of 'red leaders' in the preparatory processes and the use of mechanical spraying techniques for the rougher tasks.[31] Nonetheless, in the eyes of the West of Scotland Factory Inspectorate. the most significant development which had emerged in this particular field by 1902 was:

the extended use of pneumatic tools, especially in shipbuilding yards and engineering and boiler shops. Jobs formerly done by journeymen can now with these tools be undertaken by apprentices. In one case I heard of, a job was finished by an apprentice in three or four hours which formerly took a journeyman on an average more than a day to accomplish.[32]

Underlining this testimony, the Associated Society of Millmen argued, in their submission to the *Royal Commission on Labour,* that within the West of Scotland 'there is a number [of their members], owing to the introduction of machinery, who are almost continuously unemployed, and who are unemployed in this sense, that they have no regular work to go to, but look about the works, and get an odd job here and there where they can have it'.[33] If, therefore, technological change on the whole proceeded gradually when placed against the broad background of Glasgow's industrial structure and if it was usually attended with beneficial long-term consequences, it is still impossible to overlook the fact that in certain areas it left in its wake a residual element of craftsmen who were the direct casualties of innovation and who over time added to the city's pool of unskilled labour.

But of more general application, tradesmen could also share the same experience as a result of advancing years and declining physical powers. In Hunter's view, for example, bakers and engineering and shipbuilding workers encountered fundamental problems in securing regular employment in Glasgow once they were past middle-age.[34] Similarly, those artisans who lodged in the Charity Organisation Society's Industrial Shelter in Killearn Street in the autumn of 1907 were victims not merely of their own over-indulgence in drink but also of physical infirmity. [35] Wherever this pattern was to be found, it was usually attributed by firms to two distinct causes. It was first of all seen as an inevitable sequel to craft union insistence upon the payment of the standard rate for a specific job. In employers' eyes, strict adherence to this doctrine gave them little alternative but to discharge elderly or infirm workers whose productivity performance did not match up to this exacting measurement.[36] In addition it was alleged that Workmen's Compensation legislation made companies more discriminating in their selection of employees, with equally disastrous results for aging tradesmen.[37] Nonetheless, not all who entered the ranks of the unskilled were the unwitting victims of powerful exogenous forces. There remained a small segment of craftsmen who experienced the same fate as the result of such personal failings as irregularity of attendance and habitual drunkenness.

The juvenile labour market constituted the third major source of supply of unskilled adult male labour in the city. Indeed it was generally believed that Glasgow's seemingly intractable problem of underemployment was exacerbated by the existence of 'blind alley' occupations for school leavers. In Tawney's view, many of the difficulties which confronted the unskilled could be causally related to the engagement by city firms 'of boys between the ages of fourteen and twenty in occupations within which there will be no demand for their services as men, from which they obtain no industrial qualifications likely in any way to fit them for other occupations, and out of which they are thrust at manhood into the unskilled labour market'.[38] An identical verdict was to be delivered in the post-1900 period by the Charity Organisation Society, the Queen Margaret College Settlement's Committee on Skilled Employment, and the Scottish Trades Union Congress, which in 1911 explicitly condemned juvenile street trading as 'the cause of grave economic evils through the army of unskilled and casual workers it produces'.[39] The remarkable degree of unanimity on this issue which embraced individuals and organisations of widely differing social philosophies was summed up by the *Glasgow Herald* when it proclaimed as a received truth that 'the boy who begins with street trading, when it does not turn him into a wastrel or a criminal, is almost certain to drift into the unskilled labour market'.[40]

On the positive side, such generalisations are helpful in drawing attention to the fact that amongst the most economically deprived, where irregular work and low wages were an integral part of the life experience of the head of the household, the unskilled labour market tended to perpetuate itself in much the same way as occurred among Rowntree's 'race of the "unfit" '.[41] In particular, among those families 'who live not knowing in the morning where the food of the day is coming from' and 'where everything is uncertain in their lives', the temptation to maximise family income 'is almost overwhelming'.[42] In practical terms this meant — as with boys whose parents lived in 'farmed-out' houses — juveniles seeking work in 'the most rapidly remunerative form [of employment], which is usually unskilled'.[43] A similar trend can also be observed among families of skilled artisans and semi-skilled workers who had fallen upon hard times through the death of the principal breadwinner. More specifically, in cases where a widow was compelled to seek assistance for her offspring from the Poor Law, the evidence points overwhelmingly to the conclusion that economic necessity often compelled her to place her children in unskilled, but initially well-paid, occupations rather than apprentice them to a trade.[44] Again, truancy rates could be causally related to the social class of the head of the household, while many of those who, before and after the 1901 Scottish Education Act, took advantage of those legal provisions which enabled them to leave school at the earliest opportunity, invariably secured their first jobs in areas where there was no chance of their rising socially and economically in adult life.[45]

Nonetheless, despite the general validity of these points, it would be an error to treat the connection between juvenile and adult male unskilled work outlets in terms of a narrowly conceived unilineal model, in which the boundaries of the unskilled juvenile market were historically determined by, and coterminous with, the incidence of primary poverty in Glasgow working-class society. Perhaps the most important qualification which should be made to this monocausal explanation stems from the fact that Glasgow throughout this quarter of a century never experienced anything remotely resembling the traumatic consequences which, in Peter Hall's striking phrase, accompanied 'the vertical disintegration of production' in several of the London trades.[46] Not merely, therefore, was home-work never to assume in Glasgow the formidable proportions it did in the metropolis in the second half of the nineteenth century; it also meant that, given the city's industrial structure, there was a considerably more buoyant demand for apprentices than obtained in many other centres. Since, however, it was rare for apprentices to be taken on by employers before the ages of fifteen or sixteen, the period between leaving school and entering a trade was invariably filled by working in what were 'blind alley' occupations.[47] A 'trace-boy', for instance, employed by railway companies and carting concerns might stay 'until he is sixteen years of age, and then his father puts him to a trade', while an undefined percentage of those who had initially obtained jobs as messengers, vanboys, milkboys and in soft goods and hardware warehouses followed a fundamentally similar course of action. The juvenile unskilled market, therefore, did not simply afford employment to the children of the city's labouring population. It also provided the first openings for many boys from an artisan background who within two years were to transfer to apprenticeships in one of the city's staple industries.

Furthermore — and directly related to the preceding discussion — it was widely believed that certain occupations were inherently more likely than others to compel their adherents to seek new openings in late adolescence in the broader market for unskilled adult male labour. This thesis was outlined at length by Tawney when he analysed the relative heterogeneity of Glasgow's juvenile employment outlets and explored the causal links between unskilled adolescent and adult male employment patterns. The essence of his argument was that occupations — such as trace-boys, messengers and lorry-boys — which did not offer the school leaver the prospect of high wages, 'do not compete in attractiveness with apprenticeship' and hence did not 'tempt a boy into remaining in them till he is eighteen or nineteen'. In practice most of those who took up these jobs 'give them up before the age of sixteen'.[48] On the other hand there remained 'a large range of occupations' in which 'the wages are high, ranging from 9s to 16s a week, for boys of fifteen to nineteen years of age, with the result that, instead of leaving at fifteen, boys stay on to the verge of manhood'. Placed in this last category were 'loom-boys, doffers, or shifters in weaving factories, rivet-boys in boilershops, oven-boys in bakeries, "drawers-off" in sawmills, packers in soap works, machine-minders in furniture factories, labelling bottles in mineral water factories, turning the wheel for rope-spinners, and . . . numberless other such positions in which they [adolescents] are performing some simple operation, often as an assistant to a man'.[49] It was in these areas that the 'dead-end' job wreaked its maximum destruction on the social health of the working class, since individual workers were invariably discharged at an age when they could only enter an already glutted market.

Yet even if the emphasis of this argument can be broadly accepted as correct, there are still two points which should be borne in mind. Firstly, if the majority of vanboys and juvenile workers in warehouses were never highly remunerated, there were still within each of these occupations substantial numbers who were only dismissed in their late teens. This was usually the case with the majority of large bakeries, where vanboys were retained until they were seventeen, when 'most of them drift on to the street', and with McGeoch and Company, wholesale ironmongers in the city, who could absorb only ten per cent of their warehouse 'apprentices', although 'at least' half of them would have opted to remain with the firm if adult employment had been available.[50] Similarly, until the closing quinquennium of our period the Post Office usually dispensed with the services of its telegraphic messengers when they were beyond the age at which apprenticeship normally began, while juvenile street trading — an imprecise term which included newsboys, matchsellers, flower-sellers, and shoeblacks — was often denounced on the grounds that it destroyed all incentive among boys to seek 'regular skilled employment after this experience'.[51] It must be concluded, therefore, that these kinds of juvenile occupations powerfully supplemented the contribution made to the unskilled labour market by recruits from those 'blind alley', but highly rewarded, jobs to which Tawney devoted so much of his attention.

Secondly, while it is true that the overwhelming majority of employers of unskilled juvenile workers turned them adrift without any form of industrial training, there remained a minority who sought to retain a proportion of their more promising adolescent employees by promoting them to better-paid jobs within the adult sector of the labour market. Examples of this type of integrated pattern of employment included the promotion by J. T. Campbell and Company of errand boys into the packing departments of their 'soft goods' warehouse: the recruitment by the United Co-operative Baking Society of their drivers of light pastry vans from their vanboys; and the attempt by the Glasgow and South Western Railway Company to provide employment for their horse-boys, on attaining manhood, as carters, 'ticket collectors or porters or something like that'.[52] But if in most cases those who were the beneficiaries of what might be called a limited form of paternalism stayed firmly rooted within the unskilled sector of the labour market, there were a few areas where a limited degree of social mobility was to be recorded. Thus in some of the city's sawmills a proportion of the 'drawers-off' could legitimately aspire to fill, in adulthood, some of the better-paid, semi-skilled jobs within the industry.[53] An identical pattern can be observed among youths who started their working lives as labourers in engineering workshops. Finally, a small percentage of juveniles who began as unskilled hands in biscuit-making factories later secured apprenticeships in some of Glasgow's largest bakeries.[54] In the light of these qualifications, therefore, the social historian should beware of over-emphasising or distorting the nature of the connection between the markets for unskilled adolescent and adult male labour, for it was by no means as intimate or as uncomplicated as much early twentieth century comment tended to suggest. Expressed in another form — and to revert to an earlier part of this discussion — to obtain a balanced assessment of the principal sources of recruitment for unskilled adult occupations, it is essential to broaden our perspective to cover not merely juveniles in 'blind alley' factory jobs but also incomers to the city from rural and Irish backgrounds and those artisans who,

K

for a variety of reasons, were compelled to seek work in the unskilled market.

II

The task remains of identifying and describing the outstanding socio-economic features of the market. In this context there are at least three major themes which merit detailed consideration. In the first place there is the general question of wages and earnings. How well or how badly paid were those workers who followed occupations which could legitimately be labelled unskilled? Secondly, are we in geographical terms dealing with a highly mobile labour force? Were individuals prepared to scour the city and the outlying districts in search of employment or were they tied to a specific locality by a combination of pressures which had solidly economic as well as social roots? Lastly, to what extent did unemployment in its various guises affect those without specific skills?

The hardest of these questions to answer is that which relates to wages, since much of the extant data covers only certain jobs and/or is confined to isolated individual years. Effectively, therefore, there is little prospect of analysing any short-term swings in hourly or piece rates, reflecting in their turn intense short-run changes in the demand for labour, which might have occurred. It must be conceded, however, that this is the least serious obstacle to any attempt at delineating the general contours of wage-rates of the unskilled over time, since qualitative evidence strongly suggests that they moved relatively smoothly and within narrowly defined limits for most of the period under review. On the other hand, a much more formidable barrier to our understanding of this problem is the fact that there was no guarantee that all those who worked at a particular job were governed by a uniform system of payment. For example, hourly scales paid to labourers by Clydeside shipbuilding, engineering and boilermaking firms in 1902 were subject to considerable variations.[55] In this particular instance it can be argued that the ensuing differentials reflected in large measure corresponding differences in labour productivity, although such a conclusion does not necessarily hold true of other areas — above all tailoring in the sweated sector, foundry labouring, and carting — with which this study is concerned.[56] On the other hand, yet other sources — including Glasgow Trades Council in 1903 — refer to 'average' wages without discussing the size or representativeness of their sample, and indeed without indicating whether the resultant statistics represent a mathematical mean or are simply unweighted averages.[57] Lastly, those data which relate solely to conditions of full employment cannot be accepted as a reliable guide to actual annual earnings since they make no allowance for the pervasive depressing influence of 'broken time' on working-class living standards.

But if there is little possibility of constructing a completely authoritative picture of the chronology and movement of wage-rates and earnings in the unskilled market as a whole, there still remain a few areas where the general pattern for all or part of this quarter of a century can be clearly traced. Among others they include those working in iron foundries in the city, a group which seems to have been one of the most poorly remunerated of all categories of unskilled labourers. In 1903 it was estimated that their earnings fluctuated between 17/- and 19/- per week, although these calculations ignored the annual loss of four working weeks.[58] Over the course of the next decade evidence from a wide variety of sources indicates that despite the upward movement in retail prices no significant improvement in their money wages was to be recorded.[59] Indeed, as if to emphasise their lowly economic status, James Ferguson drew attention to the fact that those with large families who participated in the 'make work' schemes which were mounted in 1904 by Glasgow Corporation were initially better rewarded than 'the foundry or other labourer working 54 hours per week [who] receives an average 16s. to 18s. per week'.[60] Nonetheless, despite the objectivity of these comments, it would be a mistake to regard the foundry labourer's experience as untypical of other occupations in the unskilled sector of the market. Among other groupings whose earnings, when in full work, displayed a similar degree of underlying stability were the bulk of the surfacemen and platelayers employed by the North British Railway Company, who between 1899 and 1911 received from 18/- to 20/- weekly according to experience; dock and quay labourers engaged by the Allan Steamship Line whose hourly rate seems to have remained constant at 7d during the entire period 1890-1907; and shipbuilding and boilermaking labourers, the majority of whom were earning 4½d or less per hour in 1902.[61] Some sections of the unskilled workforce, including paviours and causeway labourers, and under-employed dock workers, failed even to achieve these modest standards during the decade 1893-1902;[62] but of equal importance, there were some elements which performed somewhat better, in money terms, than the norm. Bricklayers' and masons' labourers, for example, could expect to earn in the summer months 24/- per week, although this figure was to be considerably reduced during the winter months, while railway carters could secure 23/- in return for what, as late as 1908, might involve a working week of seventy-five hours.[63] It was only, however, in the post-1910 period, when the 'all union' unemployment statistics for the greater Glasgow area point to a return to conditions of full employment, that substantial wage advances were to be recorded. In 1911 most categories of dock labourers won, after a protracted strike, a rise of 1d per hour. In the following years — 1912-13 — the carters' union extracted significant improvements in pay and conditions from railway contractors and other employers, while similar gains were to be achieved by seamen and some elements of the unskilled workforce employed by Glasgow Corporation.[64] Yet even when this late surge in earnings is taken into account — and it by no means affected the entire market — it is impossible to dispute that the majority of the families of unskilled workers must have lived at or below the poverty line if they solely depended upon the income of the head of the household.

The considerable differences between skilled and unskilled labour were not, however, simply confined to the central issue of wages and earnings. In the Glasgow experience they also displayed fundamentally different patterns of mobility. It was quite common, for instance, for members of the labour aristocracy within the shipbuilding industry to travel several miles from their home to their place of employment. As McGregor Smith commented, 'Take, for example, Clydebank, a large proportion of the men come from Dumbarton, a large proportion from Govan, and a large proportion from Partick. Take Port Glasgow and Greenock shipyards, a large proportion go down from Govan, and the case is the same in Paisley, and a number of workmen go from Glasgow out to the country east by train'.[65] Again, when Singer's moved their factory from the east end of the city to Clydebank, a sizeable element of the workforce continued to live in Bridgeton and to commute daily to work, both because the margin of income which was left after meeting the necessities of life was more than sufficient to sustain the cost of travel — according to Peter Fyfe, their incomes amounted to between 30/- and 40/- per week — and also because the range of occupations open to 'the younger members of the family' was infinitely wider in Glasgow than in a medium-sized Dunbartonshire town heavily dependent upon two major industries.[66] On the other hand, workers in the unskilled market were much more tied to a particular locality. Tawney was one of several individuals who argued that builders' labourers, even within the restricted context of Glasgow, were 'very immobile indeed'; if they lived in tenements in the northern districts of the city, they would rarely cross the Clyde to seek work on contracts being carried out in the southern suburbs.[67] This verdict was endorsed by John Paterson, one of Glasgow's largest building contractors, who averred that he always found it easier to recruit labour when he was building in the central, than in the outlying, areas.[68] The same phenomenon can also be identified in the life patterns of dock labourers who were heavily concentrated in those areas — Finnieston, Tradeston and the police burgh of Govan — which were within easy reach of the major docks and wharves on the Clyde, and of the army of casual labourers who gravitated towards the city centre where their chances of securing employment were highest.[69] In short, even if certain qualifications need to be attached to A. V. Woodworth's analysis of the relatively static nature of the unskilled market, it is still possible to accept his conclusion that 'opposed to the popular notion of a restless, shifting population, ready to turn its hand to anything, the results [of his study of unemployed and largely unskilled workmen] show dull apathetic men whose passive resistance to all outside influences constitutes their most hopeless feature'.[70]

Immobility on this scale can partly be accounted for in social terms, for the attachment of the unskilled labourer to his neighbourhood seems to have been both real and lasting. Nevertheless, while the problem certainly possessed this social dimension, it is probable that the factors which had greater consequence in inhibiting labour mobility were economic in origin. In the first place there was the vexed question of travelling expenses, a point forcibly raised by

Rowntree in his discussion of the principal causes of secondary poverty among York's working-class population. In Glasgow it was thought that unskilled workmen had to live within walking distance — defined as within three-quarters of a mile — of their place of employment, since they could not afford even a modest outlay upon public transport.[71] In other words, movement from the centre to the outskirts in search of employment was to some extent ruled out on cost grounds. Another factor promoting the same end was the existence of a surplus of labour throughout the city in the building trades, which considerably reduced the incentive for 'outsiders' to seek jobs in areas where they were unlikely to be known by local foremen.[72] Finally, the families of the unskilled were drawn to the central districts partly because of the openings which were available for their children — as newsboys and deliverers of milk — to earn 2/6d to 3/- per week for 'the family purse, and that is a very grave consideration, because every shilling is a serious thing for them' — and partly because those wives of labourers who were working in the sweated trades would then be within easy reach of most of those large wholesale warehouses and firms which were involved in the domestic system of production.[73]

Geographical immobility, therefore, did not of itself necessarily depress the living standards of the unskilled. Primary poverty, as and when it manifested itself, was overwhelmingly the product of inadequate wages and the devastating effect of unemployment and under-employment upon the lives of the socially and economically deprived. Cyclical unemployment, of course, pressed with particular severity upon all unskilled workers, since they were among the first to be dismissed as the trade cycle moved on its inexorable downward course and among those sections of society least capable of insulating their families from its attendant socio-economic repercussions. Placed against this bleak backcloth, it is scarcely surprising to find that this element figured most prominently in the registration lists for relief work and charitable assistance in all the major economic crises — 1892-3, 1895, 1903-5, and 1907-10 — which beset the city in our period. In 1892-3, for example, although it was claimed that the social distress generated by 'a very considerable commercial depression' in the iron, shipbuilding and ancillary trades was in some measure offset by 'a state of great activity' in the building industry and the 'enormous amount of labouring work' available upon a multitude of projects mounted by the railway companies and the municipality, this compensatory factor made little difference to the overall trend in applications for relief.[74] Of 2,801 individuals whose cases were investigated for employment on the 'make work' schemes run by the corporation, well over 50 per cent — 1,700 in all — were from a labouring background.[75] The same problem was to recur in the opening months of 1895, when a prolonged spell of sub-zero temperatures led to a cessation of virtually all activity in the outdoor trades and produced a further intervention by the municipality and private benevolence to meet the needs of the unemployed. On this occasion more than two-thirds of those who were engaged in stone-breaking yards — 2,665 out of 3,643 — were classified as labourers.[76] This trend, once established, was to be repeated in 1904, when 80.3 per cent of those seeking work on public relief projects came from the same socio-economic grouping; in 1904-5 when the comparable figure was 63.7 per cent; and throughout 1907-10 when casual and general labourers formed easily the largest single category of workers dealt with by the Glasgow Distress Committee.[77] Incorporated within these statistics there was, of course, as some commentators pointed out, a number of individuals who were physically unfit for, or who actively avoided, periods of sustained manual toil.[78] Nonetheless, in accepting the central idea of this thesis — the existence of an 'unemployable' fringe — we must still conclude that the data, assessed as a whole, mirrored accurately enough the widespread experience of a class who, because they 'have not a pound a week' when fully employed, were quickly reduced to a state of grinding poverty at the outset of any depression.[79]

Subject to additional pressures were masons' and builders' labourers who were particularly hard hit by the downswing of the building cycle in the post-1903 period. The dimensions of the problems facing the building industry can in fact be traced in the yearly returns of the Dean of Guild Court. Whereas between 1893 and 1906 the annual average value of linings approved by the Court amounted, at current costs, to £1,749,042, that figure had plummeted to £898,105 in 1907, £894,716 in 1908, only to rise by the smallest of margins to £902,603 in 1909.[80] The period of dull trade, highlighted by these statistics, owed everything to the frenetic activities of speculative builders during the decade 1892-1901, when they built at a rate vastly in excess of current demand. The inevitable sequel to 'overbuilding' on this scale was predictable enough.[81] As Thomas Mason — himself a partner in a large contracting firm — lamented in 1907, the industry was still 'at a very low ebb, with little prospect of early improvement' since 'the number of unlet houses in the city, over 14,000, is quite unprecedented'.[82]

It would be quite mistaken, however, to attribute the incidence of social suffering in the unskilled labour market arising from unemployment exclusively to the downswing of the trade and building cycles. Contributing to the same end were the seasonal trades, although it must be stressed that seasonal work patterns did not affect the complete spectrum of unskilled occupations. There is scant evidence, for instance, that labourers in the iron, shipbuilding and engineering industries were hit by this kind of fluctuating demand for their services, even if, as occurred during January-March 1895 and March 1903, exceptionally bitter weather might lead to a modest but essentially ephemeral rise in the 'all union' unemployment statistics for the Clyde shipyards.[83] On the other hand, those workers who were broadly connected with the building trades experienced either a marked reduction in the length of their working day or a significant diminution in the demand for their services during the period running roughly from November to March. The occupations worst hit by this trend were painters, who sometimes had as many as two-thirds to seven-tenths of their members unemployed at the height of the seasonal crisis; plasterers; causewayers; paviours; all kinds of building labourers; brickmakers whose busiest months, from April to September, coincided with the peak of activity in the house-building industry; and labourers in sawmills whose numbers were reduced *pari passu* with freezing over of the Baltic and Canadian ports and the annual falling-off in demand for house timber.[84] Outside the building trades a parallel process was at work among bespoke and wholesale tailors; dockers; cabinet-makers; porters in the fruit market; and makers of jam and aerated water.[85] A minority of industries, however, reversed this chronological pattern, shedding labour in summer and recruiting extra hands when the demand for their products or services improved with the onset of cold weather. Pre-eminent among them was the gas industry, although a few other consumer-oriented producers, such as suppliers of boots and shoes, always received a powerful boost as a result of heavy falls of snow or a particularly harsh winter.[86]

It was precisely because of the undulating and unsynchronised nature of this seasonal pattern that it was in some degree possible to mitigate the impact of this kind of unemployment by 'dovetailing' jobs; that is, by transferring from an industry which experienced the nadir of its fortunes in winter to one which either then entered its 'boom' period or which, if not seasonal in the classic sense, might at that point in time have vacancies for unskilled labourers. For example, during the winter months some dockers sought work in the iron foundries, while a small element drawn from the ranks of brickmakers and sawmill labourers found employment in the municipal gasworks.[87] Again, during the 'dull' early part of any year, 'first class' tailors were employed by contractors in making up uniforms for the police and local authorities.[88] Conversely, gas work labourers would return in summer to the brickfields or in a few cases make their way to the Western Highlands to participate in the fishing season.[89] Nevertheless, in spite of a measure of success, the overall effectiveness of this process was strictly controlled by two potent exogenous constraints. Firstly, dovetailing was always likely to be of limited significance, since the prosperous months in the majority of these trades occurred in the summer. By very definition, therefore, only a minority of those who were discharged in the late autumn could hope to obtain employment in those few industries whose period of greatest activity coincided with winter-time. In addition, the concepts of seasonality and dovetailing obscure the highly imperfect nature of the unskilled labour market, and above all the dimensions of the reserve of labour problem. For each of the seasonal trades possessed contingents of casual workers who were only fully employed at the height of their short-lived 'boom' period and who for the remainder of the year circulated within the unskilled market, securing, as and when opportunity arose, temporary engagements in other industries.

It is not possible, of course, within the compass of an essay devoted to the unskilled market as a whole, to probe the character, or to chart the parameters, of Glasgow's casual workforce. Those tasks must await a further paper. Within the limited context of this discussion there are only three general points about the inter-connected questions of under-employment and the casual market which need to be made. In the first place the existence of a reserve of labour affected the entire unskilled market, and not merely the seasonal industries. As Pringle wrote in 1907, after examining the returns of the local Distress Committee, 'the short engagements and the long intervals between them indicate a very marked surplus of unskilled labour in Glasgow'.[90] Secondly, the problem of male under-employment had direct consequences for, and was causally linked with, the casual sector in the unskilled market for female labour, the significance of which relationship was underlined by Peter Fyfe, who demonstrated that the majority of married women included in his survey of 660 female workers in the notoriously irregular sweated trades were 'chiefly . . . the wives of labourers whose pay is small and whose employment is casual'.[91] Finally, despite the attempts by some early twentieth century analysts of the social scene to identify the casual workforce with character failings and to regard it as synonymous with the 'unemployable', the casual market was largely the creation of specifically economic forces at work in late Victorian and early Edwardian Glasgow.[92] The advantage to employers of a readily accessible pool of unskilled labour which imposed no additional burden upon their costs structure; their refusal to contemplate any measure for decasualising dock labour — one prominent shipowner went so far as to label the very idea 'utopian'; and the continuing imbalance between the supply and demand for unskilled hands all contributed to the immiseration of this deeply depressed section of the workforce, and helped to produce that peculiar air of 'hopelessness' which was one of the principal hallmarks of the casual market.[93] But in one sense the sufferings to which the casual worker was exposed were unique only in their magnitude compared with those which were experienced by the unskilled generally; for the rewards of economic growth were very unevenly distributed between different social classes and even within Glasgow's working-class society.

Hitherto, however, historians have largely been preoccupied with quantifying and describing the process of growth itself without exploring in sufficient detail its social dimensions. It has been the aim of this essay to make a small contribution to redressing the balance by focusing upon the relationship to the labour market of those 'hundreds and thousands' in the 'Second City of the Empire' who, during this quarter of a century, 'are miserably poor, have to work terribly hard for a bare existence, and never have enough food to eat nor enough clothes to keep them warm'.[94] For them and for the unemployed generally the campaign mounted by the 'Right to Work' movement in Glasgow after 1904 offered the enticing prospect of a better future, with its immediate concern for 'the recognition of the great principle of the right to work' and the noble vision of 'the reconstruction of society on a basis that will secure that the satisfaction of the material and intellectual aspirations of any one individual will not be dependent on the whim or caprice of another'.[95]

APPENDIX

Occupations which can be clearly identified as being the preserve, or containing an element, of unskilled male labour in the Municipal Burgh of Glasgow, 1891-1911

	1891 Census		1901		1911	
	Numbers employed	Percentage of total occupied male population	Numbers employed	Percentage of total occupied male population	Numbers employed	Percentage of total occupied male population
Civil Service Messenger and Letter Carrier	860	0.41	1,289	0.51	1,361	0.54
Inn, Hotel Servant	3,085	1.46	235	0.09	263	0.10
Others in Inn, Hotel, Eating House Service	—	—	1,243	0.50	921	0.36
Barmen	—	—	1,996	0.80	1,172	0.46
Railway Porters and Servants	2,233	1.06	2,402	0.96	1,544	0.61
Carters, Carriers and Vanmen	7,551	3.58	10,747	4.30	11,017	4.35
Warehousemen	1,588	0.75	1,738	0.69	990	0.39
Dock, Wharf Labourers	2,361	1.12	2,851	1.14	3,973	1.57
Messengers, Porters, Watchmen	6,046	2.87	6,716	2.68	7,345	2.90
Railway Labourers (not contractors)	—	—	678	0.27	2,299	0.91
Coalheavers, Coal-Porters, Labourers	468	0.22	464	0.19	753	0.30
Labourers in Engineering	—	—	—	—	2,775	1.10
Ship Painters, Ship-yard Labourers	—	—	—	—	2,381	0.94
Builders' Labourers	—	—	55	0.02	367	0.14
Bricklayers' Labourers	1,269	0.60	746	0.30	642	0.25
Masons' Labourers			1,829	0.73	1,103	0.44
Plasterers' Labourers	137	0.06	384	0.15	243	0.10
Milksellers, Dairymen	586	0.28	523	0.21	852	0.34
Carpenter, Joiner Labourers	—	—	—	—	97	0.04
Navvies, Railway Contractor Labourers	780	0.37	610	0.24	253	0.10
Paviours, Road Labourers	295	0.14	602	0.24	677	0.27
Painters, Plumbers, Decorators	3,022	1.43	4,047	1.62	3,837	1.52
Tailors	4,294	2.04	4,399	1.76	4,136	1.63
Gas Works	1,400	0.66	2,159	0.86	2,557	1.01
Scavengers	—	—	264	0.11	619	0.24
Costermongers, Hawkers, Street Sellers	505	0.24	632	0.25	878	0.35

	1891 Census		1901		1911	
	Numbers employed	Percentage of total occupied male population	Numbers employed	Percentage of total occupied male population	Numbers employed	Percentage of total occupied male population
General Labourers	12,841	6.09	13,444	5.37	7,293	2.88
Bill Posting	—	—	—	—	284	0.11
Newsboys	—	—	—	—	243	0.10
Jam, Preserves, Sweets Makers	—	—	146	0.06	455	0.18
Boot and Shoe	3,674	1.74	3,373	1.35	2,549	1.01
Factory Hands (Textiles undefined)	963	0.46	773	0.31	1,562[1]	0.62
Factory Labour (undefined)	861	0.41	417	0.17	222	0.09
Aerated Water, Ginger Beer making	272	0.13	324	0.13	291	0.11
Other Iron Goods Makers, Ironworkers (undefined)	—	—	—	—	1,040	0.41
Coachmen, Grooms, Cabmen	1,893	0.90	2,133	0.85	1,380[2]	0.55
Other Workers in Wood	120	0.06	471	0.19	344	0.14
Total Occupied Male Population	210,778	100.00	250,441	100.00	253,210	100.00

[1] Included in this category were various groups of undefined weavers.
[2] This category consists for 1911 of 'horsekeepers, grooms, stablemen'.

Notes

1.　C. Booth, *Life and Labour of the Poor in London* (London, 1889-1903, 17 vols); B. Webb, 'The Docks', in C. Booth, op. cit., iv, 1893.

2.　W. H. Beveridge, *Unemployment: a Problem of Industry* (London, 1908); N. B. Dearle, *Problems of Unemployment in the London Building Trade* (London, 1908).

3.　*Report by the Board of Supervision on the Measures taken by the Local Authorities of the Principal Centres of Population in Scotland for the Relief of the Ablebodied Unemployed during the Winter of 1893-4*. P.P. [C. 7,410], 1894, 6.

4.　B. S. Rowntree, *Poverty, a Study of Town Life* (London, 3rd ed. 1902), 32; Eleanor Rathbone, *How the Casual Labourer Lives* (London, 1909).

5.　E. Hobsbawm, 'The Nineteenth Century Labour Market', in R. Glass and Others, *London: Aspects of Change* (London, 1964); P. G. Hall, *The*

Industries of London since 1861 (London, 1962); G. Stedman Jones, *Outcast London* (London, 1971); J. Harris, *Unemployment and Politics* (London, 1972).

6.   *Board of Trade Labour Gazette, passim.*

7.   This discussion of Glasgow's occupational structure is based upon the 1891, 1901 and 1911 *Censuses of Scotland.*

8.   Ibid.

9.   *Minutes of Evidence taken before the Glasgow Municipal Commission on Housing* (1902-3), q. 12,095.

10.   Ibid., q. 13,352.

11.   *Royal Commission on Labour, Minutes of Evidence, Group A*, iii, P.P. [C. 6,984-VIII], 1893, q. 24,003.

12.   Ibid., 494.

13.   *Minutes of Evidence taken before the Glasgow Municipal Commission on Housing* (1902-3), q. 12,839.

14.   Ibid; *Royal Commission on Labour, Minutes of Evidence. Group A*, iii, P.P. [C. 6984-VII], 1893, 495.

15.   For these data, see Appendix

16.   *Fourth Report of the House of Lords Committee on the Sweating System*, P.P. (331), 1889, qq. 25,565, 25,628-30, 25,671, 25,726, 26,162-4.

17.   *Royal Commission on Labour, Minutes of Evidence, Group B*, ii, P.P. [C. 6765-II], 1892, q. 13,417.

18.   *Report of the Administration of the Glasgow Unemployed Relief Fund 1878-9* (1879), 21; A. V. Woodworth, *Report of an Inquiry into the Condition of the Unemployed conducted under the Toynbee Trust, Winter 1895-6* (1897), 26, 32-3.

19.   *Fourth Report of the House of Lords Committee on the Sweating System*, P.P. (331), 1889, evidence of Daniel McLaughlin and Frances Gallacher; *Report from the Select Committee on Home Work*, P.P. (290), 1907, evidence of Mrs Brophy, qq. 2,926-7.

20.   *Royal Commission on the Poor Laws, Appendix Vol. XXIII, Report to the Royal Commission on the Poor Laws and Relief of Distress on the Condition of Children who are in receipt of the various forms of Poor Law Relief in certain Parishes in Scotland by C. T. Parsons*, P.P. [Cd. 5075], 1910, 10.

21.   *Royal Commission on the Poor Laws, Vol. IX, Minutes of Evidence*, P.P. [Cd. 5068], 1910, 334.

22.   *Royal Commission on Labour. Minutes of Evidence, Group A*, vol. iii, P.P. [C. 6984-VII], 1893, q. 23,558; *Minutes of Evidence taken before the Inter-Departmental Committee on Physical Deterioration*, ii, P.P. [Cd. 2210], 1904, qq. 1,672-3.

23.   *Third Report of the Select Committee on Distress from Want of Employment*, P.P. (365), 1895, qq. 8,424-5, 8,431.

24.   *Organised Help*, March 1912, 740: of sixty-six men who had recently been admitted to the Charity Organisation Society's Shelter at Possilpark, twenty had come to Glasgow in the previous month. *Minutes of Evidence taken*

before the Inter-Departmental Committee on Physical Deterioration, ii, P.P. [Cd. 2210], 1904, qq. 1,665, 1672-3.

25. *Royal Commission on the Poor Laws, Vol. IX, Minutes of Evidence*, P.P. [Cd. 5068], 1910, q. 89,658; *Royal Commission on the Poor Laws, Appendix Vol. XIX A, Report by the Rev. J. C. Pringle on The Effects of Employment or Assistance given to the 'Unemployed' since 1886 as a means of Relieving Distress outside the Poor Law in Scotland*, P.P. [Cd. 5073], 1910, 61; Angela Tuckett, *The Scottish Carter* (London, 1967), 46.

26. *Royal Commission on Labour. Answers to the Schedules of Questions issued by the Royal Commission on Labour, Group C*, P.P. [C. 6795-IX], 1892, No. 418, Operative Bakers of Scotland, and No. 704, Messrs Bilsland Bros.

27. *Royal Commission on Labour. The Employment of Women*, P.P. [C. 6894-XXIII], 1893, 280-1.

28. *Forward*, 11 Sep. 1909.

29. *Minutes of Evidence taken before the Glasgow Municipal Commission on Housing* (1902-3), q. 11,451.

30. *Royal Commission on Labour, Minutes of Evidence. Group C*, ii, P.P. [C. 6795-II], 1892-3, qq. 17,983-6.

31. Ibid., q. 17,806; *Royal Commission on Labour. Answers to the Schedules of Questions issued by the Royal Commission on Labour, Group C*, P.P. [C. 6795-IX], 1892, No. 457, Scottish National Federation of House and Ship Painters, Glasgow; *Royal Commission on the Poor Laws. Appendix Vol. XI, Miscellaneous*, P.P. [Cd. 5072], 1911, 23.

32. *Annual Report of the Chief Inspector of Factories and Workshops for the year 1902*, P.P. [Cd. 1610], 1903, 126.

33. *Royal Commission on Labour. Minutes of Evidence, Group A*, ii, P.P. [C. 6795-IV], 1892, q. 16,226.

34. *Third Report of the Select Committee on Distress from Want of Employment*, P.P. (365), 1895, qq. 8,409-10.

35. *Organised Help*, Oct. 1907, 298.

36. *Royal Commission on the Poor Laws, Vol. IX. Minutes of Evidence*, P.P. [Cd. 5068], 1910, q. 89,905, 1,102-3.

37. Ibid., q. 89,772, 1,103.

38. Ibid., 329.

39. *Organised Help*, Feb. 1908, 404, Dec. 1908, 414; *Scottish Trade Union Congress Report for 1911*, 63.

40. *Glasgow Herald*, 30 Mar. 1912.

41. B. S. Rowntree, op. cit., 32.

42. *Minutes of Evidence taken before the Inter-Departmental Committee on Physical Deterioration*, ii, P.P. [Cd. 2210], 1904, q. 6,162; *Royal Commission on the Poor Laws, Vol. IX, Minutes of Evidence*, P.P. [Cd. 5068], 1910, q. 96,633.

43. *Minutes of Evidence taken before the Inter-Departmental Committee on Physical Deterioration*, ii, P.P. [Cd. 2210], 1910, 6,150-1.

44. *Royal Commission on the Poor Laws. Appendix Vol. XXIII. Report to the Royal Commission on the Poor Laws and Relief of Distress on the Condition of Children who are in receipt of the various forms of Poor Law Relief in certain Parishes in Scotland by C. T. Parsons*, P.P. [Cd. 5075], 1910, 48-50.

45. *Forward*, 5 Mar. 1910; *Annual Reports of the Chief Inspector of Factories and Workshops for 1899*, P.P. [Cd. 223], 1900, 233; *for 1900* [Cd. 668], 1901, 395; *for 1902* [Cd. 1610], 1903, 137.

46. P. G. Hall, op. cit., 55.

47. *Royal Commission on the Poor Laws. Vol. IX. Minutes of Evidence*, P.P. [Cd. 5068], 1910, 331.

48. Ibid., 331-2.

49. Ibid., 332.

50. *Minutes of Evidence taken before the Departmental Committee on the Hours and Conditions of the Employment of Van Boys and Warehouse Boys*, P.P. [Cd. 6887], 1913, qq. 5,263, 5,266-7, 5,745-7, 5,753.

51. *Glasgow Herald*, 14 Dec. 1908, Letters to the Editor; *Organised Help*, Apr. 1909, 463. The quotation is taken from this latter source.

52. *Minutes of Evidence taken before the Departmental Committee on the Hours and Conditions of Employment of Van Boys and Warehouse Boys*, P.P. [Cd. 6887], 1910, qq. 1,391-2, 5,204-8, 5,612.

53. *Royal Commission on the Poor Laws. Appendix XI. Miscellaneous*, P.P. [Cd. 5072], 1911, 55-6.

54. *Royal Commission on the Poor Laws, Vol. IX, Minutes of Evidence*, P.P. [Cd. 5068], 1910, 333.

55. *Minutes of Evidence taken before the Glasgow Municipal Commission on Housing* (1902-3), qq. 13,352, 13,388, 13,447-8, 13,452-3, 13,457-8, 13,470-1, 13,492-9.

56. For differences in wages and piece-rates in the sweated sector of the tailoring industry in Glasgow, see the evidence of D. McLaughlin, F. Gallacher, J. Mundey, C. Letham, T. Carey, H. Samuel, J. Pinto and J. Pitkeithley, *passim* in *Fourth Report of the House of Lords Committee on the Sweating System*, P.P. (331), 1889; for foundry labourers' wages see, *inter alia*, Glasgow Trades Council's Minutes, 11 Mar. 1903; for wage differences in carters' wages, see A. Tuckett, op. cit., 109.

57. Glasgow Trades Council Minutes, 11 Mar. 1903.

58. Ibid.

59. *Forward*, 4, 11 and 25 May 1912; *Royal Commission on the Poor Laws, Appendix Vol. XIX A, Report by the Rev. J. C. Pringle on The Effects of Employment or Assistance given to the 'Unemployed' since 1886 as a means of Relieving Distress outside the Poor Law in Scotland*, P.P. [Cd. 5073], 1910, 39.

60. *Corporation of Glasgow. Return of Unemployed for 1904. Report by James Ferguson, Chief Assistant of Poor, Glasgow Parish Council and Clerk in Charge of Schedules in connection with the Unemployed* (1904), 4.

61. *Forward*, 12 Aug. 1911; *Royal Commission on Labour. Minutes of Evidence, Group B*, ii, P.P. [C. 6795-V], 1892, q. 12,772; *Royal Commission*

on the Poor Laws, Vol. IX, Minutes of Evidence, P.P. [Cd. 5068], 1910, q. 89,760; *Minutes of Evidence taken before the Glasgow Municipal Commission on Housing* (1902-3), qq. 13,492-4, 13,496.

62.   Glasgow Trades Council Minutes, 11 Mar. 1903; *Royal Commission on Labour, Answers to the Schedules of Questions issued by the Royal Commission on Labour, Group C*, P.P. [C. 6795-IX], 1892, No. 566, Scottish Society of United Paviours; and *Answers to the Schedules of Questions issued by the Royal Commission on Labour, Group B*, P.P. [C. 6795-VIII], 1892, No. 361, Glasgow Branch of the National Union of Dock Labourers.

63.   Glasgow Trades Council Minutes, 11 Mar. 1903; A. Tuckett, op. cit., 92.

64.   *Forward*, 18 Feb., 24 June, 1, 8, 15, 22, 29 July, 5 Aug. 1911, 14 Sep. 1912, 25 Jan., 1, 8 Feb. 1913; A. Tuckett, op. cit., 113-14.

65.   *Minutes of Evidence taken before the Glasgow Municipal Commission on Housing* (1902-3), q. 13,441.

66.   Ibid., q. 821; *Minutes of Evidence taken before the Inter-Departmental Committee on Physical Deterioration*, ii, P.P. [Cd. 2210], 1904, q. 6,061.

67.   *Royal Commission on the Poor Laws, Vol. IX, Minutes of Evidence*, P.P. [Cd. 5068], 1910, qq. 96,610, 96,625.

68.   *Minutes of Evidence taken before the Glasgow Municipal Commission on Housing* (1902-3), qq. 7,725-8.

69.   Ibid., qq. 818-20, 6,633; *Minutes of Evidence taken before the Inter-Departmental Committee on Physical Deterioration*, ii, P.P. [Cd. 2210], 1904, qq. 6,016-7.

70.   A. V. Woodworth, op. cit., 54. This conclusion, of course, applied to all areas of the United Kingdom, Glasgow among them, which had been covered by this study.

71.   *Minutes of Evidence taken before the Glasgow Municipal Commission on Housing* (1902-3), qq. 818-9.

72.   *Royal Commission on the Poor Laws, Vol. IX, Minutes of Evidence*, P.P. [Cd. 5068], 1910, 331, q. 96,610.

73.   This quotation and information are taken from the same questions and source as Note 70.

74.   *Glasgow Unemployed Relief Fund 1892-3. Report by the Committee appointed in December 1892 by the Lord Provost and Magistrates of Glasgow to deal with the Relief of the Unemployed in the City* (1893), 1.

75.   Ibid., 4.

76.   *Third Report of the Select Committee on Distress from Want of Employment*, P.P. (365), 1895, 517-19, q. 7,913.

77.   *Royal Commission on the Poor Laws. Appendix Vol. XIX A. Report by the Rev. J. C. Pringle on The Effects of Employment or Assistance given to the 'Unemployed' since 1886 as a means of Relieving Distress outside the Poor Law in Scotland*, P.P. [Cd. 5073], 1910, 30; and *Reports by the Local Government Board for Scotland as to the Proceedings of Distress Committees in Scotland*, P.P. [Cd. 4478], 1908, 12; [Cd. 4946], 1909, Table V; [Cd. 5409], Table V.

78.   For example, *Royal Commission on the Poor Laws, Vol. IX, Minutes of Evidence*, P.P. [Cd. 5068], 1910, qq. 89,905, 90,115.

79.   *Third Report of the Select Committee on Distress from Want of Employment*, P.P. (365), 1895, qq. 8,271-2.

80.   *Glasgow Herald*, 19 Oct. 1909.

81.   For the movement of the building cycle in Glasgow, see J. Butt, 'Working-Class Housing in Glasgow 1851-1914', *The History of Working-Class Housing*, ed. S. D. Chapman (London, 1971), 71-4.

82.   *Royal Commission on the Poor Laws, Vol. IX, Minutes of Evidence*, P.P. [Cd. 5068], 1910, 1,089.

83.   *Third Report of the Select Committee on Distress from Want of Employment*, P.P. (365), 1895, q. 8,266; *Board of Trade Labour Gazette*, Apr. 1903, where A. J. Hunter's report for Mar. 1903 on the Clyde shipyards recorded that 'bad weather has seriously interfered with outside work'. The 'all union' unemployment returns for the Clydeside shipyards rose from 8.7 per cent in Feb. 1903 to 10.2 per cent in Mar., only to fall to 7.4 per cent in Apr. Overall, however, unemployment, apart from the influence of bad weather, was already of serious dimensions and was to rise still further in the second half of the year.

84.   *Royal Commission on Labour. Answers to the Schedules of Questions issued by the Royal Commission on Labour, Group C*, P.P. [C. 6795-IX], 1892, No. 457, Scottish National Federation of House Painters, Glasgow; No. 462, Scottish National Operative Plasterers' Federal Union; No. 566, Society of Scottish United Paviours; *Royal Commission on the Poor Laws, Appendix XI, Miscellaneous*, P.P. [Cd. 5072], 1911, 56; *Minutes of Evidence taken before the Glasgow Municipal Commission on Housing* (1902-3), q. 7,659; *Glasgow Herald*, 12 Dec. 1906; and Glasgow Trades Council Minutes, 11 Mar. 1903.

85.   For bespoke and wholesale tailors, see *Board of Trade Labour Gazette* monthly reports, *passim*. *Fourth Report of the House of Lords Committee on the Sweating System*, P.P. (331), 1889, q. 25,554; *Royal Commission on Labour. Answers to the Schedules of Questions issued by the Royal Commission on Labour, Group C*, P.P. [C. 6795-IX], 1892, No. 509, Alliance Cabinet Makers' Association, Glasgow and District Branch; *Minutes of Evidence taken before the Departmental Committee on the Hours and Conditions of Employment of Van Boys and Warehouse Boys*, P.P. [Cd. 6887], 1913, qq. 1,379-81, 5,484-5; *Royal Commission on Labour, Minutes of Evidence, Group B*, ii, P.P. [Cd. 6795-V], 1892, q. 12,879.

86.   *Royal Commission on the Poor Laws, Appendix Vol. XIX A. Report by the Rev. J. C. Pringle on The Effects of Employment or Assistance given to the 'Unemployed' since 1886 as a means of Relieving Distress outside the Poor Law in Scotland*, P.P. [Cd. 5073], 1910, 60-1; *Minutes of Evidence taken before the Inter-Departmental Committee on the Hours and Conditions of Employment of Van Boys and Warehouse Boys*, P.P. [Cd. 6887], 1913, qq. 5,315-6.

87.   *Royal Commission on Labour, Minutes of Evidence, Group B*, ii, P.P. [C. 6795-V], 1892, q. 12,879; *Minutes of Evidence taken before the Glas-*

gow *Municipal Commission on Housing* (1902-3), q. 7,659; *Royal Commission on the Poor Laws, Appendix XI, Miscellaneous*, P.P. [Cd. 5072], 1911, 56.

88.   *Fourth Report of the House of Lords Committee on the Sweating System*, P.P. (331), 1889, q. 25,533.

89.   *Minutes of Evidence taken before the Glasgow Municipal Commission on Housing* (1902-3), q. 7,659; *Royal Commission on the Poor Laws, Appendix Vol. XIX A. Report by the Rev. J. C Pringle on The Effects of Employment or Assistance given to the 'Unemployed' since 1886 as a means of Relieving Distress outside the Poor Law in Scotland*, P.P. [Cd. 5073], 1910, 61.

90.   *Ibid.* [Pringle Report], 63.

91.   *Royal Commission on the Poor Laws. Report by Miss Constance Williams and Mr Thomas Jones on The Effect of Outdoor Relief on Wages and Conditions of Employment*, P.P. [Cd. 4690], 1909, 247-8.

92.   Among many who identified the casual worker with character failings, was James R. Motion, see, for instance, *Third Report of the Select Committee on Distress from Want of Employment*, P.P. (365), 1895, qq. 8,115, 8,147-8.

93.   W. H. Raeburn was the Glasgow shipowner who regarded decasualisation as a utopian project. In his words, 'you might as well think you could control the action of the planets. You could never do it'. *Royal Commission on the Poor Laws, Vol. IX, Minutes of Evidence*, P.P. [Cd. 5068], 1910, q. 89,871.

94.   *Forward*, 6 Aug. 1910. Article by Priscilla E. Moulder.

95.   *Ibid.*, 7 May 1910, Address of J. C. Hendry to the Scottish Trade Union Congress. I wish to thank Bette Duncan of the University of Strathclyde for her invaluable work in helping to gather part of the material upon which this article has been based and for her general assistance in researching into the question of unemployment in Glasgow. I am also indebted to my colleagues — Dr J. Butt for his kindness in calculating the percentage data embodied in the Appendix, and Dr W. H. Fraser and Dr T. M. Devine for their critical comments. Finally, I wish to thank the staff of the Glasgow Room of the Mitchell Library, Glasgow, for their ever-helpful attitudes to my many inquiries. This paper is an expanded version of a lecture delivered to the meeting of Scottish Economic Historians at the University of Dundee on 19 Mar. 1976.

Working-Class Housing in Glasgow, 1900-39

John Butt

OVERWHELMINGLY, recent studies in labour history have been concerned with concepts of ideology and consciousness, social and occupational structure, elites and institutions, political repression, control and incorporation of the working classes — and these approaches have been very fruitful and stimulating.[1] Yet there is a case for testing the validity of political and social concepts against local experience. The effects of government social policy upon a city would be, perhaps, too diffuse a theme, and therefore this study is concerned with only one aspect — the housing of the working classes in Glasgow from the beginning of the twentieth century up to the second world war. Essentially, it examines and quantifies the inter-action between central and local government and attempts to assess the motives for, and the results of, housing policy in 'the second city of the Empire'.

I

Although detailed research — into property relations, for instance — still remains to be done, the general housing situation in Glasgow at the beginning of the twentieth century has now been reasonably established.[2] The municipal authorities, through the activities of the City Improvement Trust, were well aware of the slums, of the extent of overcrowding, and of the obvious contrasts between areas of affluence and squalor. Urban deprivation, in its housing aspects, was carefully documented in the published evidence of the Municipal Commission on the Housing of the Poor (1901-2);[3] the general Scottish housing problem was the subject of a Royal Commission appointed in 1912.[4] At the same time as this general inquiry began, Glasgow Corporation decided to monitor progress in the implementation of the recommendations of the Municipal Commission.[5]

Partly, local civic opinion expressed the view that undue commitment to expenditure on drink militated against the proper housing of the poor, and, in consequence, it had been Corporation policy since 1905 to reduce 'greatly' the number of licensed premises in working-class districts and 'to discourage' the granting of licences 'in new districts'.[6] Partly, the pressure was medical in origin. Following on the great tradition established in the nineteenth century by Dr J. B. Russell (1837-1904) and the Glasgow Health Committee, the Medical Officer of Health prepared a special report in 1910 on those municipal wards where the death rate always, or occasionally, exceeded the city average and linked, as his predecessor had done, high mortality and the general incidence of disease with poor housing.[7]

The state of repair, as well as the sanitary condition, of many tenement buildings gave cause for concern. Sir John Lindsay, the Town Clerk, estimated in 1913 that 40,000 people lived in 'uninhabitable houses' and that many other dwellings in 'congested areas' were 'in a state of structural disrepair, ruinous and should be demolished'.[8] Just before the first world war the sanitary inspector was notifying landlords of over 20,000 nuisances in their property *per annum*. Even then, this did not reveal the full extent of these problems, for statutes and bye-laws were not being enforced rigorously for fear that the immediate results of such action would be to increase the total number of homeless people within the city.[9]

Internal conditions within tenement property were often prejudicial to good health. Backlands were already recognised by 1908 as the main problem with their poorly lit and ventilated common lobbies and their concealed beds, the omnipresent but totally inadequate compromise with deficient floor-space. Yet the focus of civic inquiry was no longer so directly on the 'single end' (or one-roomed house), as it had been before 1900, but more on two-apartment back-to-back houses in tenement blocks.

The city officials — and, therefore, the Corporation — had already available to them lists of dark and poorly ventilated dwellings, and their files contained pages of concealed beds.[10] After deputations had visited Port Sunlight and the Millbank estate in London, they had already decided that garden city cottages or low-rise planned housing estates were the most satisfactory approaches to the problem of rehousing the city's working classes.[11] About what to do with the existing housing stock there was considerable debate concerning ways and means, and even the officials were not united on this matter. Peter Fyfe, the Sanitary Inspector, believed in treating slum landlords with kid gloves, giving them informal or 'courtesy' notices of at least a month before enforcing the laws against their malpractices.[12] The Town Clerk believed that currently uninhabitable houses should be purchased: some could then be put into good repair and others reconstructed to comply with the Corporation's bye-laws at a total cost of between £1 million and £1½ million. Existing statutes, he thought, should be firmly enforced so as to make 'all the houses on the market fit for human habitation'.[13]

A definite and consistent policy had to be followed. Slums, in his view, had to be abolished by demolition, compulsory purchase and reconstruction. Small improvement schemes should be undertaken as necessary by the Corporation to prevent the evolution of new slums. Under the terms of the Housing and Town Planning Act of 1909 the Corporation had power to enforce repairs and improvements on landlords who owned properties let at under £16 per annum.

Earlier private legislation endowed the city with all the necessary powers to demolish 'obstructive properties' [i.e. backlands, in particular] and to close slums, and these powers had already been used, with discretion. According to the Town Clerk, the principal aim of Corporation housing policy should be to reduce the public costs of rehousing the poor by compelling landlords to keep their properties in reasonable repair. Such a policy, if successful, would reduce demands upon the rates and the common good fund. To illustrate his position still further, it should be noted that where 'obstructive buildings' were fit for human habitation, he favoured the compulsory purchase of some of them and their demolition by the Corporation, the costs being recovered from those private landlords who gained from the resulting improvement.[14]

Alexander Walker, the City Assessor, in a percipient memorandum to the Lord Provost in June 1913, indicated that he thought that there were two policies for dealing with slums. The Corporation could decide to redevelop complete areas of the city which were most affected, and before doing this would need to acquire all the properties it was intended to demolish. This course of action (normal policy after 1945) 'may be ideal', he thought, but it would be very costly. The alternative policy combined an amalgam of strict enforcement of existing statutes relating to slum property and a willingness to accept from landlords individual properties at realistic prices. He thought 'much good might be accomplished by following the second course': it would be cheaper than wholesale redevelopment and it would distribute the Corporation's effort over the whole of the inner city. In consequence, he favoured advertising discreetly the fact that the Corporation was interested in acquiring slum property.[15]

This advice might well have brought many properties into the Corporation's hands, for in August 1913 there were 3,467 single ends unoccupied in the twenty-six wards of the old city and 13,886 two- and three-apartment houses. These empty properties were producing no income for their private landlords and in the prevailing economic circumstances could not hope to tempt tenants into taking them, for cheap public transport allowed workers in secure jobs to travel to work from more salubrious districts. Nor was there really entrenched opposition to the City Assessor's brainwave. Even the house factors' and landlords' associations, asked to make submissions to the Corporation about it in 1914, made no reasoned defence of the rights of those who owned slums, simply favouring a system of compensation for properties taken into municipal ownership.[16]

On the eve of the first world war, therefore, the Corporation became committed to a policy of piecemeal slum clearance and local improvement, a course of action entirely consistent with the earlier activities of the City Improvement Trust.[17] Already on 3 August 1911 the Corporation had resolved that the Common Good Fund might be used to buy slum backlands; this resolution, because of its financial implications, was duly modified on 28 December 1911 to allow the Fund to be used only to buy properties over which the Corporation had no statutory control.[18] An Executive Committee on Housing was constituted in 1913, combining all the departments of local government interested in slum clearance, and in the following year a *résumé* was made of the difficulties encountered during earlier activities by the City Improvement Trust in clearing slums and creating new housing schemes.[19] The principal problem had proved, undoubtedly, to be initial capital costs: for instance, before rebuilding began at all, land acquired under the terms of the private Act of 1897 had cost, on average, £9 per square yard. It was accepted that 'the problem of the rehousing of the working classes is wholly an economic one'. Moreover, the Housing Committee knew that the real costs of housing could not be recovered from rent revenues; rents could not be economic, assuming existing wage levels.[20]

II

The state of the housing market at the opening of the twentieth century gave the city authorities some grounds for complacency, but this was to evaporate fairly quickly. In 1901 the total number of houses available for occupancy (162,751) roughly equalled the total number of families (163,548) normally resident in the city, and by 1911 there were — after boundary changes — 183,960 houses as against 167,896 families.[21] Yet there was a tendency for overcrowding to increase in some working-class wards of the city between 1901 and 1911, for increasing numbers of houses were unoccupied: by 1910, 10.95 per cent of the total housing stock was uninhabited. Undoubtedly, this was one outward manifestation of a wages and employment problem in the city which became most acute after 1905.[22] Poverty, therefore, was the underlying reason for the large number of small houses, which, as we have already noticed, were empty in the years before the first world war.

Incentives to build working-class houses virtually ceased from c. 1904. The number of vacant houses induced keen competition for tenants and retarded rent movements. Landlords viewed the situation as one of excess housing capacity. Net income from house property tended to fall from 1905

Table 1.   Vacant Houses in Glasgow, 1901-1915

Year	Number	Percentage of total stock
1901	7,225	4.44
1910	19,715	10.95
1911	19,375	10.74
1912	18,623	10.33
1913	18,341	7.93
1914	13,178	5.69
1915	8,998	3.88

Sources: Butt, 'Glasgow Working-Class Housing', 61; B.P.P. 1914-16, Cd. 8111, Report of the Committee appointed to inquire into the increase of house rents (Scotland), 3-4 and 94.

because of increases in rates, interest charges and costs of repairs. Returns on city bonds were more attractive than speculations in working-class housing. The cost of labour and raw materials for building rose 25 per cent between 1905 and 1914. Thus, the supply of new working-class housing dried up entirely.[23]

Some recovery in demand was associated with the rapid development of the armaments race after 1911; this can be crudely measured by reference to the decline in the number of vacant houses. Supply began to respond only slowly, and by 1916 there were 198,405 small dwellings in a city which had been enlarged by boundary changes and had attempted to house incoming munition workers.[24] Only 1,488 houses were, however, built in the city in the four years 1912 to 1915, as Table 2 reveals. In the autumn of 1915 the Corporation decided to relax the building regulations in the hope that this action would stimulate private enterprise into providing larger numbers of new houses for the working classes.[25]

Table 2. New Houses in Glasgow, 1912-15

Year	New Houses
1912	200
1913	461
1914	373
1915	454

Source: Glasgow City Archives [G.C.A.], DTC 8/19/1/1, Executive Committee on Housing Papers, Report 12 December 1916.

Upward movements in rents were at first slight but then gathered momentum, for the war distorted the trend towards recovery of the housing market which might have caused a more energetic response to the increasing demand for working-class dwellings. Tenants, used to rent levels of 1910 (which were generally favourable to those in steady employment), were not prepared to accept increases, mostly varying between 5 and 10 per cent, and a wave of rent strikes followed. The better working-class districts were most affected by strikes because of the 'house famine' in them and also on account of the fact that wages of those residents not employed directly in the war effort (workers in wholesale and retail distribution, for instance) did not move upwards to keep pace with prices in general and rents in particular.[26]

The actions of the city Labour Party Housing Committee, formed in 1913 and consisting of representatives from every trade union and co-operative organisation in Glasgow, made these strikes effective and gave some of the post-war 'Red Clydesiders' such as John Wheatley (later M.P. for Shettleston and Minister of Health in the 1924 Labour Government), George Buchanan (later M.P. for Gorbals), John McGovern (later M.P. for Shettleston) and Neil Maclean (later M.P. for Govan) both an unrivalled opportunity to develop a wider political base and also an acute awareness of the significance of the city's housing problems. The Rent Act of 1915 was a legislative consequence of this activity organised by Labour and also formed part of a Liberal policy designed 'to kill Socialism with kindness'.[27]

Without legal controls, Glasgow's rents during the war would have gone through the roof, and thus it is reasonable to regard the Rent Act of 1915 as part of an attempt to incorporate the city's working classes within the community as a whole. By December 1916 the shortfall in the supply of houses needed to rehouse those in poor accommodation was calculated by the city authorities at 12,377: 'at the moment the supply of houses in good sanitary condition has practically been exhausted'.[28] The obstacles to improving this situation were real enough: money was dear; costs had risen; labour was scarce; and the Ministry of Munitions had imposed restrictions on building houses. The Corporation, in fact, reluctantly acted to reduce the supply of housing in the city: 2,619 visits were made by the Sanitary Inspector in 1916, for instance, to ascertain whether houses were fit for habitation; 48 demolition orders were made affecting 21 tenements in which there were 163 dwellings; 69 closing orders were served, and 264 houses closed; only in the case of 27 houses were landlords prepared to undertake the necessary repairs.[29] Had there been no war, one suspects that the scale of demolition and closure would have been greater, for Peter Fyfe was the dominant official as far as housing policy was concerned and he, as we have already noticed, had no wish to add to the ranks of the homeless.

Nonetheless, during the war the Housing Committee was responsible for closing 1,099 houses and demolishing 672. Properties mainly in Broomielaw, Tradeston and Cowcaddens were purchased, at a cost to the Common Good Fund of £25,007 3s. 3d., and demolished. In 1916 the Committee first began to consider the future of working-class housing in the city; the principal stimulus of this planning for the post-war situation was the belief that heavy unemployment would grip Glasgow's over-inflated heavy industries when peace came, and that a major slump could be avoided by the careful implementation of prepared building programmes. On 31 January 1917 a housing scheme of 92 houses occupying 13,159 square yards of ground at Garngad Road (with building regulations relaxed) was accepted by the Corporation, but permission to proceed was not received from the Ministry of Munitions until December 1917.[30] Three months earlier, in September 1917, the Government had issued a circular to local authorities offering unspecified financial assistance to those willing to build houses for the working classes. Consequently, the Committee produced a rough plan for the whole city: 47,000 houses were needed immediately, they decided, and 5,000 *per annum* for many years after that.[31]

The Government was, therefore, compelled to define exactly its financial provisions for post-war housing; this was an immense task, as more and more local authorities, both in Scotland and in the rest of the United Kingdom, indicated their willingness to provide 'houses fit for heroes'. The Government's first offer was rejected by the Scottish local authorities because in it their own financial liabilities were not delimited.[32] Eventually, it was agreed that the Government would provide all funds beyond the produce of a rate of four-fifths of a 1d in £1 rateable value for two years only.[33] The Housing Committee then began to look for sites for its prospective houses as a matter of urgency and recommended to the Corporation that ground already in civic ownership should be used. In fact land was a major problem, for the city owned only sufficient ground for about 5,000 houses. After due investigation it transpired that there was not enough vacant ground within Glasgow's boundaries to allow the Committee to fulfil its suggested programme; the fringes of the city were then examined, and a revised draft housing plan was prepared for the Scottish Board of Health. This draft plan not only allowed for the erection of new houses but also for the reconstruction of slum areas. When the estimate of Glasgow's housing needs went to the Scottish Board of Health on 15 October 1919, the Scottish Office found that 57,000 new houses were required by the city in the following categories:

> 25,948 three-apartment houses
> 25,944 four-apartment houses
> 5,108 five- or more apartment houses.

The land requirement was 5,106 acres, on which 53,500 houses would be built in areas throughout the city, but including for the first time plans for Cardonald, Castlemilk, Pollokshaws, Giffnock, Thornliebank, Millerston and Shettleston. An additional 4,000 houses would be built to replace existing slums.[34] Thus, the Corporation of Glasgow planned for a brave new world with an energy that cannot be faulted.

III

Before proceeding to examine the progress of Glasgow's housing programme in the inter-war years, it would be useful to consider the early post-war environment, national and local, in which it was conceived, at first nurtured, and then retarded. The story of how David Lloyd George won the 'coupon' election of 1918, only to become the prisoner of the Conservative backbenchers, is now well known. What is not usually emphasised is the fact that he hoped, in the immediate post-war years, to recapture the Liberal Party with a revival of the pre-war social reform programme of New Liberalism, and if, in the process, his party machine managed to assimilate left-wing Conservatives and right-wing Labour members, so much the better. It was a bold recipe for actions that he hoped would ensure for him a long tenure at No. 10 Downing Street.[35]

Inevitably, the political strains on the coalition were accentuated by promises and programmes which increased public expenditure and at the same time weakened sterling's capacity to return to the gold standard. Such a financial policy was less *directly* significant for employment opportunities than has often been supposed (since the elasticity of demand for British exports was very low in the 1920s), but it was crucial to the progress of social reforms such as house-building; a return to the gold standard depended upon maintaining high interest rates in Britain which would certainly weaken the borrowing capacity of local authorities and indirectly affect employment. The commitment of the City of London and its supporters in Parliament to the gold standard was absolute; public expenditure cuts were not long delayed after the initial euphoria which peace brought.[36]

However, Christopher Addison, one of Lloyd George's most loyal and radical Liberal ministers, piloted the Housing, Town Planning, etc. (Scotland) Act through Parliament in 1919.[37] As we have seen, this Act, which authorised housing subsidies from the Exchequer for the first time, emerged after sharp negotiations between the Scottish local authorities and the Government. It was also a consequence of Government reactions to the *Report of the Royal Commission on the Housing of the Industrial Population of Scotland (1918)*. This commission had been appointed in 1912, yet another pointer to the possibility that the war had delayed housing reform. Its findings unreservedly condemned the existing housing provision in the whole of Scotland and established its priority for action:

> Of the many social problems which, after the War, will demand treatment and solution, none is more pressing or more vital, in the interests of the welfare not only of the individual but also of the nation, than the housing problem.[38]

The Commission's comments on Glasgow's housing stock put into national circulation facts which were well known locally. There were many 'congested' areas in the city, and their condition was appalling. In older overcrowded tenements in the worst wards, such as Anderston, there were cellar ('sunk') dwellings, passages which were 'often dark, narrow and foul-smelling', so dark, in fact, that it was necessary 'to light a match in the day time to distinguish the doors', and partitions were so poorly constructed that 'there is no privacy even within the houses'.[39] In sub-divided properties, once belonging, as single houses, to wealthier occupants, overcrowding reached 'black hole of Calcutta' proportions. For instance, in Richard Street, thirty-seven single-end dwellings in one house were entered from a single stair.[40]

Made-down properties undoubtedly posed particular difficulties to housing reformers, but the principal problems were provoked by purpose-built working-class tenements which had outlived their utility. These were commonly built in great numbers in the 1860s and 1870s and usually possessed only one virtue: they had windows and were reasonably airy. Good external structure — without, however, damp course — was often offset by poor internal arrangement, inadequate lighting and deficient sanitary facilities. Many tenements, however, were ill-ventilated rabbit warrens, consisting of single ends running off long straight passages from the stairheads, as for example, in Cowcaddens. Many were pervaded by a damp, vermin-ridden mustiness, highly resistant to soap and water, no matter how energetically applied. In St. Clement's Parish, for instance, the *Report* revealed:

Ground-floor houses are most unwholesome. The smell here frequently makes visiting ladies ill, and they say it is just a breeding-ground of consumption. Not matter how clean the houses are kept, or how well they are ventilated by open windows, the damp filthy smell is there.[41]

In general, investigation exonerated the inhabitants of any responsibility for the condition of their houses. The average standard of cleanliness was good, but naturally this did depend upon personality:

While even under slum conditions some occupiers display remarkable resistance to their surroundings and keep their houses in good condition, there are others whose powers of resistance are not so strong, and who fall to the level of their surroundings. There is a remainder — we are glad to think a small and diminishing remainder — whose habits are so uncleanly, and others whose habits are so destructive, that they require to be specially dealt with.[42]

The slum environment was more than a test of working-class character; it was an affront to all those with consciences. Professional men, such as doctors, clerics, teachers and local authority officials especially, were likely to find that slums made their efforts for respectable inhabitants unavailing. Rev. David Watson, Minister of St. Clement's Church, represented most clearly and moderately this sense of outrage:

I am well aware of course that beautiful Christian homes exist even in the slums, but the expenditure of effort and watchfulness is tremendous, and the anxiety is endless. I am familiar with the 'eternal heroism of the slums' but it is a heroism that should be uncalled for in a civilised, not to say professedly Christian, country.[43]

It was the world of the single end which the Commission's witnesses most attacked. The last survey available to the Commission was undertaken in 1915, and this disclosed that there were 41,354 one-room dwellings in the city, 19.49 per cent of a total housing stock of 212,223 houses. Of the single ends, 7.12 per cent were equipped with a separate water closet; the inhabitants of the rest, 92.88 per cent, shared common closets.[44] Mrs Mary Laird of the Women's Labour League, a body representative of the better-paid members of Glasgow's working classes, spoke from personal experience of the improvisations which the one-room dwelling demanded: at births and deaths and in sickness proper care could not be given; the dead lay among the living until burial; in families containing boys and girls moral decencies were difficult, if not impossible, to observe.[45] There was general acceptance that living in single ends 'lies in the extreme margin of industrial civilisation' and should be ended as soon as the city administration found it practicable.[46] The Commission concluded from the evidence given to it:

Life in one room is incompatible with family decency; it is incapable of affording conditions for a healthy or moral family life; it involves an overwhelming burden on the occupants; it is marked by a higher disease-rate, a higher general death-rate, a higher infantile death-rate, and a higher tuberculosis death-rate.[47]

Hence, it favoured the demolition of all single ends and a decision to build no more.

Yet the reality of existence for many working-class families in the 1920s and 1930s was the environment provided by the single end. Often their experience of life in one room was temporary, for there is much evidence that many moved to better accommodation when income allowed. Newly marrieds began their life together in single ends; on the other hand, there was a more permanent group of those wage-earners with large families — often with children all of the same sex — who, faced with sharply fluctuating incomes and the omnipresent threat of unemployment, kept their cost of living down by living near to their workplace in cramped conditions. However, the very mobility of inhabitants of single ends allowed landlords to raise rents, since decontrol occurred after 1923 with vacant possession.[48]

The largest single category of housing in the city consisted of two room dwellings — 111,451 houses in 1915 or 52.5 per cent of the whole housing stock. 38.15 per cent of these houses (42,513) had a separate water closet; the inhabitants of 61.85 per cent (68,938) shared common water closets.[49] It is surely significant that in submitting an estimate of 57,000 new houses for the city in 1919, the Corporation made no provision for houses of less than three rooms. Officials and councillors were generally convinced that two room dwellings were not satisfactory, nor did they meet rising working-class expectations.[50]

Overcrowding occurred widely, even in dwellings which their inhabitants would not have considered slums. In slum areas densities per acre of 472, 620 and 700 persons were occasionally found. For the city as a whole at the Census of 1911 there were 61.9 persons per acre, but this calculation included recreational space such as parks. Because of its 'lumpiness', calculation of population density is not an entirely satisfactory measure of the extent of overcrowding; it is better to consider the whole population against the rooms provided by its housing stock. According to the Census of 1911 — the last comprehensive data available to the Commission — over 62 per cent of Glasgow's population lived in one or two room dwellings: 55.7 per cent lived in houses with more than two persons to a room, 27.9 per cent more than three to a room and 10.7 per cent more than four to a room. Using the standard of three persons to a room, over 200,000 people in the city lived in overcrowded conditions.[51]

Ticketing houses according to capacity was a long-established practice in Glasgow to control overcrowding, and visitations by the housing inspectors were regularly made at night to 22,000 ticketed houses in the city. The ticket became a symbol of degradation, real if not total, for the inhabitants of the property: 'when you have put a ticket on a house you have stamped it with a certain character which, in the eyes of the decent working classes, is very sinister'.[52]

Total degradation was reserved for the inhabitants of farmed-out houses and of the common lodging houses. According to a return made to the Local Government Board in 1914, there were 86 common lodging houses in the city, housing 13,000 people; these presented most acute problems to city administrators, and the Medical Officer spoke of them as a 'permanent sore on civilisation'. Crime and drunkenness flourished amongst this group, and they were rarely able to command regular employment. These evidences of social or society's failure were equally manifested among those who lived in farmed-out houses. These houses were not cheap: with their poor-quality furnishings they were let at 5p for the first night and 3 to 4p for each succeeding night.[53] There were 1,434 farmed-out dwellings in Glasgow in 1914, a substantial increase on the number of 1901; 981 of them were single ends, and 453 were two room houses. Their 4,000 inhabitants — if we exclude about 1,000 children — were mainly unskilled workers, subject to seasonal and casual unemployment, and people 'who have come down in the world'. The heads of family represented, according to Dr David Watson, 'the unskilled, undisciplined, vicious and degraded . . . 99 per cent are there through drink, improvidence, and laziness'. Peter Fyfe, who had closer and better experience of the problem, thought that 50 per cent of the inhabitants of farmed-out houses were there through drink, 20 per cent through illness or idleness, 10 per cent through a desire to be mobile, and 20 per cent were 'fallen women'.[54] Not surprisingly, the Corporation was concerned to control immorality, and some of the inhabitants of farmed-out houses clearly posed an acute threat to that possibility.

Glasgow's desire to improve the housing conditions, health and morality of its citizens was hampered by a number of circumstances. Land that would cost £80-£120 per acre in Dundee reached prices of between £200 and £300 in Glasgow, and the high cost of ground was a formidable restriction on building for the working classes. High building costs in a free enterprise situation led on to rents which were beyond the means of many wage-earners. In the view of the majority of the Commissioners, the commercial provision of working-class housing had ceased to be possible: 'for the housing of the working classes the State must accept direct responsibility'. By transferring public funds to the local authority, central government, they thought, might most efficiently discharge this duty and provide subsidised housing.[55]

There were many advantages in this sort of arrangement. The Local Government Board could control rent levels and prevent abuses. The building trade, employers and employees, would have greater economic security, for demand for housing would be rendered effective. Labour relations might be improved, the Commission argued, for 'the chief root of industrial unrest is the desire of the workers to establish better conditions of life for themselves and their families'.[56] The earlier rent strikes and the shop stewards' movement on Clydeside had made an indelible, and not entirely unfavourable, impression upon articulate middle-class opinion in Glasgow: 'bad housing may fairly be regarded as a legitimate cause of social unrest'. Agitation on the housing issue was not regarded as dangerous or even unwarranted. The Commission concluded:

So far as housing is concerned, we cannot but record our satisfaction that, after generations of apathy, the workers all over Scotland give abundant evidence of discontent with conditions that no modern community should be expected to tolerate. Industrial unrest, whatever be its ultimate causes, undoubtedly is stimulated, directly and indirectly, by defective housing.[57]

These views reinforced the conclusions reached by the Commission of Enquiry into Industrial Unrest in Scotland and reported in the same session of Parliament (1917-18). Workers, according to this report, were resentful of their treatment by other groups in society and by studying social and economic questions were indicating their desire for change. However, the chief cause of unrest — unemployment had not yet become an issue — was the cost of living. Closely related to the cost of food was the housing question. The stock of houses was inadequate and its quality deficient, 'a serious cause of unrest, as well as a danger to public health'. Market forces had ceased to make available enough houses to meet demand well before 1914, and the war had made matters worse. The Report was unequivocal in its conclusions:

> The industrial unrest attributable to this cause, it is strongly represented, can only be allayed by the Government taking steps to grapple with a problem which appears to have grown too great for private enterprise to meet, by in some way having land in the near neighbourhood of congested industrial districts made available on reasonable terms for building working-class houses, and by rendering financial aid for building expeditiously the urgently wanted houses.[58]

Addison's Act gave Glasgow Corporation an opportunity to put its plans for rehousing the working classes into operation, for the Act recognised the need to provide subsidies, a fact not always readily accepted by influential members of the Parliamentary Labour Party. J. H. Thomas, for instance, placed his faith in raising wage levels and considered that only the exceptional effects of the war in cutting the supply of houses justified a subsidy policy. He argued:

> The houses must be let at an economic rental. I cannot conceive it to be a good thing that the working classes should be subsidised in any way. It savours too much of charity, and in the end, is demoralising and leads to corruption.[59]

The Exchequer's open-ended financial commitment beyond the local authority's need to provide the revenue arising from a rate of four-fifths of a penny in the pound (4/5d in £1) was the source of Addison's personal decline, and his resignation in 1921 was immediately preceded by a decision by the Cabinet's Financial Committee to end housing subsidies. David Lloyd George, at first keenly supporting Addison and the cause of housing reform — one of his long-cherished interests — vacillated in the face of by-election victories by anti-waste candidates and middle-class opposition to existing tax levels. The high costs of Addison's proposals, as these became apparent, weakened political will-power generally and completely scuppered the hoped-for revival of New Liberalism.[60]

The implementation of Addison's Act injected further demand into an inflationary situation. Glasgow was quickly away: of the tenders for the first 9,000 houses approved in 1918 by the Scottish Board of Health, 6,731 were in the city. 368 timber houses were also erected, an indication of the seriousness with which the Corporation approached the housing shortage. Eventually, by 1921, 4,474 houses were built under the Addison Act, for pressure on resources prevented the completion of all these first tenders.[61] Building was not, in fact, keeping up with either rising expectations or annual wastage, for by 1921 there were 12,000 occupied houses in the city which the Medical Officer had declared unfit for human habitation.[62]

The City Chamberlain's department were clearly concerned in the period 1919-21 with the long-term effects on the Corporation's debt of the housing account; this anxiety was fed by rising interest rates and zooming costs of construction. There was evidence of combination among builders to prevent price competition for public contracts, and although information about contractors' profit margins is not readily obtainable, a Committee of Inquiry into the high cost of building working-class dwellings believed that 'opportunities presented themselves for the earning of considerable and even undue profits'.[63] The system of contracting was not conducive to lowering costs. For instance, the contractor might accept a 'lump sum' contract, i.e. his estimated costs would be paid by the local authority and, assuming that he met the terms of the agreement, the builder would also receive a profit of £40 per house. If the contractor managed to build at below the estimated cost, he received a bonus which varied between 25 per cent and 50 per cent of the difference. Should the builder overshoot his estimate, he was only penalised by up to £20 per house, and thus had a guaranteed unit profit of £20, no matter what his costs.[64] In many parts of Scotland, including Glasgow, local employers' associations submitted for contracts and then apportioned parts of the work to their members. The final price was adjusted by representatives of the Scottish Board of Health, the local authority and the employers' association. This form of contracting had resulted in very high prices, it was believed. There were also a few sliding scale contracts designed to solve the questions of rising labour and raw material costs.[65]

Cost inflation was a substantial problem, as Table 3 helps to demonstrate in the case of a few materials essential to house-building.

Table 3. Costs of Building Materials, 1914-21

Item	1914	1919	1921
Bricks per 1,000	25s	70s	110s
Cement per ton	38s	107s	123s 6d
Baths each	£5	£8	£12

Source: B.P.P. 1921 Cmd. 1411, Report of the Committee of Inquiry into the High Cost of Building Working-Class Dwellings in Scotland, 13.

Glasgow Corporation responded to rising costs in several ways. There was insufficient brick-making capacity in Scotland, and therefore the city bought a brickworks; it was estimated in 1921 that this would lead to a saving on bricks of

£37 per house. Cement costs, it was thought, could be reduced by allowing Belgian cement into the country duty-free. There was also much public agitation against 'trusts' which raised the costs of materials, notably the National Light Castings Association.[66] Labour costs had also risen remarkably since 1914 (see Table 4), and bricklayers and plasterers were particularly scarce. Had it not been for labour disputes in the shipyards, there would also have been a shortage of joiners. The trade unions in the building trades opposed dilution in any form and constantly refused to accept ex-servicemen unless they had served an apprenticeship. Attempts to improve the productivity of labour had only marginal success in a period of relatively full employment for building workers; negotiations during strikes, however, with individual unions such as the Carpenters in 1920, did succeed in getting work on housing schemes completed to schedule. Generally, the Corporation attempted to improve working conditions on its building sites so as to avoid labour disputes which would impede housing progress.[67]

Table 4. Building Trade Wages in Glasgow, 1914-20

Occupation	Standard rate per hour (s. d.)	
	1914	Nov. 1920
Bricklayers	11	
Glaziers	9½	
Joiners	10½	
Masons	10½	
Painters	10	1s 11¼d — 2s 4d
Plasterers	10	
Plumbers	10½	
Platers	10	
Labourers	7	

Source: B.P.P. 1921, Cmd. 1411, 18.

A three apartment house in a two storey block containing four such houses could cost in 1920 up to £900 (excluding land, roads and sewers), compared with £723 in 1919 and £300 in 1914. Apart from this obvious increase in cost, the standard of work produced by private contractors was often unsatisfactory. Accordingly, the Corporation decided, after investigation, that the Housing Department should establish its own Direct Labour organisation to cut the costs of housing and to improve its quality. The first housing scheme erected by Direct Labour was at Drumoyne, where 318 houses were built between March 1921 and September 1923; the actual cost was well below the estimate, a saving of £140 per house, according to John McGovern, M.P. for Glasgow Shettleston.[68]

However, the domination of Glasgow Corporation by politicians favouring private enterprise prevented the Direct Labour section from taking many contracts: some work was done at Polmadie between 1922 and 1924 and at Langlands (completed in 1926). The energies of the section were concentrated on maintenance and the construction of roads and sewers; unemployed men were recruited for these tasks, and the Unemployed Grants Committee in 1922 agreed to pay up to 60 per cent of the wage bill.[69]

After the Labour Party won control of the Corporation in 1933, the Direct Labour section began to extend its activities slowly. The quality of painterwork in 1933 was so defective that Direct Labour was used to complete some existing contracts, and in 1935, because of the amount of repairs found to be needed after plasterwork contracts had been completed by private contractors, the same principle of action was followed. Entire housing schemes were allocated to the Direct Labour section in 1936 — at Bellahouston and Queen Victoria Drive, for example — and its activities expanded greatly in the years just before the second world war.[70]

Table 5.   The Direct Labour Section and its activities, 1921-39

Date	No. of employees	Houses completed	Houses partly completed
1921-3		318	
1923-4			102
1925-6		84	
1933			232
1934			664
1935			466
1936	371	36	811
1937	1,200	262	707
1938	1,700	901	1,188
1939	2,000	1,447	376
	Totals	3,048	4,546

Source: Glasgow Corporation Housing Department, *Review of Operations 1919-47* (Glasgow, 1948), 21-3.

However, from the evidence of Table 5 it is apparent that a Direct Labour section within the Housing Department did not provide any more than a palliative for Glasgow's housing problems, but its major contribution occurred when any attempt to incorporate the working classes within the city's political consensus had least stimulus from the prospect of internal disorder.

IV

The aggregate performance of the city's housing department between the wars can be judged by reference to Table 6. Undoubtedly, most effort went into the construction of three apartment houses, and the number of one, two, and five apartment dwellings was relatively insignificant. The four apartment house ranked a poor second for most of the period, but there is a little evidence of a switch to this form of housing in the last two years of peace. Whether one considers total houses built or total apartments provided

Table 6. Houses completed by the Corporation of Glasgow, 1920-39

Year	1 Apt	2 Apts	3 Apts	4 Apts	5 Apts	Total Houses	Total Apts
1920			250	18		268	822
1921			305	51	48	404	1,359
1922			799	531	240	1,570	5,721
1923		162	1,122	833	244	2,361	8,242
1924		400	232	137	8	777	2,084
1925		324	315	198	86	923	2,815
1926		344	1,048	477	79	1,948	6,135
1927		428	2,329	859	93	3,709	11,744
1928		370	2,372	816	54	3,612	11,390
1929		278	4,659	1,379	51	6,367	20,304
1930		474	2,098	595	61	3,228	9,927
1931		472	1,823	387	3	2,685	7,976
1932		190	1,874	350	2	2,416	7,412
1933	33	288	2,079	433	10	2,843	8,628
1934	33	318	3,310	775	3	4,439	13,714
1935		762	2,386	774	4	3,926	11,798
1936	33	84	1,384	478	6	1,985	6,295
1937		12	1,066	667	96	1,841	6,370
1938			1,154	1,394	240	2,788	10,238
1939			771	1,215	201	2,187	8,178
Totals	99	4,906	31,376	12,367	1,529	50,277	161,152
Average p.a.	4.95	245.3	1,568.8	618.35	76.45	2,513.85	8,057.6

Source: Glasgow Corporation Housing Department, *Review of Operations 1919-47* (Glasgow, 1948), 65.

(perhaps the latter is a better measure of the use of capacity), peaks in the city's building cycle were reached in 1923, 1927, 1929, 1934 and 1938, and troughs were apparent in 1924, 1928 (a slight recession), 1932 and 1936-7. The movements of the city's business cycle and its amplitude conform very closely to changes in the city's building pattern, historically an almost unique phenomenon. Performance was certainly less for the period 1920-9 (21,939 houses comprising 70,616 apartments) than for the following decade (28,338 houses including 90,536 apartments).

Table 7. Corporation House-building, 1920-39, by decades

Decade	Houses %	Apartments %
1920-29	43.64	43.81
1930-39	56.36	56.18

Source: Calculated from Table 6.

An assessment of the role of the Corporation in providing houses can be made from the evidence of the total number of linings granted by the Dean of

Guild Court in the inter-war years. 73,630 linings for new houses were granted, 54,289 of which were for Corporation houses, leaving 19,349 linings for houses to be built by private enterprise. However, the Corporation gave financial assistance to private enterprise to build 10,235, leaving a balance of only 9,106 houses as the private contractors' unaided contribution. Generally the private contractors were satisfying a different market from the Corporation: only 1,529 five apartment houses were built by the city out of a total of 6,410, and none of the 972 houses of six apartments and above.[71]

Table 8.   House Linings, 1919-39

Corporation	73.73%
Private with Corporation assistance	13.9
Private alone	12.37

Source: Glasgow Corporation Housing Department, *Review of Operations 1919-47* (Glasgow, 1948), 26.

Political decisions at Westminster and at the Scottish Office in Edinburgh influenced the total picture most definitely, but local decisions still remained important. The Corporation provided six out of every seven houses built in the city between 1919 and 1939, and thus the total housing market was formed by public policy decisions relating to the payment or non-payment of housing subsidies. But the types of houses built were settled in Glasgow, subject always to the final approval of the Scottish Board of Health.[72] Three main categories were, in fact, erected: tenement houses, built in blocks, two to four storeys in height; flatted or four-in-a-block houses (i.e. a single block with four separate flats, two on the ground floor and two on the upper floor), each with direct access to the street, thus avoiding the use of closes; and cottages, semi-detached or terraced, with pend entrances or back lanes. The number of apartments could be varied within each of these categories, and a few housing schemes mixed houses of each category. Generally, schemes in the central area of the city have been composed entirely of tenements, whereas those on the periphery have demonstrated greatest diversity.[73] The statistical relationship between the various categories built between 1919 and August 1939 (49,366 houses) is given in Table 9.

Table 9.   Corporation Housing, 1919-39, by category

Category	Number	Percentage
Tenement houses	25,537	51.73
Flats	15,552	31.5
Cottages	8,277	16.77

Source: City Architect's Department.

Compared with the earlier history of working-class housing in the city, Glasgow's experience between the wars was markedly different. Tenements dominated the housing story, it is true, but they were not so high, their design and facilities were better, and their population densities were relatively low. Most remarkable was the reaction in favour of four-in-a-block flats, and cottages. Schemes like Mosspark, Knightswood and Carntyne, all begun in the 1920s, had low population densities and had more in common with the garden-suburb ideas of Ebenezer Howard than with earlier indigenous experience. In the 1930s the principal housing effort was designed to ameliorate over-crowding — especially after 1935 — as cheaply as possible, and there was, therefore, a reversion back to tenements as, for instance, in Calton or Blackhill (built 1933-8), where 74 per cent of the housing was of this type.[74]

However, the evidence presented in Table 6 shows clearly that the aim of building 57,000 houses quickly (within fourteen years was the Royal Commission's declared objective) was not fulfilled. Moreover, the shortfall was most marked in the case of four and five apartment houses, whereas the estimate of 25,948 three apartment dwellings was exceeded by 5,428. It is apparent, therefore, that housing policy was not consistently pursued.

The explanations for this, and its short-term results, are worthy of examination. They demonstrate the superficiality of the view that there was a political consensus to provide the houses needed.[75] It was the means whereby provision was to be made and the consistency of effort which really mattered. About these points there was massive political argument, and the numbers and nature of housing Acts indicate the extent of debate and the refusal to accept and to operate existing legislation.

Addison's Act was intended to be temporary, and the restoration of market forces in the Glasgow housing market led by 1924 to a marked decline in the number of houses completed, as dwellings authorised under this statute were finished. Most emphasis by Conservative administrations was placed upon reducing the financial costs of housing policy; demand in Glasgow, in these circumstances, tended to outstrip the supply of houses. John Wheatley, in the debate on the Address (16 December 1924), put the differences between Labour and Conservative administrations in reasonable parliamentary language. Labour

humbly regret that your Majesty's advisers are committed to a policy of leaving the solution of the housing problem mainly to private enterprise and the operation of occupying ownership, thus ignoring the importance of carrying out a long-term scheme of building houses to be let at rents within the means of the working classes, and failing to take every advantage for increasing employment in the building and auxiliary industries.[76]

Conservatives unreservedly argued that the solution of the housing problem could best be achieved by allowing free rein to market forces. In England and Wales response to Neville Chamberlain's Act of 1923 had been very positive: 38,000 houses (13,000 for let) had been built between July 1923 and November 1924; in the whole of Scotland, however, only 915 houses (842 for sale and 73 for let) were erected. Chamberlain hoped for better results in 1925. In mitigation, he pointed to the fact that although only 14,500 houses had been built by local authorities in the United Kingdom, under the terms of his Act, by September 1924 more than 95,000 had been built by private enterprise. He clearly relied upon a filtering up process: dwellings vacated by those who took up new houses provided by the normal operations of the market would gradually become available to the working classes; he argued that there was 'a great reservoir of houses of a standard of accommodation very much in advance of what the working man is in possession today, and these houses will eventually come within his means as their value falls'. Aiding the process of owner-occupation was consistent with the Government's general political objectives:

> The man who owns his own house is always going to be a good citizen. He is always going to be a friend of law and order. He is not going to support those who want to upset the state of society which has enabled him to become a little capitalist. . . .[77]

If Chamberlain was directly concerned with incorporating the working classes within a political consensus based on ownership, his concern was clearly with a very small minority; one suspects that he was not prepared — nor was the Government — to accept the substantial rise in public expenditure and taxation which would be essential to any direct alleviation of the housing problem in cities like Glasgow.

His back-bench supporters were even less committed to government intervention. Austen Hopkinson, M.P. for Mossley, who commonly intervened in housing debates, English and Scottish, put an unequivocal view. Housing subsidies, in his opinion, simply encouraged contractors to put up prices. Practical men always knew better than Governments of whatever party:

> If only Government could be persuaded to keep its meddling fingers out of the pie, we could have got working-class houses at an economic cost. . . . It is absolutely heart-breaking to see the way in which one Government after another prevents the housing problem from being solved.[78]

The rejection of Addison's principle of unlimited Exchequer commitment, implicit in Chamberlain's Act, did not mean the end of subsidies. In fact, the Government agreed to a subsidy of £6 per house annually for twenty years if the local authority could satisfy the Scottish Board of Health that private enterprise could not or would not build the houses.[79] Lump sums or annual subsidies on the same scale were available to individuals to build houses for private occupation, provided certain standards relating to space were met. As Table 10 reveals, the response in Glasgow to these financial opportunities was limited.

When Labour came into office in 1924, the only unquestioned success was John Wheatley. A complex but exceedingly able Red Clydesider, Wheatley combined a deep Roman Catholic commitment to social reform, a strong streak of competence and practicality, a capacity for lucid argument and negotiation mingled with a trenchant wit, and an unquestioning belief in the rightness of socialism. Arthur Greenwood joined him at the Ministry of Health, and together they made both a formidable team in Parliament and a strong empirical contribution to housing policy in the country. The deficiencies of the building industry — the shortage of materials and the lack of skilled men — were precisely pinpointed by expert inquiry, and a fifteen-year programme of house-building was envisaged. Wheatley accepted the findings of the inquiry and attempted to mobilise organised labour and the employers in the implementation of a planned resurgence of the building industry which, he thought, would greatly reduce the dimensions of the housing problem.[80]

The Wheatley Act was not doctrinaire Socialism. For instance, it extended the life of Chamberlain's £6 subsidy beyond 1 October 1925, the date fixed for its termination within the 1923 Act. However, the local authorities no longer had to prove the inadequacy of private enterprise before they could get the financial assistance themselves. Moreover, there was to be a new subsidy of £9 per annum for thirty years (£12.50 in rural districts), to be paid if the houses built met certain conditions: they must be rented to tenants who could not sub-let them; the houses could not be sold by the local authority; the rents had to be based on pre-war rents in the same area. Yet the Government left the building industry to do the job — subject only to fair wages clauses in contracts — and expected housing output under the Act to rise from 90,000 houses in the United Kingdom in 1925 to 225,000 in the period 1934-9. The supply and price of building materials was to be monitored under the Buildings Materials Bill, but the Labour Government fell before this essential element in Wheatley's plans reached the Statute Book.[81]

The Wheatley Act made substantial housing progress possible — even under Conservative administrations — until its subsidy provisions were withdrawn in 1934. As Table 10 makes clear, it was the most significant piece of legislation in Glasgow's experience between the wars, nearly 42 per cent of all houses

Table 10. Houses erected in Glasgow under Housing Acts, 1919-39[82]

Acts	House Purchase	Ordinary	Intermediate	Rehousing	Total	Percentage of 1919-39 total
1919		4,690			4,690	9.08
1923	428	2,052		6,546	9,026	17.47
1924		13,435	8,151		21,586	41.78
1930-35		868	2,961	8,001	11,830	22.89
1939		1,754	2,573	212	4,539	8.78
Totals	428	22,799	13,685	14,759	51,671	100.00

Source: Based on *Third Statistical Account, Glasgow*, ed. J. Cunnison and J. B. S. Gilfillan (Glasgow, 1958), 878, Table 81.

completed with financial assistance from Government being provided under its terms. Nonetheless, political uncertainty about subsidy policy and its future certainly affected housing operations locally. Faced with a threatened cut in subsidies, for instance as in 1929, Glasgow Corporation endeavoured to complete as many houses as possible (see Table 6) and did not put out more contracts to tender until the true situation was known. Thus, future housing progress could be jeopardised, even when other circumstances made significant advances possible.[83]

A steady fall in the cost of building between 1924 and 1935, for example, aided the fulfilment of Wheatley's housing objectives. Evidence relating to costs of three and four apartment flats is given for particular years in Table 11. The decision to end the subsidy under Addison's Act and rising interest rates

Table 11.   Cost (£) per house for flats (4 in block), 1919-39

Year	3 Apt	4 Apt	Year	3 Apt	4 Apt
1919	721	—	1930	330	366
1920	823	913	1931	325	360
1921	847	953	1932	320	358
1922	507	578	1934	298	327
1923	392	450	1935	283	318
1924	425	488	1936	320	365
1927	410	461	1937	366	417
1928	365	411	1938	400	456
1929	345	380	1939	400	456

Source: Glasgow Corporation Housing Department, *Review of Operations 1919-47* (Glasgow, 1948), 80.

in 1921 attacked demand in the public and private sectors alike, and builders' prices were already falling before the Building Costs Committee reported in that year. This fall was arrested in 1924 as Chamberlain's Act and the promise of Wheatley's Act made demand apparently buoyant once more. In Scotland, as a whole, tender prices rose by 45 per cent in that year, and the Scottish Board of Health began to refuse to approve contracts which it deemed to be too expensive.[84] As Table 6 indicates, Glasgow's house-building performance in 1924 and 1925 was very poor judged by earlier standards.

However, as the Chamberlain and Wheatley Acts made their impact on demand in the form of a steady and continuous building programme, economies of scale influenced costs more and more, as did improvements in the supply of materials and labour. The Conservative Government naturally took account of falling costs in determining the levels of subsidy, and in 1928 reduced Chamberlain's £6 subsidy to £4 and prepared to cut Wheatley's £9 subsidy to £7.50 for houses completed after 30 September 1929. The advent of the second Labour Government in the summer of 1929 saved Wheatley's subsidy entirely but allowed the reduction in Chamberlain's subsidy to stand. However, as we have already noticed, disorganisation of the housing programme had already occurred because of the political uncertainty surrounding subsidy policy.[85]

The Greenwood Act of 1930 was essentially aimed at slum clearance, as Table 10 broadly indicates. It gave cities such as Glasgow powers to clear slum areas for redevelopment and offered a subsidy of £2.50 per person rehoused for forty years. This Act significantly changed the objectives of subsidy policy. It linked the subsidy to people instead of to the houses built for them, and therefore discriminated in favour of rehousing large families. Since large families tended to be poorer than small families — and the subsidy per house increased according to the number of persons per family — the rate of subsidy rose as rent-paying capacity fell. With lower building costs and relatively higher subsidies, rehousing the slum dweller became a serious possibility although, as Table 10 makes clear, slum clearance in Glasgow had begun under the terms of Chamberlain's Act.[86]

The early thirties might have seen a greater building effort without a corresponding increase in municipal rates, had it not been for the severe depression and the cuts in public expenditure which accompanied it. Interest rates fell after 1932, and rents of under 25p per week were technically feasible without calling upon ratepayers to contribute more than the statutory rate for slum clearance.

The general story of how the National Government cut housing expenditure in Scotland, under the terms of the Housing Act of 1933, is relatively well known. Gradual reductions in subsidies, and finally the end of them in 1935 — except for slum clearance — account both for the frenzy with which Glasgow Corporation attempted to complete houses before subsidies ended (see Table 6) and for directional changes, demonstrated in Table 10, in favour of rehousing. Thus, local authorities, such as Glasgow, were left to supply demand, ineffective in the face of normal market forces, while the ordinary housing requirements of citizens were to be met by unsubsidised private enterprise with the help of building society loans guaranteed by the Government.[87]

Unfortunately, private enterprise built only to sell and — apart from slum clearance housing — Glasgow Corporation, under a Labour administration after 1933, could only supply more working-class houses by increasing the burden on the rates, already large by contemporary standards.[88] To keep the rates down, rents had to be economic and, therefore, beyond the means of the poorer-paid. Ironically, housing built under the Wheatley Act had also allowed the 'filtering up' of some poorer workers into houses left vacant by their more affluent fellows. But this process had limits, and the Housing Act of 1933 accentuated the problem of overcrowding because it gradually slowed down the pace of building as reductions in subsidies became effective.

Overcrowding outside the slums was the subject of an inquiry by the Scottish Board of Health established in 1933; its findings became the basis for the Housing Act of 1935. This re-launched subsidies for the relief of overcrowded families at £6.75 per annum for forty years for each house built. In Glasgow a survey published in 1935 showed that of 262,900 families living in the city, 82,109 (over 31 per cent) were overcrowded under the not particularly exacting standards laid down in the 1935 Act. The greatest problem existed in two apartment houses, where 46,929 overcrowded families lived. Moreover, 10,440 condemned houses were found occupied during the course of the survey. Thus, an intransigent problem remained, despite the attempts of the Corporation to deal with it: 10,695 new houses were needed so that all condemned houses could be demolished; 50,800 houses were still required to meet normal replacement levels, without dealing with the problems of the homeless or of those about to be married.[89] More generous subsidies were made available under the terms of the Housing Act of 1938,[90] and these, it was hoped, would act as an incentive to the permanent solution of the housing problem. However, the second world war frustrated the fulfilment of this objective.

V

In conclusion, it is evident that the implementation of the Corporation's housing policy was inadequate to deal with the housing requirements of the city's population. Changes in Government policy relating to housing subsidies prevented a consistent response to the major problem of an under-supply of suitable houses. In the immediate post-war period and again after 1935, the building industry's deficiencies were a marked feature of that failure. Substantial provision of subsidies simply compounded an overloading of the industry and raised costs in both periods (see Table 11).[91]

About the question of whether housing policy actually made a contribution to a general 'programme' of incorporating the working classes and reducing class awareness and identity, I can only express doubts. It is true that John Wheatley and others saw housing reform as 'the Red Cross work of the class struggle',[92] but there seem to have been as many bloodstained victims of urban deprivation after their activities as before. For the working classes in Glasgow, the reality was often the possibility of a lifetime's wait on a housing list, closed in 1933 with 80,000 names on it; a social stigma associated with being lucky enough to be rehoused from slum property; overcrowding if the rent could be paid and eviction if it could not; key money and rack-renting in small properties as rent decontrol increased the opportunities of many ruthless factors and landlords. The worship of market forces emerged as the most significant reason for intellectual disputes about, and practical differences in, housing policy. From the housing situation in the city between the wars, one would not have expected that Red Clydeside would have adopted a paler shade by 1939, and if there really was in George Square a revolutionary moment in 1919, there was no need for it to pass away.[93]

Notes

1.   Although it is invidious to particularise, I have in mind *inter alia* the work of John Foster, Eric Hobsbawm, E. P. Thompson, Neil J. Smelser and Harold J. Perkin.

2.   W. Smart, *The Housing Problem and the Municipality* (1902); H. W. Bull, 'Working-Class Housing in Glasgow, 1866-1902' (unpublished Strath-

clyde M.Litt. thesis, 1974); J. Butt, 'Working-Class Housing in Glasgow, 1851-1914', in *The History of Working-Class Housing*, ed. S. D. Chapman (Newton Abbot, 1971), 57-92; A. J. Jury, *Glasgow's Housing Centenary 1866-1966* (1966); A. Slaven, *The Development of the West of Scotland 1750-1960* (1975), 230 ff.

3.   Glasgow City Archives [G.C.A.], C3/2/18 Minutes of Evidence taken before Glasgow Municipal Commission on Housing (1902-3), passim.

4.   B.P.P. 1917-18 Cd. 8731, Report of the Royal Commission on the Housing of the Industrial Population of Scotland, Rural and Urban.

5.   G.C.A., DTC 8/19/1, Executive Committee on Housing Reports, 21 Mar. 1912.

6.   Ibid., 31 Aug. 1905.

7.   Ibid., Report on Insanitary and Obstructive Buildings, 1910.

8.   Ibid., Report by Town Clerk, 1913.

9.   Ibid., Report by Peter Fyfe on the Housing Question, 1914.

10.   Ibid., Medical Officer of Health's Reports on Insanitary Buildings, 1908-10.

11.   Ibid., Report of Deputation on visit to English housing estates, 12 Dec. 1912.

12.   Ibid., Peter Fyfe on the Housing Question, 1914.

13.   Ibid., Sir John Lindsay on the Housing Question, 1913.

14.   Ibid., W. E. Whyte and W. Gordon, *Law of Housing in Scotland* (1938).

15.   G.C.A., DTC 8/19/1, City Assessor's Memorandum to the Lord Provost, June 1913.

16.   Ibid., Housing Report, Aug. 1913; Submission by House Factors and House Owners, 1914.

17.   Cf. especially H. W. Bull, op. cit.; C. M. Allen, 'The Genesis of British Urban Redevelopment with general reference to Glasgow', *Economic History Review*, Second Series, xviii, 1967-8, 711-30.

18.   G.C.A., DTC 8/18, Notes on Housing, 1920.

19.   Ibid., DTC 8/19, Statement re difficulties encountered in connection with housing schemes, 1914.

20.   Ibid.

21.   Butt, op. cit., Table 2.1 on p. 60.

22.   B.P.P., 1914-16, Cd. 8111, Report of the Committee appointed to inquire into the increase of house rents (Scotland), 3.

23.   Ibid., 3-4.

24.   Ibid., 4-5.

25.   G.C.A., DTC 8/19/1/1, Executive Committee on Housing Papers, Report, 12 Dec. 1916.

26.   B.P.P., 1914-16, Cd. 8111, 5-98.

27.   P. Rowland, *Lloyd George* (1975), 237, 278 and 450; R. K. Middlemas, *The Clydesiders* (1965), 61-2; D. Kirkwood, *My Life of Revolt* (1935), 58, 108-110.

28.   G.C.A., DTC 8/19/1, Report on Housing, 12 Dec. 1916.
29.   Ibid., Report on Housing for year ending 31 Dec. 1916.
30.   Ibid., DTC 8/18, Notes on Housing, 1920.
31.   Ibid.
32.   Ibid., City Chamberlain's Notes, Aug. 1919.
33.   Annual Report of the Scottish Board of Health, 1919.
34.   G.C.A. DTC 8/18, Estimate sent to Scottish Board of Health, 15 Oct. 1919; Abstract of areas suitable for building, 1919.
35.   P. Rowland, op. cit., 463, 466 and 508.
36.   B. W. E. Alford, *Depression and Recovery? British Economic Growth 1918-1939* (1972), 30-9; R. S. Sayers, 'The Return to Gold 1925', chap. xii in *Studies in the Industrial Revolution*, ed. L. S. Pressnell (1960); *The Gold Standard and Employment Policies Between the Wars*, ed. S. Pollard (1970).
37.   9 and 10 Geo. V, ch. 60.
38.   Cd. 8731 (1917-18), para. 22.
39.   Ibid., para. 28.
40.   Ibid., para. 413.
41.   Ibid., para. 414.
42.   Ibid., para. 625.
43.   Ibid., para. 626.
44.   Ibid., para. 572.
45.   Ibid., para. 646.
46.   Ibid., paras. 671-2.
47.   Ibid., para. 674.
48.   Ibid., para. 667; my judgments here have also been greatly influenced by the unpublished work of J. Dillon who studied the Springburn housing situation in this period and by the researches of J. McKee who is currently examining the housing of the working classes in Polmadie. Cf. also *Report of the Inter-Departmental Committee on the Rent Restriction Acts*, Cd. 5621 (1937-8), 16.
49.   Cd. 8731, para. 572.
50.   G.C.A., DTC 8/18, Estimate to Scottish Board of Health.
51.   Cd. 8731, paras. 707, 711, 728.
52.   Ibid., paras. 794-804.
53.   Ibid., paras. 822-831.
54.   Ibid., paras. 844-857.
55.   Ibid., paras. 1592, 1924, 1938.
56.   Ibid., para. 2223.
57.   Ibid., paras. 2223-2230.
58.   B.P.P. 1917-18, Cd. 8669, paras. 3-8.
59.   J. H. Thomas, M.P., *When Labour Rules* (Glasgow, 1929), 66-74.
60.   P. Rowland, op. cit., 510 and 540; B. B. Gilbert, *British Social Policy 1914-39* (1970), 48-50 and 137-58; E. D. Simon, *The Anti-Slum Campaign* (1933), 3-14; C. Addison, *The Betrayal of the Slums* (1922), passim.
61.   *Hansard*, 14 Nov. 1918; G.C.A., DTC 8/18/2, Scottish Board of Health

to Town Clerk, 9 Dec. 1921; Glasgow Corporation Housing Department, *Review of Operations, 1919 to 1927* (Glasgow, 1928), 5-7.

62. G.C.A., Medical Officer of Health Report, 1921; DTC 8/18, 1920-2, Wm McMurdo to Town Clerk, 30 Mar. 1920.

63. B.P.P. 1921, Cd. 1411, Report of the Committee of Inquiry into the High Cost of Building Working-Class Dwellings in Scotland, 1-10.

64. Ibid., 11.

65. Ibid.; cf. also James Stewart, M.P. for Glasgow St. Rollox: 'In Glasgow today we have reached that stage when builders are not making offers. There is now no competition', *Hansard*, 16 Dec. 1924.

66. Cd. 1411 (1921), 13-17.

67. G.C.A., DTC 8/18/1920-2, Peter Fyfe to Town Clerk, 1 Apr. 1921; DTC 8/18/1922-3, Neil Livingstone to Town Clerk, 6 Jan. 1922.

68. Cd. 1411 (1921), p. 26; Glasgow Corporation Housing Department, *Review of Operations 1919-47* (Glasgow, 1948), 20-1; *Hansard*, 14 and 22 June 1933; G.C.A., DTC 8/18/1922-3, Statement of Progress as at 31 Aug. 1923.

69. G.C.A., DTC 8/18/1922-3, City Chamberlain to Town Clerk, 11 Feb. 1922; Director of Housing to Town Clerk, 4 Feb. 1922; *Review of Operations 1919-47*, 21-2.

70. *Review of Operations 1919-47*, 22-3.

71. Ibid., 26.

72. G.C.A., DTC 8/18/1922-3. This source reveals constant communication between the Corporation and the Scottish Board of Health regarding all aspects of municipal housing: contracts, tenders, rents, building supplies, house factors, tenants.

73. Cf. Roger Smith, 'Multi-dwelling Building in Scotland, 1750-1970: A study based on housing in the Clyde Valley', in *Multi-Storey Living: The British Working Class Experience*, ed. Anthony Sutcliffe (1974), 217-222, especially Table F.2.

74. Smith, op. cit., 219; G.C.A., DTC 8/18/1922-3, Statement of Progress as at 31 Aug. 1923; *Third Statistical Account: Glasgow*, 881-2, Table 85.

75. Cf. B. B. Gilbert, op. cit., vii.

76. *Hansard*, 16 Dec. 1924.

77. Ibid.

78. Ibid.

79. R. D. Cramond, *Housing Policy in Scotland 1919-1964: A Study in State Assistance* (Glasgow, 1966), 14; 13 & 14 Geo. V, ch. 24.

80. R. W. Lyman, *The First Labour Government 1924* (1957), 110-127; R. K. Middlemas, op. cit., 35-41, 46-54, 136-9, 145-152. Wheatley had published a pamphlet in Oct. 1913 called *Eight Pound Cottages for Glasgow Citizens* in which he argued that the profits made by Glasgow Municipal Tramways should be used to subsidise rents.

81. 14 and 15 Geo. V, ch. 35; Lyman, op. cit., 115 ff.; Gilbert, op. cit., 199-200; Middlemas, op. cit., 155-9.

82.   The categories — Ordinary, Intermediate and Rehousing — were adopted in the 1930s to distinguish between levels of rent:

i   Ordinary houses were let at economic rents.

ii   Intermediate houses were let at sub-economic rents to families living in overcrowded conditions, after a means test.

iii   Rehousing was the category provided by higher subsidies for slum clearance. Dwellings were, therefore, let at particularly low rents, subject again to a means test.

83.   This is apparent from annual reports issued by the Scottish Board of Health. Cf. also R. D. Cramond, op. cit., 17-18.

84.   R. D. Cramond, op. cit., 15-16; Annual Report of Scottish Board of Health, 1924.

85.   R. D. Cramond, op. cit., 17.

86.   20 and 21 Geo. V, ch. 40. Chamberlain's Act of 1923 gave a 50 per cent subsidy for slum clearance; cf. E. D. Simon, op. cit., 15-41.

87.   Annual Reports of Scottish Board of Health, Cd. 4469, 1934 and 1935; cf. also speech of A. N. Skelton, Under Secretary for Scotland, reported in *Hansard*, 22 June 1933.

88.   *Review of Operations 1919-1947*, 27-8; *Third Statistical Account: Glasgow*, 879, Table 83.

89.   B.P.P. 1936, Cd. 5171, Department of Health for Scotland, Housing Overcrowding Survey of 1935, Table III; *Review of Operations 1919-1947*, 29-34.

90.   R. D. Cramond, op. cit., 23; Annual Report of the Department of Health for Scotland, 1938, Cd. 5968.

91.   H. W. Richardson and D. H. Aldcroft, *Building in The British Economy between the Wars* (1968), 123-6, and 174 ff.

92.   *Hansard*, 16 Dec. 1924.

93.   I am grateful to my colleagues, Professor J. T. Ward, Dr W. H. Fraser and Dr J. H. Treble for their comments and help and to Mrs E. M. Thrippleton who typed this essay.

Some Aspects of the 1926 General Strike in Scotland

Ian MacDougall

IN Scotland, as it seems elsewhere in Britain, trade unions made virtually no preparations for a General Strike until a few days before the Strike began on Tuesday, 4 May. The Scottish Trades Union Congress, though an autonomous body, awaited a lead from the British T.U.C. — a lead that did not come until the eve of the Strike.

To an enquiry in February 1926 from the S.T.U.C. General Council about the attitude of the T.U.C. toward maintenance of essential services in the event of large industrial disputes, Citrine, the acting general secretary, replied that the T.U.C. General Council's Special Industrial Committee was 'not in a position to make a declaration of policy on the subject at the moment'.[1] As Joseph F. Duncan, president of the S.T.U.C. in 1925-6, afterward put it: 'Until a strike was decided on by the T.U.C. we did not know what to do.'[2]

A fortnight before the Strike began, the S.T.U.C. annual congress passed unanimously an emergency resolution supporting the miners' struggle to defend their existing conditions, and calling on the British and Scottish T.U.C.s to continue their co-operation with the Miners' Federation in preventing any lowering of working-class conditions.[3] The first part of another resolution, moved by Peter Kerrigan, Communist leader of the Minority Movement in Glasgow, was also carried, calling for 'effective preparations' by the working class against 'the Capitalist Offensive', which preparations should include support by the S.T.U.C. General Council for the Workers' Industrial Alliance — the projected defensive alliance of unions in heavy industry and transport. But the second part of this resolution, which instructed the General Council to discuss with the Scottish Co-operative Wholesale Society means of concerting co-operative and trade union resistance to the capitalist attack, was struck out and replaced by an amendment from the General Council itself. This asked the Council to keep in touch with the British T.U.C. 'in any effort to resist the capitalist attack'.[4] A second motion by Kerrigan, endorsing the formation of Workers' Defence Corps and instructing the General Council not only to help form them but to take the lead in coordinating them in Scotland under unified control, was defeated by a large majority.[5] Directly the Congress was over, the General Council sent its secretary, William Elger, to London to find out what steps the British T.U.C.

was taking in the developing crisis. A few days later the S.T.U.C. General Council was represented by Elger and its president, Peter Webster, at the Farringdon Hall conference of trade union executives which approved the calling of the General Strike.[6] On the question of preparations for a big industrial struggle, then, the S.T.U.C. lay very much in the shadow of the T.U.C.

Among trade unions and trades councils in Scotland, only those where left-wing influence was dominant or strong appear to have urged preparations in the months or weeks before the General Strike began. Thus Glasgow Trades and Labour Council, which had affiliated the previous year to the Minority Movement, agreed on 24 March by 102-88 votes to press the T.U.C. and Labour Party to set up Workers' Defence Corps.[7] Aberdeen Trades Council's executive committee received two circulars in January and March from the Minority Movement, and agreed on 19 April to recommend a resolution urging 'effective preparations . . . by the working class', and in particular support for the Workers' Industrial Alliance.[8] Douglas Browett, a tramwayman and activist in Aberdeen in 1926, long afterward recalled that before the General Strike he had urged that the T.U.C. make preparations such as setting up emergency organisations, creating a system of couriers, and providing for publication of a Strike bulletin, 'but nothing concrete emerged locally from this'.[9] In Fife, Lochgelly Trades and Labour Council, which was not affiliated to the Scottish T.U.C., called a conference early in the spring to prepare for the approaching crisis. The conference set up a Central Committee of Action for Fife, Kinross and Clackmannan.[10] Methil and District Trades and Labour Council held 'a large and enthusiastic' meeting of delegates in the last week of April to discuss unity of action, and agreed that a Workers' Defence Corps be set up.[11] A few miles to the west, at Thornton, local activists arranged shortly before the Strike for a large store of petrol to be gathered for use by motor cycle messengers.[12] In Lanarkshire, where the Minority Movement was strong, some twenty-three Councils of Action had been set up by the end of April, and energetic attempts were made by William Allan, president of the Scottish Section of the Minority Movement and member of the executive of the Lanarkshire Miners' Union, as well as by other militant local leaders, to arouse awareness and make preparations for the impending struggle.[13]

In addition to the Minority Movement and the Communist Party,[14] more militant sections of the Independent Labour Party in Scotland also urged preparations in advance of the Strike. The author of a women's column in the Edinburgh weekly independent labour paper *Labour Standard* on 7 November 1925 called on workers to store oatmeal, flour, macaroni, sago, lentils and other foodstuffs in their homes in preparation for the struggle. The paper frequently used its editorials to press for action in preparation for a renewed struggle in May, calling in December 1925, for example, for 'unceasing effort' to strengthen the Workers' Industrial Alliance and the General Council of the T.U.C.: 'by next May they *must* be fool-proof'.[15]

Despite exhortations or activities such as these, the general situation in Scotland until two or three days before the Strike began was one of lack of preparation by the organised working-class movement. In addition to the failure or refusal of the T.U.C. to provide any lead, there was a disinclination among some rank and file trade unionists to believe that a big industrial upheaval would in fact occur. As a militant Fife miner later recalled: 'I don't think many people, because of bitter disappointments in the past, actually felt that the General Strike would take place. A number of us decided to hold a meeting on the Sunday prior to the General Strike at Denbeath Bridge, Methil. We had to cancel it for lack of attendance. But we had a meeting the next Sunday when the Strike was on, and one could hardly see the back of the crowd.'[16] In Lanarkshire, too, some miners had 'believed up to the last moment that the Strike would not be called'.[17]

In contrast, preparations by the Government were well advanced in Scotland before the Strike began on 4 May. As early as 7 August 1925, only a week after Red Friday, the Cabinet had agreed that a permanent headquarters be set up in each area of the country where detailed emergency arrangements could be worked out.[18] A representative of the Scottish Office was always present at the meetings of officials concerned with the Emergency Organisation that were held fortnightly from November at the Home Office in London under the chairmanship of Sir John Anderson, permanent under-secretary. These meetings discussed such business as the listing of volunteers and the availability of heavy motor vehicles and cars that could be loaned to the police.[19] The Government's proposed arrangements for Scotland were set out in Circular No. 2,076 of 21 November 1925 from the Scottish Office to local authorities. The basic aim of these arrangements was to create 'a decentralised organisation designed to secure the maintenance of services essential to the well-being of the community'. The whole scheme was to go into operation directly an emergency was declared. An emergency headquarters would be set up in Edinburgh by the Scottish Office under a minister (the lord advocate, William Watson, K.C., M.P., was appointed) acting for the secretary of state and other government departments. This headquarters was to work in close co-operation with the local authorities, the sheriffs, the Post Office and other departments that normally extended over the whole of Britain. A headquarters branch was to be set up at Glasgow, centre of the Western Division, with Sir Arthur Rose, a leading public administrator, as district commissioner. Other district commissioners, acting under the instructions of headquarters in Edinburgh, would be appointed at Inverness, Aberdeen, Dundee, and Edinburgh itself, with responsibility for these centres and their surrounding counties. Each district commissioner was to have a staff dealing with questions of transport, food, and if necessary voluntary workers, and would co-operate closely with local officials of government departments dealing with shipping, docks, petrol supplies, postal services, and coal. District commissioners and their staffs were to keep in touch with the town and county councils in their areas, and local authorities were asked to co-operate with their district commissioner in running enrolment centres for voluntary workers. Questions of food distribution and road transport were to be handled by district food and road officers and by road haulage committees, with a road commissioner at Scottish headquarters. Vehicles were where necessary to be transferred from less to more important services, on the orders of the district commissioner or road officer. Supply and distribution of coal, and control of the consumption of gas and electricity were also provided for. Maintenance of law and order was, of course, to be the responsibility of the police, but local authorities 'might co-operate, for instance, in securing able-bodied citizens of good character to serve as special constables'. Local authorities were thus expected to be responsible for maintaining local public utility services, and to co-operate with the national emergency organisation in transport and distribution of coal; while, unless plans had to be altered, the government would be responsible for shipping, railway and postal communications, and docks and harbours where the local authority was not already the Port authority.

The immediate response from local authorities to this Scottish Office circular was in most cases a bare acknowledgement.[20] Only one or two councils, as at Aberdeen and Lochgelly, expressed 'open opposition' to the proposals.[21]

By 15 April 1926, when a conference of the Scottish Emergency Organisation, the naval and military authorities, and the Ministry of Transport, was held in Edinburgh, the government's preparations appear to have been complete with one exception. Questions such as daily liaison among the authorities, protection of vulnerable points and of food convoys, petrol and road transport, yeast supplies, movement of troops, the role of the O.M.S. (Organisation for the Maintenance of Supplies), and even the concentration of explosives at four places — Ardeer, Polmont, Camilty Mill, and Crombie — had been discussed and in most cases settled.[22]

The one aspect of the government's preparations which remained incomplete until a couple of days before the General Strike began was the supply of voluntary workers or, as trade unionists regarded them, blacklegs. As early as September 1925 the Scottish Office had been offered the services in an emergency of the Fascists in Glasgow. Their leader, the Earl of Glasgow, informed Sir John Gilmour, the secretary of state, that the Glasgow Fascists had been divided into two groups. One consisted of 'special service men' — motor and train drivers, ship winch workers, and those who knew how to work coal mine pumps or electricity and water power plants. The other group contained all the remaining Fascists, who were ready 'to take on as special constables'. The Earl claimed that the Fascists numbered 2,000, and that recruits, especially working men and unemployed, were daily enlarging this number.[23] The secretary of state and his officials, while anxious to obtain lists of Fascists willing to volunteer, were careful in their dealings with the Earl to emphasise that Fascists must volunteer for emergency work as individuals, and that the government could not have any official connection with them as an organised group. Eventually, on 16 February 1926, the Earl of Glasgow agreed with Sir Arthur Rose that 'in the event of trouble his men will join the Roll of Voluntary Workers as individual volunteers'.[24]

The Roll of Voluntary Workers had existed in Glasgow for some years before 1926 'with the simple aim of enrolling persons willing to maintain services in an emergency'.[25] A division of labour had been agreed at the beginning of January between Scottish Office officials and Colonel A. C. H. Maclean, organiser in Scotland of the Organisation for the Maintenance of Supplies: the Roll of Voluntary Workers to enrol volunteers in Glasgow, the O.M.S. to do so elsewhere in Scotland.[26] The Roll of Voluntary Workers appear to have enlisted about 2,000 volunteers before the General Strike began.[27] Some other volunteers were provided in Glasgow by the National Citizens' Union, which claimed in the April 1926 issue of its quarterly, *The Citizens' Journal*: 'We are not strike-breaking. We are only anxious to save the nation.'

Although the General Council of the 'strictly non-political and non-party' O.M.S. in Scotland was formed on 23 February 1926, 'it was not until 17th April that it really came into the open, through the appeal made by the President, The Earl of Stair'.[28] By then, or shortly afterward, the O.M.S. had opened over a score of branches in Scotland, including six in Edinburgh, seven in Roxburghshire and Selkirkshire, five in Fife and Kinross, and one in Dundee. The public appeal by the Earl of Stair on 17 April for O.M.S. volunteers 'brought in a very considerable response'. On the day before the General Strike began, a branch was opened in Peebles, but efforts to open one a few days earlier at Lanark were 'absolutely stultified'. Other branches were about to be formed at Dumfries, Alloa and Dumbarton, but the Strike began before they had taken shape.

In his subsequent report on the work of the O.M.S., Captain A. R. Dunlop, its general secretary in Scotland, identified four obstacles to recruitment before the Strike. One was apathy, 'the almost universal opinion . . . held up to the last moment, that a general strike would be avoided'. Thus enrolment at Dundee, where an O.M.S. branch was opened on 9 April, was at first 'somewhat slow'. Another obstacle was 'suspicion that the O.M.S. was a Tory organisation'. A third was the view that the O.M.S. was 'intruding upon the prerogative of the Government whose duty it was to take measures in advance to prevent the stoppage of essential services'. Finally, the O.M.S. seemed before the Strike not to be a body that 'offered any special attractions. It asked people to volunteer beforehand to do what they fully intended to do when the emergency arose (but which in the minds of the majority was very doubtful) and which it was known the authorities had made preparations for'.[29] Dunlop was reported early in March to be 'mournfully' describing O.M.S. recruitment in Edinburgh as 'sticky'.[30] Precisely how many volunteers the O.M.S. had enrolled in Scotland before the Strike began is not clear, but it must have been at least several hundreds.

II

When the General Strike began at midnight on Monday, 3 May, the response in Scotland by those unions called out by the T.U.C. in support of the miners appears to have been generally very strong, though, of course, allowance must be made for some exaggeration in reports from either side. Among transport unions, the railwaymen seem to have come out solidly. Members of A.S.L.E. & F., who in Glasgow and west of Scotland numbered about 2,500, were reported to be 'practically out to a man'.[31] The News Bulletin issued by head office of the National Union of Railwaymen on the evening of 4 May indicated that, in a random list of almost forty Scots branches, only Forres with four and Polmont with three had members who refused to strike. At Aberdeen, the position was said to be, 'On Strike, 1,200; Blacklegs — nil';[32] at Perth, 1,500 were reported on strike, and only four men working;[33] at Thornton Junction in Fife, only one N.U.R. member refused to strike — an elderly man allegedly hoping for promotion to locomotive inspector;[34] at Glasgow and the surrounding district, where the N.U.R. strength was about 25,000, the union delegate told Glasgow Trades and Labour Council on 5 May that 'their members were out 100 per cent'.[35] At Stranraer, where several hundred railwaymen were employed, all but four struck work; and at Stirling, 'only about a dozen' railwaymen out of some 500 N.U.R., A.S.L.E. & F., and Railway Clerks Association members did not strike — indeed the strikers claimed that only one driver and one clerk had reported for work on 4 May. Castle Douglas was perhaps unique in having so high a proportion as half (fifteen out of thirty-three) of its railwaymen remain at work.[36]

The General Strike was the first national strike that the Railway Clerks Association had ever taken part in, but the response by its members was 'highly gratifying'. At Aberdeen, Edinburgh, and at Glasgow — where over 2,000 were out — the strike by the railway clerks was said to range from '80 per cent to absolute solidarity'.[37] On the other hand, an anonymous article published after the Strike, while admitting that 86 per cent of all L.M.S. employees in Scotland went on strike on 4 May, claimed that only 37 per cent of the company's clerks did so.[38]

An indication of the solidity of the railwaymen's response was provided by the number of trains running in the first few days of the Strike. At Dumfries, only two engines had moved by the fifth day; at Elgin and Galashiels for the first two days and at Peterhead for the first three, there were no trains at all; and throughout all nine days of the Strike, there was only one train at Stranraer and at Fraserburgh.[39] On the entire L.N.E.R. system in Scotland only two trains ran on the first day of the Strike, and only about seven on the L.M.S. lines.[40]

Among road transport workers, members of the Transport and General Workers' Union were reported to have responded solidly.[41] Union organisation was weak among busmen, but some private bus companies did not run buses after the first day or two of the Strike, and the S.M.T. bus company based on Edinburgh and the Lothians did not run any buses at all throughout the Strike, as the risk of stone-throwing in mining areas was too great.[42] The Scottish T.U.C. claimed in the middle of the Strike that, 'During the last two days unorganised workers on road transport and buses have been throwing in their lot with the strikers in large numbers.'[43] But some members of the other chief road transport union in Scotland, the Scottish Horse and Motormen's Association, showed reluctance to respond to the T.U.C.'s call, and the Association came in for a good deal of sharp criticism from other strikers.[44]

Rather more precision is available concerning the response by municipal tramwaymen. At Aberdeen, at least 600 of the total Tramways Department staff of 639 appear to have struck work; and the Edinburgh and Glasgow tramwaymen were said to be 'practically all out'.[45] In Edinburgh all but 196 of the 1,180 drivers and conductors employed on the trams and corporation buses struck work at midnight on 3 May. At Dundee no trams at all ran between 4 and 10 May.[46]

The response by dockers was complete. At Aberdeen, 818 were said to be on strike on 4 May and there was only one blackleg.[47] At Glasgow, where the men were 'solid', employers were reported to have offered to pay blacklegs sixteen shillings per shift but 'there were no takers'.[48] There seems to have been a similarly solid response in Dundee; the Methil docks were reported 'deserted'; at Leith, all 2,000 dockers, as well as virtually all the dredgermen, plate-layers, labourers, and cranemen came out.[49] At Grangemouth, where normally about 2,000 dockers were employed, 'a Sabbatic calm rested over the docks' on 4 May.[50] In Orkney, Kirkwall dockers struck work after the weekly vessels bringing supplies to the island had been unloaded.[51]

Among the printing unions, which had also been instructed by the T.U.C. to cease work from 4 May, the Scottish Typographical Association was not affiliated to the T.U.C. It had therefore not been represented at the Farringdon Hall conference of union executives in London between 29 April and 1 May. Nonetheless the Executive Council of the S.T.A. had already decided that week-end to instruct its members to give a fortnight's notice from 8 May. When, however, the T.U.C.'s instructions were received on 3 May, the S.T.A. Executive was hurriedly recalled to Glasgow to decide whether the Association should observe its agreement with employers, including the necessary fort-night's notice, or obey the T.U.C.'s instructions. After a lengthy debate it was unanimously agreed to carry out the latter, and the response by members was 'nearly 100 per cent'. At Dundee, for example, only one member out of 450 refused to strike.[52]

Other printing unions also appear to have responded very well in Scotland.[53] In the newspaper industry, however, the National Union of Journalists was not affiliated to the T.U.C. Its five branches in Scotland, as elsewhere, were instructed by the Union's Emergency Committee by telegram on 3 May that they were not on strike and were not being called on to abandon normal duties. But they were not to do work of other departments in producing newspapers, or to continue their own work if non-union labour were introduced into other departments. An explanatory letter from H. M. Richardson, general secretary, on 4 May instructed journalists not to supply copy where any printers remained at work in defiance of their own unions' instructions to strike. Glasgow branch of the Journalists obeyed head office instructions, but Edinburgh branch 'claimed complete liberty of action for all members', and Dundee branch by a three-to-one majority repudiated the instructions altogether.[54] The response of the Fife branch of the union is not known, but two-thirds of the Aberdeen branch members were still on strike on 12 May.[55]

The response by the printers and pressmen considerably affected publication of newspapers in Scotland during the Strike. Of some 210 Scots daily, evening or weekly papers (excepting technical and church publications) normally published in 1926, it has so far proved possible to examine 138. Of these, seventy-four were able to appear during the Strike, though in the case of twenty-five, in smaller format only, or with fewer pages or less than usual frequency. Sixty-four papers were unable to publish at all.

Of unions in other industries called out in the 'first line' by the T.U.C., the iron and steel workers responded well in Scotland, the only refusals to strike being at Wishaw, Lugar, and Gartsherrie.[56] At Gartsherrie, what seems to have been a tradition of paternalism and deference[57] expressed itself in 'vigorous resentment' of pickets and the singing by the non-strikers' womenfolk of *God Save the King* 'and other patriotic airs'.[58]

Among the building trades the response by some unions is less certain. Under the T.U.C. instructions 'all commercial and luxury building' was to be stopped, together with the making of equipment for such building, but work on housing was to continue.[59] The Amalgamated Union of Building Trade Workers complained that other building unions remained at work on jobs where its own members were called out, because 'there was more desire to protect the funds of their unions by our comrades in other trades than to apply the desires of the T.U.C.'.[60] How far this was the case in Scotland, where the A.U.B.T.W. had 2,500 members,[61] is not clear. But in Glasgow, the Central Strike Co-ordinating Committee found it difficult to restrain building trade workers employed on housing from joining the Strike when it began; and members of the Operative Masons and Monumental Building Workers' Association of Scotland appear to have stopped work.[62] In Edinburgh the response of the building trades was described by the Official Strike Bulletin as 'solid'; and subsequently the local weekly *Labour Standard* claimed that although 'most of their members should, under T.U.C. instructions, have remained at work few would tie themselves down to work, and every means by which they could find excuse for joining in the fight was explored so that the first week-end saw practically the whole of the masons, bricklayers, plasterers, plumbers, and joiners lined up to resist depression'.[63] The only building union about whose response any substantial quantitative evidence survives was the Scottish Painters' Society. A sub-committee of its Executive Council decided on 3 May that all members employed in the industry, including all working on housing, should strike — but not until Thursday, 6 May. District Committees of the Society were to decide whether work on hospitals should continue.[64] On 5 May, however, the Society agreed to allow members working on subsidised housing to remain at work.[65] Of the total Society membership of 6,500, over 5,000 were estimated to have gone on strike.[66]

The initial confusion in the building trades was paralleled by that in the engineering industry. Engineering workers engaged in maintenance work were to stop wherever other workers were instructed to strike, as were those making or installing machinery for producing or supplying fuel that could be used as a substitute for coal. But all other engineering, as well as shipbuilding, workers were meantime to continue at work.[67] It was not surprising that, as foundry workers in Glasgow reported to the Trades Council, 'some confusion had taken place'. Their National Executive had instructed them to stop, but later sent another telegram that they should remain at work. 'The men had actually stopped in certain shops.'[68] On the first day of the Strike, Glasgow Central Strike Co-ordinating Committee decided to send a deputation to the General Council of the S.T.U.C. to point out that engineering and shipbuilding workers on Clydeside could not reach their places of work because of the transport strike, and to urge that all such workers should be instructed to join the Strike. The General Council received the deputation next day and wired the British T.U.C. : 'Circumstances have arisen in Scotland which make it exceedingly difficult to keep moulders, engineers and shipbuilders at work. Feeling is so strong that we advise these sections be officially asked to cease work.' But the T.U.C. replied on 6 May that its earlier instructions be followed meantime.[69] The decision not to call out all engineering and shipbuilding trades at the beginning of the Strike was criticised in some quarters. The Glasgow I.L.P. leader, Patrick Dollan, for instance, later described it as 'an error in tactics'. Dollan considered that the engineers' and shipyard workers' 'militant qualities would have strengthened the strike movement in the Clyde area . . . (where it) was a long way short of a General Strike'. Districts such as Govan, Partick, Clydebank, Renfrew, Greenock, Port Glasgow and Paisley were only partially affected by the withdrawal of labour until the engineers and shipbuilders were all called out on the morning of the last day of the Strike.[70] Whether the T.U.C.'s decision was merely a tactical error or a deliberate attempt to prevent the Strike from becoming more militant by keeping at work many thousands of workers on the 'Red Clyde' is a matter for conjecture. There seems at any rate little doubt that many of those workers did want to come out at the beginning of the Strike. 'The only difficulty we have had,' reported the General Council of the S.T.U.C. to the T.U.C. on 7 May, 'has been with the men engaged in engineering and shipbuilding. The difficulty there has been to keep them at work.'[71]

III

Applying the T.U.C.'s plan and making the Strike effective in Scotland was the responsibility of the General Council of the Scottish T.U.C. This had been agreed at meetings of the T.U.C. General Council immediately after the Farringdon Hall conference of union executives of 29 April-1 May.[72] The S.T.U.C. General Council met in continuous session from the morning of 3 May until 15 May, and conceived its task as being 'to see that the policy laid down by the British T.U.C. is carried out loyally'.[73] This task appears not to have been one that put the S.T.U.C. General Council's own loyalty under much strain, since like its counterpart in London the dominant influences upon it, especially James Walker of the Iron and Steel Trades and Joseph F. Duncan of the Farm Servants, were distinctly 'moderate'. It instructed that local strike committees be formed to take responsibility for the conduct of the Strike in their respective areas. Each committee was to consist of a representative from every union involved in the stoppage and one from any existing trades council, with sub-committees to cover each industry concerned.[74] Almost as soon as the Strike began, the General Council established a network of communications by road between Carlisle, meeting point with the British T.U.C. network, and Aberdeen, with the S.T.U.C. office in Glasgow as the focal point. Relay stations along these lines of communication became collecting and distributing centres for every strike committee within the area. Through the network were distributed the S.T.U.C. official bulletins issued on 5, 6, 7 and 8 May to local strike committees and trades councils, and also from the first day of its publication on 10 May the S.T.U.C. Strike paper, *Scottish Worker*, which replaced the official bulletins. Back through the network to the General Council in Glasgow came information, reports, requests for decision. Messages, instructions, papers and enquiries were carried in either direction by couriers arranged by local strike committees or the General Council and travelling by car, motor cycle or push bike. Only urgent messages were telephoned or telegraphed.[75] The system appears to have become increasingly effective in ensuring both that strike committees were informed of T.U.C. and S.T.U.C. decisions and to some extent of reports coming in from other localities, and that the General Council of the S.T.U.C. was kept in touch with main developments in the districts in Scotland.

Local strike committees, based generally on the trades councils and unions directly involved in the stoppage, had already begun hurriedly to be formed in the forty-eight or so hours before the Strike began. In Glasgow, on the initiative of the Industrial Committee of the Trades Council, there was set up on 3 May a Central Strike Co-ordinating Committee, with full powers to organise the Strike in the city on the lines laid down by the T.U.C. and S.T.U.C.[76] The area covered by the Co-ordinating Committee, which met continuously each day between 4 and 15 May, ran as far as Alexandria on the north side of the Clyde and Greenock on the south'.[77] Fifteen or sixteen Area Committees were set up in the city itself on the initiative of Peter Kerrigan and other militant members of the Central Strike Co-ordinating Committee which, with its thirty or so regularly attending members, was felt to be too unwieldy a body. The Area Committees, composed of local representatives of unions on strike, public representatives from the wards and parliamentary divisions, and in at least one case of Co-operative and Unemployed organisations, did 'splendid work . . . and it was generally after they adopted certain measures that the Central Committee fell into line'.[78] In Edinburgh, too, it was the Trades Council that took the initiative, forming its seven-man Industrial

Committee into the nucleus of a Central Strike Committee at the week-end 1-2 May, before instructions had come from the T.U.C. or S.T.U.C. This Strike Committee grew rapidly with the addition to it of two delegates from each union on strike, and pressure of business soon obliged the Committee to form sub-committees that dealt with the Strike in each respective industry.[79] At Aberdeen, the Strike Committee appears to have been similarly composed to that at Edinburgh.[80] At Methil, the Trades Council, which was under militant left-wing influence, formed itself on 1 May into a Council of Action and, in addition to the normal sub-committees, set up one to deal with Workers' Defence, and another with Class War Prisoners' Aid.[81] The Methil Council of Action appears to have been one of several that were co-ordinated through Fife and Clackmannan.[82] In Lanarkshire, where Communist Party and Minority Movement influence was strong as in Fife, a similar formation and co-ordination of Councils of Action existed, the central Council for the county having some forty delegates.[83] Generally, it took a day or two from the beginning of the Strike before local strike committees were functioning smoothly; but one of the features of the Strike was the enthusiasm and practical skill of local strikers in rapidly developing their strike organisation despite lack of preparation.

The government's Emergency Organisation also functioned relatively smoothly, and certainly did not lack volunteers for work during the Strike. Immediately the state of emergency was declared on 1 May, the Emergency Organisation in Scotland itself began to recruit volunteers, as well as taking over the lists of O.M.S. and other volunteers. Part of the pre-Strike agreement between the Scottish Office and the O.M.S. had been that O.M.S. enrolment cards should collate easily with those of the Emergency Organisation, 'to simplify handing over'.[84] A total of around 25,000 volunteers was enrolled in Scotland.[85] In addition to those listed before the Strike by the O.M.S., the Roll of Voluntary Workers, the Fascists, and the National Citizens' Union, some firms offered the services of their employees. In Glasgow, for instance, 1,000 were thus offered.[86] Thousands of other volunteers were enrolled from among students at the four Scottish universities. At St Andrews, virtually the entire body of 650 matriculated students, together with many members of staff, volunteered; at Edinburgh, over 2,000 of the 3,953 students did so; and at Aberdeen, between 300 and 500 volunteered out of 1,399.[87] At Glasgow, although the number of student volunteers is uncertain, it was probably a few hundreds out of a total student body of 4,489 — a distinctly smaller proportion than at the other Scottish universities. How far that was a result of, how far a reason for, the University's not giving to those who volunteered examination concessions as generous in scope as those given at the other three universities, is also uncertain. Whereas at Glasgow the Senate agreed to ignore absences from classes by volunteers between 3 and 17 May,[88] the other three universities went further. The Aberdeen Court agreed on 11 May that 'all possible steps will be taken to secure that the academic interests of such students as volunteer for service will not suffer'.[89] At St Andrews, in the interests of volunteers, Degree examinations were postponed for a week in June and Honours examinations until September.[90] And at Edinburgh, absences of volunteer students were to be ignored and those unable to sit examinations that term were to be allowed to do so in September 'or another convenient time'.[91]

Students at several other institutions of higher education also volunteered. A dozen from Heriot-Watt College in Edinburgh helped maintain the city's electricity supply; in Glasgow some students volunteered from the Technical College and College of Art.[92] A few volunteers were drawn even from among older schoolboys at several fee-paying schools in Glasgow, Edinburgh and Aberdeen.[93]

The government's Emergency Organisation in fact had far more volunteers than it could use. The 1,000 employees offered by firms in Glasgow were not put to work at all, as was the case indeed with all but 2,000 of the 16,000 volunteers enrolled in that city; of the 2,000 Edinburgh University student volunteers, only 1,000 were actually given work to do.[94] The government's need was really for volunteers who could drive railway engines or help maintain supply at electricity power stations. There was no shortage of less skilled volunteers, willing to work as conductors on trams or buses, as stokers at power stations, or as lorry drivers, dock labourers, or special constables. Volunteers not given work were nonetheless useful not only as evidence of support for the government, but also as a reserve army of labour, available to 'deter' potential strikers. Thus the Glasgow bakers were said not to have joined the Strike because they believed that if they did so they would within hours be replaced by voluntary labour.[95] The government achieved through its Emergency Organisation and its army of volunteers the maintenance of emergency services of food supply, and a partial or at least skeleton service of trams, buses and trains. Except at Wick (where bakers were so seriously handicapped by shortage of yeast that one of them had to motor cycle the 500-mile round journey to Aberdeen for supplies),[96] nowhere in Scotland does there appear during the Strike to have been any notable shortage of food, milk or petrol. This fact, together with the increase after the first couple of days in the number of trains, trams and buses running — even though services remained below or well below normal — helped keep up the morale of government supporters and even persuaded some of the uncommitted that if the government was not winning the Strike it was not obviously losing it.

Class consciousness, very often expressed as 'patriotism', or a wish for 'adventure', generally motivated government volunteers. *The Fettesian*, magazine of the private fee-paying Fettes College in Edinburgh (one of whose distinguished former pupils, Sir John Simon, on 6 May in the House of Commons denounced the Strike as illegal), commented afterward that: 'The miners themselves behaved in far too level-headed a manner to satisfy the average Fettesian who was just dying to be called out.'[97] Among students at Edinburgh University, Jennie Lee, later a Labour M.P. but at that time herself a student, 'began to hear normally good-natured young fellows talk with unholy glee of the pleasure it would give them to run a tank through some of our mining villages'.[98] Most volunteers appear to have worked without payment, though meals and cigarettes were usually provided free. But in some cases 'patriotism' paid well. Thus £5 per week was paid to volunteers employed at Glasgow docks, and Edinburgh Corporation paid tramway voluntary workers double time.[99]

The light-hearted spirit with which many student volunteers were imbued expressed itself in rhyme in the Aberdeen University magazine *Alma Mater*:[100]

> My friend Jimmy drove a 'bus
> When the Strike restricted us.
> Di immortales! Sic Transit!
> My friend Dick conducted it.
>
> Down the Gallowgate, up Mounthooly,
> Hullaballoo! The Wild and Woolly!
> Tricky fox-trotting in the Spital
> (O Methusaleh! Cattle kittle!)
>
> All the passengers they annexed
> Stepped out at the stop before next.
> All the policemen were nonplussed,
> And all the pedestrians bit the dust. . . .
>
> All the passengers who survive
> Thank your stars you are still alive!
> (My friend Jimmy, and my friend Dick,
> Di immortales! Transit! (Sic)).

Risks were indeed run by many of those who ventured to travel during the Strike by bus, tram or train. In some cases the risks arose from the unfamiliarity of blackleg drivers with the route or with safety procedures, or from their determination to arrive at their destination *malgré tout*. 'The gates at a level crossing near Prestonpans,' reported the *Scotsman*, 'were run into by a passenger train, the driver having apparently failed to observe that they were shut.'[101] The most serious railway accident in Britain during the Strike occurred in St Margaret's Tunnel outside Waverley Station, Edinburgh, on 10 May, when a blackleg train passed signals at danger and smashed into some refuse wagons. Three people were killed and eight injured. Thirty-six of the rescuers were temporarily gassed by an escape from pipes broken in the smash.[102] Safety conditions on the railways are suggested in the fact that the driver of the passenger train involved in the accident was the assistant works manager at Cowlairs Depot, Glasgow; the fireman of the refuse train was a medical student; the assistant signalman in the nearest signal box was a blackleg miner; and 'three signal boxes on that section of the line . . . were not manned, as no one was available to act as signalman'.[103] In other cases, risks arose from the hostility of strikers or their supporters to the running of transport during the Strike, despite the instructions and exhortation of the T.U.C. and S.T.U.C. to restrict themselves to peaceful picketing. A train from Anstruther to Edinburgh on 7 May was 'suddenly swept off the main line on to a branch line leading to some collieries' near Cameron Bridge: strikers or their supporters had shifted the points. The train had to stand in a siding for two hours while the points were returned to the correct position, and during that time 'hundreds of strikers from the Leven district appeared and insulted the passengers with shouts and threats of physical violence'. The passengers, shouting 'Shame!' and 'Un-British!', had to hurl themselves to the floors of the carriages as stones were thrown at the train.[104]

Stoning of trams and buses also was frequent and widespread in the industrial areas, and consequently, at Johnstone, for example, 'some drivers took liberties with speed and at times accidents were narrowly avoided'.[105] At Cambuslang, trams ran a gauntlet of stone-throwers on either side of the main street, and six policemen travelling on one tram had to lie under its seats for protection; other strikers stopped buses, turned the passengers out, and went for a joy ride through the countryside.[106] Here and there more drastic action than stoning was taken. Part of a railway line at Omoa in Lanarkshire was blown up, and a bridge or culvert at Blackridge in West Lothian was mined by an experienced quarryman but the calling off of the Strike cancelled demolition.[107]

IV

While large numbers of anti-Strike volunteers were not in fact given emergency work to do, many strikers also found themselves kicking their heels. 'They pulled us out, and we just wandered through the streets. We had nothing to do. We made sure that everybody on Strike was out but after that we just waited.'[108] The T.U.C. official Strike policy of dampening down any tendency to militancy that was reiterated daily south of the Border in the *British Worker* — 'Do any odd jobs that want doing about the house . . . a good walk every day will keep you fit. *Do something.*'[109] — was largely repeated in the *Scottish Worker*, published from 10 May by the S.T.U.C. General Council as its official Strike paper: 'Don't encourage inflammatory propagandists: they may be in the enemy's service. . . . Don't express your views in unnecessarily provocative language. This Strike will be won hands down if you keep cool heads, stout hearts, stolid discipline and exemplary conduct.' Ironically, this last bit of advice was supplemented on the last day of the Strike, a few hours before its calling off, by the exhortation not to grumble or express pessimistic opinions.[110] In about a dozen places in Scotland, including Banff, Perth, Grangemouth, Ayr and Bo'ness, strikers were reported to have organised concerts, dances, or football matches — though Carstairs strikers appear unique in having arranged a football match versus the police.[111] The confidential report by the T.U.C. Intelligence Committee to the General Council on 11 May that 'concerts, whist drives, etc.' were being organised in most centres seems to be rather an overstatement of the position in Scotland at least. Perhaps the Strike did not last long enough for a more widespread need to be felt for organised recreation or socials.

If strikers did not, except at Carstairs, find themselves versus the police in sport, they often did so in picketing. Picketing was one activity in which large numbers of strikers were in some places engaged. It was by no means always accompanied by difficulties or conflict: 'We picketed three works this morning, and got them all to stop work — about 2,000 men.'[112] But picketing, especially of transport, was often a source of conflict between strikers and blacklegs or police; and fracas arising from the running of trams, buses, lorries and trains were widespread and sometimes serious in the industrial — especially mining — areas of Scotland. The running of trams in Glasgow prompted a march into the city on 6 May by some 500 miners from Cambuslang and Newton, intent on strengthening the pickets at the tramway depots at Ruby Street and Paton Street. A 'fierce struggle' with police ensued and sixty-six people were arrested.[113] At Tranent in East Lothian on 7 May a road-picketing incident led to a serious mêlée during which police were forced to retreat to the police station. It was then besieged by a crowd of over 1,000 and all the windows smashed.[114] In the second week of the Strike, on 10 May, a 'brutal assault'[115] by police on a picket at Muiredge resulted in Methil Council of Action immediately increasing from 150 to 700 the strength of its already formed Workers' Defence Corps, under the control of former wartime army warrant officers and N.C.O.s. 'There was no further interference by the police with pickets.'[116]

Most of the riots and disturbances that occurred during the Strike, as at Aberdeen, Glasgow, Edinburgh, Methil, Tranent, Airdrie and elsewhere, arose from the running of, or attempts to run, blackleg transport. The T.U.C. General Council emphasised that there should be peaceful picketing, no obstruction, and no provocation of the police by pickets.[117] In some cases, at Methil for example, the evidence suggests that it was the police who were provocative, not the pickets. But in many cases strikers and other workers ignored T.U.C. instructions, so determined were they to stop transport, except lorries carrying strike committee permits. Thus at Aberdeen on 6 May 'some Corporation buses manned by students but without police escort were captured by strikers and driven back to the depot', and later that day police made a baton charge on a crowd, some of whom were stoning tramcars.[118] At Glasgow, the serious riots and disturbances each day between 5 and 8 May arising mainly out of attempts to stop trams, buses, trains and lorries from running resulted in hundreds of arrests.[119] On 5 and 6 May similar disorders occurred in Edinburgh and baton charges by foot and mounted police on large crowds at the Tron produced a score of arrests.[120] At Airdrie, the running on 10 May of an empty tramcar driven by an inspector led to its being surrounded and 'good naturedly' rocked on its wheels by a large crowd. On the following day an announcement that buses would be run attracted a large crowd. Police then 'lost their heads and made a baton charge', and there were several arrests.[121]

Among the results of such conflicts, one was the large number of arrests made and the subsequent criticism of sentences imposed; another was the putting under pressure in some areas of the resources of the police. Though the precise number of arrests made in Scotland arising from the Strike appears not to be available, it certainly amounted to several hundreds. A survey of press reports in May and early June of arrests and court hearings indicates that there were about 300 arrests in Glasgow, at least eighty in Stirlingshire, Clackmannanshire and West Lothian, over seventy in Fife, a mere half-dozen in Aberdeen, but 108 in Edinburgh.[122] This list is obviously not exhaustive, since it omits some court cases dealt with as late as July,[123] as well as all arrests made in such industrialised areas as Lanarkshire, Dunbartonshire, Ayrshire, Renfrewshire, Dundee, and East and Midlothian. Sir John Gilmour, secretary of state, told the House of Commons on 20 June that up to the 11th of that month 409 people had been sentenced for Strike offences in Scotland to imprisonment without the option of a fine.[124] Since many of those convicted were fined, and some charged were found not guilty or not proven, or had the cases against them dropped, a conservative estimate of the total number of arrests would be 600 or 700. Thus there appears to have been a relatively higher number both of arrests and of sentences to imprisonment in Scotland for Strike offences than in England and Wales, where 632 sentences of imprisonment were imposed by 10 June.[125] Sentences imposed in Scotland on convicted Strike offenders were considered by strikers and supporters to be often excessive. The Edinburgh Central Strike Committee, for example, protested during the Strike about 'the savage sentences being imposed upon workers in the present dispute'.[126] When Labour M.P.s pressed in the Commons on 17 June for an enquiry into the arrests and convictions, one instanced the sending to prison for three weeks of a mother of five children and also a young pregnant wife, both convicted of stoning a blackleg tramcar at Cambuslang, although 'it was impossible for anybody to give evidence of identification correctly in these two particular cases'.[127]

Road picketing and disturbances put the police in some areas under pressure. In Glasgow, for instance, they were said to be on duty for sixteen or eighteen hours every day, and had to call for reinforcements from quieter areas such as Perthshire, which sent twenty officers on 10 May.[128] In Scotland generally, large numbers of volunteers were enrolled as special constables in addition to the normal complement of about 11,000 specials, to assist the 6,500 or so regular police.[129] Thus 600 specials were enrolled at Aberdeen, 900 in Dunbartonshire, 300 at Arbroath, 1,500 in Renfrewshire, 2,000 in Glasgow, 400 at Kirkcaldy, and in Edinburgh the strength of the special constabulary at the end of 1926 was said to be 5,200 — ten times as many as a year earlier.[130] Some of these special constables were formed into motor patrols or 'flying squads', to deal with road picketing. In Edinburgh, for instance, 350 specials were employed in that way.[131] Armed with batons and wearing white brassards, the specials, drawn as they were in many cases from student and even schoolboy volunteers, on the whole contributed to tension and animosity between police and strikers or their supporters. 'We weren't welcomed with a friendly smile from the inhabitants on our beats,' reported a student 'special' on his experiences in Edinburgh. 'Their greetings mainly consisted of presents in the form of stones, bottles, jugs, and even . . . of a stove, a rum jar (empty), a fender etc.'[132] Nonetheless, despite the disturbances, picketing incidents, and riots, the police did not become so hard pressed, nor the character of the conflicts between them and the strikers become so serious, that active military intervention had to be invoked.

Armed soldiers, sailors, and (at least at Montrose) airmen,[133] armoured cars, tanks, and warships were all part of the government's preparations for dealing with trouble if it arose. There was a flurry of army and naval movements at the weekend before and in the first two or three days during the Strike. The battleship *Warspite* arrived at the Tail of the Bank on the Clyde early on 3 May and was joined there later that day by a second battleship, *Hood*, and on the morning of 12 May, the last day of the Strike, by the aircraft carrier *Furious*. H.M.S. *Comus*, a light cruiser, lay at Princes Dock in Glasgow throughout the Strike.[134] In the Forth, the battleship *Royal Sovereign* took up position off Rosyth, and the destroyer *Seraphis* tied up at Leith Docks on 5 May, to be joined three or four days later by another destroyer, *Storm Cloud*.[135] Army movements were similarly precautionary. In the west, there was a build-up of troops at Glasgow and Hamilton. Summoned by an urgent message dropped by aeroplane on the Sussex Downs near their camp at Crowborough, the 2nd Battalion of the South Staffordshire Regiment arrived by ship at the Clyde on 7 May. Two companies went to Maryhill Barracks, Glasgow, where the 1st Battalion Royal Scots were already billeted; the rest of the South Staffs. went to Hamilton. The troops at Maryhill were reinforced by the transfer from Northern Ireland on 10 May of the 1st Battalion Northumberland Fusiliers, and by the arrival of a squadron of the 13/18 Hussars from Edinburgh.[136] To Edinburgh from Portsmouth, 400 men of the 1st Battalion of the Duke of Wellington's Regiment were hurriedly brought by ship on the evening before the Strike began, to reinforce the 1st Battalion King's Own Scottish Borderers and the greater part of the 13/18 Hussars.[137] From Fort George the 2nd Battalion of the Black Watch were rushed south between 4 and 6 May 'in all kinds of vehicles, including a charabanc-de-luxe and a steam-coal wagon'. Two companies of the Battalion were stationed at Stirling, and two at Donibristle in Fife.[138] Those at Stirling were joined on 6 May by about 160 men of the Royal Tank Corps and a dozen armoured cars.[139] In addition to these troops, there were, of course, smaller groups of infantry in their normal stations at regimental depots in Glasgow, Stirling, Edinburgh, Inverness, and elsewhere, as well as units of the Artillery, Engineers, and Signals, at Leith, North Queensferry, and Dunbar.[140]

Direct intervention by the armed forces in the Strike was, however, extremely limited. Here and there troops were placed on guard at docks, railways, power stations, oil or petrol storage points, and explosives dumps. Soldiers were sent midway through the Strike to guard Portobello Power Station and St Margaret's locomotive sheds in Edinburgh; some were sent to patrol L.N.E.R. railway lines after stone-throwing incidents; others guarded explosives at Polmont and Ardeer; marines as well as soldiers stood sentry at dock gates in Glasgow; some sailors guarded oil tanks along the Forth and Clyde Canal, while others, after the holding up of a train by pickets at Leven in Fife on 7 May, rode next day on the footplate of the engine.[141] If the Strike had continued beyond 12 May it is possible that a proposal to employ ratings as firemen on railway engines at Glasgow and Edinburgh would have been adopted.[142] But as it was, the military and naval forces at the government's disposal remained a very largely uncommitted and relatively unobtrusive reserve throughout the Strike.

V

Rumours of mutiny among troops at Maryhill Barracks, Glasgow, and at Donibristle in Fife, circulated during the Strike. In neither case is there any confirmatory evidence.[143] But such rumours were among the many of all kinds that spread. Thus at Dumbarton it was rumoured that trenches were being dug in the streets — and indeed they were, but only for new electric cables; at the village of Eddleston in Peeblesshire rumour had it that eighteen policemen had been killed in the riots in Edinburgh.[144] Naturally, rumours abounded where hard news was scarce, and one of the features of the Strike was the hunger for news of what was happening.

To provide news, convey information, and keep up the morale of strikers, local strike committees in the more important centres produced their own strike bulletins. These were usually a single foolscap or quarto duplicated sheet, selling at ½d. or 1d. each. Their publication illustrated the initiative and enterprise with which the Strike was conducted at local level. At Aberdeen, the first issue of the British Worker — Aberdeen Edition, as it was titled, was on 6 May. It contained main items of local Strike news and an appeal to 'Keep Calm'. It appeared daily thereafter, and developed after the Strike into a printed paper, altering its title on 24 May to *The Aberdeen Citizen* and continuing afterward as an evening paper. During the Strike, the circulation of the British Worker—Aberdeen Edition was restricted to the city and did not extend into the surrounding districts.[145] In Fife, Strike bulletins were issued at Methil, Kirkcaldy and Dunfermline. An unusual feature of the Kirkcaldy bulletin was that it contained advertisements by local shopkeepers.[146] Paisley Strike Bulletin was written with more verve than most: 'Foot and Mouth Disease — Position normal. Hand to Mouth Disease — Position likely to improve after Strike treatment'; and with reference to the incident that ostensibly had prompted the government to break off pre-Strike negotiations with the T.U.C.:

> Let heat, light, food and fuel fail
> But Spare, O! Spare the *Daily Mail*.[147]

The Paisley Bulletin was distinguished too by the inclusion from its second or so issue onward of a daily cartoon by 'G. Whiz' — John Gallacher, brother of

William Gallacher of the Communist Party. One cartoon depicted a bloated capitalist grasping a Union Jack — 'Remember the Constitution' — confronted by a miner with meagre wages in outstretched palm — 'Remember ours.'[148] The Edinburgh Official Strike Bulletin was one of the first to appear. It was published every day from 4 until 13 May, the cost of paper, stencils, etc., being met from a special fund raised through an appeal by the Strike Committee which, within the first twenty-four hours of the Strike, had brought in £200. The Bulletin was distributed through the Lothians by motor cycle couriers. Its daily circulation, at first 5,000 or 7,000, had reached 12,000 copies by the end of the Strike. On the second last day of the Strike, the Edinburgh Strike Committee, convinced that it could 'easily dispose of several times as many' copies, and anxious to publish a more weighty rival to the non-union anti-Strike *Scotsman* and *Evening Dispatch*, but faced with production problems, sent a deputation to the S.T.U.C. General Council in Glasgow to ask permission to print the Strike Bulletin. Permission was refused, on the grounds that printing was contrary to the Strike instructions of the T.U.C. Instead, the S.T.U.C. General Council offered to let the Edinburgh Strike Committee reprint the S.T.U.C.'s own Strike paper, the *Scottish Worker*, provided the work was done by an Edinburgh printing shop under trade union or co-operative control. The proviso could not be met and with the calling off of the Strike next day nothing more was done.[149]

This decision by the S.T.U.C. General Council illustrated the rigidity with which it applied the T.U.C.'s Strike policy, a policy that prevented the appearance of a considerable section of the capitalist press but also of virtually all labour papers too. In its Daily Bulletin of 6 May, the S.T.U.C. General Council asked local strike committees to send it copies of any bulletins they issued, reminding them that 'Printers are on strike and only duplicators may be used.' At its first emergency session on the morning before the Strike began, the General Council had considered an offer by *The Worker*, printed in Glasgow as the organ of the Minority Movement, to 'place the paper under the full control of any authorised Strike Committee'. There was also an offer by the Glasgow independent labour weekly, *Forward*, to include S.T.U.C. material in a special strike bulletin. But the General Council decided to take no action on either offer, on the grounds that 'the general plan of action included withdrawals of all Printing Trades' and 'no exceptions were to be made'. *Forward* was not published at all during the Strike, but *The Worker* refused to cease publication and, together with the *Workers' Weekly*, appeared in cyclo-styled form. This brought down upon its publishers the censure of the General Council, which summoned them before it but without result.[150] Even when on the first day of the Strike the General Council learned that the anti-Strike daily and evening papers in Glasgow were combining to produce the *Emergency Press*, it decided to take 'no action meantime'.[151] Two days later, leaders of the printing unions on the Glasgow Central Strike Co-ordinating Committee appeared before the General Council to propose publication of a printed news sheet that would be produced voluntarily by union labour. The General

Council, however, decided 'that no News Sheet intended for the general public be printed'. At the same time, by a majority of one, the General Council decided to take no action on a proposal to ask newsagents not to distribute the *Emergency Press*.[152] Yet another appeal to the General Council to publish a Strike paper was received on 7 May from Glasgow Central Strike Co-ordinating Committee. Again the decision was to take no action.[153] It was only that afternoon, when couriers from the British T.U.C. had reached the S.T.U.C. office with instructions that 'newspapers be published in various centres', that the S.T.U.C. General Council at last agreed to arrange for publication from 10 May of an official Strike organ, to be titled the *Scottish Worker*. The paper was to be printed by the trade union-controlled Civic Press in Glasgow, with *Forward* Printing and Publishing Company contributing its stock of newsprint and giving other practical help. The printing unions agreed that members work on the *Scottish Worker* without payment. J. F. Duncan, one of the dominant members of the General Council, was appointed editor, and a staff of journalists, including Emrys Hughes, Tom Dickson and John S. Clarke, recruited.[154] But on 9 May the Strike Publicity Committee of the General Council of the British T.U.C. prohibited publication of the *Scottish Worker* and insisted that its own *British Worker* be reprinted in Glasgow. Copy was to be brought by courier from Newcastle to Glasgow and there must be 'no cuts or additions' in the text. The S.T.U.C. General Council, in a rare display of independence, declared this proposal 'utterly impracticable'. Later that day a compromise was reached by which the T.U.C. agreed that publication of the *Scottish Worker*, which was already on the machines, should go ahead but that three pages of copy from the *British Worker* would be sent each morning to Carlisle by 4 a.m., to be collected by courier and reprinted in Glasgow. The fourth page of the paper was to be filled with Scottish news, and it was suggested that the title of future issues of the paper be *Scottish Edition of the British Worker*. In addition, the S.T.U.C. General Council guaranteed that the paper would not be concerned with policy but would reprint all statements of policy issued by the British T.U.C.[155] The first issue of the *Scottish Worker* duly appeared on 10 May. But the arrangement to reprint the *British Worker* copy in Glasgow broke down because of the impossibility of sending it speedily enough by road from London. The copy sent from London on 9 May did not reach Glasgow until the afternoon of 11 May. The S.T.U.C. General Council therefore decided to carry on with publication of the *Scottish Worker* and it appeared each day until 15 May.[156]

The first issue of the *Scottish Worker* was of 25,000 copies, but the demand for news was so great that, despite problems of newsprint supply, the paper's last issue five days later reached 75,000 copies. It circulated in all the main centres in Scotland. Although it was independently published by the S.T.U.C. and was not merely a local edition of the *British Worker* — which, like the government newspaper *British Gazette*, did not circulate at all in Scotland — the *Scottish Worker* made clear in its first issue that it did not concern itself with deciding Strike policy or discussing the general situation, and that the British

T.U.C. was solely responsible for the direction and control of the Strike.[157] As soon as they were received by telephone or otherwise, official pronouncements by the British T.U.C. General Council were reprinted word for word in the *Scottish Worker*.[158] As in the *British Worker*, the impression was conveyed that everything was going well, and the content of the *Scottish Worker* reflected the wish of E. L. Poulton, chairman of the Strike Publicity Committee of the T.U.C. General Council, when he had said in his telephone conversation with the S.T.U.C. General Council on 9 May:

We have a report lying on my desk now saying that your people are wanting to extend the Strike in all kinds of ways. Will you see that all that stuff is kept out and nothing provocative put in. The Negotiating Committee are sitting now and do not want a word said which will prevent them from continuing.[159]

When the Strike was called off by the T.U.C. General Council on Wednesday, 12 May, the statement telephoned by the *British Worker* to the S.T.U.C. General Council for insertion next day in the *Scottish Worker* contained no reference to the refusal of the Miners' Federation to accept the Samuel Memorandum as the basis for ending the Strike. When J. F. Duncan complained that the blackleg *Emergency Press* in Glasgow contained that information, he was told by the *British Worker* that the statement telephoned was the instruction of the T.U.C. General Council. So the *Scottish Worker*, in the wake of the deception practised in the *British Worker*, did not reveal the divergence between the Miners' Federation and the T.U.C. General Council until two days after the Strike was ended.[160]

VI

The announcement, about 1 p.m. on Wednesday, 12 May, by the T.U.C. General Council that the Strike was being called off immediately and unconditionally was at once received over the radio in Scotland.[161] The *Aberdeen Evening Express*, the Glasgow *Emergency Press*, and other anti-Strike newspapers rushed out editions containing the news. But some hours passed before most or all of the strikers heard the news or had it officially confirmed by their own unions or the T.U.C. or S.T.U.C. Since in many areas the Strike was as strong as ever, many strikers at first assumed that, as on Red Friday, the government had given way. Thus at Kilmarnock 'it was freely stated in certain quarters that the Government had capitulated and acceded to all the requests of the T.U.C. and the Miners' Federation', and speakers at an open-air meeting in the town declared the Strike was 'a great victory for the workers'.[162] At Keith, the news that the Strike was over was greeted with cheers from the railwaymen, who 'marched to the station in a body, headed by a piper and a drummer'.[163] In Edinburgh 'everyone, of course, thought it was a victory';[164] and at Kirkcaldy a 'victory social' was held in the Labour Halls.[165]

Even as late as the following day, a local railwaymen's leader told a mass meeting at Motherwell that 'concessions had undoubtedly been won for the miners, and he thought they could all go back to work glad at heart'.[166] In other places, the first unofficial news of the ending of the Strike was received sceptically by strikers. At Bellshill it came 'as a great surprise and its authenticity was much doubted for a time'; at Aberdeen, Montrose, Grangemouth and Stirling the initial reaction was similar.[167] The Edinburgh Official Strike Bulletin was issued with a 'stop press' item at 2.30 p.m., that 'All strikers must . . . pay no attention to newspaper special editions or wireless news stating that the Strike has been finished. Please spread this information with all rapidity.'[168] The Falkirk Central Strike Committee posted a notice outside its headquarters: 'S.T.U.C. official message. No confirmation of settlement as reported by wireless. Strike still on. Stand fast.'[169] Even stronger scepticism was expressed by 'the more ardent strikers' at Kirkintilloch, where a youth tore down a notice of the wireless message that the Strike was off with the remark, 'There's one damned lie gone.'[170] Some strikers, on the other hand, evidently feared the worst from the first announcement over the wireless. Thus, at Hamilton the miners' union offices were 'besieged by miners all anxious for an official statement' and there were 'ruffled tempers'.[171] At Montrose, when railwaymen at a meeting addressed by the writer and local town councillor Hugh MacDiarmid heard the news, they burst into tears — as did Mac-Diarmid.[172] At Bathgate a motor cyclist, said to be carrying a T.U.C. message that the Strike was still on, was greeted with cheers from 'a section of the more extreme element'.[173]

Once confirmation reached strikers later in the afternoon or evening, however, scepticism or the assumption of victory gave way in many cases to bewilderment, rage, or despair. At Aberdeen, one striker afterward recalled there had been 'complete bewilderment'. The belief that the strikers had won soon changed 'to the belief that we had been sold down the river. What we could not understand was why the Strike had been called off when from day to day it was getting stronger'.[174] In the Vale of Leven, where militant influence was strong, 'the T.U.C. wires were greeted with furious boos and hissings'.[175] At Johnstone, which had a reputation as a town 'harbouring diehards of the deepest red', the news came 'as a shock to many'.[176] At Edinburgh, a feeling of shock and betrayal was experienced by some, including Jennie Lee, who had been helping the local Strike Committee: 'That evening, while the Central Strike Committee attended to the last funeral rites on the floor above us, we younger ones were huddled together in a corner of our improvised office, stunned and listless, demoralised by the utter absolute fiasco of it all. We ended the day with a cursing competition. I was shocked by the language I suddenly discovered I knew.'[177]

Denunciations, and demands for an enquiry into the calling off of the Strike, began to be made more or less immediately by the more militant. On the afternoon of 12 May Motherwell Council of Action sent a telegram of protest to the T.U.C., and when no reply had been received, followed it up with a letter

P

which said that 'the workers of Motherwell had been stunned by the blow'.
On 20 May, by which date still no reply had been received, the Council agreed
to call for a special Scottish Trades Union Congress to hear a statement of the
reasons for calling off the Strike. During the discussion, one delegate called
on the General Council of the T.U.C. to resign en bloc, and another described
the General Council as 'cowards and traitors who carried out the greatest piece
of treachery in history'.[178] Laughter and applause from his audience at
Bannockburn a week after the Strike greeted a sally by J. R. Campbell, editor
of the *Workers' Weekly*, that those who collected cigarette cards could now go
in for another hobby — collecting T.U.C. explanations for calling off the
Strike: there was a new one every five minutes.[179] Coatbridge Trades Council
condemned 'the action of the T.U.C. in calling off the General Strike before
receiving adequate guarantees that all grades of workers should resume work
on the same conditions as they left'.[180] Similar resolutions were passed by
Rutherglen Trades Council and by the Joint Committee of Lanarkshire Trades
Councils,[181] as well as by the Trades Council in Glasgow, where the Central
Strike Co-ordinating Committee had already on 12 May expressed 'keen
resentment' at the absence of any satisfactory explanation for the calling off
of the Strike.[182] Criticism was also expressed by, among others, the Organising
District Delegates of the Amalgamated Engineering Union at Edinburgh and at
Paisley, a Govan branch of the Woodworkers, and Clydebridge and Woodside
branches of the Iron and Steel Trades Confederation, the latter of which
suggested withdrawal of the Confederation from the T.U.C.[183] The Scottish
Typographical Association believed that 'Instinct told the workers they had
been hopelessly beaten, and what was much worse to bear was the suspicion that
they had been misled.'[184] When C. T. Cramp, Industrial General Secretary
of the National Union of Railwaymen, addressed a crowded meeting of railwaymen on 30 May at the St Andrew's Halls in Glasgow, he and the other
members of the platform party 'were greeted with a volley of groans, catcalls,
uncomplimentary remarks, and much booing'. The first speaker, an organiser
named Marsh, 'was forced to sit down in dismay' when the hostile audience
drowned his remarks 'in a general chorus of "Awa' hame. Give us Cramp.
Produce the body"'. When Cramp rose to say he could not provide reasons for
the calling off of the Strike because he was not a member of the T.U.C. General
Council, he was greeted with 'a concerted remark of "Did ye no' ask Jimmy
[Thomas]?"' Eventually, Cramp and the platform party retired 'amidst a storm
of protest'.[185] Not all strikers or trade unionists in Scotland felt so strongly as
those quoted here. But many ordinary workers appeared to have shared the
view of the president of the Scottish Bakers' Union, when the absence of
guarantees for the return to work at the end of the Strike became known, that
'we have been sold'.[186]

Was the Strike weakening in Scotland by the time it was called off? The
evidence points in both directions. On the one hand, it is clear that there were
substantial returns to work by tramwaymen and a limited return here and there
by printers, railway clerks, and some strikers in other trades. At Glasgow,

Aberdeen, Dundee, Paisley, and Johnstone, tramwaymen had returned to work in considerable numbers. At Glasgow, where the morale of some of the 4,000 tramwaymen had been shaken from the beginning of the Strike by the running of a skeleton service of trams manned by students and other volunteers, seventy-eight drivers and conductors were reported to have returned to work on 10 May, 305 on the 11th, and altogether 900 by the time the Strike ended. The number of trams running almost doubled from 219 on 8 May to 400 on 11 May,[187] so that by the last day of the Strike roughly half the normal service was running, many of the trams manned, of course, by student and other volunteers. At Aberdeen, nine 'of the older and more experienced drivers' returned to work on 10 May; by the night of 11 May over 100 had returned, and there was a further large breakaway next day with the presentation to the tramwaymen of an ultimatum by the lord provost on behalf of the Town Council Emergency Committee, either to return by 12 noon or be dismissed. By noon 223 tramwaymen were officially stated to have returned to work, though 376 remained on strike.[188] At Dundee, where no trams at all had run since the beginning of the Strike, some tramwaymen returned to work on 10 May and the first trams ran that day. On 11 May the remaining strikers decided 'almost unanimously' to return to work the following day.[189] At Edinburgh there was a drift back to work by some tramwaymen from 11 May, and 'it was only with difficulty that large sections . . . were prevented from breaking away'.[190] At Perth, the tramwaymen's strike remained solid until 12 May, only two men breaking away, but three hours before the Strike was called off non-union tramwaymen returned to work.[191] At Johnstone, the tramwaymen had 'broken away altogether'.[192]

Returns to work by other groups of workers before the Strike was called off appear distinctly more limited than those by the tramwaymen. Among other transport workers, railwaymen appear not to have weakened except very marginally. Thus some signalmen in Dumfries district 'applied for reinstatement'; one man returned at Annan, and most of the porters at Wemyss Bay Station; at Keith, 'a few more' railwaymen went back each day; a driver returned at Peterhead; several men did so at the end of the first week at Buckie, and some railway guards at Elgin on 8 May; at Edinburgh 'some of the fainthearted were dribbling back'; at Bo'ness and Linlithgow some members of the N.U.R. tried to return to work on 10 May, but were dissuaded by pickets.[193] Even among railway clerks, returns to work seem to have been very limited: twenty-three clerks returned at Dundee, thirty at South Leith Station in Edinburgh, 'some' at Montrose, and two at Banff Harbour.[194] A newspaper report on 12 May implying a return by railway clerks at Selkirk was contradicted two days later by the statement that the men had never been on strike at all.[195] Among carters and lorrymen, some returns were reported on 11 or 12 May at Montrose and Perth, and there were threats to go back by non-union men at Edinburgh, in whose case the Trades Council recommended strike payments be given on condition they joined the union.[196] At Stirling, eighteen non-union bus drivers and conductresses returned to work on 10 May, but no buses were run.[197] At Greenock, sixty street paviours returned midway through the Strike.[198]

So far as printers were concerned, some at Aberdeen, Inverness, and at one shop in Montrose returned on 11 May. At Arbroath, 'a few of our spineless members fell to the wiles of their employers'; at Paisley also 'several returned', at Greenock only one did so. Those employed on the *Orkney Herald* and the *Orcadian* had returned on 7 May; all but two at the *Fife Herald and Journal* at Cupar on 11 May; and those at the *Banffshire Herald* decided on 11 May to return.[199] The *Edinburgh Evening News*, which had not been published since the day before the Strike began, appeared on 12 May, and 'its printers had already decided to go back to work before the Strike was called off'. At Edinburgh, too, the paperworkers evidently broke away.[200] In the Borders, the printers played cox and box: those at Galashiels, Kelso, Selkirk and Peebles had at first refused to strike without giving a fortnight's notice, but were persuaded by their union to strike from 10 May; those at Hawick had struck work on 4 May, but resumed three days later.[201]

These waverings or returns to work appear to constitute the bulk of the available evidence for the view that the Strike in Scotland was at its maximum or actually declining in strength by 12 May. There was, on the other hand, an extension of the Strike that morning by the calling out by the T.U.C. of the 'second line' of unions — those in the engineering and shipbuilding industries. How large an extension of the Strike resulted thereby in Scotland is difficult to assess accurately because of the rather scrappy and impressionistic nature of the surviving evidence it has so far been possible to consult. 'The men have awaited the instruction impatiently, and all over the country they have received their marching orders with enthusiasm and a sense of relief.' This claim by the *British Worker* on 11 May would appear to have had a good deal of justification when applied to the 30,000 or so workers in engineering and shipbuilding on the Clyde.[202] It is supported also by the testimony of the strongly anti-Strike *Scotsman*, which reported on 13 May that 'Men in the shipyards and marine engine shops came out pretty generally yesterday.' A different view of the response was presented, however, by the *Emergency Press*, which estimated that 'fully 75 per cent of the men were at work' in the shipbuilding and engineering industries on the Clyde when the Strike was called off later that day. And at Aberdeen the *Press and Journal* claimed that 'Only a small percentage responded.'[203] Until surviving evidence can be more widely examined, allowances should no doubt be made both for some exaggeration on either side of the argument and also for the non-appearance in the 'second line' of the Boilermakers' Society, whose Executive Council had decided to hold a ballot of members before taking action.[204]

As well as the strengthening of the Strike, to whatever degree, by its eleventh hour extension to the engineering and shipbuilding workers, there was a steady increase of its pressure upon industries whose workers were not called out at all by the T.U.C. These industries were affected, in some cases quite seriously, by either lack of transport — particularly rail transport — or shortage of coal, or both. Potteries, stone quarries and granite yards, shale mining, rubber works, textile mills, and even agriculture and fishing, all to one extent or another had their production hampered.[205] Had the Strike continued beyond 12 May there is little doubt that in these and other industries where workers had not been called out by the T.U.C. such difficulties would have worsened and the impact of the Strike would have become correspondingly heavier.

'Thousands of members will be victimised as the result of this day's work.' Ernest Bevin's foreboding at the calling off of the Strike on 12 May[206] proved well founded so far as strikers in Scotland were concerned. The failure of the T.U.C. General Council to ensure that there would be no return to work without the maintenance of trade union agreements and conditions resulted in or contributed to the widespread victimisation suffered by strikers even after the virtual resumption of the Strike during 13 and 14 May by unions resisting attacks on members' pre-Strike conditions. Even in industries where, as to some extent on the railways, employers were, or may have been, prevented by the continuing coal stoppage from re-employing immediately all those who had gone on strike, there is evidence of victimisation. Indeed it was said to be 'rampant' among railwaymen in Scotland.[207] For example, twelve of the twenty-eight L.N.E.R. senior grade railwaymen victimised were in Scotland. They included three stationmasters, a yardmaster, and four inspectors. Of the twelve, five were employed at Edinburgh — 'all Churchmen, and three of them are elders'.[208] The treatment of these men was raised in the Commons on 20 May by Drummond Shiels, M.P. for Edinburgh East, and their case was still being agitated in August by local railwaymen, evidently without success.[209] That no railwaymen guilty of violence or intimidation would be re-employed — a relevant clause in the railway settlement agreed on 14 May between companies and unions — was said to have been interpreted by some local officials on the L.M.S. to include participation in the work of local strike committees.[210] A week after the calling off of the General Strike, over 2,000 men employed at railway workshops in Glasgow threatened a strike unless shop stewards 'whose return to work had been delayed' were re-employed en bloc.[211] The sincerity of the railway companies' claim to be unable, because of the continuing coal stoppage, to re-employ rapidly all pre-Strike staff was questioned by railway trade unionists in Scotland: 'Cases have been reported of men working up to sixteen hours on duty and at one loco depot a complete list of the overtime worked during the first week after the settlement has been tabulated and sent to Unity House. This list will prove that not half of the men required have so far been started.'[212] At Edinburgh, six months after the Strike it was reported that 'some very shady tactics' were still being used by the railway company to prevent reinstatement of an activist of N.U.R. No. 1 Branch; and the issue of victimisation of local railwaymen remained on the agenda of Aberdeen Trades Council as late as March 1927.[213]

Tramwaymen suffered a more palpable amount of victimisation than railwaymen, since there was less ostensible justification for not re-employing them after the Strike on the plea of the continuing coal stoppage. At Perth the foreman of the Corporation tram sheds, with twenty-one years of service to his credit, was singled out for dismissal, the decision being defended by the lord provost on the grounds that the foreman had had 'the choice of being loyal to the Corporation or loyal to his Trade Union'.[214] At Kilmarnock, where all tramwaymen had struck work, all lost their jobs; the Town Council decided not to resume the tram service, .which had been making a loss before the Strike.[215] At Edinburgh, a measure of the extent of the victimisation was that fifty-seven voluntary workers were given permanent jobs as tram drivers or conductors at the end of the Strike. Some of the city's tramwaymen had still not been reinstated six months afterward, although it appears that three of these men were refused re-employment because of their conviction for Strike offences.[216] At Aberdeen, where 376 tramwaymen had remained on strike after the expiry of the lord provost's ultimatum at 12 noon on 12 May, 182 had still not been reinstated a fortnight later. One striker long afterward recalled that about half-a-dozen tramwaymen, including himself, were not allowed by the Corporation to return to work until a year after the Strike.[217] At Glasgow, Labour town councillors struggled for seven months to secure the reinstatement of 316 employees of the Tramways Department, one of them a wartime hero with the Victoria Cross.[218] But the men's reinstatement appears to have taken place only at the beginning of 1927, after the Tramways manager, described as a 'local Mussolini', decided to go into retirement.[219] In the course of the struggle, a Labour councillor brought an action for slander against the manager, the Tramways Committee itself by a majority of one agreed to review the manager's terms of employment, and the Town Council meeting had twice to be adjourned in disorder, so much was feeling inflamed on the issue.[220]

Some strikers in numerous other industries were also victimised, and there were attempts by some employers — not all of which were successful — to reduce wages or lengthen hours or enforce non-unionism. Pickering's carriage and wagon works at Wishaw attempted unsuccessfully to extend its working week from 44 to 47 hours.[221] At Falkirk, some transport workers were told they would be reinstated only if they accepted a reduction in wages of 1d. an hour for men and ½d. for women.[222] 'A considerable number' of the members of the Amalgamated Engineering Union and other unions were not re-employed at two foundries at Dundee, 'and it was quite noticeable that amongst all these . . . was practically every shop steward in these works'.[223] Singers sewing machine factory at Clydebank locked out 1,000 workers for joining the Strike on its last day and had announced, it was claimed, that 'they were to be re-organised which . . . means made proof against trade unionists'.[224] Bakers who had gone on strike at Hawkhill Bakery, Edinburgh, in protest against being asked to supply blackleg workers during the Strike, were victimised.[225] Building trade workers employed by Glasgow Corporation Parks Department were refused reinstatement.[226] In Orkney, storemen employed by three shipping companies were forced into non-unionism.[227]

Non-unionism was enforced fairly widely in the newspaper industry. Morning and evening newspapers in Aberdeen, Dundee, Edinburgh, and, excepting the *Daily Record* and *Evening News*, in Glasgow, as well as some of the weekly or bi-weekly papers, refused after the Strike to employ trade unionists, and the *Edinburgh Evening News* became an open shop.[228] Altogether over thirty newspapers and periodicals were affected and they included the *Glasgow Herald, Bulletin, Glasgow Evening Times, Aberdeen Press and Journal, Evening Express*, and *Dundee Courier and Advertiser*.[229] Despite a lengthy struggle, conducted with support from the Scottish T.U.C. and trade unionists generally, against the non-union newspaper proprietors, the printing unions lost considerable numbers of members, some of them in 'a demonstration of treachery by rushing back to work as non-unionists'.[230] The Scottish Typographical Association lost about one-tenth of its membership;[231] the National Society of Operative Printers and Assistants (N.A.T.S.O.P.A.) suffered 'a serious setback' in Glasgow, Dundee and Aberdeen;[232] Glasgow branch of the National Union of Journalists lost almost half its members.[233] In the paper-making industry, too, non-unionism was imposed on hundreds of workers employed in mills at Denny and, in Aberdeenshire, at Stoneywood, Mugiemoss, Donside and Culter.[234]

It is scarcely surprising that opinion afterward among trade unionists in Scotland was divided over the General Strike. 'An unwise and costly blunder' in the eyes of some,[235] to others it seemed 'a memory of unselfish devotion, of unflinching courage, of unlimited faith in the power of the workers'.[236] Many of those who retained some such memory of the Nine Days would no doubt have approved the terse view of the A.E.U. Organising District Delegate at Dundee, who wrote: 'There are some who say that we have seen the last General Strike. Let us prepare for the next.'[237]

Suggestions for further reading

Margaret Morris, *The General Strike* (London, 1976)

G. A. Phillips, *The General Strike: The Politics of Industrial Conflict* (London, 1976)

Jeffrey Skelley, *The General Strike 1926* (London, 1976)

Doris Hatvany, 'The General Strike in Aberdeen', *Scottish Labour History Journal*, No. 10, June 1976

John McLean, 'The 1926 General Strike in Lanarkshire', *Our History*, Spring 1976, Pamphlet 65

Paul and Carol Carter, 'The Miners of Kilsyth in the 1926 General Strike and Lockout', *Our History*, Spring 1974, Pamphlet 58

Notes

1.   Minutes of the S.T.U.C. General Council (henceforward S.T.U.C. G.C. Mins), 8 Feb. and 8 Mar. 1926.

2.   Interview with J. F. Duncan, 18 Apr. 1963.

3.   *S.T.U.C. Annual Report 1926*, 95-6.

4.   Ibid., 139-140.

5.   Ibid., 117-120.

6.   *Report of S.T.U.C. General Council 1927*, 7.

7.   *Glasgow Trades and Labour Council Annual Report 1925-6*, 6; Mins of Council, 24 Mar. 1926.

8.   Mins of Aberdeen Trades Council, 20 Jan. and 3 Mar. 1926, and mins of its executive committee, 19 Apr. 1926.

9.   Interview with Douglas Browett, Apr. 1963.

10.   *West Fife Echo*, 21 Apr. 1926; S.T.U.C. G.C. Mins, 8 Feb. 1926.

11.   *Fifeshire Advertiser*, 1 May 1926.

12.   Letters, 14 and 27 Oct. 1963, from David Laing, an A.S.L.E. & F. branch official at Thornton in 1926.

13.   Paul Carter, 'The West of Scotland', in *The 1926 General Strike*, ed. J. Skelley (London, 1976), 113; John McLean, 'The 1926 General Strike in Lanarkshire', *Our History*, Spring 1976, 7-8.

14.   L. J. Macfarlane, *The British Communist Party* (London, 1966), 160-1; James Klugmann, 'Marxism, Reformism and the General Strike', in Skelley, op. cit., 61-71.

15.   *Labour Standard*, 19 Dec. 1925.

16.   John McArthur, unpublished reminiscences, tape-recorded by Ian MacDougall, 1968-71.

17.   *Hamilton Advertiser*, 15 May 1926.

18.   Scottish Record Office (henceforward S.R.O.), H.H. 56/17, Reports of government conferences, 1925-6.

19.   Ibid.

20.   Ibid.

21.   Ibid.; *Scotsman*, 4 May 1926.

22.   S.R.O. H.H. 56/17 and H.H. 56/21.

23.   S.R.O. H.H. 56/18, letter, 21 Sep. 1925, from Earl of Glasgow to Sir John Gilmour.

24.   S.R.O. H.H. 56/18, letter, 17 Feb. 1926, from Sir Arthur Rose to P. J. Rose.

25.   S.R.O. H.H. 56/18, memorandum by P. J. Rose for secretary of state for Scotland, 25 Sep. 1925; *Edinburgh Evening News*, 1 May 1926.

26.   S.R.O. H.H. 56/18, note of discussion on 9 Jan. 1926.

27.   S.R.O. H.H. 56/18, letter, 9 Mar. 1927, from R. J. Cairns to J. W. Peck.

28.   S.R.O. H.H. 56/18, report by Captain A. R. Dunlop, general secretary of O.M.S. in Scotland.

29.   Ibid.

30.   S.R.O. H.H. 56/18, letter, 4 Mar. 1926, from C. Campbell to J. W. Peck.

31.   *Scotsman*, 4 May 1926; *British Worker*, 8 May 1926, quoting John Bromley, general secretary.

32.   British Worker — Aberdeen Edition, 21 May 1926.

33.   Mins of Stirling and District Trades and Labour Council General Strike Committee, 7 May 1926; *Railway Review*, 4 June 1926.

34.   Interview with John Cameron, N.U.R., Thornton, 31 July 1963.

35.   Mins of Glasgow Trades and Labour Council, 5 May 1926; *Scotsman*, 4 May 1926.

36.   *Kirkcudbrightshire Advertiser*, 7 and 14 May 1926; *Stirling Observer*, 11 and 18 May 1926; *Stirling Journal*, 6 May 1926.

37.   *British Worker*, 6 May 1926; quotations from letter, 6 May 1926, from George Latham, R.C.A., to E. L. Poulton, T.U.C. General Council, in T.U.C. Intelligence Committee correspondence file (henceforward T.U.C. I.C. file).

38.   G.H.R.L., 'Some experiences of a blackleg', *Glasgow Academy Chronicle*, June 1926, 101.

39.   *Dumfries and Galloway Courier and Herald*, 8 May 1926; *Elgin Courant*, 21 May 1926; *Buchan Observer*, 11 May 1926; *Border Telegraph*, 11 May 1926; *Galloway Gazette*, 15 May 1926; *Fraserburgh Herald*, 12 May 1926.

40.   *Scotsman*, 5 May 1926.

41.   Report from T. & G.W.U. to T.U.C. General Council, 5 May 1926, in T.U.C. I.C. file.

42.   Report, 7 May 1926, from S.T.U.C. to T.U.C. Intelligence Committee; *Labour Standard*, 22 May 1926.

43.   *British Worker*, 10 May 1926.

44.   Report, 7 May 1926, from S.T.U.C., op. cit.; *Labour Standard*, 22 May 1926.

45.   Report, 25 May 1926, by Tramways manager, in Aberdeen Town Council correspondence file, May-Aug. 1926, item 35a; *Aberdeen Press and Journal*, 13 May 1926; quotation from Report, 7 May 1926, from S.T.U.C., op. cit.

46.   *Edinburgh Town Council Mins*, 1 July 1926, and accompanying *Report by Lord Provost's Committee*; *Scotsman*, 11 May 1926.

47.   British Worker — Aberdeen Edition, 21 May 1926.

48.   *British Worker*, 5 and 6 May 1926.

49.   *College Echoes*, St Andrews University Magazine, new series, xxi, No. 12, 28 May 1926, 189-190; *Fifeshire Advertiser*, 29 May 1926; *Minutes of Leith Docks Commission*, 11 June 1926 (report by convener of Emergency Special Committee).

50.   *Grangemouth Advertiser*, 8 May 1926; *Scotsman*, 6 May 1926.

51.   *Scotsman*, 6 May 1926.

52.   *Scottish Typographical Association Annual Report 1926*, 23-4, 59.

53.   See, e.g., letter, 6 May 1926, from general secretary, N.A.T.S.O.P.A., to T.U.C. in T.U.C. Publicity Committee files; Mins of Glasgow Branch N.A.T.S.O.P.A., 11 June 1926; *Labour Standard*, 24 July 1926; *British Worker*, 10 May 1926.

54.   F. J. Mansfield, *Gentlemen, the Press!* (London, 1943), 426-8.

55. *Aberdeen Press and Journal*, 12 May 1926.
56. *Report of Iron and Steel Trades Confederation*, June 1926, 124.
57. See above, p. 50.
58. *Airdrie and Coatbridge Advertiser*, 15 May 1926.
59. Memorandum by T.U.C. General Council, 1 May 1926.
60. *A.U.B.T.W. Trade Circular*, No. 60, June 1926, 14-15.
61. *S.T.U.C. Annual Report 1926*, 12.
62. Peter Kerrigan, 'Glasgow', *Plebs*, xviii, No. 10, Oct. 1926, 366; Mins of Glasgow Trades and Labour Council, 5 May 1926.
63. Official Strike Bulletin, 4 May 1926; *Labour Standard*, 22 May 1926.
64. Letter, 4 May 1926, from D. MacLean, general secretary, in T.U.C. I.C. file.
65. S.T.U.C. G.C. Mins, 6 May 1926, morning session.
66. *Scottish Painters' Journal*, June 1926, 1-2.
67. Memorandum by T.U.C. General Council, 1 May 1926.
68. Glasgow Trades and Labour Council Mins, 5 May 1926.
69. S.T.U.C. G.C. Mins, 5 and 6 May 1926, morning sessions.
70. P. J. Dollan, 'The Strike on the Clyde', *Socialist Review*, June 1926, 19.
71. T.U.C. I.C. file on Progress of Strike, No. 6, 10 May 1926.
72. S.T.U.C. G.C. Mins, 3 May 1926, morning session.
73. Ibid.; S.T.U.C. General Strike Daily Bulletin, No. 2, 6 May 1926.
74. S.T.U.C. Circular, 5 May 1926, to trades councils and General Strike committees.
75. Ibid.
76. Glasgow Trades and Labour Council Mins, 5 May 1926.
77. *Glasgow Trades and Labour Council Annual Report 1926-7*, 8-9.
78. Peter Kerrigan, op. cit., 366; Glasgow Central Strike Co-ordinating Committee Mins, 4 and 5 May 1926; *Workers' Weekly*, 21 May 1926; Susan Bhaumik, 'Glasgow', in *The General Strike*, ed. M. Morris (Harmondsworth, 1976), 399-403.
79. *Edinburgh Trades and Labour Council Annual Report 1926-7*, 9; *Labour Standard*, 22 May 1926; interview, 1959, with Tom Drummond, chairman of the Strike committee.
80. Interviews, Apr. 1963, with R. A. R. Fraser, vice-chairman of Aberdeen Trades Council, and G. R. McIntosh, secretary of the Strike Committee; Doris Hatvany, 'The General Strike in Aberdeen', *Scottish Labour History Journal*, No. 10, June 1976, 7.
81. Emile Burns, *The General Strike, May 1926: Trades Councils in Action* (London, 1926), 143.
82. *West Fife Echo*, 21 Apr. 1926; S.T.U.C. G.C. Mins, 8 Feb. 1926; *Plebs* typewritten and MS reports on the Strike, in Edinburgh Public Library Reference Department, on microfilm.
83. *Workers' Weekly*, 21 May 1926; John McLean, op. cit., 9-10.
84. S.R.O. H.H. 56/18, discussion, 9 Jan. 1926, between Scottish Office officials and Col. A. C. H. Maclean, O.M.S.

85.   *Scotsman*, 18 May 1926, quoting lord advocate.
86.   S.R.O. H.H. 56/18, letter, 9 Mar. 1927, from R. J. Cairns to J. W. Peck.
87.   *St Andrews University Calendar 1927-8*, 649; *College Echoes*, op. cit., 189; *Edinburgh University Calendar 1926-7*; *The Student*, xxii, No. 10, 2 June 1926, 242-3; *Aberdeen University Review*, xiii, No. 39, July 1926, 266; *Aberdeen University Calendar 1927-8*, 789; Aberdeen University Court Mins, 11 May 1926.
88.   Glasgow University Senate Mins, 20 May 1926.
89.   Aberdeen University Court Mins, 11 May 1926.
90.   *Emergency Press*, 14 May 1926.
91.   Edinburgh University Senatus Mins, 6 May 1926.
92.   *Edinburgh Town Council Mins*, op. cit.: *Emergency Press*, 6 May 1926.
93.   See, e.g., *Glasgow Academy Chronicle*, June 1926, 101, 116; *Edinburgh Academy Chronicle*, xxxiii, No. 5, June 1926, 84; *Aberdeen Grammar School Magazine*, June 1926, 255.
94.   S.R.O. H.H. 56/18, letter, 9 Mar. 1927, from R. J. Cairns to J. W. Peck; *The Student*, op. cit., 242-3.
95.   S.R.O. H.H. 56/18, Cairns to Peck, op. cit.
96.   *Scotsman*, 12 May 1926.
97.   *The Fettesian*, xlviii, No. 5, June 1926, 133-4.
98.   Jennie Lee, *Tomorrow is a New Day* (London, 1939), 81.
99.   *British Worker*, 15 May 1926; *Edinburgh Town Council Mins*, op. cit.
100.   xliii, No. 18, 26 May 1926, 319.
101.   *Scotsman*, 6 May 1926.
102.   *The Thistle, Quarterly Journal of the Royal Scots*, 2nd new series, ii, No. 1, July 1926, 17.
103.   *Railway Gazette*, 22 Oct. 1926, reporting the official enquiry into the accident; *Labour Standard*, 22 May 1926; *Scotsman*, 13 May 1926; Edinburgh Official Strike Bulletin, 11 and 12 May 1926.
104.   *Scotsman*, 8 May 1926.
105.   *Paisley Daily Express*, 18 May 1926.
106.   Reminiscences, 1963, of Dan Docherty, Cambuslang, tape-recorded by Jean McCrindle.
107.   G.H.R.L., 'Some experiences of a blackleg', op. cit., 102; *Motherwell Times*, 14 May 1926; interview, 23 Oct. 1963, with a veteran member of the Workers' Union at Airdrie in 1926.
108.   Dan Docherty, op. cit.
109.   *British Worker*, 6 May 1926.
110.   *Scottish Worker*, 10, 11 and 12 May 1926.
111.   M. Morris, *The General Strike*, op. cit., 56.
112.   Letter, 5 May 1926, from James Jarvie, secretary, Lanarkshire Joint Trades Industrial Committee, to W. Citrine, T.U.C., in T.U.C. I.C. file.
113.   *Emergency Press*, 7 May 1926.

114. *Haddingtonshire Courier*, 21 May 1926.

115. *Leven Advertiser*, 25 May 1926, quoting a resolution at Wemyss Parish Council.

116. Emile Burns, op. cit., 143; John McArthur, op. cit.

117. *British Worker*, 5 May 1926.

118. *Aberdeen Press and Journal*, 7 May 1926; telegram, 7 May 1926, from Aberdeen Trades Council to W. Citrine, T.U.C., in T.U.C. I.C. file.

119. *Emergency Press*, 5, 6, 7 and 10 May 1926.

120. *Scotsman*, 6 and 7 May 1926; *Emergency Press*, 6 May 1926.

121. *Airdrie and Coatbridge Advertiser*, 15 May 1926; quotation from interview with Mr H. Maxwell, Airdrie, 1963.

122. *Scottish Worker*, 10 May 1926; *Scotsman*, 10 May 1926; *Emergency Press*, 6, 7, 8 and 10 May 1926; *Falkirk Herald*, 15 May 1926; *Stirling Observer*, 18 May and 1 June 1926; *Bo'ness Journal*, 21 May 1926; *West Lothian Courier*, 21 May 1926; *Alloa Advertiser*, 22 May 1926; *West Fife Echo*, 26 May and 2 June 1926; *Dunfermline Journal*, 22 May, 12 June and 3 July 1926; *Fife Free Press*, 15, 22 and 29 May and 5 June 1926; *Kirkcaldy Mail*, 1 June 1926; *Fifeshire Advertiser*, 29 May 1926; *Aberdeen Press and Journal*, 7, 12, 13 and 19 May 1926; *Chief Constable of Edinburgh, Annual Report 1926*, 16.

123. See, e.g., *Scotsman*, 10 July 1926.

124. *Hansard*, 20 June 1926, column 2473.

125. Statement by W. Joynson-Hicks, home secretary, in Commons, 10 June 1926.

126. Edinburgh Official Strike Bulletin, 11 May 1926.

127. *Hansard*, 17 June 1926, column 2506.

128. *Emergency Press*, 11 May 1926; *Perthshire Advertiser*, 12 May 1926.

129. *Report of H.M.'s Inspector of Constabulary for Scotland*, 1925, 3-4.

130. *Aberdeen Press and Journal*, 13 May 1926; *Kirkintilloch Herald*, 26 May 1926; *Arbroath Herald*, 14 May 1926; *Paisley Daily Express*, 14 May 1926; *Scotsman*, 21 May 1926; *Southern Press*, 21 May 1926; S.R.O. H.H. 56/18, Report by Captain A. R. Dunlop, O.M.S.; *Chief Constable of Edinburgh, Annual Report 1925*, 24, 1926, 27, 31.

131. *Scotsman*, 11 May 1926.

132. R.M.K., 'With the Special Constables', *The Student*, op. cit., 241; see also *Aberdeen Grammar School Magazine*, op. cit., 255, for reference to a schoolboy ' "special" whose only regret was that he had no occasion to use his baton'.

133. *Montrose Review*, 7 May 1926.

134. *Greenock Telegraph*, 3 and 12 May 1926; *Emergency Press*, 5 May 1926.

135. *Dunfermline Journal*, 15 May 1926; *Scotsman*, 6 and 10 May 1926.

136. *The Staffordshire Knot*, Regimental Journal, No. 4, 1926, 20-2; *The Thistle*, op. cit., 4-5; *Highland Light Infantry Chronicle*, xxvi, No. 3, July 1926, 157-8.

137.   *Scotsman*, 4 May 1926; *The Iron Duke, Regimental Magazine of the Duke of Wellington's Regiment*, July 1926, 218.

138.   *The Red Hackle, Black Watch Regimental Magazine*, 2, No. 22, July 1926, 23, 36; *Stirling Journal*, 6 May 1926.

139.   *Stirling Observer*, 11 and 18 May 1926; *The Red Hackle*, op. cit., 42.

140.   *Army, Navy and Air Force Gazette*, xlvii, No. 3462, 29 May 1926, 254.

141.   *Labour Standard*, 22 May 1926; *The Thistle*, op. cit., 7, 17; *Scotsman*, 12 May 1926; *Stirling Observer*, 11 May 1926; *Govan Press*, 21 May 1926; *Kilsyth Chronicle*, 14 May 1926; *Kirkintilloch Herald*, 12 May 1926; *Fifeshire Advertiser*, 29 May 1926.

142.   S.R.O. H.H. 56/21, note of telephone message from Mr Gresley, chief engineer, L.N.E.R., 12 May 1926.

143.   *The Staffordshire Knot*, op. cit., 21; *Kirkcaldy Times*, 26 May 1926; P. J. Dollan, op. cit., 19-26.

144.   *Dumbarton Herald*, 19 May 1926; *Peeblesshire News and County Advertiser*, 14 May 1926.

145.   Doris Hatvany, op. cit., 9; *Scottish Typographical Association Annual Report 1926*, 53.

146.   Emile Burns, op. cit., 123, 143; interview, John Cameron, op. cit.

147.   Paisley Strike Bulletin, n.d. (c. 6 and 7 May 1926).

148.   Ibid., n.d. (c. 7 or 8 May 1926).

149.   *Edinburgh Trades and Labour Council Annual Report 1927*, 9; Edinburgh Official Strike Bulletin, 12 May 1926; letter, 8 May 1926, from Gerald Crawford, secretary, Edinburgh Strike Committee, to T.U.C., in T.U.C. I.C. file; *Plebs*, xviii, No. 7, July 1926, 255-6; S.T.U.C. G.C. Mins, 11 May 1926, afternoon session.

150.   S.T.U.C. G.C. Mins, 6 (morning session) and 12 May 1926; *S.T.U.C. General Council Report 1927*, 7; *Workers' Weekly*, 21 May 1926.

151.   S.T.U.C. G.C. Mins, 4 May 1926, afternoon session.

152.   Ibid., 6 May 1926, afternoon session.

153.   Ibid., 7 May 1926, morning session.

154.   Ibid., 7 May 1926, afternoon session; *S.T.U.C. General Council Report 1927*, 9; William Elger, 'The Scottish Worker', *Labour Magazine*, Aug. 1926, 162-3; interview with J. F. Duncan, op. cit.

155.   S.T.U.C. G.C. Mins, 9 May 1926.

156.   Ibid., 11 May 1926, afternoon session.

157.   *S.T.U.C. General Council Report 1927*, 8, 9-10; *Scottish Worker*, 10 May 1926.

158.   *S.T.U.C. General Council Report 1927*, 10.

159.   Typed copy of telephone message from Poulton to W. Elger, general secretary, S.T.U.C., 9 May 1926, 6.10 p.m., in T.U.C. files on *British Worker*.

160.   S.T.U.C. G.C. Mins, 13 May 1926, morning session; *Scottish Worker*, 14 May 1926.

161.   See, e.g., *West Lothian Courier*, 21 May 1926.

162.   *Kilmarnock Standard*, 15 May 1926.

163. *Banffshire Herald*, 15 May 1926.

164. Arthur Woodburn, private report, n.d. (? June 1926), to *Plebs*, on microfilm in Reference Department, Edinburgh Public Library.

165. *Fifeshire Advertiser*, 15 May 1926.

166. *Motherwell Times*, 14 May 1926.

167. *Hamilton Advertiser*, 15 May 1926; *Aberdeen Press and Journal*, 13 May 1926; *Montrose Review*, 14 May 1926; *Grangemouth Advertiser*, 15 May 1926; *Stirling Journal*, 13 May 1926.

168. *Scotsman*, 13 May 1926.

169. *Falkirk Herald*, 15 May 1926.

170. *Kirkintilloch Herald*, 19 May 1926.

171. *Hamilton Advertiser*, 15 May 1926.

172. Hugh MacDiarmid, *The Company I've Kept* (London, 1966), 158.

173. *Scotsman*, 13 May 1926.

174. Douglas Browett, op. cit.

175. R. W. Postgate, E. Wilkinson and J. F. Horrabin, *A Worker's History of the Great Strike* (London, 1927), 87.

176. *Paisley and Renfrewshire Gazette*, 15 May 1926.

177. Jennie Lee, op. cit., 83; interview, Tom Drummond, op. cit.

178. *Motherwell Times*, 28 May 1926.

179. *Stirling Observer*, 27 May 1926.

180. *Coatbridge Leader*, 29 May 1926.

181. S.T.U.C. G.C. Mins, 14 June 1926.

182. *Glasgow Trades and Labour Council Annual Report 1926-7*, 9; Mins of Glasgow Trades and Labour Council, 14 May 1926.

183. *A.E.U. Monthly Journal*, June 1926, 24, 26; *A.S.W. Monthly Journal*, June 1926, 319; *Confederation Report*, quarter ending 30 Sep. 1926, 153-4.

184. *Scottish Typographical Association Annual Report 1926*, 27.

185. *Forward*, 5 June 1926.

186. *Report of Annual Delegate Meeting, Scottish Bakers' Union 1926*, 7.

187. Peter Kerrigan, op. cit., 365; *Scotsman*, 12 and 13 May 1926; *Emergency Press*, 10 and 11 May 1926.

188. *Scotsman*, 11 May 1926; *Aberdeen Press and Journal*, 12 and 13 May 1926; Aberdeen Tramways manager's report, op. cit.

189. *Emergency Press*, 11 May 1926; *Scotsman*, 12 May 1926.

190. *Minutes of Edinburgh Town Council*, op. cit., and information provided, 1959, by Transport Department; quotation from Arthur Woodburn, op. cit.

191. *Perthshire Constitutional and Journal*, 12 May 1926; letter, n.d. (? June 1926) from secretary, Perth Trades Council, to *Plebs*, in Reference Department, Edinburgh Public Library, on microfilm.

192. R. W. Postgate, *et al.*, op. cit., 93.

193. *Dumfries and Galloway Courier and Herald*, 8 May 1926; *Dumfries and Galloway Standard*, 12 May 1926; *Greenock Telegraph*, 12 May 1926; *Banffshire Herald*, 15 May 1926; *Aberdeen Press and Journal*, 13 May 1926;

Banffshire Journal, 11 May 1926; Arthur Woodburn, op. cit.; *Linlithgowshire Gazette*, 21 May 1926.

194.   *Emergency Press*, 8 May 1926; *Edinburgh and Leith Observer*, 22 May 1926; *Montrose Review*, 14 May 1926; *Aberdeen Press and Journal*, 12 May 1926.

195.   *Scotsman*, 12 and 14 May 1926.

196.   *Montrose Standard*, 14 May 1926; *Perthshire Constitutional and Journal*, 12 May 1926; S.T.U.C. G.C. Mins, 10 May 1926, morning session.

197.   *Stirling Journal*, 13 May 1926.

198.   *Emergency Press*, 8 May 1926.

199.   Ibid., 12 May 1926; *Aberdeen Press and Journal*, 11 May 1926; *Montrose Standard*, 14 May 1926; quotations from *Scottish Typographical Association Annual Report 1926*, 55-6, 67, 71; *Orcadian*, 13 May 1926; *Fife Herald and Journal*, 12 May 1926.

200.   Arthur Woodburn, op. cit.

201.   *Southern Reporter*, 13 May 1926; *Hawick Express*, 14 May 1926.

202.   S.T.U.C. G.C. Mins, 5 May 1926, morning session; Report, 7 May 1926, from S.T.U.C. G.C. to T.U.C., in T.U.C. I.C. file; *Emergency Press*, 11 May 1926.

203.   *Emergency Press*, 13 May 1926; *Aberdeen Press and Journal*, 14 May 1926.

204.   *Scotsman*, 12 May 1926.

205.   See, e.g., *Bo'ness Journal*, 7 May 1926; *Kirkcudbrightshire Advertiser*, 14 May 1926; *Elgin Courant*, 21 May 1926.

206.   A. Bullock, *Ernest Bevin* (London, 1960), i, 337.

207.   *Railway Review*, 4 June 1926.

208.   *Scotsman*, 28 June 1926, letter from J. Allan, secretary, Edinburgh No. 4 Branch, N.U.R.

209.   *Hansard*, May 1926, column 532; *Scotsman*, 14 Aug. 1926.

210.   *Railway Review*, op. cit.

211.   *Scotsman*, 19 May 1926.

212.   *Railway Review*, op. cit.

213.   Edinburgh No. 1 Branch, N.U.R., Mins, 14 Nov. 1926; Aberdeen Trades Council Mins, 2 Mar. 1927.

214.   *Perthshire Courier*, 8 and 21 June 1926.

215.   *Kilmarnock Standard*, 22 May 1926.

216.   *Edinburgh Evening Dispatch*, 20 May 1926; *Labour Standard*, 6 Nov. 1926 and 15 Jan. 1927.

217.   Aberdeen Tramways manager's report, op. cit.; Douglas Browett, op. cit.

218.   *Mins of Glasgow Town Council* and *Tramways Committee*, 5 May-15 Dec. 1926 *passim*; *Forward*, 5 June 1926.

219.   Quotation from Peter Kerrigan, op. cit., 367; *Mins of Glasgow Tramways Committee*, 2 Feb. 1927.

220.   *Glasgow Town Council Mins*, 27 May and 23 Sep. 1926; *Mins of*

Glasgow Tramways Committee, 4 Aug. 1926; *Scotsman*, 30 July 1926.
221. *Associated Blacksmiths' Society Second Quarterly Report*, Mar.-June 1926, 4696-7; *A.E.U. Monthly Journal*, June 1926, 26.
222. *Falkirk Herald*, 15 May 1926.
223. *A.E.U. Monthly Journal*, op. cit., 20.
224. Glasgow Central Strike Co-ordinating Committee Mins, 13 and 17 May 1926; *Scotsman*, 17 May 1926; quotation from A.E.U. Glasgow District Committee report by H. Luckhurst, 13 May 1926.
225. *Scottish Union of Bakers: Report of Annual Delegate Meeting, June 1926*, 11.
226. Glasgow Central Strike Co-ordinating Committee Mins, 14 May 1926.
227. *Orkney Herald*, 19 May 1926.
228. *Scottish Typographical Association Annual Report 1926*, 28; *Edinburgh Evening News*, 14 May 1926.
229. *S.T.U.C. Annual Report 1927*, 21; *Labour Standard*, 24 July 1926.
230. *Scottish Typographical Association Annual Report 1926*, 28.
231. Ibid., 110, 120-3.
232. *N.A.T.S.O.P.A. Journal*, Aug. 1926, 4.
233. *The Journalist*, July 1926, 161.
234. *Scotsman*, 22 May 1926; *Aberdeen Press and Journal*, 18 May 1926.
235. *Scottish Typographical Association Annual Report 1926*, 64-5.
236. *Labour Standard*, 22 May 1926.
237. *A.E.U. Monthly Journal*, op. cit., 23.

The New Left in Scotland[1]

William Thompson

IN spite of a virtually unaltered structure of property distribution and persistent reservoirs of poverty and deprivation, the mid-1950s found the masses in Britain enjoying hitherto unprecedented levels of real income and welfare provision.

Ultimate credit for these advances was claimed and usually conceded to lie with the Labour government of 1945-50, a fact going a long way to explain the dominance exercised in the political and industrial wings of the labour movement by the political philosophy which the leaders of that movement represented. Characteristic of that philosophy was a stringent attachment to the constitutional properties, implying the firm separation of industrial and political action together with commitment to the mixed economy and market relations for the foreseeable future. It embodied in addition active membership of the Atlantic alliance with a foreign policy established on the premises of likely Soviet aggression and nuclear deterrence. The left wing within the official movement, most publicly represented by Aneurin Bevan, very weak in the trade unions and only relatively stronger among the constituency parties, differed in degree rather than on fundamentals. Its challenge was to *policies*, domestic or foreign, rather than to institutional structures. Thus, vehement opposition was expressed to British acquiescence in the intransigence of U.S. diplomacy, to German rearmament, to the extent to which resources were absorbed by military requirements; but the constitutional processes which produced these realities were not called into question. From this viewpoint, social progress in Britain lay in the extension and furtherance of the measures initiated by the postwar government.

The political stance of the Communist Party, stigmatising the economic, state and cultural structures as engines directed to warmongering and exploitation of the working class at home and abroad, lacked public credibility, not least because of the Party's identification in public consciousness as the apologist and would-be imitator of the Soviet government, towards whose record and postures hostility and suspicion had been cultivated by all the agencies of information and education since the initiation of the cold war. Nevertheless, in certain trade unions and in certain areas the Communist Party remained influential and respected, thanks to its members' militancy and the memory of their role during the thirties and the War years.

In Scotland all the foregoing tendencies were emphasised and exaggerated. Poorer and grimmer in every respect than the British average — in spite of regional policy — political and social issues drew sharper lines among the politically aware, corresponding positions were more clearly defined. Right-wing union leadership was entrenched deeper, the labour left even weaker than its English counterpart, and conversely the Communist Party proportionately more numerous and strongly based in the labour organisations. This was nowhere truer than among the miners and in the mining areas, West Fife above all, where a Communist M.P. was returned until 1950.

The beginnings of the dissipation of the cold war atmosphere, at any rate in its more congealed forms, can be traced in the events of 1956 — events which initially seemed much more likely to thicken it: Krushchev's denunciation of Stalin's practices and behaviour, followed by the political upheavals in Poland, the brief civil war in Hungary, the Anglo-French-Israeli invasion of and subsequent withdrawal from the Suez area. These events crystallised and gave form to changes in the political mood among articulate elements in the British labour movement.

West Fife provided the most clear-cut and organisationally defined example, an outcome explained by the existence in that area of a particularly strong and deep communist tradition combined with an unusually impregnable right-wing control in the local Labour Parties. Ugly stories circulated of corruption and misuse of office. It was hinted that individuals used their trade union connexions to gain positions in the Labour Party which were then cashed as a profitable niche in the Co-op. machinery. The nature of the constituency Labour Party was exemplified by the circumstance that its M.P., William Hamilton, had drafted the only constituency resolution supporting West German rearmament to the 1954 Labour Party conference.[2]

The origins of the Fife Socialist League can be identified even prior to the Hungarian events. In the town of Lochore, in June 1956, Lawrence Daly, the secretary of the Glencraig N.U.M. branch, a member of the Communist Party's Scottish Committee, former chairman of the Scottish N.U.M. youth committee and S.T.U.C. youth advisory council, publicly renounced his Party membership. The analysis on which he based his decision concentrated upon two principal criticisms of the Communist Party.[3] He indicted it first of all for total subservience to the Soviet leaders at the expense of principle or consistency, instancing the denunciation of Stalin following the 20th Congress as being no less unprincipled than the previous adulation: 'The most disgusting and disgraceful somersault in political history'. Secondly, and partly because of this, the Communist Party in Britain could never hope to be a serious political force. Though it might exert some influence in industrial affairs, the generality of British workers would not alter their assessment of the party on the political level. The Communist Party did not possess a single M.P. or control so much as one parish council, and the position was unlikely to alter. In August Daly repeated his explanation before an audience of miners in Lochore.

Daly's action provoked a very extensive correspondence in the local newspaper, the *Times for Lochgelly and District*, where he had first publicly announced his decision. He was criticised in a restrained and civil fashion by the local Communist Party organisations, but some of his former party associates, writing in their own names, denounced him with exceptional venom. P. C. Walters, from Bowhill, a county councillor, declared that:

All you have done is add another name to the sorry list of forgotten failures who don the mantle of prophet to vent their anti-Communism.[4]

The uproar following on the fighting in Hungary could not fail to embitter relations even further. Continuing in his line of approach, Daly organised a public meeting in Lochgelly for Peter Fryer, the dissident correspondent of the *Daily Worker*. In the same month he defeated Tommy Stewart, a Communist Party member, for the position of pit delegate at Glencraig colliery. This action attracted a measure of criticism on the grounds that Stewart had filled the office admirably, and a non-communist correspondent, one William King, accused Daly of contesting the position 'in furtherance of his own aspirations'.[5] In reply Daly accused the Party of having vetoed the compromise that he and Stewart had agreed upon.[6] Stewart himself wrote to affirm that Daly would give good service as pit delegate but that he would be unable to alter the progressive policies of the Scottish N.U.M.[7]

By 1957, when Daly's letters were putting 'Communist' in quotes when referring to the C.P.G.B. or its representatives and even characterising it as the 'British Kremlinist Party', throughout the country mass resignations from the Communist Party were taking place. Among these, a group based principally on the north of England, composed chiefly of university lecturers, founded the *New Reasoner*, 'a quarterly of socialist humanism', concerned mostly at first with a moral critique of the communist experience, but asserting as well a claim for a new socialist 'humanist' politics, morally orientated and hostile to bureaucratic solutions. The journal's editors were the labour historians John Saville and E. P. Thompson. Contact was soon established with the movement in Fife, where the ground was prepared for the formal inauguration of the Fife Socialist League in March.

The expressed political analysis and aims of the F.S.L. corresponded fairly closely to those of the Labour Party left. A survey of the duplicated monthly journal it published from early 1960 indicates a coverage of local and national political issues, including the N.U.M. and unilateralism, the conduct of the sitting M.P., the attitude of local councillors to rent arrears, seamen's strikes, capital punishment, short biographies of labour and socialist pioneers. The slant of practically all articles is that of straight reporting from a radical standpoint. Analysis at an abstract theoretical level was not emphasised. The following paragraph, from an article entitled 'Alfred the Grate' — on the Coal Board's appeal for Saturday working — indicates the prevalent tone of *The Socialist*:

That is one of several reasons why Robens' appeal for Saturday working at selected pits should be rejected. The lower-paid miner desperately needs that extra shift's earnings, but he knows well that if he or his union yields to the temptation his right to a decent wage for a five-day week will be ignored. Firm action indeed will be needed to secure it. Within the next few months the union will be free from the shackles of compulsory arbitration. That does not mean that the miners should then have a head-on clash with the Coal Board on every issue that divides them.[8]

The principal planks in the League's public platform were: unilateral nuclear disarmament especially, extension of public ownership — with workers' control developed and bureaucratic management curbed, and Scottish devolution. In spite of its origins as a Communist Party breakaway, one element which seems to have disappeared from its thinking and programme is a distinctively Marxist approach, either implicit or explicit. At any rate there is little evidence of one in its published material.

The F.S.L.'s first major breakthrough came in the local elections of 1958, when Daly secured election to the Fife County Council for the Ballingry division, the largest in the county, with 1,085 votes against Labour (525) and the Communist Party (197):

Opinion in the League was divided. The trained dialectitians cautiously forecast either a narrow defeat or (less likely) a narrow victory. The 'inexperienced' new recruits declared that we would win comfortably. The result was astounding. . . . This demonstrated not only the depth of the workers' disgust with the Labour Party but also their readiness to choose an alternative where Tory candidates could not reap advantage from a split vote.[9]

The new councillor went on to make arrangements for the publication of a twice-yearly bulletin on council affairs folowed by a public meeting for reporting back and promoting discussion.

Given the international events of 1956, an upheaval in the West Fife labour movement was most likely inevitable, but that it took the form of an independent electoral organisation owed everything to local circumstances. Its foundation preceded the emergence of the new left on a national scale whose basic political positions corresponded to some extent with its own. It was to be expected that links would be established rapidly — in fact Daly and his colleagues had been distributing the *Reasoner*, predecessor of the *New Reasoner* and published by the same team, as early as 1956. The general election of 1959, which the League decided to contest with Lawrence Daly as candidate, saw the connexion reinforced considerably.

In No. 10 of the *New Reasoner* (autumn 1959, the last one to appear), John Saville justified the decision of several on the editorial board to support Daly's candidature, perceiving no inconsistency in doing so while at the same time working for official Labour candidates in their own constituencies. The argument he presented accepted that the promotion of internal change in the Labour Party was the only viable long-term strategy and went on to assert that support for a dynamic and popular socialist against a sclerotic Labour machine in a constituency with very specific local characteristics might well contribute to this end. The F.S.L. was also approached at this point by the newly-created Socialist Labour League, whose journal, the *Newsletter*, Peter Fryer edited at that time, but rejected a formal compact.

In the outcome, the election campaign achieved a modest success. Daly recorded 4,886 votes (against Hamilton's 25,000), pushing the Communist Party into third place (3,826). More significantly, the F.S.L. established a valuable network of contact and influence both in the constituency and the local labour movement.

The formation of New Left nuclei in Scotland, more specifically affiliated to the national movement than was the Fife group, was furthered considerably by the circumstances of the election.

The decision by some of the *New Reasoner* team to support Daly's contest is only one instance of the extended political discussion generated around this event among activists on the labour left. The debate concerned itself in particular with the shortcomings of the official leadership's approach towards social and economic reconstruction, an approach expressed in the anti-nationalisation outlook and Atlantic diplomacy postures identified with the party leader, Gaitskell. A counterpart to the *New Reasoner, Universities and Left Review*, based on Oxford and created by youthful socialist radicals, though examining socio-economic themes such as the ownership patterns in British industry and finance, placed its emphasis on a critique of the prevailing norms of British culture. It was technically an extremely professional production, edited by the West Indian sociologist, Stuart Hall. Further stimulus to the creation of organised groupings was furnished by the Labour Party's mediocre electoral performance. Outbid in the rhetoric of expanding affluence, the Party suffered its third successive electoral defeat in 1959. The impending merger of the two New Left journals in the same year, not to mention the commencement of university sessions, contributed to the atmosphere of new initiatives and departures.

Preceded for some time in the main Scottish centres by the sale of the journals and other literature, following and stimulated by the development of a Campaign for Nuclear Disarmament network, New Left clubs appeared almost simultaneously in more than one area. Both the Glasgow club,[10] which replaced an earlier, unsuccessful attempt, and the Aberdeen one, were founded in the late autumn of 1959. Edinburgh Universities and Left Review Club, already in existence, changed its title accordingly.[11] Dundee, however, lacked any such organisation for a further year.

None of these groups was large in numbers. The Aberdeen club, for example, included thirty-one members after seven months.[12] Participants' memories suggest that the corresponding figure for Glasgow was around fifty. The social composition of both was very heavily weighted towards academic personnel. Most active in establishing the Aberdeen Left Club were Sandy Hobbs, a postgraduate psychologist, and Ken Alexander, one of the original *Reasoner* group and latterly lecturer in political economy at Aberdeen University. Over fifty per cent of the membership were connected with the university, and the original committee comprised two university lecturers, two mature students (one of them a communist), Sandy Hobbs as secretary-treasurer, and a draughtsman.[13] The latter was a prominent Labour Party activist, Robert Hughes, later M.P. for the North Aberdeen constituency.

Among the other founders was an ex-communist bookseller currently active in the Liberal Party.

The clubs were, in their own estimation, primarily propagandist and educational organisations. The adopted aims and initial activities of the Aberdeen club exemplify this.[14] The defined objectives were to provide a discussion forum for socialists, and secondly to attract people to socialism. These objectives were to be pursued through a monthly public meeting with addresses by a range of labour movement, New Left and literary figures. The initial programme included Stuart Hall, now editor of *New Left Review*, E. P. Thompson, Mervyn Jones, novelist and New Left spokesman on disarmament, Ron Meek, Glasgow University economist and frequent contributor to the *New Reasoner*, John Saville, Judith Hart, M.P. for South Lanark and associated with the Glasgow New Left, and V. G. Kiernan, historian.[15] Hamish Henderson, folk musician, and Hugh MacDiarmid had also been proposed.[16] Study groups comprising a 'small, active membership', loosely composed, were established as research bodies. Three such were originally intended, taking nationalisation and workers' control, class in contemporary society, and socialism and the novel as their themes.[17] The former two were actually convened, respectively by Ken Alexander and Derek Allcorn, a sociologist.[18]

The meetings of the Edinburgh club follow a similar pattern, covering 'Developments in Modern Capitalism' with Ron Meek and Duncan Hallas as speakers, Ken Alexander on 'A Socialist Wages Plan', and 'A Socialist Scotland', addressed by Lawrence Daly. Study groups existed here too, on the Central African Federation and Edinburgh housing.[19]

Similar features are revealed in the Dundee club, established a year later in the autumn of 1960. Here the moving spirit and provisional secretary was a sociologist, David Riddell, the first guest speaker — to an audience of thirty-five — being Ken Alexander, who conducted discussion round the theme of 'socialism in relation to the world in the sixties', which, the subsequent press release pointed out, was aimed to promote the new unilateralist policy adopted by the Scarborough conference of the Labour Party.[20]

The patterns of activity revealed by this sketch tend to confirm the conclusion that the Left Clubs saw their primary role for the most part as a propagandist one, disseminating the concept of socialism by meeting and journal. Precise objectives were never defined, and no effort made to organise systematically to gain positions or influence in the labour movement. Possibly, Ken Alexander has surmised,[21] this abstention was a product of the way New Left members regarded Communist Party activities in that direction. Perhaps surprisingly in view of the occupational status of so many of its members, one avenue which the New Left did not try to exploit, though it might have done so with relative facility, was that of gaining elected positions in the academic machinery and exploiting them as platforms for agitation and propaganda. Still, the higher education environment was a very different world in those days from what it subsequently became.

Nevertheless, individuals active in the New Left were simultaneously and effectively engaged — as individuals — in their local Labour Party organisations. Judith Hart has already been referred to, though following her election, her contact with the Glasgow Left Club was perforce minimal. One constituency in which a pronounced influence was exercised was the North Angus and Mearns Constituency Labour Party. Though the region is chiefly rural, returning Conservative M.P.s, three functioning Labour Party branches existed in the towns of Stonehaven, Brechin — where it was based on the engineering industry — and Montrose, dominated by the railwaymen. Evidence of the constituency's firmly left-wing orientation is to be found in its record of votes and resolutions on the contentious issues of the day. Bob Hughes, later on the committee of the Aberdeen Left Club, stood as parliamentary candidate in 1959, while two of the most active party workers were Ken Alexander and Mary Klopper — like Alexander an ex-communist — for a short time Scottish secretary of the Left Clubs and subsequently the Labour Party adviser on Algeria. No formal contacts, however, existed between this constituency organisation and any of the Left Clubs.[22]

Regardless of possible reasons or justifications for the lack of any organised New Left presence in the labour movement, such absence may well have contributed substantially to what was probably the most severe defeat the Left sustained at that time, the failure to hold the majority vote in favour of unilateral British nuclear disarmament won at the Scarborough Labour Party conference of 1960. The one external organisation among which Left Club adherents were consistently and energetically at work was the Campaign for Nuclear Disarmament. Any cursory inspection of the movement's literature makes it plain that the unstable international nuclear balance constituted its major theoretical and political preoccupation. It would not be unjust to regard the New Left as constituting, in some respects, the left wing of C.N.D., and concluding that its major role was to promote — though as stressed above not in any systematic or organised fashion — the case for nuclear disarmament in the labour movement. An extensive overlap between leading individuals in the Left Clubs and C.N.D. can be observed. Regular appearance at anti-nuclear demonstrations, on platforms and in organising committees, was the basic political fare of the New Left membership. This was no less true of the Fife Socialist League than it was of any of the other groups. Unilateral nuclear disarmament featured as Lawrence Daly's leading demand in his 1959 election campaign; the issue was covered, in one way or another, in practically every number of the *Socialist*. Daly's election agent in his parliamentary contest had been Will Warren from Oxford, who was a member of the Direct Action Committee and imprisoned in 1960 for participating in the sit-in at the Foulness nuclear base.[23]

Moreover, it is in this particular field that the New Left's influence on the course of political events — and specifically that of the F.S.L. — is probably most identifiable. It is to be expected that the League's leading members, considering who they were, would have some standing not only in their own localities but in the Fife area of the Scottish N.U.M., and through it exercise a leverage on national N.U.M. policy.

In the context of the nuclear disarmament debate this proved significant. By 1959 the unilateralist idea was making considerable headway in the trade union movement, but one element opposing it as a diversion from the serious business of international disarmament agreements was the Communist Party. At the N.U.M. national conference of 1959 a unilateralist resolution sponsored by the Derbyshire miners was defeated, in part because of opposition from Scotland. According to *The Socialist* of June 1960:

> A clean-cut demand that Britain should give up the Bomb *now* was embarrassing as Communists would be told to give the same advice to the Russians. It was much easier to get workers to agree with the C.P.'s demand for international agreement to ban the bomb. But in 1959 the Aldermaston march doubled in size and the mighty Transport and General Workers' Union led by Frank Cousins threw its weight behind the unilateralists. The demand grew loud and clear for a British lead *without* waiting on international agreement. The C.P., which always claims to be the 'vanguard of the working class', had become the guard's van! It applied the brakes via the Scottish N.U.M. to the Derbyshire resolution for unilateral renunciation. Thereby the C.P. aided Gaitskell and his friends. It soon saw its mistake — but just a little too late. A few weeks earlier, in June 1959, Lawrence Daly, on behalf of the Glencraig N.U.M. branch, had got up at the Scottish Conference and proposed that Derbyshire should be supported — but to no avail.

The following year, however, with other unions having adopted a unilateralist stance, and the Paris summit talks having collapsed in the U-2 fiasco, the Glencraig demand became the central feature of a composite resolution accepted by the Scottish conference. Scotland supported Derbyshire in July, and at Scarborough in October the miners' vote was cast against Gaitskell. *The Socialist* of June — this before the outcome was known — was gratified but cautious:

> We are *not* saying that Lawrence Daly has made possible a major change in Labour Policy. We are saying that such a change is now possible because Lawrence Daly *and thousands of other people* have kept up the fight in a variety of ways.

In the nature of things, the activities of all the Left Clubs were highly localised. Central direction of any sort was almost altogether absent, and theoretical guidelines — so far as they existed — developed only through the consensus of the *Review* — so far as it reached the membership. Nor, lacking any apparatus to establish or implement a common policy or line of action, could it have been otherwise. Yet the commitment to decentralisation among New Left organisations appears to have exceeded even what the circumstances of necessity dictated.

National conferences took place on at least three occasions between 1960 and 1962, resulting in the election of a national committee with various national officers. These conferences, however, adopted no programmes, and neither the national committee nor its officers possessed any executive authority.

At the gathering convened in London during May 1960, Daly, the only Scottish delegate to contribute to the discussion, argued forcefully for the preparation of a common programme and the introduction of improved organisational methods, including regular publication of a bulletin, without, he emphasised, establishing a bureaucratic machine.[24] In addition he referred to the F.S.L. as a political party, not a Left Club. Perhaps he envisaged it as making serious inroads on Labour Party strength, whose sterility in many parts of Scotland he emphasised, though noting that particular tactics would have to be adapted to the prevailing situation.

These same proposals were indeed adopted by the conference, which instructed the newly elected national committee to develop a broad, permissive and not obligatory policy statement, and to publish a bulletin. Moreover, education and propaganda were to be developed in collaboration with the *Review* and the regional committees, and a financial levy was to be fixed at the rate of £1 per club per year plus £1 for every 50 members.

Even this modest degree of centralisation proved impossible to accomplish. Only two issues of the bulletin, *Viewpoint*, ever succeeded in appearing. Subsequent letters and circulars make it evident that the national committee found it wholly impossible to raise more than a fraction of the agreed affiliation fees. The next conference, in December 1960, at Stockport, demonstrated that even a common political stance, let alone organisational expertise, was beyond the capacities of the Left Clubs.

On that occasion, the Scottish delegates, though not Lawrence Daly, were more in evidence than they had been in March. One session was chaired by the Glasgow delegate Neil Carmichael. The main business centred on the draft statement of aims drawn up by the national committee in accordance with the previous resolution. After an introductory reference to the political failure of the labour movement, four paragraphs rejected capitalist ownership, nuclear weapons and cold war alliances, racialism and anachronistic laws concerning personal relations. Paragraph six associated culture and politics, demanding that culture be freed from the distorting effects of capitalism. The prescription for New Left action in paragraph eight was based on the assertion that socialism could not be founded upon 'narrow administrative remedies' but only on 'a common vision of a new society'. The clubs consequently were to establish the case for socialism by fostering an 'alternative way of life' through the practice of socialist values and comradeship.[25]

In the event the conference refused to adopt any statement of aims, a decision in line with the sentiments of the Scots. At a meeting of the Scottish regional committee following the March conference, doubt was expressed on 'the good sense of some of the decisions taken', and the Edinburgh representatives in particular objected to the notion of a committee established in London drawing up a policy statement. Nevertheless, the report of the conference was accepted 'with reservations' and Neil Carmichael appointed to be Scottish regional representative on the co-ordinating committee.[26] When the Scottish committee met again in October to discuss the draft proposal, the recorded opinions of the clubs and the Fife Socialist League were almost unanimously opposed to adoption. St Andrews club formed the only exception and even here, its most prominent member and representative on the Scottish committee, Les Honeyman, was against it personally.[27] It has been suggested that there was suspicion among the clubs of the motives of those who had advanced the proposal and produced the document. The target of these suspicions were the ex-communist founders of the movement, who, some thought, aspired to create an alternative Communist Party on an unacceptable model. Lawrence Daly, however, as noted, on behalf of the F.S.L. supported the Scottish rejection of the draft, an action which would nevertheless seem to contradict his stand at the March conference for sharper direction and tighter organisation in the clubs.

Channels of communication did, of course, exist. As previously indicated, the common viewpoint of the clubs, so far as there was one, was expressed through the *Review.* All the Scottish clubs handled *New Left Review,* but it would be an exaggeration to suggest that they noticeably influenced it in any manner. Arrangements made for a substantial Scottish contribution to N.L.R. never came to fruition. The Scottish committee meeting previously referred to reviewed the proposed articles from Scottish authors. They covered education (J. Christie), highland economics, the Scottish literary scene (Edwin Morgan), the Scottish theatre (Alex. McCrindle). In the last case the editor had failed to make the necessary arrangements with the author, and Daly undertook to protest at the next editorial board meeting. None of the planned material ever did get printed in the *Review.*

Nevertheless, Scottish authorship did occur from time to time in N.L.R., generally as subsidiary items or book reviews. Daly and Carmichael reported in the same issue, No. 4, the former on the progress of the F.S.L. and the latter on the Scottish apprentices' strike of 1960. Ron Meek reviewed W. W. Rostow's famous *Stages of Economic Growth.*[28] Roy Wilkie, also from the Glasgow club, dealt with assessments of Chinese development.[29] Martin Baillie surveyed Picasso's artistic career[30] and Lawrence Daly discussed Arthur Horner's autobiography.[31]

In May 1961 strike action broke out for the first time among Scottish teachers, when 5,000 out of the 7,000 employed in Glasgow came out in protest at inadequate salaries and government threats to reduce qualifications for teaching employment. Norman Buchan used his account of these developments to examine the steady erosion of teaching conditions by government policy and to advocate the continuation and intensification of the action.[32] In N.L.R. 9, Ken Alexander exhibited what in retrospect looks like prophetic abilities when he commenced under the title 'Premier Wilson's Plan' (Harold Wilson had just stood for the party leadership) with:

> It was a cynic who last November said to a 'Campaign for Unity' supporter, 'I am more politically advanced than you; I've got a petition which says "Wilson must go".' . . . A leader closer to the trend of Party opinion who would give loyalty *to* as well as expect loyalty *from*, would be a great improvement. At this point we return to Mr Wilson who probably sees himself and is certainly seen by many in the Party as filling this bill.

The article goes on to criticise the Harold Wilson economic proposals expounded in a *New Statesman* article of 24 March 1961 for neglecting the question of trade union participation, making a fetish of increased investment without considering the political implications, and speaking ambiguously on the question of nationalisation.

In addition to Lawrence Daly, one other spokesman of the Fife Socialist League appeared in the pages of the *Review*.[33] John Keenan, an active member of the F.S.L. and a regular contributor to the columns of *The Socialist*, entered the debate on the chapter written by E. P. Thompson for the book published by the New Left, *Out of Apathy*. This was entitled 'Revolution' and set out Thompson's interpretation of the New Left's potential. Keenan congratulated him for making an unassailable case for the necessity of socialist revolution, then criticised his argument for refusing to take account of the possibility that ruling class resistance might not be overcome except by force and violence:

If the declared purpose is to change completely the nature of our society then there must be preparation and provision for the worst that can happen. Revolution requires careful and detailed planning. It requires resolute and effective leadership of the kind that will not baulk at 'smashing' (regrettable though that would be) should it become necessary.

Distribution of *New Left Review* in Scotland does not appear to have been very extensive. Aberdeen had an order for thirty-three, of which, through 1960 and 1961, increasingly larger numbers of each issue remained unsold.[34] Comments made at the time indicated some degree of disillusionment with the magazine, an impression that N.L.R. had neither the analytical depth of the *New Reasoner* nor the impact and pertinence of U.L.R. The Dundee figure was twelve. Correspondence between these two clubs and the business manager makes it plain that serious problems of payment and distribution were encountered, and that accounting procedures in London were bad.

The circulation of the organisation's spokesmen among the clubs' membership represented a further medium of contact and dialogue. Summer and weekend schools featuring these individuals on political themes were popular, likewise speaking tours by them of the regional clubs. Scotland was well represented in this respect, as noted. There were evidently problems, however, financial and otherwise in this connexion. The 1960 A.G.M. of the Aberdeen club noted a need to reduce the number of outside speakers in the following year's programme. Disappointment was expressed that their contribution had concentrated more on raising morale by means of generalised rhetorical inspiration than opening up a searching examination and debate on national issues. When responding to a request from the newly formed Dundee Left Club to make such an arrangement on their behalf, Neil Carmichael explained that:

We in Glasgow have frankly been disappointed with the contributions made by some visiting speakers from the south. . . .

and went on to recommend the use of local talent:

. . . Ken Alexander was stimulating, informed, but at the same time feeling his way through the problems of the 1960s — which is surely the reason for Left Clubs. . . .[35]

The action and consequence of the Scottish Left Clubs Co-ordinating Committee could not be other than very limited. Intended to convene three times per annum (April/May, August/September and January), it served to enable views to be exchanged between club representatives and organised a regional school on *Out of Apathy* in the summer of 1960. Its first secretary was Jean McCrindle of the Glasgow club, a W.E.A. tutor-organiser, also active in the newly formed Young Socialists. She was followed in May 1962 by Mary Klopper, who, communicating the change to the clubs, expressed her conception of their function: they should provide facilities for local research and contributions to national publications as well as creating social contacts and entertainment independent of the 'capitalist bourgeois world', for:

> It is only on our own ground that we can analyse as well as describe and present the case for a radical socialist transformation on an openly anti-Gaitskellite and anti-Stalinist basis.[36]

By the time these lines were written, however, their tone was at complete variance with the realities of the situation, whether in Scotland or elsewhere. In the course of 1962 the New Left evaporated entirely as a political force, by the end of the year it no longer existed as an organised entity of any sort.

The simultaneous collapse at the centre and in the local clubs is remarkable, considering how tenuously the clubs were connected to the *Review* or to the national committee. There was no intrinsic reason why their functioning and activity should have been affected, far less paralysed, by the crisis in the affairs of the *Review* which culminated in a reconstitution of the editorial board and the eventual eviction from it of the original founders of the movement.[37] The parallel dissolution of the C.N.D.'s strength and the extinction of the F.S.L. — most autonomous of all the New Left's affiliates — indicate that the political climate had after a few years changed in a manner unfavourable to broad radical movements outside the political mainstream. The failure to consolidate the unilateralist victory at Scarborough, followed by reversal a year later with consequent demoralisation, intensifying crisis in the Conservative Party with the probability of Labour victory in an impending election, political weariness after several years of intense activity without much apparent result — without doubt all these were contributory factors, though their precise relationship is obscure.

Such developments were evident in the national conference convened in March 1962 between the reconstruction of the N.L.R. board and the removal of the old guard. The fact that this gathering was occasioned by 'the remaining members of the original national committee having for some time wished to resign because of heavy pressure of work . . .'[38] set the tone. Attendance was thin; only thirteen clubs were represented, together with the F.S.L., the only organisation present from Scotland.

In his opening address, Edward Thompson put the best face he could upon the difficulties. Characterising the New Left as a left-wing equivalent of the Fabian Society, he presented the editorial changes as a technical device to surmount obstacles arising from the impossibility of frequent board meetings and an over-expensive format. He further promised that the new *Review* would eschew an inner jargon and, 'In general there will be less culture-and-communications and more direct criticism and writing.'

No doubt it was consistent with Daly's background, both in his Communist Party career and in the F.S.L., that he should have been the only delegate to advance proposals designed to salvage a coherent national organisation from the prevailing muddle. The points he now made fairly clearly echoed his views expressed at the March 1960 conference. Summing up previous developments by expressing his sense of debt to those 'who have carried on the fight against organisational chaos in the New Left', he went on to propose the creation of a National Society of Socialists advancing 'a clear policy', though not necessarily putting up parliamentary candidates:

It would be able to identify with international trends and hope to gain the support of those now leaving the Labour Party in disillusion.[39]

The appeal met with some sympathy but little enthusiasm. Delegates who referred to it showed themselves most aware of its dangers in terms of 'vanguardism'. Some felt a more appropriate occasion would come in five years or so, but that in the meantime the clubs were the best bet for keeping grassroots politics alive, as constructive work was still possible in most Labour Party organisations. It was pointed out that parliamentary candidates were already standing on independent unilateralist platforms 'and there was no need to duplicate either the effort or the odium'.[40] The conference concluded with the formation of a fresh co-ordinating committee of which no more is heard, and advice to clubs favouring Lawrence Daly's proposal to contact him personally. Nine delegates present at the conference itself had expressed interest in establishing a committee for this purpose, but little appears to have come of it.

If Daly was disappointed by the response of the Left Clubs conference, he found no greater encouragement on his home ground. Since mid-1961 the F.S.L. had been, by his own account, moribund. *The Socialist* managed to appear only three times in the first half of the year, and the May issue was the final one. In spite or because of these circumstances, however, Daly made to his 350 readers an approach of the same sort as he had propounded at the conference, though scarcely in a manner that could be considered the most effective, even given the available resources. The front page of *The Socialist* of March 1962 contained an assessment of the political scene entitled 'Britain after Orpington', concluding that the Liberal success in that bye-election must be attributed to the party's image of radicalism, from which followed the inference that the electorate were seeking, though confusedly, radical initiatives. Gaitskell's nuclear policy was indicted again, and the page ended with the statement that: 'Those who can see this are getting out of the Labour Party fairly fast these days.'

The article appears at first sight to terminate there but, though there is no 'continued on . . .', in fact a concluding paragraph is to be found tucked obscurely on the back page in these terms: 'For them and many other Socialists, the question is "Where do we go from here?" In our view the time is ripe for the creation of a new Socialist *Party* with complete political electoral and organisational independence. All who agree should write to me so that proposals may be considered.' Not surprisingly perhaps, given the situation and presentation, little interest was elicited, though maybe the fact that he got only *one* reply is somewhat startling, more so the fact that it came from outside Fife. This was printed in the last number of *The Socialist* (May 1962) and was unfavourable to the suggestion. The writer, Ian Taylor of Edinburgh, expressed surprise to see Daly quoting the Orpington result in justification: '. . . I can't imagine that a constituency, previously held by Sir Waldron Smithers would return any sort of Socialist M.P., nor that its behaviour can be a useful guide to our movement.' He went on to adduce certain positive reasons for maintaining a Labour Party connexion:

> The Scarborough decision was a tremendous boost: it was too easily come by though, and not nearly enough work and organisation followed it. The reversal at Blackpool could be foreseen long before. Yet there was a large left contingent among the delegates. . . .
> [with reference to Polaris] . . . the voting on the neutralist resolution did show that there was more than a mere nucleus of delegates interested in a Socialist foreign policy. This body of opinion can be most effectively strengthened by working inside the Labour Party.

And again:

> Another important consideration is the Young Socialist movement facing difficulties and very much in need of assistance from Socialists inside the Labour Party. . . . I hope you will encourage other correspondents to try the L.P. a bit longer — else we feel, the New Left will be the Old Left writ small.

It was advice which Daly himself appears to have accepted not very long afterwards, for by September he had arrived at the conclusion that the Fife Socialist League was no longer viable. In a circular to his supporters sent over his own name[41] he related the disintegration of the League's activity, emphasising that '*interest has practically disappeared*', and that due to apathy the F.S.L. was viewed as a purely local phenomenon. It had proved impossible to break out on to a national level of organisation, though 'I have encouraged every step that others have taken away from the Labour Party,' believing that a fair number of people were in the mood for such an endeavour. The experiences outlined above had convinced him, however, that no real basis existed and certainly no one was available to undertake the organisational groundwork. Therefore, 'I have argued with less and less conviction for the formation of a new, national, independent Socialist organisation,' and he had come to accept that socialists would do best to support the Labour Party in view of its potentialities in the forthcoming election, for

> . . . with a good majority there would be no excuse for the rejection of radical policies . . . it seems to me that the enthusiasm engendered would revive the rank and file so much that Left policies would have more chance of support.

Conversely, to be held responsible for defeat at the election by splitting the vote would strengthen the right wing. Moreover, it would become possible to gain admission to Scottish and national Labour Party conferences. It had been put forcefully to Daly that if a strong left spokesman had represented the N.U.M. at the 1962 Scottish Labour Party conference, the vote on Polaris might have gone in favour of the unilateralists.

It followed from these considerations that '. . . the Fife Socialist League should be disbanded and a public declaration made that we are doing this in the interests of unity and victory at the next General Election'. Daly and his fellow F.S.L. councillor George MacDonald would continue as Labour councillors and fight inside the Labour group, some of whose older leaders were near retirement. A New Left club or group would be set up in West Fife to promote the sales of *Tribune* and *N.L.R.* Thus ended the oldest, most proletarian, best established and most politically successful element in the Scottish (or British) New Left, which was simultaneously fading from the scene.

There are few manifest occurrences or phenomena in which it is possible to trace the long-term influence or significance of the New Left, even less so in a restricted area like Scotland. In Glasgow and Edinburgh and on the Aberdeen-Dundee axis contact and communication with organisations and sympathetic individuals in the labour movement were certainly maintained, but it is impossible to discern any concrete effect on policy or behaviour that can be distinguished from the general advance of anti-nuclear sentiment marking these years. More noticeable are the active members of the Left clubs who later went on to fill leading positions in the labour movement or public life.

Ken Alexander, following his appointment as professor of Economics at Strathclyde University, was, like many of his colleagues in the *Reasoner* group, to play a distinguished role in academic life, reaching the positions of a celebrated commentator on the Scottish economy and a government-appointed director of Fairfield's shipyard and the U.C.S. consortium. After the drowning of the aged M.P. Hector Hughes, Bob Hughes (no relation) was elected to the safe seat of Aberdeen North, subsequently becoming an under-secretary at the Scottish Office. Neil Carmichael of Glasgow won the parliamentary by-election at Woodside in the autumn of 1962. Both his selection by the constituency party and his electoral victory were at least partly due to individuals formerly associated with the Glasgow New Left, by then regrouped in the Woodside Young Socialists. He too was a future member of the Wilson governments, as was Norman Buchan, elected at West Renfrew in 1964, likewise a pillar of the Glasgow club. Lawrence Daly's accomplishments were even more noteworthy. In 1964 he defeated a communist candidate, Guy Stobbs, to succeed another communist, John Wood, as general secretary of the Scottish area of the N.U.M. and from there went on to become national secretary of that key union. It would be idle to pretend that the reputation and standing he acquired during his time in the F.S.L. were unconnected with these achievements.

The Fife Socialist League was, of course, a unique departure, nothing resembling it appeared anywhere else in Britain, and its relatively large numerical basis, its organised structure and political activism remained an anomaly within the tendency of the New Left. If the New Left was ever to have become the political force which at one time appeared conceivable, similar bodies would have needed to be established in many other places, for organisations of this sort represented the most hopeful avenue for the penetration of the New Left's notions into the broader movement. But though the New Left, like C.N.D., attracted from all age and social levels, its strongest appeal was to the educated youth. Scotland, with the exception of Fife, conformed to the same pattern and exhibited no distinctive characteristics. In certain respects this phenomenon has persisted ever since, in the form of the anti-Vietnam war movement and the student insurgence of the later sixties and seventies, though these were and are undoubtedly much more diffuse in political outlook and even less coherent organisationally. Lawrence Daly in one sense at least was consistent. Among his stated reasons for quitting the Communist Party was the assertion that it possessed no future as a major political presence, and when he called for the winding up of the F.S.L., he repeated the same argument in respect to it. In doing so he was voicing a feeling increasingly prevalent among the New Leftists, that the Party's existence as an organised grouping was a distraction from more relevant work in the mainstream of the Labour Party and unions. Such an approach is understandable as there were genuine fears of its evolution towards the status of a political sect such as the I.L.P. or the S.P.G.B. Nevertheless, in the confusion and disarray which fell upon the Left once the postures and direction of the 1964-70 Labour governments had become clear, it is at least conceivable that a surviving New Left in an organised form, above all the F.S.L., could have provided an appropriate focus for the assertion of counteracting tendencies aiming at the establishment of different policies. While the disappearance of all the components of the New Left (other than the *Review* in its changed form) was probably unavoidable in the circumstances, those who regret the political outcome of the later sixties may also regret its abrupt and possibly premature demise.

Suggestions for further reading

Little has been published on the British New Left of the 1956-62 period and nothing at all on its Scottish components. For the movement generally, see the issues of *New Reasoner* and *Universities and Left Review* and the early numbers of *New Left Review*. In 'An Open Letter to Leszek Kolakowski', *Socialist Register 1973*, E. P. Thompson discusses the 'purge' of the N.L.R. editorial board in 1962. For an all-round statement of the New Left's political position, see the essays in *Out of Apathy* (London, 1960), and for a critical assessment of the movement the chapter, 'Marxism and the British Intelligentsia' in *The Coming British Revolution* by Tariq Ali (London, 1972).

Notes

1. The following account is based principally upon documents and letters kindly made available by Mr A. Hobbs, the first secretary-treasurer of the Aberdeen Left Club and later secretary of the Dundee Left Club. Lawrence Daly, secretary of the National Union of Mineworkers, who figures prominently here, willingly agreed to discuss his role in the Fife Socialist League, but was prevented from doing so by illness. Others who contributed their recollections were Neil Carmichael and Mrs June Wall of the Glasgow Left Club and Professor K. Alexander of the Aberdeen one.

2. *N.L.R.* 4, July-Aug. 1960.

3. Letters to *Times for Lochgelly and District* (henceforward *Lochgelly Times*), 28 June 1956, 12 July 1956, 9 Aug. 1956.

4. *Lochgelly Times*, 5 July 1956.

5. Ibid., 27 Dec. 1956.

6. Ibid., 10 Jan. 1957.

7. Ibid., 17 Jan. 1957.

8. *The Socialist*, Feb. 1961.

9. *N.L.R.* 4, July-Aug. 1960.

10. Formation mentioned in letter from Judith Hart to Ken Alexander, 17 Nov. 1959.

11. Undated circular outlining programme for winter, 1959, signed by David Wilkie, secretary.

12. Secretary-treasurer's report, 31 May 1960.

13. Ibid.

14. Ibid. Undated account of inaugural meeting.

15. Secretary-treasurer's report.

16. Undated account.

17. Undated public hand-out.

18. Secretary-treasurer's report.

19. Undated winter, 1959, programme.

20. Press release, undated.

21. Conversation with author, 1974.

22. Ibid.

23. *The Socialist*, June 1960.

24. Report of conference in *Viewpoint*, bulletin of the Left Clubs, No. 1, July 1960.

25. Report of Dec. 1960 conference.

26. Minute of Scottish Committee meeting, Glasgow, 4 June 1960.

27. Undated note of Scottish Committee meeting on 29 Oct. 1960.

28. *N.L.R.* 6, Nov.-Dec. 1960.

29. *N.L.R.* 3, May-June 1960.

30. *N.L.R.* 6.

31. *N.L.R.* 9, May-June 1961.

32. *N.L.R.* 10, July-Aug. 1961.

R

33. *N.L.R.* 5, Sep.-Oct. 1960.
34. Undated note.
35. Neil Carmichael to David Riddell, 7 Sep. 1960.
36. Circular to Scottish Clubs, 29 May 1962.
37. A partial account is given by E. P. Thompson in the *Socialist Register*, 1973.
38. Minute of conference.
39. Ibid.
40. Ibid.
41. Circular to supporters, 12 Sep. 1962.

Guy Alfred Aldred, Antiparliamentarian, 1886-1963: a Memoir

John T. Caldwell

MANY older Glaswegians will remember Guy Aldred. For fifty years his knickerbockered figure was a familiar sight in the streets of Glasgow, and often his powerful voice could be heard above the traffic din, rising from the midst of huddled shadows at a street corner. Senior citizens of distinction can remember the days of their youth being enlivened and enlightened by his oratory.

Guy Aldred was a heretic in religion, politics, and social convention, and few could make heresy more alluring. He was against the institutions of Church and State, and more immediately against parliamentary socialism. He considered these two words contradictory by definition and fraudulent by implication.

Aldred came to speak in Glasgow in 1912. The radical tradition of the city appealed to him. He settled there in 1920 and became a Glaswegian by adoption. He was born in London on 5 November 1886. His father, Alfred Aldred, was a naval lieutenant who resigned his commission to write for the stage. Early in 1886 he met a nineteen-year-old parasol maker, Ada Holdsworth. She was seven months pregnant when he married her, and, as the union was socially unsuitable, left her on the church steps and went back home with his widowed mother. Seven weeks later a boy was born. It was Guy Fawkes day, so they called him Guy.

Guy was brought up in his maternal grandfather's house. He attended the Hugh Myddleton School in Clerkenwell, leaving at fifteen and starting work with the National Press Agency. He was already a precocious theologian and a natural preacher.

By the time Guy was seventeen he was an agnostic and at eighteen an atheist. He was also a member of the Social Democratic Federation, and unpaid parliamentary correspondent for their organ *Justice*. This appointment confirmed him in the antiparliamentary convictions he was developing. He left the S.D.F. after a year — in August 1905. Then for a time he assisted in running *The Voice of Labour*, organ of the Industrial Union of Direct Action. By this time he was searching for an organisation in sympathy with his ideas. In 1906 he formed the first of his Communist Propaganda Groups. There were several of these groups in London, and eventually in Wales, the North of England and Scotland.

In 1908 Aldred formed a free-love union with Rose Witcop, and in 1909 their son Annesley was born. The baby was only a few months old when Guy was jailed for publishing the *Indian Sociologist*, a paper which had been banned following the assassination in London of a Government official by an Indian patriot. Aldred believed neither in political assassination nor in political suppression.

This imprisonment brought him the friendship of Sir Walter Strickland, a baronet who lived in self-imposed exile from Britain, and who travelled the world, friend and benefactor of suppressed nationalities. The friendship between the anarchist and the aristocrat lasted till the older man's death in 1938, when he left enough money for the establishment of the Strickland Press in Glasgow.

When he came out of prison in July 1910, Aldred revived his groups and started a monthly paper, *The Herald of Revolt*. As it carried a column of Scottish Notes, presumably it circulated north of the border. In 1912 the Glasgow Clarion Scouts invited Aldred to speak in the Pavilion Theatre, followed by a Scottish tour of nine meetings. The radical traditions and proletarian atmosphere of Glasgow appealed to Aldred, and, having given up his job on the *Daily Chronicle* to devote all his time to socialist propaganda, he returned often to the city.

His meetings were well attended. His youth — he was twenty-five — his vigour, his oratory, his mighty polemics, his personality were all magnetic. Specially interested were the Socialist Labour Party, founded in 1903 under the influence of James Connolly. They were among the major socialist organisations in Scotland, and their industrial unionism made them sympathetic to Guy's antiparliamentarism.

Another interested group were the anarchists. They had their origin in the Socialist League of William Morris. At their inception in 1895 they had fifty members, and although for a time outshone by their Paisley counterparts, carried on an energetic propaganda, bringing to the city such notables as Peter Kropotkin, Emma Goldman, and Voltairine de Cleyre. In 1912 they had a patron in George Davidson, director of Kodak Camera Company. He supplied them with headquarters in Buchanan Street, and financed the publication of a paper, *The Anarchist*. The editor was George Barrett, who died of consumption in 1919 aged thirty-four.

The Anarchist first appeared on May Sunday, 1912. Intended to strengthen the group, it caused dissension in the ranks. The editorial board became a caucus, holding private meetings and having unofficial dealings with the Freedom group in London without consultation with the other members. The secretary, Angus MacKay, resigned in protest, and when Aldred formed the Glasgow Communist Propaganda Group, many disgruntled anarchists were among the first members.[1]

Aldred was booked for another Clarion mission in 1913. By the time the war broke out he had a number of groups in Lanarkshire, Fife, and Aberdeen.

Aldred had described the 1913 Basle Labour and Socialist Congress as a gathering of careerists and potential traitors to the workers' struggle: 'The socialists of Europe have betrayed the workers of the world. . . . The syndicates of France have united with the social democrats of Germany to deluge Europe with proletarian blood.'[2] He denounced as a warmonger Blatchford, who had sent forth another Clarion call to the youth of Britain: 'It is the duty of every British citizen to support the government, especially Lord Kitchener and Winston Churchill. . . .'

The title of *The Herald of Revolt* was changed to *The Spur* — 'Because the Workers need a Spur.' The first editorial said: '. . . The workers must think and act. Anarchists, socialists, and Trade Unionists in every district must merge into a single unit to control the situation. . . .'

Guy Aldred took no part in the industrial disputes on the Clyde — from which many careers were made. The workers had no country to fight for. National states had been contrived by emerging capitalism, they had no substance in reality; and patriotism had been fostered among the dispossessed to make them defend their masters' wealth and power. He condemned the munition makers as assassins of their own kindred. He castigated workers' leaders who were prepared to condone this mass murder, making it an excuse to be paid twopence extra an hour.

In 1916 Aldred was called up for military service. He did not respond and when he was charged he caused two court adjournments while advice was sought on whether or not he was a married man by Scots law of habit and repute. A Scottish advocate, Mr Steadman, told the court that he could say 'without hesitation' that Guy Aldred was married according to Scots law. The magistrate who had sought the advice promptly rejected it: 'It is for me to say whether or not he is married; and I say he isn't.' Guy was fined five pounds and handed over to the military authorities to face the first of four courts martial.

The next three years were spent in prison with brief spells of liberty under the Cat and Mouse Act. He was constantly on work and discipline strike and spent much of his time in the punishment cells. In a Home Office report he was named as a leader of the Wandsworth Prison riot in 1919.[3] But we must leave his prison experiences for another essay. Let us consider his political assumptions.

It was Aldred's contention that Marxism was antiparliamentary, and international. It had been driven within national confines with the fall of the Paris Commune and the persecution which followed. From this situation arose social democracy, as a wing of the parliamentary system. Hence the betrayals of socialist aspirations, the promotion of capitalist economism, and the acceptance of war.

This situation was not created by Marx, but it was welcomed by him. The defeat of the French enabled him to shift the centre of European activity from France to Germany, and so get rid of the Proudhonists and Bakuninists. When the Franco-Prussian war was imminent Marx wrote to Engels, 20th July,

1870, 'The French need a thrashing. Is Prussia victorious, then state power will be centralised, thus centralising the German working-class. German preponderance will shift the centre of the West European Labour Movement from France to Germany. . . . Its preponderance over France would be the preponderance of our theory over the one of Proudhon.'[4]

This wish of Marx was realised in 1871 when France was defeated. Engels wrote, in the 1895 preface to *Class Struggles in France*, 'As Marx predicted, the war of 1870-1871, and the fall of the Commune, shifted the gravity of the European Labour movement from France to Germany.' This, said Aldred, brought Engels to the ridiculous deduction that 'The successful employment of the parliamentary vote entailed the acceptance of an entirely new tactic by the proletariat, and this has undergone rapid development. It has been realised that the political institutions in which the domination of the burgeoisie is incorporated offer a fulcrum whereby the proletariat can work for the overthrow of these very institutions. The social democrats have participated in the elections to the various diets, municipal councils, industrial courts . . . consequently the bourgeoisie and the government have become much more alarmed at the constitutional, rather than at the unconstitutional activities of the workers, dreading the results of the elections more than the results of rebellions.' Thus, remarked Aldred, the leadership of the movement passed to Kautsky, notorious for his weary theorising, practical reaction, and renegadism.

Guy Aldred blamed Engels for fostering parliamentary socialism as opposed to commune socialism after the death of Marx. The early Social Democratic Federation was unsure of this point, according to Belfort Bax. There were those who believed in political action and those who were convinced that anything beyond propaganda, tempered by occasional direct action, was of the bourgeoisie. Aldred saw in 1906 what became indisputable twenty years later, that to make socialism a matter of electoral power was to make it a conserving force within the system, not a power to overthrow it.

Guy Aldred was in prison when the Russian Revolution took place. The excitement inside was greater than outside. What was essential now was solidarity. There must be unity. The Groups of the United Kingdom must federate into a British section of the Third International. In February 1918 Aldred smuggled a statement out of Brixton Prison. This called for 'A sense of reality to grow out of our differences.'[5] He was released from prison in August 1918 and arrested again to face his fourth court martial. The following January he was set free under the Cat and Mouse Act after a seven-day hunger strike. His most able colleague Henry Sara was also free. They got down to work at once.

In March 1919 the Socialist Labour Party issued a manifesto calling for a Communist League. It advocated the formation of the workers' own Party to form Councils.[6] A Unity Conference was held, and the Communist League was established by an amalgamation of S.L.P. local Groups and Communist

Propaganda Groups. Aldred and Sara set out to carry the message throughout Britain. They were both arrested and returned to prison — as they could be, without trial, under the Act.

Aldred was released in May, after another hunger strike. In Glasgow the welcoming celebration was two-fold. It also marked — by a Night of Frolic, Dancing, and Games — the opening of Liberty Rooms, 13 Burnbank Gardens, off Great Western Road, as the group's headquarters. Later this was renamed Bakunin House and became probably the best-known socialist centre in Glasgow.

The Communist League had a short-lived organ, *The Communist*.[7] The pen of Aldred was much in evidence. Correspondents addressed him as 'the Organiser', though there is no note of an official endorsement of this office. He was undoubtedly the outstanding personality of the organisation.

Sylvia Pankhurst was the outstanding personality of the Workers' Socialist Federation organ, *The Workers' Dreadnought*. She suggested a merger between the Communist League and the Workers' Socialist Federation to form a British Communist Party. Negotiations were slow in getting under way. At a congress of its groups the W.S.F. declared itself the British Communist Party (British section of the Third International).[8] Sylvia had formed her Communist Party without Lenin's blessing, though she was in his favour and expected her action to be endorsed. But her group was antiparliamentary and federalist, as were most of the groups outside the two parliamentary parties of the left. It was assumed a new Communist Party would be likewise in character. Lenin had other ideas and called for a Unity Conference of many of these smaller groups. The result was the formation of the Communist Party of Great Britain.

This party leapt on to the stage of history in a series of somersaults which were to become characteristic. One backwards leap changed its members from antiparliamentarians to parliamentarians, and another from strong opponents of the Second International to adherents, via the Labour Party, to which they must seek affiliation. The third contortion was painful enough to draw forth futile protests. The constituent groups had to kill themselves off and become submerged in an amorphous mass membership of sloganisers orchestrated from a Soviet score.

To rescue commune-ism from the rising tide of opportunism, Aldred brought together the Communist Propaganda Groups and sympathetic anarchist comrades into an Antiparliamentary Communist Federation, with headquarters at Bakunin House. He had gained from the experience of the Socialist League of Morris that an organisation of workers cannot be maintained on purely negative principles. Polemics against parliamentarians was not enough, there must be action. He proposed a programme based on the tactic of the Sinn Fein in 1918. They had put up candidates at the general election for the Westminster parliament but the elected members had assembled in Dublin, had declared themselves the first *Dail Eirann*, and as the Government of Ireland had declared war on the English invader.[9]

Aldred drew a parallel between the invaded nation of Irish and the invaded nation of the workers. Disraeli had said that there were two nations, the rich and the poor. Let the nation of the poor use the electoral machinery of their masters, the nation of the rich, to establish their own Government. Let the workers put forward candidates pledged not to go to the legislature of the enemy but to remain with the people, forming an Assembly of the Workers' Republic.

The new organisation insisted on having a journal of its own. *The Spur* was Aldred's personal mouthpiece. So an editorial board was elected and eventually the new paper appeared in February 1921. It was called *The Red Commune*, and was entirely the work of the editorial board. Aldred was in London at this time. The paper published the A.P.C.F. manifesto based on the 'Sinn Fein tactic'. It also reported a speech by Colonel Cecil L'Estrange Malone, M.P., who had been imprisoned for six weeks for writing that the House of Commons was the kept harlot of the capitalist press.

On 2 March 1921 there were raids, almost simultaneously, on Bakunin House and on Aldred's London flat. Aldred was arrested and brought to Glasgow. The federation secretary, Jenny Patrick, and the chairman of the editorial board, Douglas McLeish, were also arrested. Later the printer of *The Red Commune* was added to the bag. Aldred was kept in custody in Duke Street prison for four months awaiting trial. The others were allowed bail.

The trial opened on 10 June 1921 in the Glasgow High Court amid a great deal of excitement. On the calendar of cases were two murder trials, and several charges of mobbing, rioting, illegal drilling, and possession of arms. Recently there had been an affray immortalised for a few years thereafter in some quarters in a ballad entitled 'The Smashing of the Van'. This commemorated an I.R.A. attack on a prison van, which resulted in the arrest of a Father McRory in Abercromby Street and in disturbances resulting in High Court appearances.

The eight-page indictment against Aldred and his confederates boiled down to a charge of advocating the establishment of a communist republic by a method involving the destruction of parliamentary government by Sinn Fein candidature. Aldred defended himself and his comrades. He did not deny the publication of the paper, but maintained that it was 'good in law'. The jury took twenty minutes to reach a verdict of guilty, with one dissension. Aldred was sentenced to one year's imprisonment. The remand period was not taken into account. The other accused were each sentenced to three months.

Aldred served his time in Barlinnie Prison, where John MacLean was a fellow convict. MacLean was the only parliamentarian of that time whom Aldred did not accuse of place-mongering. There is an assertion in MacLean's Gorbals address: 'To get a Scottish Workers' Republic I will not go to the London House of Commons, but stay in Scotland, helping the Scots unemployed, standing by those at work, educating in the Scottish Labour College, and carrying the Revolutionary Propaganda all over Scotland (and

England too).'[10] In another part of the statement he says, 'To carry out such a work effectively I have resolved to stay in Scotland even if the winner, and so will adopt the Sinn Fein tactic.'   If we also note that one of MacLean's last slogans was 'Let Glasgow flourish by the preaching of the Revolutionary Word',[11] we may suppose that Aldred and MacLean had discussions in Barlinnie, for there is an Aldred undertone in this line of action. In Barlinnie Aldred wrote an essay, 'The Word to the World'. To Aldred and MacLean there could be no question of the *Word* standing for theological mysticism, or even Feuerbachian *essence*; it was the standard-bearers' challenge in a very real struggle.

Aldred came out of prison in time to stand for the Shettleston division of Glasgow in the 1922 General Election. The prospect was not encouraging. The A.P.C.F. had not propagated the idea, nor in any way prepared the ground while he was absent. *The Spur* had been allowed to collapse, and *The Red Commune*, on which the comrades had insisted to show their independence from the dominant personality of Aldred, had not gone into a second issue. The anarchist faction had asserted its opposition to the use of the ballot box even as a weapon against parliamentarism. So *The Red Commune* episode caused Aldred to lose sixteen months in his mid-thirties, and to wreck the plan on which the A.P.C.F. had been founded. This, however, is a criticism which Aldred never made, either in speech or in writing.

Repudiating the election campaign as a group, the comrades still helped, unenthusiastically, as individuals. John McGovern, later I.L.P. candidate for the division, was Aldred's election agent. In his autobiography he confesses his lack of interest. Guy worked as usual with titanic energy, but considering the indifference of the group and the bad press, the extent of his defeat is not surprising. He polled 400 votes.[12] This put him in the category of freak candidates, and the image stuck to him. Despite the low poll, his meetings had been attended with so much enthusiasm that in a maiden speech in the House of Commons, Edwin Scrymgeour (who had defeated Churchill at Dundee) warned the House to beware of this man Aldred who was cheered to the echo when he was committing himself to the most drastic line of action.[13]

Margaret Sanger, pioneer advocate of birth control, was touring the United Kingdom under the auspices of the New Generation League with Bertrand Russell and Guy Aldred among the speakers. She had known Rose and Guy from pre-war times, and in 1920 Aldred had arranged a meeting for her on Glasgow Green. She describes the audience in her autobiography: about two thousand 'shipyard workers in caps and baggy corduroys (who) stood close together, listening in utter stillness, without cough or whisper'. In the evening she spoke to a 'ladies only' gathering in Bakunin House.

On 22 December 1922, Aldred was prosecuted for publishing Margaret Sanger's pamphlet, *Family Limitation*. He had taken the precaution of having a printed slip inserted into every pamphlet. This was a declaration to be signed by the purchaser stating that he/she was over twenty-one, considered artificial family limitation justified, and wished to know the various hygienic methods which could be adopted, and 'undertakes to keep this booklet out of the hands of unmarried persons under the age of 21'.

A few years earlier in the United States William Sanger had been tricked into handing one of his wife's booklets to a government officer. After confinement without bail he was sentenced to thirty days' imprisonment and fined 150 dollars. In passing sentence the judge had said, 'Your crime is not only a violation of the laws of Man, but of God as well. . . . If some people would go around urging Christian women to bear children instead of wasting time on women's suffrage this country would be better off.' Now this menace had struck Britain. Four detectives were detailed to obtain copies of the pamphlet (price sixpence) without signing the form, thus acquiring evidence of indiscriminate publication. With predictable efficiency and justifiable falsehoods — since the nation's moral health was at risk — the officers succeeded.

Among the witnesses Aldred called for the defence was Sir Arbuthnot Lane, consultant surgeon to Guy's Hospital. This eminent authority said that the booklet should be in the hands of every young person about to be married. 'Would you allow a boy of sixteen to read it?' asked the somewhat shaken magistrate. 'This is nothing to some of the things they read,' retorted Sir Arbuthnot. The magistrate ordered the books to be destroyed 'in the interests of the morals of society'.[14] At this point in their lives Aldred and Rose parted company. She continued her birth control work by opening a clinic in London. But the authorities were watching her. When she was editing *The Spur* during the war, they had not brought up the point that she was technically an alien, having come to the country when she was five years of age. Now they used this in a threat to deport her to Russia, where (not even knowing the language) she would have been imprisoned as an anarchist. To defeat the plot Aldred agreed to go through a form of civil marriage. Rose Witcop died in London in July 1932. Shortly after that Aldred let it be known that he and Jenny Patrick, the secretary of the A.P.C.F., were living together in a free love association.

Aldred could not be without a paper for long and on May Sunday, 1923, the first issue of *The Commune* appeared. The name was a challenge to the Party concept, and proclaimed the ideal of *The Commune*. Its masthead proclamation was of loyalty to the Fourth International. This should not be confused with the later (Trotskyist) Fourth. This one was essentially anti-parliamentary and in vigorous opposition to the Third.

One of the first tasks of *The Commune* was to engage in a Glasgow Green free speech struggle. Glasgow Green is the ancient common land of the citizens of Glasgow.[15] Here women bleached their linen, young people played games, butchers slaughtered their cattle, and villains and heroes were hanged; and here the citizens foregathered to talk. In 1916 a bye-law had been passed forbidding meetings on the Green, but it was not enforced. Glasgow Green had been the venue for great gatherings in the past. Here the Labour movement laid its foundations. Now, in 1924, with a Labour secretary of state, William Adamson, the bye-law was applied. MacLean was dead but the group founded by him, the Scottish Workers' Republican Party, was very active; so was the A.P.C.F. They both, independently, defied the ban.

The Communist Party sneered at this defiance by Aldred's 'anti-panties', and the late John MacLean's 'claymore communists'. Willie Gallacher said in *The Worker* that the opposition to the ban was a 'stunt pure and simple'. *The Worker* editor, Aitken Ferguson, published an article under the banner: GIMME THAT MONUMENT. The reference was to the Nelson column where the proscribed meetings were taking place. *The Worker* article agreed with the Parks Committee that meetings should be banned, and gave reasons: '. . . a Catholic layman proving that the only way to heaven was via the Catholic faith. . . . I.L.P., B.S.P., S.L.P., and so many other P.s hurtling defiance at each other.'[16]

Members of the A.P.C.F. and the other groups defying the ban were charged by the police. Then followed arrests and imprisonments. Aldred gave notice of appeal and conducted his own case and that of the other accused. He submitted that the Act under which the bye-law was framed contained a provision that no bye-law could be based on this Act if such bye-law was repugnant to the laws of Scotland. The Green, Aldred maintained, was a traditional meeting-place of the people. The bye-law was not only repugnant to the laws of Scotland, it had been fitfully and capriciously enforced. The Lord Justice Clerk agreed that as the bye-law stood, a small boy could be prosecuted for playing a jew's harp on the Green. The appellant had argued his case well, but while his Lordship was not enamoured of the bye-law he failed to see how it was repugnant to the laws of Scotland to regulate the admitted right of public speaking. The case against the accused was upheld, but changes in the bye-law were indicated.

There was a federation of antiparliamentary groups in London and there were several autonomous groups in the North of England. Glasgow was the nerve-centre of the Federation's activity. This was Aldred's home base; here — as an obituary writer wrote much later — he bestrode the political scene like a colossus. Every night his voice was heard, denouncing the capitalist system, or the blight of religious superstition, and just as frequently blasting the careerist traitors of the Labour Party, the compromisers of the I.L.P., and the hirelings of the Communist Party. Every month *The Commune* appeared, giving permanence to the denunciations of his tongue. He declared himself 'The Red Scourge' because he whipped the charlatans out of the temple of socialism.

There were three A.P.C.F. groups in Glasgow, the Central Group, and the Eastern and Springburn branches. Bakunin House, Burnbank Gardens, was the headquarters of the Federation, and there was a Bakunin Press bookshop in Buchanan Street. The Springburn branch hired a hall for its business meetings, but the Eastern branch had a shop in Shettleston Road — Ye Olde Redde Book Shoppe — as some humorous comrade named it. It was also advertised as The Red Spot in the East. Practically all the A.P.C.F. members lived in poverty, in the worst of grey crumbling tenements, but it was a cheerful band of robust individuals, with no self-pity and little sentiment. Speakers came and went; the most enduring were Guy Aldred, James Murray, Willie McDougall (still active in 1977, in his mid-eighties), and Charlie Doran. From Paisley, Hamilton, Blantyre, Coatbridge, and Burnbank came other stalwarts in the cause.

In the late twenties and early thirties there was much activity involving conflict with the police. The city was being modernised to accommodate the motor car. Traffic lights were being erected at street corners where public meetings had been held since Chartist times. Foremost in the struggle to retain these sites were the A.P.C.F. and the Scottish Workers' Republican Party. In 1929 the Glasgow University students' magazine *Ygorra* published a photograph of Barlinnie with the caption: 'Headquarters of the Communist Party Antiparliamentary Confederation, where non-workers of the world unite.' Aldred described this as a disgraceful picture, sneering at the free speech struggle of the common people. As the students had blacklegged on the trams during the General Strike there was not much love lost between the Town and the Gown.

In 1931 the Green again became a free speech battleground. As a result of Aldred's challenge in 1922, that portion of the Green outside the gates known as Jail Square was exempted from the 1916 bye-law prohibiting meetings. In March 1927 Glasgow Corporation made application to the Sheriff Principal to revert to the 1916 bye-law, by which they hoped to clear meetings from outside the gates as well as from inside. Aldred appeared at the hearing on 29 March and opposed the town clerk's application. He complained that no Labour town councillor had protested against this closure of meetings on an historic site where they themselves had gathered support for the establishment of the Labour movement. He said the application of this bye-law was contrary to the good government of the city; this so-called act of regulation was, in practice, an act of prohibition.

In July 1931 a number of meetings were held on the Green without a permit and the speakers were booked by the police. A Free Speech Council was formed, and in Central Halls, Bath Street, at a conference of 'workers and workless', composed of delegates from several Groups, a Council of Action was set up on an A.P.C.F. resolution. *The Commune* had lapsed, but Aldred launched a new paper, *The Council*. There were some broken heads in this campaign. McGovern, having his wounds dressed in a police cell, was told that the 'city is in a grip of terror. The boys are smashing windows and looting in every street'.[17] This time the Communist Party was taking part.

Aldred saw no point in leading the workers into baton charges. He saw no value in sensation. The bye-law had to be removed or amended. To this end he carried a test case involving nine accused to the High Court. As a result of this appeal, the offending bye-law was scrapped and another substituted. This bye-law gave the right of public speaking in such parts as are set aside in parks and open spaces. Jail Square, however (which had enchanted William Morris as a modern forum of philosophical citizens), was lost to the flowerbeds.

The part set aside for public discussion without a permit was the Old Bandstand site. Aldred was accused by the other groups in the Council of Action of having compromised. As they had no ideas beyond banner-waving and abusive chanting, it was obvious that Aldred had taken the better course. To establish the right gained, Maxton, McGovern, Jean Mann and Aldred held a meeting at the Old Bandstand on May Sunday, 1932. After that the Green was forgotten by all except Aldred.

Aldred wanted to press for the establishment of speaking sites in every park. He would hold a referendum in the city to assess the strength of public opinion on the closing of Jail Square and the right of public speaking. He would do this by standing for every ward in the city at the next municipal election. However, the A.P.C.F. refused to support any ballot-box activity. Aldred retorted that to place antiparliamentarians above socialism was to destroy socialism. Labour parliamentarism had been discredited, 'now let us preach socialism'. What was required was a united socialist movement. In the February 1933 issue of *The Council*, Guy Aldred announced that he had left the A.P.C.F.

This was the time of hunger marches. Aldred opposed them. A unity of articulate workers was what was needed. Careerist politicos were marching the people all the way to London for a look at Westminster, thereby acknowledging its right and power. The workers should stay at home and form their own local councils, backed by their power as producers. A United Socialist Movement was inaugurated and its first manoeuvre was the nominating of Guy Aldred for fourteen wards in the city. There were thirty-four wards, but various factors prevented nomination in all of them. In his election address Aldred 'outlined the history of bye-law 20'. He explained: 'I am not seeking Town Council honours, and I shall pursue none of the usual methods of obtaining votes. If you realise the vital nature of these questions you will vote for me as a protest against the studied neglect of your citizen rights by the Lord Provost, the Magistrates and the Councillors of the City of Glasgow, without distinction as to their political complexion. . . . When the Town Council enacts bye-laws in the terms of certain statutes, those bye-laws are binding not only upon the citizens of Glasgow, but also upon the Members of the Council. . . .'

Aldred concluded a vigorous campaign with a 'final rally' in the City Hall. To a heckler who shouted that the old 'anti-panty' was turning his coat, Aldred pointed out that to dissipate his energy over fourteen wards was not the way to get a seat on the Council. The result was over a thousand votes for Guy Aldred. As his referendum covered only half the city and for every vote cast there would be possibly three sympathisers not prepared to lose their vote, it could be reckoned that around six thousand responsible citizens knew and appreciated Aldred's attitude to free speech in the parks.

Aldred's propaganda never ceased, he never took a holiday. The next eruption was a paper called *Attack!* and an outburst of leaflets denouncing the Empire Exhibition held in Bellahouston Park in 1938. Aldred was incensed at the effrontery of the government in staging this display of imperial wealth and power in a city of despairing unemployment; where the poorly dressed and half-starved overcrowded the crumbling tenements; where two shillings a week was allowed to feed a child — and one pound was required to feed a police-man's horse. He poured forth torrents of vituperation on the Labour parliamentarians in the House and the Council for not condemning but actually supporting this parade of colonial exploitation as a boon to the workers of Glasgow.

Another of his concerns at this time was the Morison Committee report on the Scots law of marriage. He wrote in the *Glasgow Evening Times* of 25 January 1937: 'The doctrine of marriage by interchange of consent is the most rational and most moral doctrine of marriage in the world. . . . Because marriage is a spiritual union and not a union of bodies the Scots irregular marriage requires consent, actual, living, ever-present consent and consecration. . . . It requires no ceremony. . . . Real marriage is not a rite, but a fact. . . .' He put his point of view before the Morison Committee in Edinburgh.[18]

With the outbreak of the Spanish Civil War in July 1936, meetings were held every night, bigger and more excited gatherings than at any time since the General Strike. It was not a simple conflict with Fascists on one side and Communists on the other. The Spanish government was anarcho-syndicalist, for Marxism had not gained a hold on the Iberian peninsula. It was the aim of the Stalinist communists to develop their power in Spain and take over from the Syndicalists. It was an ancient conflict expressed in modern terms. A further conflict arose between the Trotskyists and the Stalinists. In the streets of Glasgow this struggle was expressed in the antagonisms of the Anarchists (that is, the rump of the old A.P.C.F., now called the Anarchist Federation) and the United Socialist Movement (Aldred's group) on the side of the Syndicalists; the I.L.P. supporting the P.O.U.M. (Workers' Party of Marxist Unity) and the Communist Party attempting to take over the entire anti-fascist left.

This broke into open conflict in the streets of Barcelona in May 1937. Two of Aldred's colleagues, Jenny Patrick and Ethel Macdonald, had gone to Spain to work for the Government. Jenny escaped from Madrid before the city fell. Ethel was a victim of the Communist putsch and was imprisoned. With pressure from Aldred, the British consul secured her release. When she arrived back in Glasgow a welcoming crowd of 300 met her at Central Station. To them she said, 'I went to Spain full of hopes and dreams. . . . I return full of sadness, dulled by the tragedy I have seen.'

At a full meeting held in the McLellan Galleries on 'Spain — a Lost Horizon', she attacked the Stalinists for their power-struggle behind the lines while the Spanish people were being slaughtered. It was a stormy meeting and there were several ejections. The audience in the main knew only of a straight-forward fascist-communist conflict, and were bewildered by Ethel Macdonald's contentions and accusations; they did not realise that this was a continuing struggle that went back to the days when Bakunin wrote of 'the two Communisms', and had been fought ruthlessly in the Soviet Union till Stalin crushed all opposition to his personal power.

When Frank Leech, the leading figure in the Glasgow Anarchist Federation, died about two years later the organisation fell into the hands of two speakers of great wit but little understanding. It is to this group that Woodcock refers when he says in his book *Anarchism*: 'As late as the 1940s I encountered a group of anarchist working men in Glasgow for whom Stirnerism was a belated gospel.' When these two orators emigrated at the end of the war, the anarchist movement in Glasgow came to an end — for the time being — and the link with William Morris was broken.

When Sir Walter Strickland died in 1938, Aldred was his beneficiary. As Strickland's money had been invested in what were now enemy countries, most of it was lost, but enough was recovered to establish the Strickland Press in George Street opposite Albion Street. Here during the war years Guy Aldred published his monthly paper *The Word*, and a stream of pamphlets from his restless pen. He also published fifty pamphlets written by the twelfth Duke of Bedford. These were not socialist but pacifist, stressing the need for money reform. The Duke also wrote a column in *The Word*. The association was formed because the Duke could not easily find a publisher for his courageously unpopular views.

The association developed into a friendship which lasted twelve years. On several occasions when he came to Glasgow to address a meeting, the Duke stayed, not with Aldred in the Baliol Street tenement where Guy and Jenny Patrick had lived since the closure of Bakunin House, but in Gibson Street, three stairs above Smith's bookshop, where Ethel Macdonald and J. T. Caldwell lived. This was considered more convenient than Aldred's house.

When the Duke died in a shooting accident in 1953, Guy Aldred wrote in *The Word*: 'Nothing I could pen could express my personal loss at the untimely death of a good companion. No words of mine can restore the Duke to the fold of the living. He has passed, and the struggle must go on. Everyone knows that there existed a strong personal friendship between us. I took the Chair at the first pacifist meeting he held in Glasgow — in St Andrew's Halls on Friday, March 29th 1940. The Strickland Press published all his heretical speeches in the House of Lords; the most simple, brave and useful speeches ever made in that assembly. . . . His zeal for truth, and his willingness to defend heresy, even heresy with which he did not agree, made him a brave and a great man.'[19]

Wartime blackout put an end to outdoor meetings, but Aldred spoke regularly in Central Halls for the United Socialist Movement and was a frequent guest speaker for other organisations. For a time he was chairman of the Glasgow No Conscription League. He appeared many times before the tribunals in support of conscientious objectors.

After the war, from 1946-48 Aldred promoted the idea of world government. The office at George Street became the headquarters of the World Federalists. He explained his thinking to a meeting in Central Halls on 7 April 1946: 'Surely it is evident that our past propaganda is getting out of touch with the world of fact. In a world where distance is annihilated we must alter the focus of our vision. In a world growing smaller we must develop an all-embracing world outlook. We must propagate the idea of a world republic, with world citizenship. Nationalism must end. What we require is the direct representation of the people as world citizens in a non-national assembly. . . .'

Aldred promoted the idea in *The Word* and at public meetings. He also seized the chance of the general election to stand as a World Government candidate for Glasgow Central. He claimed that forty-four members of parliament supported the idea of World Federalism, but none of them dared open association with him. The idea soured for Aldred when distinctions began to be made between 'peace-loving' nations and 'bully' nations, and world government took on the form of an anti-Soviet alliance. The Korean war obliterated Aldred's hopes. There was no sense in pursuing a dream.

His World Government candidatures did not lessen the vigour of his anti-parliamentary propaganda. Every election campaign was a powerful denunciation of 'careerist charlatans'. Between 1946-62 he fought six general elections.[20] He had no idea of being 'successful'. To him success was measured by the amount of propaganda he could spread by free postage, publicised meetings, and press coverage. It was always a struggle to raise the necessary cash, but the alternative was to slide into a routine of meetings in relative obscurity.

There were common features in every contest. One of these was the distribution of a card on which was printed a pledge to resign — if elected — on demand from the constituents. There was also a statement that he would not represent a party, but the residents of the division. He would accept no more as salary than the sum reckoned to be the average national wage — at that time £5 weekly; and this sum should also be the pension rate for the elderly. He would press for this to be the rate for M.P.s, with legitimate expenses allowed under careful scrutiny. His ultimate aim was to have workers' representatives boycott Westminster.

With the victory of the Labour Party in 1945, the top members of the smaller, older, and at one time more dynamic Independent Labour Party felt the cold breeze of obsolescence blow over them and hurried to the warmth of success. At a national convention of the I.L.P. a motion for reaffiliation to the Labour Party was defeated by a narrow majority. James Maxton, most revered figure in the I.L.P., was against the motion; his colleague and election agent, James Carmichael, was in favour, according to *Forward*. Fenner Brockway wrote in *Socialist Leader*, 3 August 1946: 'Maxton understood the significance of Labour's victory last June yet he could not identify himself with its government because that would have meant a denial of his prophetic vision.'

Maxton had no ambition except to remain parliamentary member for Bridgeton, as he had been for a whole generation. Knowledge of impending death would, in any case, have made him cherish vision rather than consider the futile pursuit of a career. Two of the five Glasgow town councillors had already deserted; the two members of Parliament, John McGovern and Campbell Stephen, were waiting for Maxton to die so that they would feel 'free'.

Maxton died on 26 June 1946. The writ for the Bridgeton election was issued on 16 August. James Carmichael was nominated by the I.L.P. as candidate. It was an absurd situation. Carmichael was in favour of re-affiliation to the Labour Party. He could have joined as an individual member, but he would have joined without status. It was to his advantage that he let the I.L.P. make him an M.P. before his defection, then he would bring with him the Bridgeton division as a present to the Labour Party. Yet the Labour National Executive appointed John Wheatley to stand against Carmichael for a seat they would get in any case. This, said Guy Aldred, who stood as an Independent Socialist, was splitting the Labour vote — something *he* was accused of doing — and might easily result in this Labour stronghold being lost to the Conservatives. He issued a leaflet asking James Carmichael to answer the question: Did he intend to 'jilt' the I.L.P. and join the Labour Party if elected? It would have been inexpedient to supply the truthful answer, so Carmichael gave none, except by his action. He won the seat and by December had joined the Labour Party. So had McGovern, who had pleaded with the people of Bridgeton to elect Carmichael as I.L.P. member of Parliament, for that had been Jimmy Maxton's dying wish. A fellow defector had been Campbell Stephen, I.L.P. member for Camlachie (Glasgow), but a heart attack removed him from the scene and Camlachie fell vacant. Campbell Stephen had won Camlachie as an I.L.P. candidate, so the I.L.P. considered it their constituency, but he had died while a member of the Labour Party, so the Labour Party considered it their seat. The I.L.P. candidate was Annie Maxton, sister of Jimmy. At Bridgeton much had been made of 'the Maxton tradition', and many dewy-eyed tributes made to Maxton's memory. Carmichael had denounced the 'Labour brass-hats', expressing the opinion that they needed 'kicked in the right direction'. Now, having kicked himself in the right direction, he was one of them. The Maxton tradition was forgotten and Annie Maxton accused of being an inter-loper. She evidently had not learned the lesson, 'If you can't beat them, join them.' The seat was lost to the Conservatives.

Guy Aldred fought this seat as an independent socialist. This time he did not end at the bottom of the poll. He had 345 votes. The Liberal had 321. When the election was over, Aldred booked the Bridgeton Town Hall in the heart of I.L.P. territory to denounce this parliamentary socialist hypocrisy. It was a big meeting, but the audience came more to hear the mighty wrath of Aldred than to express any indignation of their own. Carmichael had served his own interest. Most of them would have done the same. Aldred's faith in the integrity of the 'common people' was unshakable.

Aldred had not forgotten his pledge made at the Central division election. A reference to his programme is made in a report appearing in *The Bulletin*, describing a meeting in London Road: 'A stout figure, carelessly dressed in a knickerbocker suit, prepares for his oration by sucking a throat pastille, then he mounts the platform. The practised street orator scorns the microphone as artificial. . . . Almost at once he is calling for old age pensions of £5 per week . . . **and what is good** enough for old age pensioners is good enough for Guy Aldred

s

if, and when, he is an M.P. He makes it very clear that it would be no personal favour for him to get into Westminster. . . . There is no pleading for votes with Aldred. He tells the people that if he is not at the top of the poll the loss will be theirs.'

In its 'Pertinent and Otherwise' column *The Bulletin* brought out two essential points in Aldred's programme. Under the heading 'Loose Talk', the paper said: 'That was a pretty shocking proposal that Guy Aldred made in Bridgeton the other night. He said, you remember, that if ten electors could propose a man for Parliament, it was only fair that ten electors should be able to call him to account after he was in. Golly, it is as well Parliament isn't sitting, or there would be some questions asked about that. What a way to carry on. Where does he think he is? In a democracy? But apparently Guy wasn't fooling because he said that if he was returned and people started taking a dim view of him, he'd call a public meeting, and if the general vote was agin him, he'd resign. . . . Seriously, though, this chap Aldred simply isn't playing the game . . . now the man is saying that he wants only £250 of the £1,000 salary if he is elected and the rest can go to a trust fund for the benefit of the constituency.'

Guy Aldred stood at three further parliamentary elections, the last being in 1963. There was no pause in his activity during the intervening years, and many Glaswegians became acquainted with his distinctive figure on his daily journey to and from the Strickland Press.

In May 1959 Ethel Macdonald became the victim of an illness which slowly, dreadfully, relentlessly led to complete paralysis. On 1 December 1960 she died in Knightswood Hospital, Glasgow. The press remembered that she had been in the news some years earlier and gave her headline obituaries — the *Glasgow Evening Citizen*: 'SCOTS SCARLET PIMPERNEL DIES: She became a legend in Spain.' The article recalled that Ethel Macdonald had been an announcer for the English-speaking department of Barcelona Radio, and her audience had been worldwide. When, following the communists' May attack on the anarchists, she had been arrested she engineered several escapes of fellow detainees, hence the appellation 'Pimpernel'. The loss of Ethel Macdonald to the Strickland Press was very great; to her comrades the personal loss was incalculable.

After the war town planners were let loose in Glasgow with blueprint and bulldozer, and, for better or worse, George Street fell victim to their schemes. The *Evening Citizen* for 13 May 1961 carried a headline: 'NOW *THE WORD* IS HOMELESS — After 22 years it has to move from George Street.' The text read, in part: 'Glasgow's amiable knickerbockered anarchist, Guy Aldred, is having to find new printing headquarters for *The Word*, organ of the United Socialist Movement. He has been given notice to quit his George Street premises after 22 years' tenancy, but cannot find anywhere else to go. . . .'

Glasgow Corporation were not helpful in finding Aldred other premises. Hoardings went up round the doomed property, bulldozers began their dusty meal at the corner of Montrose Street. Aldred said he would sit tight till suitable accommodation was offered. The Corporation sent engineers to assess the cost of dismantling the machinery for ejection — presumably into the street. Aldred still sat tight. Plaster dropped on to the paper as it was being fed to the machine; rain plopped into buckets. The air grew pungent with the odour of damp and decay; then, a bluff having been called, Aldred was given the keys of a shop in Montrose Street.

Now the demolition could continue unimpeded. The *Glasgow Herald* for 29 March 1962 described the passing of George Street: 'The grey block of buildings in George Street, now rapidly disappearing midst clouds of dust and falling debris as demolition men clear the way for Glasgow's latest development scheme, has a history curiously compounded of respectability and religious fervour. Yesterday the workmen were hard at it with their pickaxes at No. 136 — once the site of the Kale Kirk, which belonged to a small independent sect and was so called because the members of the congregation were always given platefuls of kale, whether as part of a secret ritual or simply as sustenance is uncertain. Soon the bulldozers will move on to the site of the tenement (demolished about 1930) which was the birthplace of Sir George Burns, co-founder of the Cunard Line, then relentlessly on round the corner to the little blue organ factory in North Portland Street, which was once a Quaker meeting house. Even the building recently vacated by a left-wing press in George Street (once considered a very superior residential quarter) seems already to have moved into the distant past. Through the greased windows can be seen some tracts and pamphlets they left behind them, including one on *Dogmas Discarded.*'

The misfortunes of the press, which tore at Guy privately, were not evident in his public activity. His speaking and writing went on, and his office was as often as ever a resort for the desperate and fearful seeking advice, or the assurance of his strong personality.

The Word dealt with most of the main issues of the time. One of these was the campaign for nuclear disarmament. Aldred was not a member of the C.N.D., nor did he take part in their demonstrations. He had a distrust of parades, believing their emotionalism was exploited by the insincere. But the object of the organisation had his sympathy, and when in late autumn 1962 a member of his audience suggested that he take advantage of the forthcoming Woodside by-election to launch an attack on the American use of Holy Loch as a nuclear base, he agreed, although he had no money and less means than ever of raising any.

There were six candidates for Woodside. Neil Carmichael, son of James Carmichael, was the Labour Party choice, and favourite to win. He said the over-riding issue was the need for jobs; a quarter of a million people had left Scotland over the past ten years to find security. Other Scottish M.P.s gave him their support, although, as the *Glasgow Herald* put it, 'Most of these do not endorse Mr Carmichael's overstepping the party line on unilateral nuclear disarmament.'

Asked if he would support the Labour Party's policy on defence if elected,

Carmichael said, 'The party's policy on defence is clearly printed in my election address. At Westminster I shall accept the Labour Party standing orders.' The Conservative candidate, Norman Glen, accused Carmichael of having accepted advice from the party to change his views in case his unilateralist position might damage the Labour vote. Carmichael replied that his views were well known and that within the Labour Party he would reserve the right to persuade his colleagues that his point of view was the right one.

It was, however, on this point of difference with the Labour Party that Carmichael got most of his campaign support. The Woodside Young Socialists, naturally vigorous, noisy and enthusiastic, were unilateralists in the extreme, and very much in favour of getting the Americans out of Holy Loch. To merit their support Carmichael had to speak their language — some of the time. To appease the party he had to accept the party's standing orders — some of the time. To confound Mr Glen's accusation of performing a *volte face* he had to add a rider to his acceptance of the standing orders to the effect that he would endeavour to subvert them. It was not a happy position to be in.

Aldred let it be known that he had sent a telegram to Earl Russell, leader of the Committee of 100: 'Strongly protest against the Committee of 100 supporting the working for the official Labour Party candidate at Woodside who has accepted the official Labour defence policy in opposition to myself. I am the anti-militarist and peace candidate.' Russell replied: 'I have no knowledge of the activities you mention. Suggest you approach the Scottish Committee of 100.'[21]

Some of the Young Socialists explained to Guy that Carmichael was 'a good lad. One of ourselves'. He could do more to get the Yanks out of Holy Loch by working from the inside than otherwise. This was a tune Guy had heard many times before.

A pen picture of Aldred during the campaign was given by Edward Ashton of the *Scottish Daily Mail* under the heading 'KNICKERBOCKER POLITICIAN': 'He has been called the "Knickerbocker politician" because of his unshakable loyalty to that Victorian fashion (probably the only conservative ingredient in his make-up). He has been hated, feared, reviled and imprisoned for his political beliefs. But today, by that odd switch of feeling that only the British public can manage, Guy A. Aldred, Independent Socialist candidate in the Woodside by-election, is regarded with a good-natured tolerant affection. None of the other candidates can even begin to match the experience and record of Aldred. . . . It is impossible to believe that this vigorously articulate man is seventy-six years old. There is not much grey in the dark hair brushed straight back. The black fuzzy eyebrows twitch as he emphasises a point. But the real gold is in the flow of words. The voice has the slightly brassy, carrying note of one who has learned his public speaking in tough street-corner, pre-microphone days when a man with a message had to make himself heard through his own fervour and lung power. . . . The reason for Aldred's private strength and public ineffectiveness lies, I think, in the fact that he is always the non-conformist who cannot compromise. . . .' The accompanying full-length photograph of Guy Aldred standing in a busy street was headed: 'WHAT A GUY!'

Polling took place on 22 November, the worst day of a dreadful month. Fog swirled like a river of filthy mist in the streets. The Young Socialists created a little liveliness outside the polling stations, but inside an almost palpable apathy hung on the silence. The vote counting took place that evening in the Sheriff Court Buildings. Guy expected around the usual 400, perhaps a few more since this was a farewell appearance. The barest flicker of disappointment crossed his face when the result was announced — Guy Aldred 134. As expected the seat was won by Neil Carmichael.

Outside, through the thick cold fog came the exultant cries of the Young Socialists telling the world that the Labour man was a jolly good fellow. Shadowy shapes showed them carrying him shoulder high to his car and depositing him inside — and off he went to Westminster. He is still there; and the Yanks are still at Holy Loch. After that excitement Woodside was a dull place for the Young Socialists. They soon dispersed as life called them on their separate ways. Guy Aldred went back to his work in the Strickland Press. He had seen it all before.

There followed a winter still remembered for its severity, yet Aldred never missed a day at his office. He carried on despite a bad cold; then most unexpectedly one bitter January night, he had a heart attack. Although he recovered and was able to get back to his desk, this was the beginning of a fatal decline. But he would not give up without a struggle. When he was no longer able to stand the strain of a two-hour public meeting he made a tape recording at home and, sitting on the platform while it was played, he then answered questions. Thus four of his speeches have been preserved.

The last recorded lecture was called 'Vision and Reality'. It was played to an audience in Central Halls, Bath Street, Glasgow, on 7 July 1963. The previous month he had asked his audience to come 'Down to Earth'. The title was topical because the first sputniks were hitting the headlines. Now he wanted to show that *on* earth dwells and *from* earth arises all the spirituality that man experiences, because it comes from himself and is part of his creative evolution. There is always implicit in Aldred's social analysis the belief in an improved human being creating and reacting to a better society.

He tried to convey to his socialist, atheistic audience that man's highest dreams were not impaired by a materialist conception, but were thereby given a reality. In 'Vision and Reality' he begins with a definition that makes the Greek meaning of vision of greater significance than the Latin. The latter means simply 'to see', the former means the same with an added implication, arising from philosophical usage, 'to see with the mind'. Aldred said:

'Its real definition is really *idea*, rather than vision. Nevertheless the word *idea* means intellectual understanding which is *subjective*, and is distinct from *objective* reality. Reality relates, not to subjective understanding but to objective observation. It is a concept of things as they are: it is factual. Vision means sailing on uncharted seas which represent the mind, setting out from the base of reality, finding its own way, venturing forth, and as a result discovering new realities.

'We tend to despise the use of the word Vision. It is regarded with disapproval and contempt. Nevertheless it is to men of vision that reality owes its development, and owes its worth to the people, whether they possess vision or not. All the realities around us, all the differences in our lives from that of our forefathers; the development of the man from the brute animal, is due to the faculty of Vision.

'In the beginning Man was a product of brute reality. He possessed no *soul* — and that does not mean some supernatural manifestation of something which has *descended* into Man. It is an expression of Man reaching upwards. It means that the animal has developed a new understanding and has therefore changed into a new being. But it is a growth from roots, it is a plant standing upright, stretching upwards, it is a challenge to dull reality. It becomes a part of a new Reality. It represents a mighty growth, a great power, fostering a new world.

'. . . Each generation is to some extent led by that Vision. Always man is seeking the Promised Land. Always the Vision arises on the horizon. Always, therefore, he is sailing uncharted seas in search of Utopia. And the Utopians are the real founders of scientific society; the *real* founders of a *real* world: a world that will one day be an abode of fairness and beauty for all mankind.

'It was Vision that inspired Isaiah to prophesy the triumph of righteousness. He was scorned and rejected. It was Vision that led Jesus to the Cross. He also was despised, till at last he was deified, and in that deification his Vision became the stock-in-trade of priests. Today, those of us who think, are scornful of that Vision, debased into priesthood. Yet, behind that imposture is the history of righteousness in poverty and misery, opposing the false realities of purple and fine linen, and the alleged riches of life. . . . It is the story of the struggle of science as well as of art for a world wherein science and art will work together for a fuller life and of leisure and beauty for all mankind. . . .

'Do not think I speak without experience. I speak with great bitterness. . . . I have challenged the cravens of fact, and those who have debased themselves before fact, before the chimera of Reality; and I have stood for truth. Of course I am bitter. I am bitter at the lack of support. I am bitter because I am growing old, and the voice I have used for so long has not had the effect it should have had. In this I am wrong. There should be no bitterness, for I know that finally the Cause shall triumph.

'And so I have finished, comrades. A very poor, limp ending to my address, but if you will take these seeds and plant them within your own minds and in the minds of your neighbours they will probably yield a greater harvest than yielded by this lecture delivered by me. I am probably not the best Sower, but someone other than myself will cultivate the seed that I have scattered, and gather in the harvest that I will never see, and in the reaping there will be well-being for all mankind. That is all.'[22]

The following month Guy decided that if he could sit in Baliol Street and talk into a microphone, he could just as well sit on the platform and speak direct to the audience. The lectures for August, September, and October were spoken extempore from the platform in Central Halls, Bath Street.

The last meeting took place on Sunday, 6 October 1963. Guy spoke for an hour, his voice as powerful as ever, but at the end he was exhausted and had to be helped to a waiting taxi. Ten days later he died in the Western Infirmary. There was no funeral; he had bequeathed his body to the Anatomy Department of Glasgow University.

So Aldred's long and active life ended. He had been, as Edward Ashton said, hated, feared, reviled, and imprisoned for his beliefs. When he died he had ten pennies in his pocket and the Strickland Press had three pounds in the bank. This accorded with his conviction that an agitator who dies rich has been a traitor to his cause. His faith in the intrinsic virtue of the people remained steadfast. In one of his darkest hours, when Ethel Macdonald died, he wrote:

'I see no kindness, no friendship, no regard for mankind, no purpose in the universe. It is a miracle that cannot be explained. It seems to be a wonderful evolution from cause to effect, although there seems to be no cause and the effect is without intelligence or aim. So, for my part, I do not believe in God. That was also the belief of Ethel. . . . Yet for some strange reason a contradiction arises within us. We *do* change the world. One generation merges into another. The hopes of yesterday's heroes and martyrs become the inspiring slogans of today, passed on to the heroes of tomorrow . . . in this frame of sorrow I turn from the lifeless body of my colleague to associate with those in whom still dwells the consciousness of being. . . .'

That is what he wrote when Ethel died: that is what he believed; and in that belief Guy Aldred died.

Suggestions for further reading

Some passages in this essay are taken from the manuscript of 'The Red Evangel', a biography of Guy A. Aldred, by J. T. Caldwell.

Guy Aldred material is housed in Glasgow's Mitchell Library, Glasgow University Library, University of Strathclyde Library, and Baillie's Library.

Aldred was founder-editor of the following journals (monthly, except when otherwise stated): *Herald of Revolt* (1910-14); *The Spur* (1914-21); *The Red Commune* (organ of the A.P.C.F.; one issue, 1921, suppressed); *The Commune* (1923-9); *The Council* (1931-3); *Attack!* (one issue, 1934); *The United Socialist* (one issue, 1933); *Regeneracion* (24 issues duplicated, then 4 issues typescript, fortnightly, 1936); *News From Spain* (one issue, 1937); *The Word* (one issue, May 1938, then May 1939-October 1963; continued under different editor till May 1969).

Aldred was the author of over fifty long pamphlets. He selected a number of these and published them as *Essays in Revolt* (1940, 2 vols.).

Autobiographical: *Dogmas Discarded* (2 pamphlets, 1940). *No Traitor's Gait!* (issued in parts at varying intervals between 1954 and 1963; unfinished). Contemporary news reports will be found in Aldred's press-cutting books in Baillie's Library, Glasgow.

Trials for sedition, in *Rex v. Aldred* (Glasgow, 1948).

Notes

1. See letter from Angus MacKay in *The Herald of Revolt*, May 1913.
2. *The Spur*, Sep. 1914.
3. R. M. Fox, *Smoky Crusade* (London, 1938), 273; John W. Graham, *Conscription and Conscience* (London, 1922), 306; *The Spur*, Jan. and Feb. 1919, and account of Inquiry in issue for June 1919.
4. Guy Aldred, 'The Reactions of Marx', in *The Commune*, Nov. 1926, quoting John Spargo, *The Life of Karl Marx*.
5. *The Spur*, Mar. 1918.
6. Ibid., Mar. 1919.
7. There seem to have been only three issues, of which Nos. 2 and 3, for July and Aug. 1919, are bound with *The Spur*. The League was inaugurated at the Communist Club, London, on 16 Mar. 1919. See *The Spur*, Apr. 1919.
8. The Congress met on 19 June 1920 in London — see *The Spur*, July 1920. For this British Communist Party's call to Aldred and others for unity, see *The Spur*, Sep. 1920.
9. See *The Spur*, Jan. 1921, for text of programme.
10. Nan Milton, *John Maclean* (London, 1973), 208.
11. See advertisement of meeting at Glasgow Green in *Forward*, 20 Oct. 1923.
12. G. A. Aldred, *Socialism and Parliament, Part One* (Glasgow, 1940), 74; John McGovern, *Neither Fear nor Favour* (London, 1960), 55-56, gives an unsympathetic account of the election and the A.P.C.F.
13. *Hansard*, 23 Nov. 1922, col. 87.
14. G. A. Aldred, *No Traitor's Gait!* (Glasgow, 1963), vol. 3, part 1.
15. Duncan McLellan, *Glasgow Public Parks* (Glasgow, 1894), 9-40, quoted by Aldred in *The Council*, July 1932.
16. *The Worker*, 9 and 16 Aug. 1924; *The Council*, Dec. 1931.
17. McGovern, op. cit., 74.
18. For precis of evidence submitted by Aldred, see his *Studies in Communism* (Glasgow, 1940), 59-63. For newspaper correspondence on Scots marriage, see G. A. Aldred, *Letters to the Editor, 1904-39* (Glasgow, 1940), 43, 45-48.
19. *The Word*, Nov. 1953.
20. Each election is fully reported in the contemporary issue of *The Word*.
21. *The Word*, Dec. 1962.
22. Excerpt from John T. Caldwell, *The Red Evangel* (unpublished biography of Aldred).

Index

Aberdeen, 9, 13, 18, 176, 181, 182, 196; Communist Propaganda Group in, 226; constituency, North, 18, 211, 221, South, 21; General Strike, 1926, in, 171, 172, 175, 176, 177, 179, 180, 181, 182, 184, 185, 187, 191, 193, 194, 195, 196, 197; Labour Committee, 19, 21; Liberals, 18, 19; Lord Provost of — see Lewis, Andrew; May Day at, 11, 19; Minority Movement, 171; New Left Club, 211, 212, 213, 217, 221; Radicals, 18; Town Council, 18, 173, 193; Trades Council, 4, 6, 8, 13, 17, 18, 20, 22, 23, 84, 94, eight hours day and, 11, 12, 19, General Strike, 1926, and, 171, 180, 195, labour representation and, 17, 18, 19, 21, unskilled workers and, 7, 8, 9, 91, 94; trade unionism in, 1, 7, 8, 91, 92, 93, 94, 109; University, 180, 182, 211; Workmen's Protective and Benefit Society, 7

Aberdeenshire, 19, 21, 90, 91, 197

Acts and Bills: Agricultural Holdings (Scotland) Act, 1883, 99; Agricultural Holdings Amendment Act, 1908, 99; Agricultural Wages (Regulation) (Scotland) Act, 1937, 101; Ballot Act, 1872, 98, 99, 107; Building Materials Bill, 1924, 162; Burgh Reform Act, 1832, 84; Cat and Mouse Act, 1913, 227, 228, 229; Cattle Diseases Prevention Act, 1866, 99; Combination Acts, 1799 and 1800, 98; Conspiracy and Protection of Property Act, 1875, 98; Corn Laws, repeal of, 1846, 98, 103; Criminal Law Amendment Act, 1871, 4, 17; Education Act, 1870, 106; Education (Scotland) Act, 1872, 68, 74, 1901, 125; Eight Hour Bill, 1887, 11, 1889, 12; Employers and Workmen Act, 1875, 98, 107; employers' liability, 20; Employers' Liability Act, 1880, 76; Factory Extension and Workshop Regulation Acts, 1867, 16; Glasgow Corporation Private Act (1897), 146; Ground Game Act, 1880, 99; Home Rule Bill, 1894, 80; Housing Acts, 1919-39, 101, 160, 162; Housing (Scotland) Act, 1919, 150, 154, 155, 160, 163; Housing Act, 1923, 160, 161, 162, 163, 164, 1924, 162, 163, 164, 1930, 163, 1933, 164, 1935, 164, 1938, 165; Housing and Town Planning Act, 1909, 144; Hypothec Abolition Act, 1894, 99; labour legislation, 1874-80, 17; Bills on taxation of land values, 1906-08, 84, 86; Master and Servant Acts, 15, 98, 107; Mines Act, 1860,

Acts and Bills: *continued*
39; Permissive Bills, 15; Public Library (Scotland) Act, 1867, 13; Reform Act, 1867, 68, 98, 1884, 98, 107; Rent Act, 1915, 147, 148; Riot Act, 77; concerning Scotland, 23; Trade Union Act, 1871, 4, 98; truck, 39; Unemployed Workmen Act, 1905, 115; Unemployment Insurance Act, 1920, 101; Union, Act of, 1800, 68; Veto Bills, 15; Workmen's Compensation, 124

Adamson, William, M.P., 232

Addison, Dr Christopher, M.P., 150, 154, 155, 160, 161, 163

aerated water makers, 133, 136

Africa — see Algeria; Central African Federation; Nigeria

Agricultural and Forestry Section, Scottish, Transport and General Workers' Union, 90, 109

Agricultural Labourers' Union, 91, 94, 96

Agricultural Society, Highland and, 96, 103, 104

Agricultural Workers, National Union of, 109

agriculture, 93, 94-97, 99, 100, 101, 102, 108, 194; *see also* Acts and Bills; animals; crofters; farm servants; hours of labour; land; Royal Commission

Airdrie, Lanarkshire: General Strike, 1926, at, 184; mineowners at, 43; miners' strikes at, 32, 33, 34, 35, 36, 39, 40, 41, 42, 48, 49, 52, 54, 58; miners' unions at, 43; procurator fiscal of, 50; Sheriff Substitute at — *see* Tennent, Hugh

Aldermaston, Berkshire, 214

Aldred, Alfred, father of Guy, 225

Aldred, Annesley, son of Guy, 226

Aldred, Guy Alfred, antiparliamentarian, 225-45 passim

Alexander, J., colliery manager, 55

Alexander, Kenneth J. W., economist, 211, 212, 213, 216, 217, 221

Alexandria, Dunbartonshire, 179

Algeria, 213

Alison, Sir Archibald, Sheriff of Lanarkshire, 1, 29, 48, 49, 50, 52, 54

Allan Steamship Line, 129

Allan, Matthew, Scottish Operative Masons, 3, 4

Allan, William, Engineers, 1

Allan, William, Minority Movement, 171

Allcorn, Derek, sociologist, 212